Everyday Mathematics®

The University of Chicago School Mathematics Project

Assessment Handbook

The McGraw·Hill Companies

The University of Chicago School Mathematics Project (UCSMP)

Max Bell, Director, UCSMP Elementary Materials Component;
Director, *Everyday Mathematics* First Edition
James McBride, Director, *Everyday Mathematics* Second Edition
Andy Isaacs, Director, *Everyday Mathematics* Third Edition
Amy Dillard, Associate Director, *Everyday Mathematics* Third Edition

Authors

Jean Bell, William M. Carroll, Amy Dillard, Kathleen Pitvorec

Teacher in Residence

Soundarya Radhakrishnan

Photo Credits

©Gregory Adams/Getty Images, cover, *top right;* ©Getty Images, cover, *center;* ©Tony Hamblin; Frank Lane Picture Agency/Corbis, cover, *bottom left.*

Permissions

The quotes on pages 4, 5, 8, and 35 are reprinted with permission from *Knowing What Students Know: The Science and Design of Educational Assessment* © 2001 by the National Academy of Sciences, courtesy of the National Academies Press, Washington, D.C.

Contributors

Jason Gil, Elizabeth Meza, Carol Pankau, Roel Vivit; Huong Banh, Mary Ellen Dairyko, Sharon Draznin, Nancy Hanvey, Laurie Leff, Fran Moore, Denise Porter, Herb Price, Joyce Timmons, Jenny Waters, Lana Winnet, Lisa Winters

This material is based upon work supported by the National Science Foundation under Grant No. ESI-9252984. Any opinions, findings, conclusions, or recommendations expressed in this material are those of the authors and do not necessarily reflect the views of the National Science Foundation.

---

www.WrightGroup.com

Printed in the United States of America.

Send all inquiries to:
Wright Group/McGraw-Hill
P.O. Box 812960
Chicago, IL 60681

ISBN 0-07-604590-0

5 6 7 8 9 POH 12 11 10 09 08 07

Contents

Philosophy of Assessment in *Everyday Mathematics* 1

Introduction 1
Balanced Assessment 2
What Are the Purposes of Assessment? 2
What Are the Contexts for Assessment? 3
What Are the Sources of Evidence for Assessment? 4
What Content Is Assessed? 5
Creating a Balanced Assessment Plan 7
Ongoing Assessment 8
Ongoing Assessment—Informing Instruction 9
Ongoing Assessment—Recognizing Student Achievement 10
Writing/Reasoning Prompts for Math Boxes 15
Portfolios 16
Periodic Assessment 18
Written Assessments 19
Mid-Year and End-of-Year Written Assessments 20
Progress Check Written Assessments 20
Oral and Slate Assessment 20
Student Self Assessment 21
Open Response Tasks 21
External Assessment 24
Record-Keeping 25
Class Checklists and Individual Profiles of Progress 25
Options for Recording Data on Checklists 27
Assessment Management System . . . 28
Introduction 28
Frequently Asked Questions 31
Recommended Reading 36
***Everyday Mathematics* Goals** 37

Assessment Overviews 51

Unit 1 52
Unit 2 60
Unit 3 68
Unit 4 76
Unit 5 84
Unit 6 92
Mid-Year Assessment Goals 100
Unit 7 102
Unit 8 110
Unit 9 118
Unit 10 126
Unit 11 134
Unit 12 142
End-of-Year Assessment Goals 150

Assessment Masters 153

Glossary 313

Index 315

Philosophy of Assessment in *Everyday Mathematics*®

Introduction

Too often, school assessment tends to provide only scattered snapshots of student achievement rather than continuous records of growth. In *Everyday Mathematics*, assessment is like a motion picture, revealing the development of each student's mathematical understanding over time while also giving the teacher useful feedback about the instructional needs of individual students and the class.

For assessment to be useful to teachers, students, parents, and others, the *Everyday Mathematics* authors believe that …

- Teachers need to have a variety of assessment tools and techniques to choose from so students can demonstrate what they know in a variety of ways and teachers can have reliable information from multiple sources.
- Students should be included in the assessment process. Self assessment and reflection are skills students will develop over time if they are encouraged.
- Assessment and instruction should be closely aligned. Assessment should assist teachers in making instructional decisions concerning individual students and the class.
- Assessment should focus on all important outcomes, not only on outcomes that are easy to measure.
- A good assessment program makes instruction easier.
- The best assessment plans are developed by teachers working collaboratively within schools and districts.

Everyday Mathematics offers many opportunities for assessing students' knowledge and skills. This handbook describes the *Everyday Mathematics* assessment resources and serves as a guide for navigating through those resources and helping you design and implement a balanced classroom assessment plan.

Balanced Assessment

When planning a balanced assessment, begin by asking several basic questions:

- *What are the purposes of assessment?*
- *What are the contexts for assessment?*
- *What are the sources of evidence for assessment?*
- *What content is assessed?*

What Are the Purposes of Assessment?

The purposes of assessment serve three main functions: to support learning, to measure achievement, and to evaluate programs. Each purpose is integral to achieving a balanced assessment plan.

Formative assessment supports learning by providing information about students' current knowledge and abilities so you can plan future instruction more effectively. Formative assessment encourages students to identify their areas of weakness or strength so they can focus their efforts more precisely.

Summative assessment measures student growth and achievement. A summative assessment might be designed, for example, to determine whether students have learned certain material by the end of a fixed period of study.

Program evaluation means judging how well a program is working. A school district, for example, may want to identify schools with especially strong mathematics programs so their successes can be replicated in other schools with weaker programs. Program evaluation makes this possible.

Assessment tools and techniques often serve more than one purpose. Assessments built into a curriculum might give teachers information they can use to plan future instruction more effectively or prepare progress reports. District administrators might use this information to allocate professional development resources.

Purposes of Assessment

Formative Assessment	Summative Assessment	Program Evaluation
◆ Used to plan instruction ◆ Helps students to reflect on their progress	◆ Used to measure student growth and achievement ◆ Helps determine if students have learned content	◆ Used to evaluate overall success of the math program

What Are the Contexts for Assessment?

Assessment occurs in a variety of contexts.

- **Ongoing assessment** involves gathering information from students' everyday work. These assessments can take place at the same time as regular classroom instruction.
- **Periodic assessment** consists of formal assessments that are built in to a curriculum, such as an end-of-unit Progress Check.
- **External assessment** is independent of the curriculum. An example of an external assessment is a standardized test.

Everyday Mathematics supports all three contexts for assessment, and it provides tools and materials for ongoing and periodic assessments that you can use to create a balanced assessment plan.

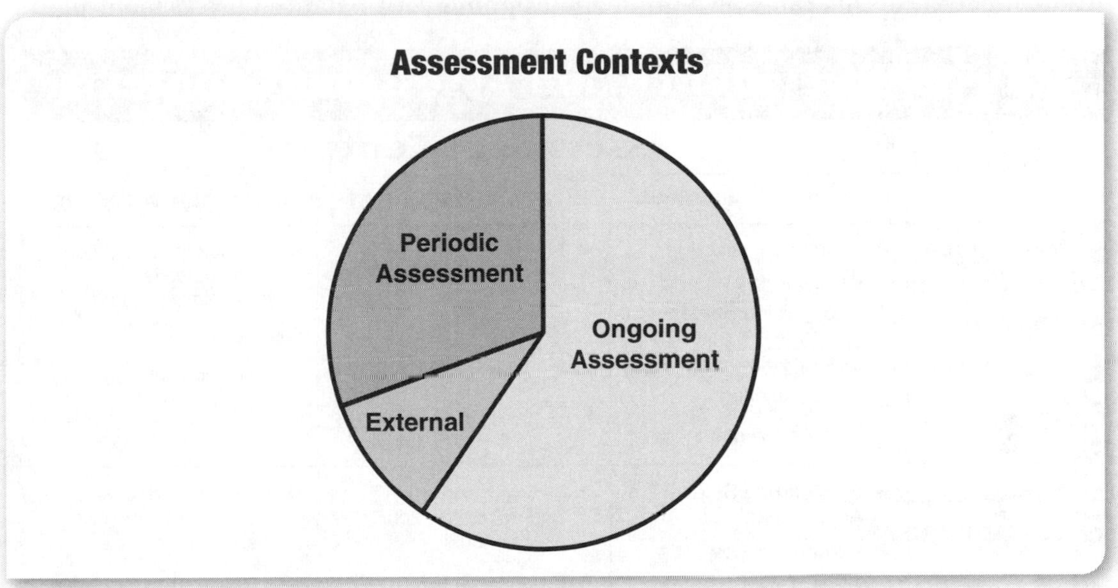

The sizes of the sections of the circle in the figure above are meant to be suggestive, but the exact proportions of ongoing, periodic, and external assessments will vary depending on your grade level, the time of year, state and district mandates, and many other factors.

What Are the Sources of Evidence for Assessment?

Assessment is a process of reasoning from evidence.

(Pellegrino, Chudowsky, and Glaser 2001, 36)

The evidence for assessing what students know is indirect because we cannot know exactly what they are thinking. Evidence about students' knowledge and capabilities comes from observing students while they are actively engaged and from analyzing the products of their work. Whatever conclusions we may make about students' thinking must be based on **observations** or **products.**

The table below shows the different contexts for assessment and the sources of evidence used for each context. Specific assessment tasks in *Everyday Mathematics* are included. Use this table as a guide in designing your balanced assessment plan.

Sources of Evidence and Assessment Contexts

Sources of Evidence	Assessment Contexts: Ongoing Assessment	Assessment Contexts: Periodic Assessment	Assessment Contexts: External Assessment
Observation	◆ Informing Instruction notes ◆ Recognizing Student Achievement notes for • Mental Math and Reflexes ◆ "Kid watching"	◆ Progress Check Oral/Slate Assessments	◆ Classroom observations by resource teachers or other outside experts
Product	◆ Recognizing Student Achievement notes for • Journal pages • Exit Slips • Games record sheets • Math Boxes ◆ Writing/Reasoning prompts ◆ Portfolio opportunities	◆ Mid-Year and End-of-Year written assessments ◆ Progress Check Written Assessments ◆ Student Self Assessments ◆ Open Response problems	◆ Standardized tests mandated by the school district or the state

Each context for assessment (ongoing, periodic, or external) can yield evidence through observations or products.

- ◆ Observing students as they are doing their daily work can provide a great deal of information about their understandings, skills, and dispositions; this kind of ongoing observational assessment may be considered "kid watching."
- ◆ A written assessment that is included as part of a curriculum is an example of a periodic product assessment.
- ◆ A classroom visit by an outside expert who will observe particular students is an example of an external assessment using observational evidence.

What Content Is Assessed?

> *Assessment does not exist in isolation, but must be closely aligned with the goals of curriculum and instruction.*
>
> **(Pellegrino, Chudowsky, and Glaser 2001, 36)**

In recent years, national organizations and most states have issued detailed sets of learning goals and standards, which provide useful guidance about what content is important to learn and, therefore, important to assess. Aligning assessment, curriculum, and instruction with standards and goals increases coherence in the system and produces better outcomes. To help teachers understand the structure of *Everyday Mathematics* and therefore better understand what to assess, the authors developed Program Goals, which are organized by content strand and carefully articulated across the grades. Below are the six content strands and their related Program Goals:

Everyday Mathematics Program Goals

Number and Numeration

- ◆ Understand the meanings, uses, and representations of numbers
- ◆ Understand equivalent names for numbers
- ◆ Understand common numerical relations

Operations and Computation

- ◆ Compute accurately
- ◆ Make reasonable estimates
- ◆ Understand meanings of operations

Data and Chance

- ◆ Select and create appropriate graphical representations of collected or given data
- ◆ Analyze and interpret data
- ◆ Understand and apply basic concepts of probability

Measurement and Reference Frames

- ◆ Understand the systems and processes of measurement; use appropriate techniques, tools, units, and formulas in making measurements
- ◆ Use and understand reference frames

Geometry

- ◆ Investigate characteristics and properties of two- and three-dimensional geometric shapes
- ◆ Apply transformations and symmetry in geometric situations

Patterns, Functions, and Algebra

- ◆ Understand patterns and functions
- ◆ Use algebraic notation to represent and analyze situations and structures

Program Goals are threads that weave the curriculum together across grades. "Compute accurately," for example, is a Program Goal. Children in *Everyday Mathematics* are expected to compute accurately. The expectations for a student achieving this goal in Grade 2 are obviously different from what is expected from a student in Grade 6. For this reason, the Program Goals are further refined through Grade-Level Goals.

Grade-Level Goals are guideposts along trajectories of learning that span multiple years. They are the big ideas at each grade level; they do not capture all of the content covered. The Grade-Level Goals describe how *Everyday Mathematics* builds mastery over time—first through informal exposure, later through more formal instruction, and finally through application. Because the Grade-Level Goals are cumulative, it is essential for students to experience the complete curriculum at each grade level. The example below shows the development of Grade-Level Goals for addition and subtraction procedures.

Grade K	Use manipulatives, number lines, and mental arithmetic to solve problems involving the addition and subtraction of single-digit whole numbers.
Grade 1	Use manipulatives, number grids, tally marks, mental arithmetic, and calculators to solve problems involving the addition and subtraction of 1-digit whole numbers with 1- or 2-digit whole numbers; calculate and compare the values of combinations of coins.
Grade 2	Use manipulatives, number grids, tally marks, mental arithmetic, paper & pencil, and calculators to solve problems involving the addition and subtraction of 2-digit whole numbers; describe the strategies used; calculate and compare values of coin and bill combinations.
Grade 3	Use manipulatives, mental arithmetic, paper-and-pencil algorithms, and calculators to solve problems involving the addition and subtraction of whole numbers and decimals in a money context; describe the strategies used and explain how they work.
Grade 4	Use manipulatives, mental arithmetic, paper-and-pencil algorithms, and calculators to solve problems involving the addition and subtraction of whole numbers and decimals through hundredths; describe the strategies used and explain how they work.
Grade 5	Use mental arithmetic, paper-and-pencil algorithms, and calculators to solve problems involving the addition and subtraction of whole numbers, decimals, and signed numbers; describe the strategies used and explain how they work.
Grade 6	Use mental arithmetic, paper-and-pencil algorithms, and calculators to solve problems involving the addition and subtraction of whole numbers, decimals, and signed numbers; describe the strategies used and explain how they work.

All assessment opportunities in *Everyday Mathematics* are linked to specific Grade-Level Goals. The curriculum is designed so that the vast majority of students will reach the Grade-Level Goals for a given grade upon completion of that grade and as a result will be well prepared to succeed in higher levels of mathematics. The complete list of Program Goals and Grade-Level Goals begins on page 37 of this handbook.

Creating a Balanced Assessment Plan

In *Everyday Mathematics,* assessment is primarily designed to help you

- learn about students' current knowledge and abilities so you can plan future instruction more effectively—formative assessment; and
- measure students' progress toward and achievement of Grade-Level Goals—summative assessment.

Although there is no one right assessment plan for all classrooms, all assessment plans should provide a balance of assessment sources from different contexts. See the chart on page 4 of this handbook for specific assessment tasks in *Everyday Mathematics* that support the different sources and contexts.

Planning Tips

Do not try to use all the assessment resources at once. Instead, devise a manageable, balanced plan. Choose those tools and techniques that best match your teaching style and your students' needs.

Consider the following guidelines:

- Start small.
- Incorporate assessment into your daily class routine.
- Set up an easy and efficient record-keeping system.
- Personalize and adapt the plan as the year progresses.

Your assessment plan should be designed to answer these questions:

- How is the class doing?
- How are individual students doing?
- How do I need to adjust instruction to meet students' needs?
- How can I communicate to students, parents, and others about the progress being made?

The following sections of this handbook provide further details about the tools and techniques you can use to develop a balanced assessment plan. Using these tools, you can support student learning, improve your instruction, measure student growth and achievement, and make the most of your experience with *Everyday Mathematics.*

Ongoing Assessment

No single test score can be considered a definitive measure of a student's competence. Multiple measures enhance the validity and fairness of the inferences drawn by giving students various ways and opportunities to demonstrate their competence.

(Pellegrino, Chudowsky, and Glaser 2001, 253)

An integral part of a balanced assessment plan involves gathering information from student's everyday work. Opportunities for collecting ongoing assessment in the form of observations and products are highlighted in *Everyday Mathematics* through Informing Instruction and Recognizing Student Achievement notes.

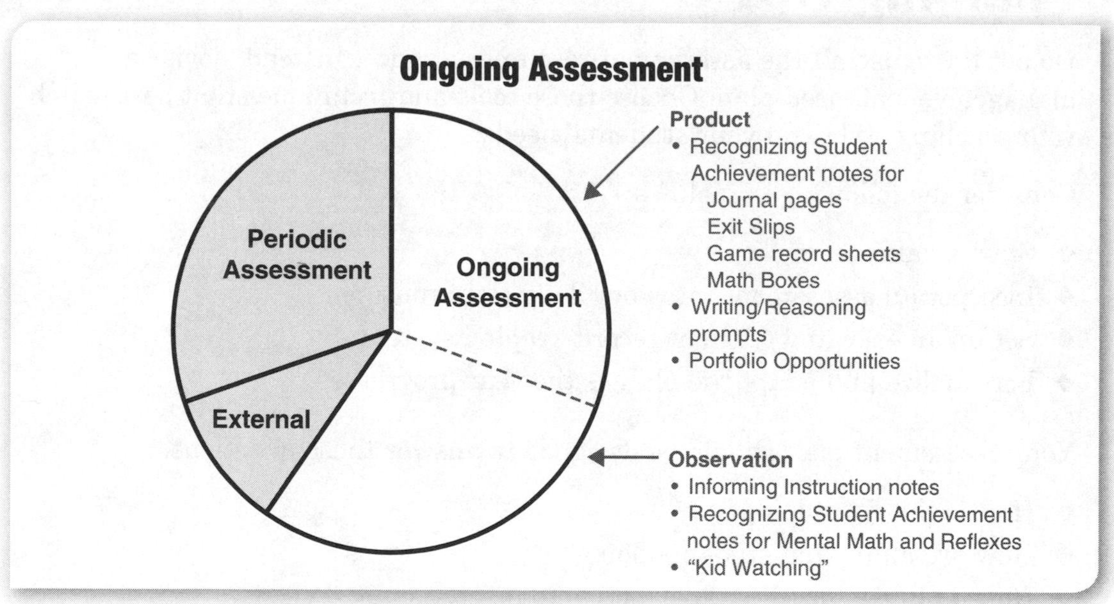

Ongoing Assessment—
Informing Instruction

Informing Instruction notes are designed to help you anticipate and recognize common errors and misconceptions in students' thinking and alert you to multiple solution strategies or unique insights that students may offer. These notes suggest how to use observations of students' work to effectively adapt instruction.

Ongoing Assessment: Informing Instruction

When base-10 blocks were used in Unit 2 to model whole numbers, the cube was the ONE, the long was 10, the flat was 100, and the big cube was 1,000. Watch for students who may not have made the transition to using base-10 blocks to model fractions with the flat as the new ONE. Draw a sketch of a flat on the board and label it ONE. Throughout the lesson, draw and label sketches to support students' transition to the new ONE.

Ongoing Assessment: Informing Instruction

Watch for students who recognize the inverse relationship between multiplication and division and solve the problem by thinking "4 times what number equals 32?" Have them write an open sentence to represent their thinking. $4 * x = 32$

Ongoing Assessment—Recognizing Student Achievement

Each lesson in *Everyday Mathematics* contains a Recognizing Student Achievement note. These notes highlight specific tasks that teachers can use for assessment to monitor students' progress toward Grade-Level Goals.

These tasks include:

- Journal pages (written problems—sometimes including explanations)
- Mental Math and Reflexes (oral or slate)
- Exit Slips (explanations of strategies and understanding)
- *Everyday Mathematics* games (record sheets or follow-up sheets)
- Math Boxes (written practice problems)

Each Recognizing Student Achievement note identifies the task to gather information from, the concept or skill to be assessed, and the expectations for a student who is *making adequate progress* toward meeting the specific Grade-Level Goal.

Math Journal 1

Journal page 30 Problem 6 ★

Use **journal page 30, Problem 6** to assess students' ability to give equivalent names for whole numbers. Students are making adequate progress if they are able to name the box and generate correct mathematical expressions involving one or more of the basic four arithmetic operations. Some students may give mathematical expressions involving grouping symbols or exponents.

[Number and Numeration Goal 4]

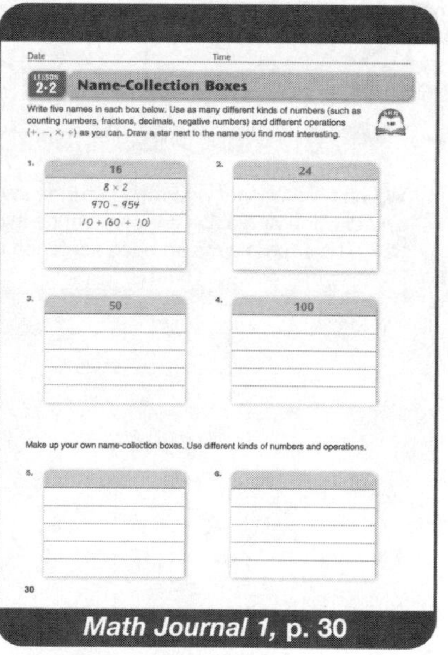

Date Time

LESSON 2·2 Name-Collection Boxes

Write five names in each box below. Use as many different kinds of numbers (such as counting numbers, fractions, decimals, negative numbers) and different operations (+, −, ×, ÷) as you can. Draw a star next to the name you find most interesting.

1. 16: 8 × 2; 970 − 954; 10 + (60 ÷ 10)

2. 24

3. 50

4. 100

Make up your own name-collection boxes. Use different kinds of numbers and operations.

5.

6.

30

Math Journal 1, p. 30

Sample 2 Recognizing Student Achievement Mental Math and Reflexes

Ongoing Assessment: Recognizing Student Achievement

Mental Math and Reflexes ★

Use **Mental Math and Reflexes** to assess students' ability to express the probability of an event as a fraction. Students are making adequate progress if they express the expected probability with a fraction. Some students may write the fraction in simplest form, for example, rename $\frac{20}{100}$ as $\frac{1}{5}$.

[Data and Chance Goal 4]

Mental Math and Reflexes 

Pose probability questions. Have students write the appropriate fractions and basic probability terms on their slates. *Suggestions:*

●○○ There are 5 red and 5 blue blocks in the bag.

What are the chances of picking a red block? $\frac{5}{10}$, $\frac{1}{2}$, or 50-50 chance

A blue block? $\frac{5}{10}$, $\frac{1}{2}$, 50-50 chance

A green block? $\frac{0}{10}$, impossible

●●○ There are 3 red, 1 blue, and 2 green blocks in the bag.

What are the chances of picking a red block? $\frac{3}{6}$, $\frac{1}{2}$, 50-50 chance

A blue block? $\frac{1}{6}$, unlikely, or very unlikely

A green block? $\frac{2}{6}$, $\frac{1}{3}$, unlikely

●●● There are 25 red, 25 blue, 20 green, and 30 yellow blocks in the bag.

What are the chances of picking a red or a blue block? $\frac{50}{100}$, $\frac{1}{2}$, 50-50 chance

A green block? $\frac{20}{100}$, $\frac{2}{10}$, $\frac{1}{5}$, unlikely

A yellow block? $\frac{30}{100}$, $\frac{3}{10}$, unlikely

Sample 3 Recognizing Student Achievement Exit Slip

Ongoing Assessment: Recognizing Student Achievement

Math Log or Exit Slip

Use a **Math Log** or an **Exit Slip** (*Math Masters,* page 388 or 389) to assess students' ability to predict the outcomes of an experiment and test the predictions using manipulatives. Have students write about how the predicted outcomes for the cube-drop experiment compare with the actual results. Students are making adequate progress if their responses include the following:

- ▷ Some predictions are closer than others to the actual results.
- ▷ Predictions are *expected* results, not exactly what will happen.

Some students may be able to use the results to predict future events. For example, what might happen if the cube were dropped 500 times?

[Data and Chance Goal 4]

Name Date Time

Exit Slip

Name Date Time

Exit Slip

389

Math Masters, p. 389

Sample 4 Recognizing Student Achievement Game Record Sheet

Ongoing Assessment: Recognizing Student Achievement

***Math Masters* Page 485**

Use ***Math Masters*, page 485** to assess students' ability to calculate the probability of an event. Students are making adequate progress if they are able to calculate the total number of items in the bag and express the probability of an event as a fraction. Some students may use a strategy when replacing *x* and *y* to earn the most possible points for each turn.

[Data and Chance Goal 4]

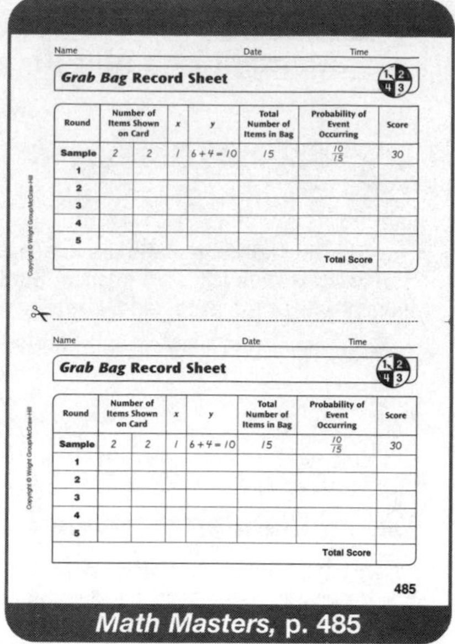

Name Date Time

Grab Bag **Record Sheet**

Round	Number of Items Shown on Card		x	y	Total Number of Items in Bag	Probability of Event Occurring	Score
Sample	2	2	1	6 + 4 = 10	15	$\frac{10}{15}$	30
1							
2							
3							
4							
5							
						Total Score	

Name Date Time

Grab Bag **Record Sheet**

Round	Number of Items Shown on Card		x	y	Total Number of Items in Bag	Probability of Event Occurring	Score
Sample	2	2	1	6 + 4 = 10	15	$\frac{10}{15}$	30
1							
2							
3							
4							
5							
						Total Score	

485

Math Masters, p. 485

Sample 5 Recognizing Student Achievement Math Boxes

Ongoing Assessment: Recognizing Student Achievement

Math Boxes Problems 2a–2d ★

Use **Math Boxes, Problems 2a–2d** to assess students' ability to compare numbers up to 1 billion. Students are making adequate progress if they can insert > and < symbols to make true number sentences. Some students may be able to solve Problem 2e, which involves exponential notation for powers of 10.

[Number and Numeration Goal 6]

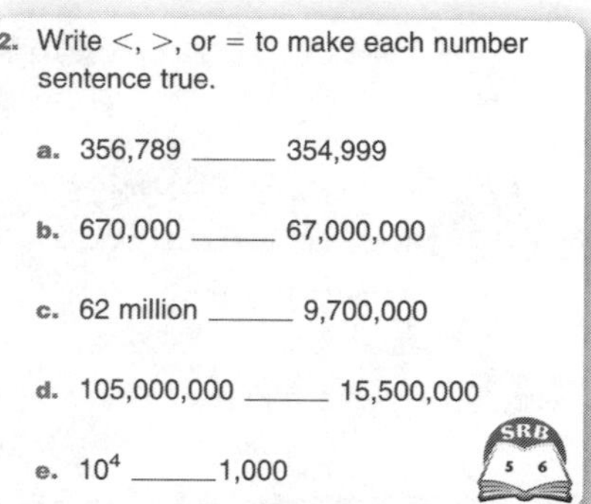

2. Write <, >, or = to make each number sentence true.

a. 356,789 ______ 354,999

b. 670,000 ______ 67,000,000

c. 62 million ______ 9,700,000

d. 105,000,000 ______ 15,500,000

e. 10^4 ______ 1,000

SRB 5 6

The Recognizing Student Achievement tasks were chosen with the expectation that the majority of students will be successful with them. Students who are making *adequate progress* as defined by a Recognizing Student Achievement task are on a trajectory to meet the corresponding Grade-Level Goal. Based on student progress toward Grade-Level Goals, you may choose to use Readiness activities or Enrichment activities to modify your instructional plan to meet an individual student's needs. See the chart on the next page for how to understand and use the results of the Recognizing Student Achievement tasks.

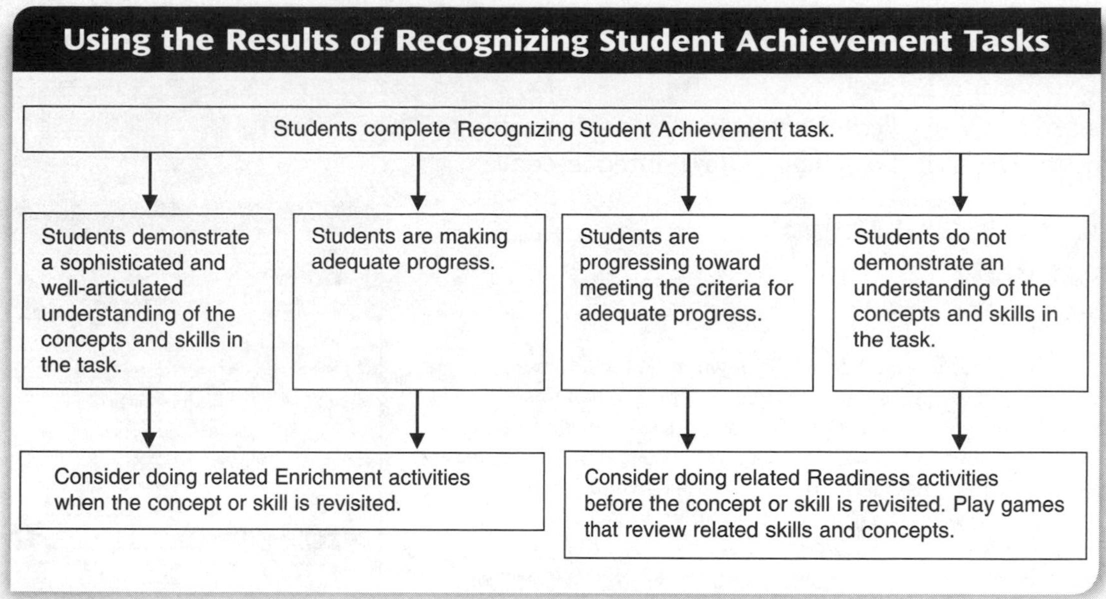

Sample Recognizing Student Achievement

The following example illustrates how to implement further Enrichment or Readiness for a given Recognizing Student Achievement task.

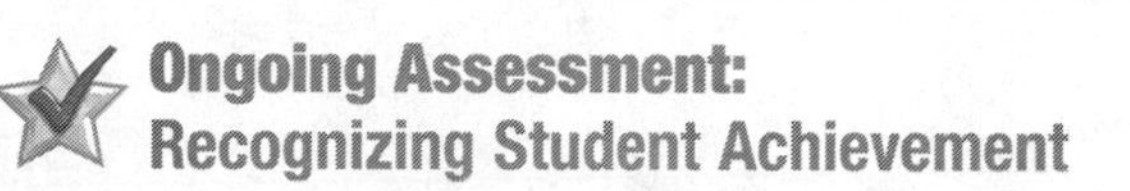

Ongoing Assessment: Recognizing Student Achievement

Journal page 83 Problem 1

Use **journal page 83, Problem 1** to assess students' ability to compare decimals through hundredths. Students are making adequate progress if they are able to solve Problems 1a–1f correctly. In Problem 2, some students may demonstrate the ability to compare decimals beyond hundredths or decimals less than 0.

[Number and Numeration Goal 6]

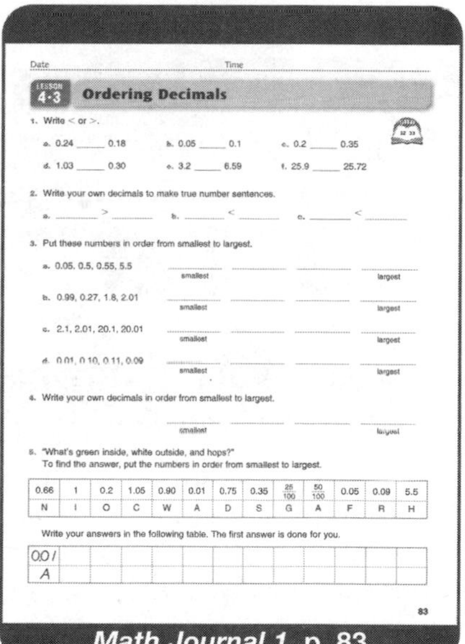

Date Time

LESSON 4·3 **Ordering Decimals**

1. Write < or >.

a. 0.24 ____ 0.18 b. 0.05 ____ 0.1 c. 0.2 ____ 0.35

d. 1.03 ____ 0.30 e. 3.2 ____ 6.59 f. 25.9 ____ 25.72

2. Write your own decimals to make true number sentences.

a. ____ > ____ b. ____ < ____ c. ____ < ____

3. Put these numbers in order from smallest to largest.

a. 0.05, 0.5, 0.55, 5.5 ____ ____ ____ ____ (smallest … largest)

b. 0.99, 0.27, 1.8, 2.01 ____ ____ ____ ____ (smallest … largest)

c. 2.1, 2.01, 20.1, 20.01 ____ ____ ____ ____ (smallest … largest)

d. 0.01, 0.10, 0.11, 0.09 ____ ____ ____ ____ (smallest … largest)

4. Write your own decimals in order from smallest to largest.

____ ____ ____ ____ (smallest … largest)

5. "What's green inside, white outside, and hops?"
To find the answer, put the numbers in order from smallest to largest.

0.66	1	0.2	1.05	0.90	0.01	0.75	0.35	$\frac{25}{100}$	$\frac{50}{100}$	0.05	0.09	5.5
N	I	O	C	W	A	D	S	G	A	F	R	H

Write your answers in the following table. The first answer is done for you.

0.01												
A												

83

Math Journal 1, p. 83

Sample Enrichment

If students are *making adequate progress,* consider using the Enrichment activities in this lesson, if applicable, or related lessons.

▶ Solving a Decimal Magic Square Puzzle

15–30 Min

(*Math Masters,* p. 117)

To apply students' understanding of place value and addition of decimals, have students complete a magic square. Students use estimation to place decimals so that the sum of the numbers in each row, column, and diagonal of the magic square is equal to 6.5. Have students describe how they decided to place the decimal points; for example, "I knew that on the diagonal, the 80 had to be 0.80 because the sum is 6.5, and 8 and 80 are each greater than 6.5."

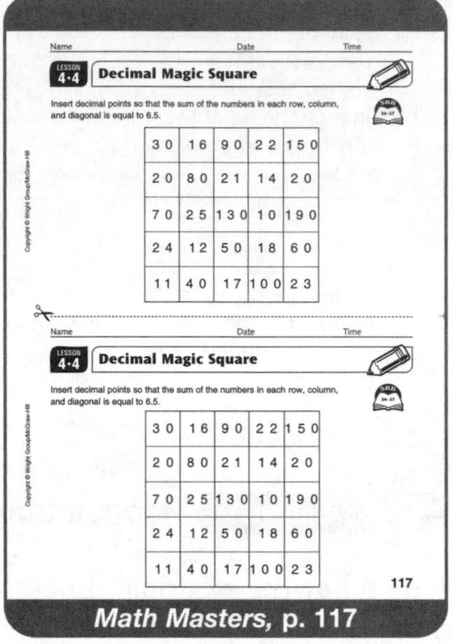

Name Date Time

LESSON 4·4 **Decimal Magic Square**

Insert decimal points so that the sum of the numbers in each row, column, and diagonal is equal to 6.5.

3 0	1 6	9 0	2 2	1 5 0
2 0	8 0	2 1	1 4	2 0
7 0	2 5	1 3 0	1 0	1 9 0
2 4	1 2	5 0	1 8	6 0
1 1	4 0	1 7	1 0 0	2 3

Name Date Time

LESSON 4·4 **Decimal Magic Square**

Insert decimal points so that the sum of the numbers in each row, column, and diagonal is equal to 6.5.

3 0	1 6	9 0	2 2	1 5 0
2 0	8 0	2 1	1 4	2 0
7 0	2 5	1 3 0	1 0	1 9 0
2 4	1 2	5 0	1 8	6 0
1 1	4 0	1 7	1 0 0	2 3

117

Math Masters, p. 117

Sample Readiness

If students are *not making adequate progress,* consider using the Readiness activities before teaching related lessons.

READINESS

▶ Investigating a Decimal Version of the Number Grid

SMALL-GROUP ACTIVITY

5–15 Min

(*Math Masters,* p. 427)

To explore the use of a visual organizer for understanding the base-ten place-value system for decimals, have students use a decimal version of the number grid.

Have students compare the number grid poster with the decimal version. Ask: *What are some similarities and differences?* Possible answers: Patterns in the digits are similar in that the hundredths digit stays the same as you move down a column, and the tenths digit stays the same as you move across a row. The numbers increase by 0.01 as you move a step to the right; the numbers increase by 0.1 as you move a step down.

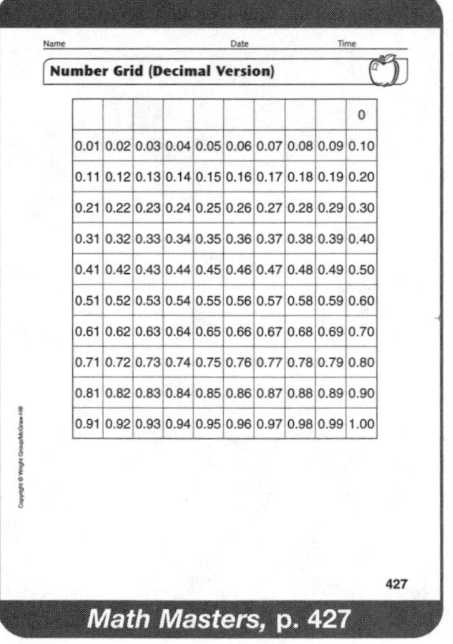

Name Date Time

Number Grid (Decimal Version)

									0
0.01	0.02	0.03	0.04	0.05	0.06	0.07	0.08	0.09	0.10
0.11	0.12	0.13	0.14	0.15	0.16	0.17	0.18	0.19	0.20
0.21	0.22	0.23	0.24	0.25	0.26	0.27	0.28	0.29	0.30
0.31	0.32	0.33	0.34	0.35	0.36	0.37	0.38	0.39	0.40
0.41	0.42	0.43	0.44	0.45	0.46	0.47	0.48	0.49	0.50
0.51	0.52	0.53	0.54	0.55	0.56	0.57	0.58	0.59	0.60
0.61	0.62	0.63	0.64	0.65	0.66	0.67	0.68	0.69	0.70
0.71	0.72	0.73	0.74	0.75	0.76	0.77	0.78	0.79	0.80
0.81	0.82	0.83	0.84	0.85	0.86	0.87	0.88	0.89	0.90
0.91	0.92	0.93	0.94	0.95	0.96	0.97	0.98	0.99	1.00

427

Math Masters, p. 427

Writing/Reasoning Prompts for Math Boxes

Every unit contains suggestions for prompts to use with Math Boxes problems. Use these prompts in a number of ways: (1) Collect student responses to these prompts on Exit Slips. (2) Request that students keep a math notebook where they record their answers to Math Message problems, Exit Slip prompts, and Writing/Reasoning prompts for Math Boxes problems. (3) Have students record responses on Math Log or Exit Slip masters and then add them to their portfolio collections.

Portfolio Ideas

Writing/Reasoning Have students write a response to the following: *Explain how you found the value of S in Problem 4e.* Sample answer: Since I knew the whole (2.43) and one of the parts (1.06), I subtracted 1.06 from 2.43 to find the value of *S*.

4. Solve each open sentence.

a. $5.9 - T = 5$ $T =$ ______

b. $9.4 - K = 3$ $K =$ ______

c. $0.81 - M = 0.43$ $M =$ ______

d. $F - 2.1 = 6.8$ $F =$ ______

e. $2.43 = S + 1.06$ $S =$ ______

f. $R - 12.2 = 4.65$ $R =$ ______

SRB 148

Portfolio Ideas

Writing/Reasoning Have students write a response to the following: *In Problem 4, is* $\overrightarrow{TC}$ *another name for* $\overrightarrow{CT}$*? Explain why or why not.* No. Sample answer: The endpoint of ray *CT* is point *C*, so ray *TC* is not the same as ray *CT*. The first letter in the name of a ray is the ray's endpoint.

Portfolios

Portfolios are a versatile tool for student assessment. They help students reflect on their mathematical growth and help you understand and document that growth. Portfolios are part of a balanced assessment plan in that they:

- emphasize progress over time;
- involve students more directly in the assessment process as they participate in selecting work and explaining what the work demonstrates; and
- document strengths and weaknesses in a student's mathematical development.

Portfolio Ideas is the symbol used to indicate opportunities to collect students' work for portfolios. Several portfolio opportunities are highlighted in each unit, but in addition to highlighted opportunities, you and your student can choose from the variety of work in daily lessons to add to students' portfolios.

Consider asking students to write about their selected works. Two optional masters, Sample Math Work and Discussion of My Work, are provided for this.

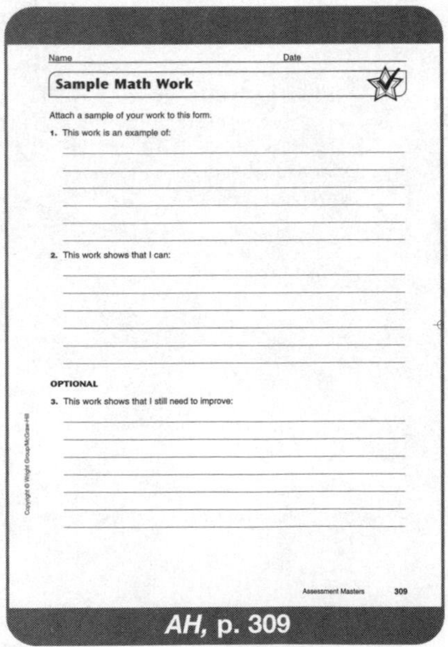
Name Date

Sample Math Work

Attach a sample of your work to this form.

1. This work is an example of:

2. This work shows that I can:

OPTIONAL

3. This work shows that I still need to improve:

Copyright © Wright Group/McGraw-Hill

Assessment Masters 309

AH, p. 309

Name Date

Discussion of My Math Work

Attach a sample of your work to this page. Tell what you think is important about your sample.

Copyright © Wright Group/McGraw-Hill

310 Assessment Handbook

AH, p. 310

See pages 304–311 in this book for additional masters that you might ask students to complete periodically and incorporate into their portfolios. *For example:*

- ◆ Evaluating My Math Class
- ◆ My Math Class
- ◆ Weekly Math Log
- ◆ Number-Story Math Log

You may also ask parents to complete a *Parent Reflection* page (*Assessment Handbook,* page 312) for inclusion in students' portfolios.

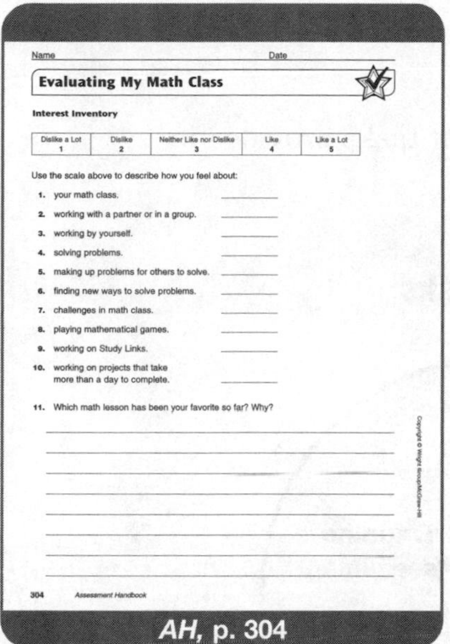

Name Date

Evaluating My Math Class

Interest Inventory

Dislike a Lot	Dislike	Neither Like nor Dislike	Like	Like a Lot
1	2	3	4	5

Use the scale above to describe how you feel about:

1. your math class.
2. working with a partner or in a group.
3. working by yourself.
4. solving problems.
5. making up problems for others to solve.
6. finding new ways to solve problems.
7. challenges in math class.
8. playing mathematical games.
9. working on Study Links.
10. working on projects that take more than a day to complete.
11. Which math lesson has been your favorite so far? Why?

304 Assessment Handbook

AH, p. 304

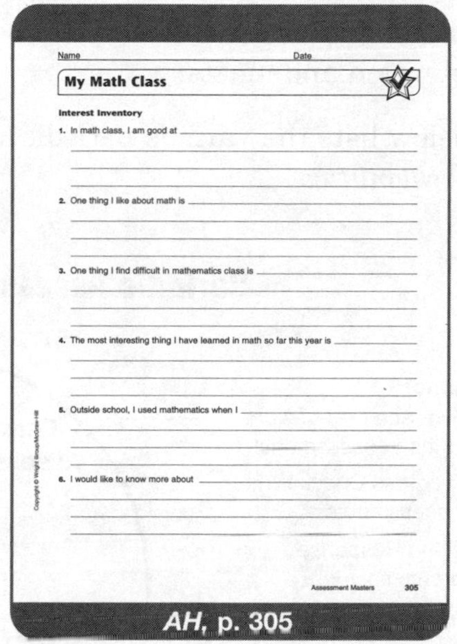

Name Date

My Math Class

Interest Inventory

1. In math class, I am good at
2. One thing I like about math is
3. One thing I find difficult in mathematics class is
4. The most interesting thing I have learned in math so far this year is
5. Outside school, I used mathematics when I
6. I would like to know more about

Assessment Masters 305

AH, p. 305

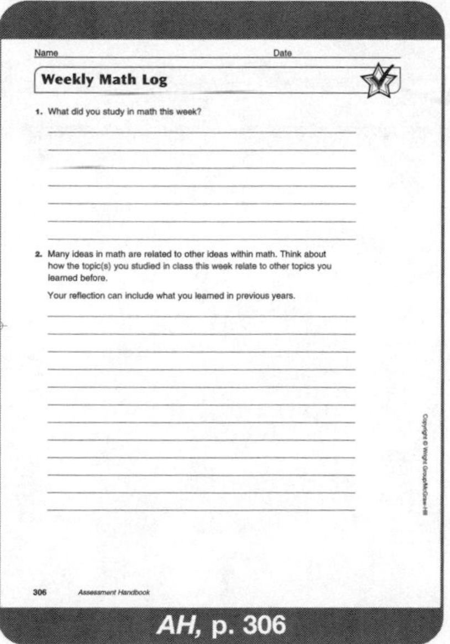

Name Date

Weekly Math Log

1. What did you study in math this week?
2. Many ideas in math are related to other ideas within math. Think about how the topic(s) you studied in class this week relate to other topics you learned before.

   Your reflection can include what you learned in previous years.

306 Assessment Handbook

AH, p. 306

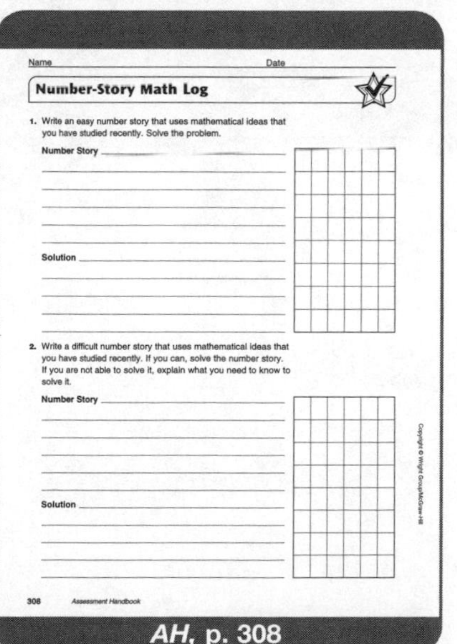

Name Date

Number-Story Math Log

1. Write an easy number story that uses mathematical ideas that you have studied recently. Solve the problem.

   Number Story

   Solution

2. Write a difficult number story that uses mathematical ideas that you have studied recently. If you can, solve the number story. If you are not able to solve it, explain what you need to know to solve it.

   Number Story

   Solution

308 Assessment Handbook

AH, p. 308

Periodic Assessment

Periodic assessments are another key component of a balanced assessment plan. Progress Check lessons and Mid-Year and End-of-Year written assessments require students to complete a variety of tasks, including short answer questions, open response problems, and reflection questions. These tasks provide you and your students with the opportunity to regularly review and reflect upon their progress—in areas that were recently introduced as well as in areas that involve long-term retention and mastery.

The figure below lists the various periodic assessment tasks provided in *Everyday Mathematics*.

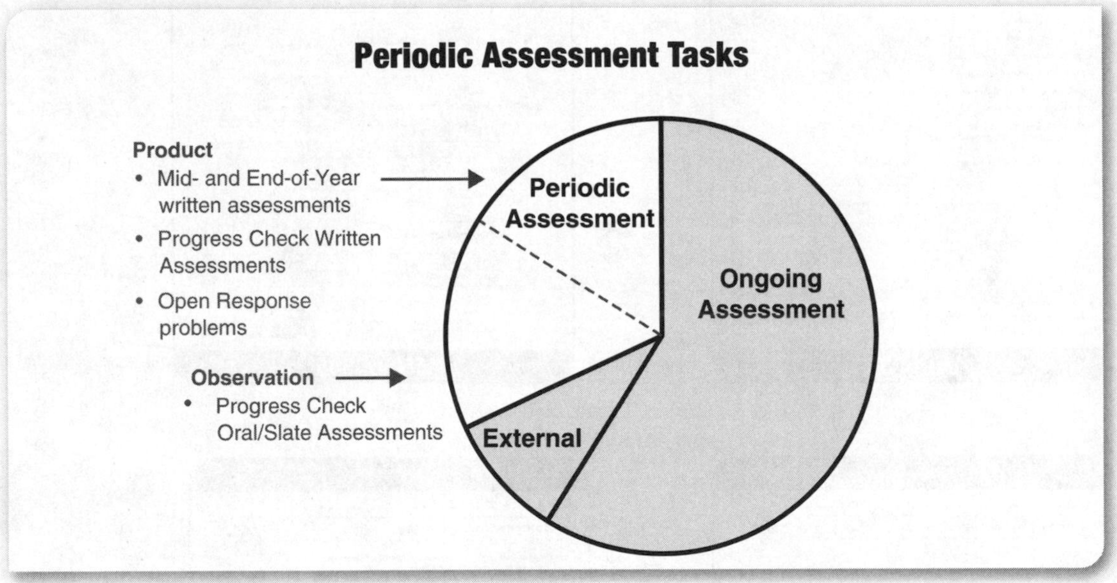

Written Assessments

Experts in assessment distinguish between summative and formative purposes of assessment. Summative assessment measures student growth and achievement so you can determine whether students have learned certain material. Formative assessment provides information about students' current knowledge and abilities so you can plan future instruction more effectively.

Accordingly, all *Everyday Mathematics* periodic written assessments include two parts:

- Part A is designed for summative purposes. The questions provide teachers with information on how students are progressing toward Grade-Level Goals. The questions can be used in the same way as Recognizing Student Achievement notes. Students *making adequate progress* toward Grade-Level Goals should do fairly well on this section.

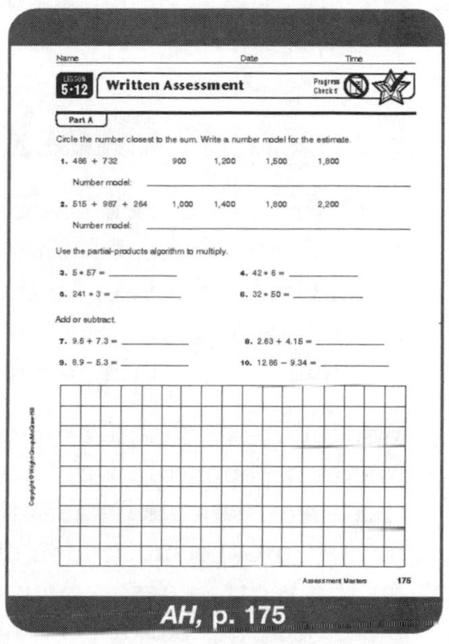

Name Date Time

LESSON 5·12 **Written Assessment** Progress Check 5

Part A

Circle the number closest to the sum. Write a number model for the estimate.

1. 486 + 732   900   1,200   1,500   1,800

   Number model: ______

2. 515 + 987 + 264   1,000   1,400   1,800   2,200

   Number model: ______

Use the partial-products algorithm to multiply.

3. 5 * 57 = ______
4. 42 * 6 = ______
5. 241 * 3 = ______
6. 32 * 50 = ______

Add or subtract.

7. 9.6 + 7.3 = ______
8. 2.63 + 4.15 = ______
9. 8.9 − 5.3 = ______
10. 12.86 − 9.34 = ______

Assessment Masters 175

AH, p. 175

- Part B is designed for formative purposes. The questions can be used to establish baselines for documenting student growth over time. The questions also assist teachers in their long-term planning in the same way as Informing Instruction notes help teachers in planning lessons.

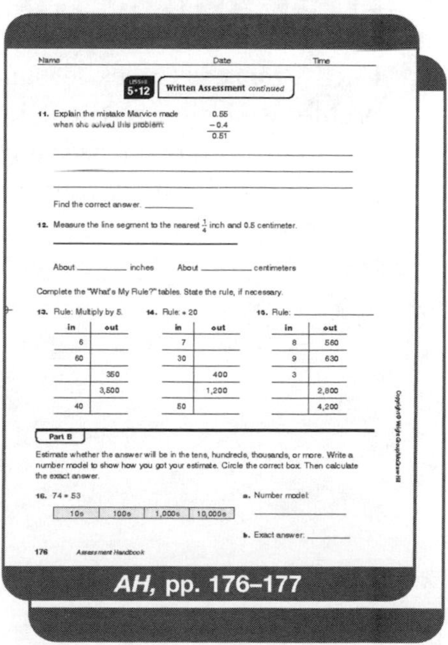

Name Date Time

LESSON 5·12 **Written Assessment** *continued*

11. Explain the mistake Marvice made when she solved this problem:

$$\begin{array}{r} 0.55 \\ -\,0.4 \\ \hline 0.51 \end{array}$$

Find the correct answer. ______

12. Measure the line segment to the nearest $\frac{1}{4}$ inch and 0.5 centimeter.

About ______ inches   About ______ centimeters

Complete the "What's My Rule?" tables. State the rule, if necessary.

13. Rule: Multiply by 5.

in	out
6	
60	
	350
	3,500
40	

14. Rule: * 20

in	out
7	
30	
	400
	1,200
50	

15. Rule: ______

in	out
8	560
9	630
3	
	2,800
	4,200

Part B

Estimate whether the answer will be in the tens, hundreds, thousands, or more. Write a number model to show how you got your estimate. Circle the correct box. Then calculate the exact answer.

16. 74 * 53

10s	100s	1,000s	10,000s

a. Number model: ______

b. Exact answer: ______

176 Assessment Handbook

AH, pp. 176–177

Mid-Year and End-of-Year Written Assessments

To provide a snapshot of how students are progressing toward a broader range of Grade-Level Goals, the program includes two comprehensive written assessments at each grade level—Mid-Year written assessment and End-of-Year written assessment. These written assessments include summative and formative components that cover important concepts and skills presented throughout the year. The Mid-Year and End-of-Year written assessments provide additional information that you may wish to include in developing your balanced assessment plan.

Progress Check Written Assessments

Each Progress Check lesson includes a Written Assessment incorporating tasks that address content from lessons in the current and previous units. The Grade-Level Goals addressed in the Written Assessment are listed at the beginning of the lesson. These assessments provide information for evaluating student progress and planning for future instruction.

Written Assessments are one way students demonstrate what they know. Maximize opportunities for students to show the breadth of their knowledge on these assessments by adapting questions as appropriate. Beginning on page 51 in the unit-specific section of this handbook, there are suggested modifications for the Written Assessments that will allow you to tailor questions and get a more accurate picture of what students know.

Oral and Slate Assessment

Each Progress Check lesson features an Oral and Slate Assessment that includes problems similar to those in Mental Math and Reflexes, which appears in each lesson. You may choose to manage the collection of information from these problems differently than you do with the daily practice. For example, you may give the problems to small groups of students at a time or have students record their answers on paper rather than on slates.

Student Self Assessment

Each Progress Check lesson includes a Self Assessment master that students complete. These Self Assessments are part of a balanced assessment plan as they allow:

- students to reflect on their progress, strengths, and weaknesses;
- teachers to gain insights into how students perceive their progress; and
- teachers and students to plan how to address weaknesses.

The Self Assessment engages students in evaluating their competency with the concepts and skills addressed in the unit. For each skill or concept, students check a box to indicate one of the following:

- I can do this on my own and explain how to do it.
- I can do this on my own.
- I can do this if I get help or look at an example.

If students feel as though they need help or do not understand, consider talking with them about how they may learn more about the concept or skill. Look to related Readiness activities in Part 3 of lessons and to games for ideas about further developing students' understanding.

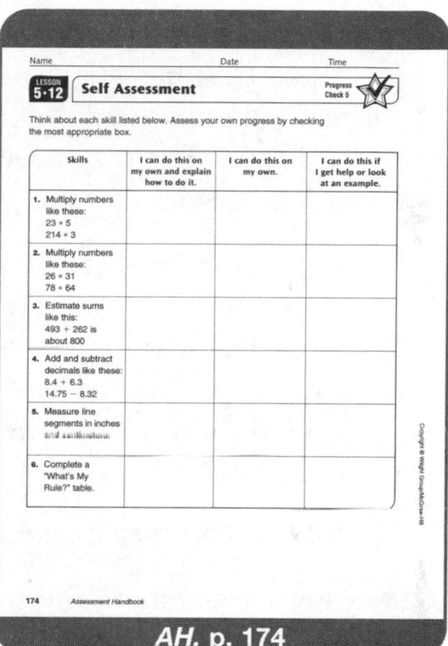

Name Date Time

LESSON 5•12 **Self Assessment** Progress Check 5

Think about each skill listed below. Assess your own progress by checking the most appropriate box.

Skills	I can do this on my own and explain how to do it.	I can do this on my own.	I can do this if I get help or look at an example.
1. Multiply numbers like these: 23 * 5 214 * 3			
2. Multiply numbers like these: 26 * 31 78 * 64			
3. Estimate sums like this: 493 + 262 is about 800			
4. Add and subtract decimals like these: 8.4 + 6.3 14.75 − 8.32			
5. Measure line segments in inches [illegible]			
6. Complete a "What's My Rule?" table.			

Copyright © Wright Group/McGraw-Hill

174 *Assessment Handbook*

AH, p. 174

Open Response Tasks

Each Progress Check lesson includes an Open Response task linked to one or more Grade-Level Goals emphasized in the unit. These Open Response assessment tasks can provide additional balance in an assessment plan as they allow students to:

- become more aware of their problem-solving processes as they communicate their understanding, for example, through words, pictures, or diagrams;
- apply a variety of strategies to solve the longer tasks;
- further demonstrate their knowledge and understanding through application of skills and concepts in meaningful contexts; and
- be successful on a variety of levels.

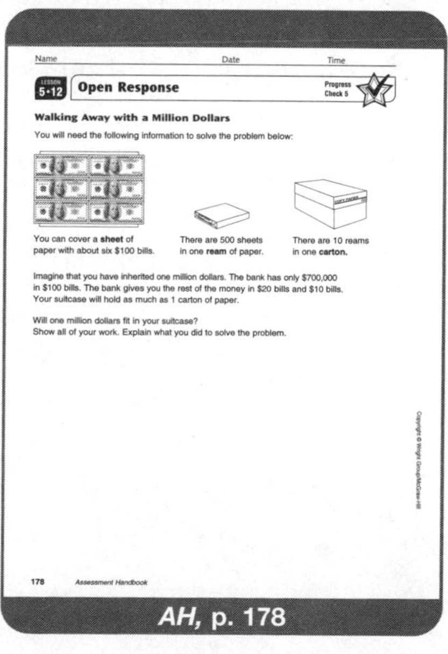

Name Date Time

LESSON 5•12 **Open Response** Progress Check 5

Walking Away with a Million Dollars

You will need the following information to solve the problem below:

You can cover a **sheet** of paper with about six $100 bills.

There are 500 sheets in one **ream** of paper.

There are 10 reams in one **carton.**

Imagine that you have inherited one million dollars. The bank has only $700,000 in $100 bills. The bank gives you the rest of the money in $20 bills and $10 bills. Your suitcase will hold as much as 1 carton of paper.

Will one million dollars fit in your suitcase?
Show all of your work. Explain what you did to solve the problem.

Copyright © Wright Group/McGraw-Hill

178 *Assessment Handbook*

AH, p. 178

The Open Response tasks have been selected with the following points in mind:

- The problem context makes sense to students.
- The skill level of the problem is appropriate for students.
- The problem involves mathematics in which students have a foundation.
- The mathematics of the problem is important to the grade level. The problem addresses one or more Grade-Level Goals for the grade.
- The problem has connections to the real world that students have experience with.
- The problem may not be a multistep problem, but the solution strategy involves several steps.
- The problem may have more than one correct solution.

In the unit-specific section of this handbook that begins on page 51, each Open Response task has suggested implementation strategies, a sample task-specific rubric, and annotated student samples demonstrating the expectations described in the rubric. The unit-specific section also includes suggestions for adapting the Open Response task to meet the needs of a diverse group of students.

The sample rubrics are on a 4-point scale. The top two scores (4 points and 3 points) are designated for student work that demonstrates success with the task. The bottom two scores (2 points and 1 point) are designated for student work that does not demonstrate success with the task; 0 points are reserved for situations where students have made no effort to understand or solve the problem.

In general, the sample rubrics focus on assessing the following items:

- whether the mathematics students use is correct;
- whether the solution strategy makes sense, is reasonable, addresses the problem, and may lead to a successful solution;
- whether the explanation of the strategy is clear and easy to follow; and
- whether the solution is correct (or correct except for minor errors).

Walking Away with a Million Dollars Rubric

4	Determines that $1,000,000 will fit in the suitcase and describes in numbers or words the number of dollars or number of bills required for each kind of bill. Shows all computation and provides clear justification in numbers or words for why $1,000,000 will fit in the suitcase. Clearly explains how the estimate is calculated.
3	Determines that $1,000,000 will fit in the suitcase and describes in numbers or words the number of dollars or number of bills required for each kind of bill. Shows computation steps, but there might be some errors. Provides some justification for why $1,000,000 will fit in the suitcase. Explains how the estimate is calculated.
2	Might determine that $1,000,000 will fit in the suitcase, but there might be errors in calculating the number of dollars or number of bills required. Shows computation steps, but there might be errors or steps might be missing.
1	Might restate some of the facts and perform some of the computation, but there might be errors. There might be evidence of major misunderstandings in interpreting the problem.
0	Does not attempt to solve the problem.

You may want to work with other teachers from your grade level to apply the *Everyday Mathematics* rubric to your students' work or to create rubrics for scoring these tasks. Consider the expectations of standardized tests in your area when creating or applying a rubric and modify this sample rubric as appropriate. For more student involvement, consider having them participate in developing a list of expectations for a Level-4 paper.

External Assessment

Outside tests, which are one example of external assessment, are generally tests given at the school, district, or state level, or are nationally standardized tests. Most teachers are familiar with the standardized tests that have multiple-choice responses. The frustrating aspect of this type of test is that it analyzes a narrow range of mathematical thinking and does not assess the depth and breadth of the mathematical knowledge that should be attained in a well-implemented *Everyday Mathematics* classroom.

Everyday Mathematics can help your students function more effectively in testing environments. For example, some Math Boxes problems have been tailored to help prepare students for the formats of an outside test. Even without such preparation, *Everyday Mathematics* students generally do just as well on the computation sections of standardized tests. However, they do much better on concepts and problem-solving sections than students in traditional programs.

More recently, some district and state tests have included performance assessments or open-ended components. *Everyday Mathematics* presents varied mathematics tasks that prepare students for these testing situations: problems requiring students to explain their thinking, writing prompts designed to help students explore content more deeply, and richer Open Response tasks that may require an entire class period for students to solve. If you have a choice in your district, encourage the use of these performance-based or open-ended assessments. They better depict the depth of your students' understandings, as well as their abilities to communicate mathematically, solve problems, and reason.

Performance-based assessments developed at the school or district level probably provide the best opportunities to gather information about student achievement in local classrooms. Teams of teachers and administrators can develop assessments and rubrics that enhance the learning process rather than focus on narrow thinking used only in a small portion of mathematical activities. At some grade levels, these assessments can be used exclusively. When standardized testing is mandatory at a certain grade level, performance-based assessments can provide a better picture of the mathematical education occurring in the classroom than other types of standardized tests.

Record-Keeping

If you teach *Everyday Mathematics* as intended and use the techniques described in this book, you will soon have a vast amount of information about students' mathematical skills and understanding. This section of the handbook offers several tools to help you organize and record this information.

Class Checklists and Individual Profiles of Progress

Each lesson in *Everyday Mathematics* identifies a suggested ongoing assessment opportunity in the form of a Recognizing Student Achievement note. These notes highlight specific tasks from which teachers can collect student performance data to monitor and document students' progress toward meeting specific Grade-Level Goals. Each unit in *Everyday Mathematics* contains a Progress Check lesson with suggested periodic assessment tasks. A wealth of assessment information can be collected from these and other sources.

To help you keep track of students' progress in areas that are important to your school and district, checklists for individuals and for the class are provided beginning on page 246 of this handbook. There are Class Checklists for each unit and for each quarter. There are Individual Profiles of Progress for each unit. These checklists provide an organizational system for recording the information you collect to assess student progress on Grade-Level Goals.

The unit checklists include places to record information gathered from the Recognizing Student Achievement notes and from the Progress Check lesson in the unit. The checklists identify the related Grade-Level Goal for each Recognizing Student Achievement task. There is an additional column in which you can add your comments or other notes. To simplify data entry, these checklists are organized according to lesson number.

The quarterly checklists include places to record information gathered throughout the quarter from the Recognizing Student Achievement tasks. To simplify the process of aggregating data in meaningful ways, these checklists are organized according to mathematical strand.

You may prefer using the Class Checklists (on the right) to gather and organize information, transferring selected information to the Individual Profiles of Progress sheet for each student's portfolio or for use during parent conferences.

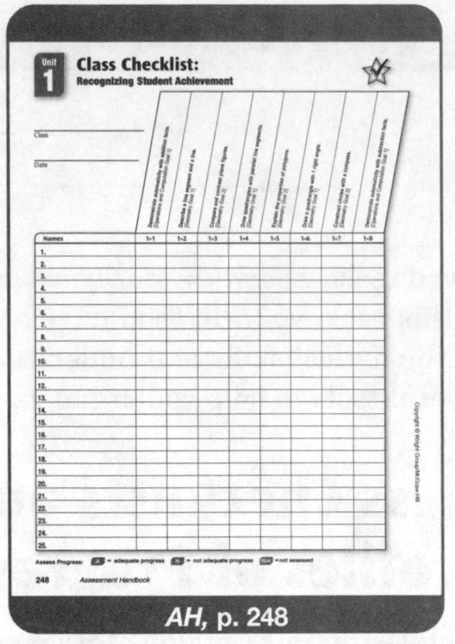

Unit 1 **Class Checklist:**
Recognizing Student Achievement

Class

Date

Names	1-1	1-2	1-3	1-4	1-5	1-6	1-7	1-8
1.								
2.								
3.								
4.								
5.								
6.								
7.								
8.								
9.								
10.								
11.								
12.								
13.								
14.								
15.								
16.								
17.								
18.								
19.								
20.								
21.								
22.								
23.								
24.								
25.								

Assess Progress: A = adequate progress N = not adequate progress N/A = not assessed

248 Assessment Handbook

AH, p. 248

Checklist Flow Chart

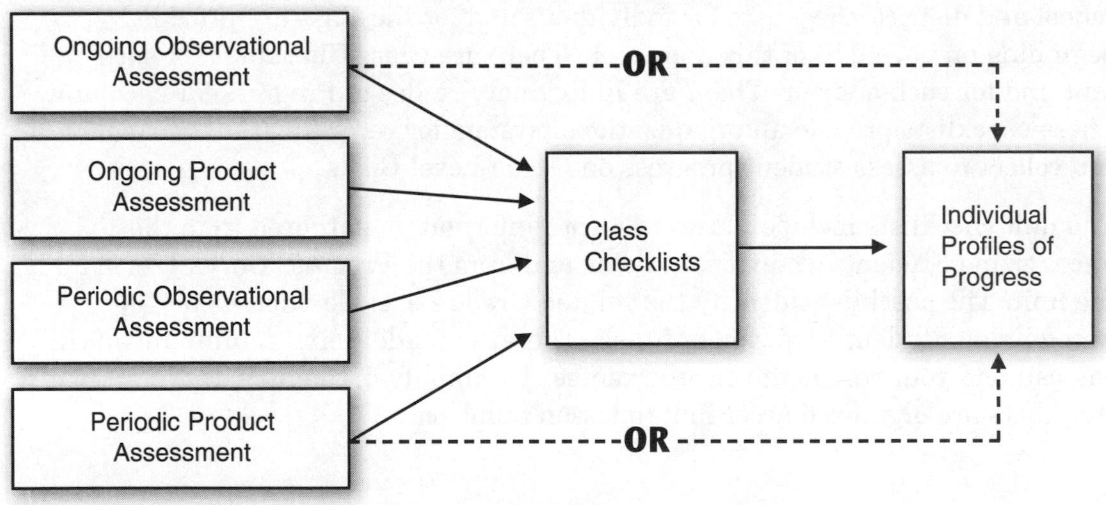

The Individual Profiles of Progress, Class Checklists, and Quarterly Checklists can be found in the Assessment Masters beginning on page 246 of this handbook. Blank checklists have been provided as well.

Options for Recording Data on Checklists

There are several different record-keeping schemes for checklists. Two such schemes are described below.

Option 1

Because Recognizing Student Achievement suggestions include descriptions of the expectations for *making adequate progress,* consider recording this information on a checklist using the following:

A	Student is making adequate progress toward Grade-Level Goal.
N	Student is not making adequate progress toward Grade-Level Goal.

Or

✓	Student is making adequate progress toward Grade-Level Goal.
–	Student is not making adequate progress toward Grade-Level Goal.

Option 2

As the teacher, you can decide how you define what is *making adequate progress* and what is not. For example, if you use a 4-point rubric like the sample below, you may decide to define 3 or 4 points as *making adequate progress* and 1 or 2 points as *not making adequate progress.*

4 points	Student is making adequate progress. Student solves the problem correctly and demonstrates a sophisticated and well-articulated understanding of the concept or skill being assessed.
3 points	Student is making adequate progress. Student solves the problem correctly with only minor errors and demonstrates a developmentally appropriate understanding of the concept or skill being assessed.
2 points	Student is not making adequate progress. Student appears to understand some components of the problem and attempts to solve the problem. Student demonstrates an understanding of the concept or skill being assessed that is marginally short of what is expected.
1 point	Student is not making adequate progress. Student appears to not understand the problem but makes some attempt to solve it. Student demonstrates an understanding of the concept or skill being assessed that is significantly short of what is expected.
0 points	Student does not attempt to solve the problem.

Assessment Management System

Introduction

The *Everyday Mathematics* Assessment Management System is an electronic tool that assists educators in monitoring and documenting student progress toward meeting *Everyday Mathematics* Grade-Level Goals.

Record-Keeping

You can use the tool to enter student performance information for the following *Everyday Mathematics* assessments:

- Ongoing Assessment: Recognizing Student Achievement
- Progress Check: Oral and Slate
- Progress Check: Written Assessment
- Progress Check: Open Response
- Mid-Year Assessment
- End-of-Year Assessment

You can also easily complement the assessments provided in *Everyday Mathematics* by adding student performance data from tasks you design or from the many other tasks in the *Everyday Mathematics* curriculum.

Features

The *Assessment Management System* includes many features for supporting your balanced assessment plan. *For example:*

- All the suggested *Everyday Mathematics* assessment tasks are built into the system. Clicking a lesson number will bring you directly to the corresponding assessment task.
- As long as you assign a Grade-Level Goal to the assessment task, any other tasks that you create or that you use from the curriculum are incorporated into the system.
- A variety of data-entry options allow you to record general student performance, detailed-scoring information, and text comments for each of your students. You can determine the level of specificity that best suits your assessment needs.

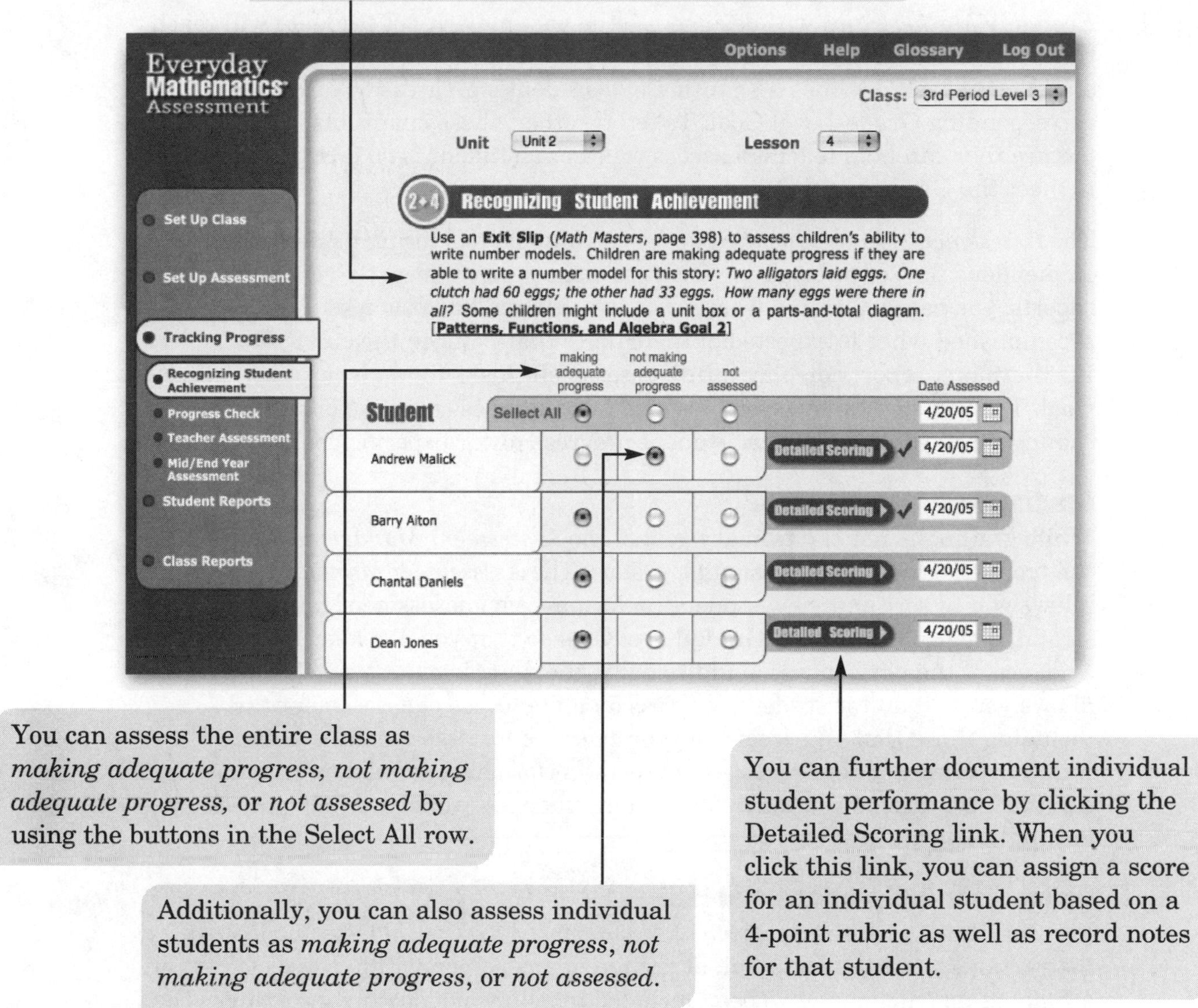

Student Reports

Once you have entered student assessment data, the *Assessment Management System* provides you with a variety of ways to sort and organize the information. *For example:*

- Class and individual reports show student performance data on specific assessment tasks.
- Class and individual reports show student performance data sorted by content strand, Program Goal, or Grade-Level Goal.
- Class and individual reports are based on time frames that you create, which allows you to tailor the reports to correspond with your district's marking periods.

These reports can then be viewed electronically or printed for distribution.

Monitor Student Progress

Everyday Mathematics was designed so the vast majority of students will reach the Grade-Level Goals for a given grade upon completion of that grade. Each assessment task provides a snapshot of a student's progress toward the corresponding Grade-Level Goal. Taken together, these snapshots form a moving picture that can help teachers assess whether a student is on a trajectory or path to meet the Grade-Level Goal.

The *Assessment Management System* is a valuable tool for managing the tremendous flow of information about student performance. By viewing the reports, you can determine whether or not children have successfully accomplished what is expected of them up to that point in the curriculum. Furthermore, reports display future assessment tasks for a given Grade-Level Goal. This function allows you to see additional assessment opportunities coming up so you can monitor student progress toward specific goals.

Grading Assistance

While grading is not the primary goal of the *Assessment Management System,* the tool can assist you in assigning grades. The *Assessment Management System* allows you to sort and view student performance on assessment tasks by content strand, Program Goal, and Grade-Level Goal so that you can keep documented evidence of the performance. Additionally, the *Assessment Management System* allows you to monitor student progress on many types of assessment tasks, including those that you create so your evidence for assessment is based on multiple sources. These records of student performance, combined with the careful observations you make about your students' work, will help you assign fair and accurate grades.

Online User Instructions and Help

For assistance with the *Assessment Management System* and specific feature instructions, click the Help link at the top of any screen within the tool. Text and animated instructions have been included to help you smoothly incorporate the *Assessment Management System* into your balanced assessment plan.

Frequently Asked Questions

1. **Do the Grade-Level Goals summarize all the concepts and skills that are covered each year?**

   No; Although the Grade-Level Goals reflect the core of the curriculum at each grade level, they are not comprehensive. They do not capture all the content that is addressed each year. Nor are they a list of activities that are completed each year. Some grade-level content supports future Grade-Level Goals that are not articulated at the given grade level.

2. **With all these Grade-Level Goals, how will I know when I'm simply exposing students to a concept or skill?**

   The *Everyday Mathematics* curriculum aims for student proficiency with concepts and skills through repeated exposures over several years. The *Teacher's Lesson Guide* alerts teachers to content that is being introduced for the first time through Links to the Future notes. These notes provide specific references to future Grade-Level Goals and help teachers understand introductory activities at their grade level in the context of the entire K–6 curriculum.

   All the content in *Everyday Mathematics* is important, whether it's being experienced for the first or the fifth time. The *Everyday Mathematics* curriculum is similar to an intricately woven rug, with many threads that appear and reappear to form complex patterns. Different students will progress at different rates, so multiple exposures to important content are critical for accommodating individual differences. The program was created so it is consistent with how students learn mathematics. It builds understanding over a period of time, first through informal exposure and later through more formal and directed instruction. For students to succeed, they need the opportunity to experience all that the curriculum has to offer in every grade.

3. There are a lot of lessons in my grade-level materials. Do I have to finish all of them? For example, I teach second grade. Automaticity with *0, *1, *2, *5, and *10 facts is not a Grade-Level Goal until third grade. Can't I just skip all of the second-grade lessons that cover multiplication facts?

Everyday Mathematics was created to be consistent with how students actually learn mathematics, building understanding over time, first through informal exposure and later through more formal instruction. Because the Grade-Level Goals are cumulative, it is essential for children to experience the complete curriculum at each grade level. Students in *Second Grade Everyday Mathematics,* for example, participate in many hands-on activities designed to develop an understanding of multiplication. This makes it possible for students to achieve multiplication goals in third grade.

4. Do I need to keep track of progress on Program Goals?

Program Goals are the threads that weave the content together across grade levels and form the skeleton of the curriculum. The Program Goals are further refined through the Grade-Level Goals. *Everyday Mathematics* provides a variety of tools you can use to assess student progress on the Grade-Level Goals throughout the year. Because every Grade-Level Goal is related to a Program Goal, you are gathering information at this less-specific level as well. This allows great flexibility in reporting to parents. Depending on how your district requires you to aggregate data, you can look broadly at content strands, more closely at Program Goals, or specifically at Grade-Level Goals using the suggested assessments in *Everyday Mathematics*.

5. What do the authors mean by "adequate progress"?

Students who are making adequate progress as defined by a Recognizing Student Achievement note are on a trajectory to meet the Grade-Level Goal. Such students have successfully accomplished what is expected up to that point in the curriculum. If students continue to progress as expected, then they will demonstrate proficiency with the Grade-Level Goal upon completion of the year.

The performance expectations described in the Recognizing Student Achievement notes for any given Grade-Level Goal progress developmentally throughout the year. The level of performance that is expected in October is not the same as what is expected in April. The term *adequate progress* describes the level of competency that the majority of students can be expected to have at a particular time. The authors of *Everyday Mathematics* chose the Recognizing Student Achievement tasks with the expectation that the majority of students would be successful with them, which is in line with the expectation that the vast majority of students will successfully reach the Grade-Level Goals for their grade level.

6. **Do students have to complete all of the Recognizing Student Achievement tasks before I can know whether they are making adequate progress?**

   Each lesson in *Everyday Mathematics* contains a Recognizing Student Achievement note. These notes highlight specific tasks from which teachers can collect student performance data to monitor and document students' progress toward meeting specific Grade-Level Goals. Each Recognizing Student Achievement note addresses part of a Grade-Level Goal. The suggested assessment tasks build a complete picture over time for each Grade-Level Goal. If students perform well on one or two Recognizing Student Achievement tasks for a goal, that may not provide enough information about the goal in its entirety. Teachers are the experts in their classrooms. If you choose to not do some of the Recognizing Student Achievement tasks, consider collecting similar information from tasks you designate to assemble a complete picture for each Grade-Level Goal.

7. **Can I use only Math Boxes to collect assessment information? They seem to have all the skills in them.**

   Everyday Mathematics includes a variety of assessment tasks to ensure that all students have sufficient opportunities to demonstrate what they know. Some students best demonstrate their knowledge through pencil-and-paper tasks, some through performance tasks, and some through explanations and demonstrations. The assessment tasks in the program have been chosen to accommodate a range of learners. Using only one tool might limit what you are able to learn about your students.

8. **I understand that *Everyday Mathematics* provides a Recognizing Student Achievement task for every lesson. May I choose my own instead of or in addition to the ones designated by the curriculum? If I don't think the results of a particular Recognizing Student Achievement task accurately reflect what a student knows, what should I do?**

   The Recognizing Student Achievement tasks and Progress Check questions occur at carefully chosen points, based on the opportunities for distributed practice that occur throughout the program. Assessment tasks were also designed to vary the ways in which students are assessed for each Grade-Level Goal.

The *Everyday Mathematics* authors respect teachers as professionals and expect that teachers will use their professional judgment when assessing students. If a particular Recognizing Student Achievement task does not adequately assess student achievement, the teacher may choose to disregard it. The *Everyday Mathematics* authors also anticipate that students' performances on tasks that are not identified in Recognizing Student Achievement notes will often provide useful information regarding their progress toward a particular Grade-Level Goal. Teachers should feel free to link such tasks to appropriate Grade-Level Goals and include them in their assessment stories.

9. I understand the different record-keeping options that were presented in this handbook. My district, however, evaluates students by assigning traditional letter grades. How should I evaluate student performance?

Because local assessment systems are based on local norms and values, it would be impossible to design a system that would apply universally. But the authors of *Everyday Mathematics* recognize that many teachers are required by their districts to give traditional grades. And although it is impossible to design a single grading system that will work for everyone, there are some broad principles to follow:

- Grades should be fair and based on evidence that can be documented.
- Evidence for grading should come from multiple sources.
- Grades should be based on content that is important. They should not be based only on the content that is most easily assessed.
- The grading system should be aligned with both state and local standards and with the curriculum.

10. Suppose a student makes adequate progress on the majority of Recognizing Student Achievement tasks and Progress Check questions for a given Grade-Level Goal throughout the year. At the end of the year how likely is it that the student will have achieved the Grade-Level Goal?

The Recognizing Student Achievement and Progress Check tasks supply a great deal of data on which teachers can base inferences about students' achievement of Grade-Level Goals. In the case of a consistent pattern of adequate progress on assessment tasks for a given Grade-Level Goal, one can reasonably conclude that the student has in fact achieved the given goal. As with any assessment, however, inferences based on positive performance are more straightforward than those based on negative performance. That is, if a student performs well, the most straightforward conclusion is that the student has probably mastered the material; whereas if a student performs poorly, there are many possible explanations, only one of which is a lack of mastery.

Teachers should also recognize that inferences about what students know should always be considered provisional, because the inferences are fallible, based as they are on incomplete information, and because students are constantly growing and changing.

According to *Knowing What Students Know*:

> *... by its very nature, assessment is imprecise to some degree. Assessment results are estimates, based on samples of knowledge and performance drawn from the much larger universe of everything a person knows and can do. . . . Assessment is a process of reasoning from evidence. Because one cannot directly perceive students' mental processes, one must rely on less direct methods to make judgments about what they know*
>
> (Pellegrino, Chudowsky, and Glaser 2001, 36)
>
> *An assessment is a tool designed to observe students' behavior and produce data that can be used to draw reasonable inferences about what students know.*
>
> (Pellegrino, Chudowsky, and Glaser 2001, 42)

Recommended Reading

Black, Paul, and Dylan Wiliam. "Assessment and Classroom Learning." *Assessment in Education* (March, 1998): 7–74.

______. "Inside the Black Box: Raising Standards Through Classroom Assessment." *Phi Delta Kappan* 80, no. 2 (October, 1998): 139–149.

Bryant, Brian R., and Teddy Maddox. "Using Alternative Assessment Techniques to Plan and Evaluate Mathematics." *LD Forum 21,* no. 2 (winter, 1996): 24–33.

Eisner, Elliot W. "The Uses and Limits of Performance Assessment." *Phi Delta Kappan* 80, no. 9 (May, 1999): 658–661.

Kulm, Gerald. *Mathematics Assessment: What Works in the Classroom.* San Francisco: Jossey-Bass Publishers, 1994.

National Council of Teachers of Mathematics (NCTM). *Curriculum and Evaluation Standards for School Mathematics.* Reston, Va.: NCTM, 1989.

______. *Assessment Standards for School Mathematics.* Reston, Va.: NCTM, 1995.

______. *Principles and Standards for School Mathematics.* Reston, Va.: NCTM, 2000.

National Research Council. Committee on the Foundations of Assessment. Pellegrino, James W., Naomi Chudowsky, and Robert Glaser, eds. *Knowing What Students Know: The Science and Design of Educational Assessment.* Washington, D.C.: National Academy Press, 2001.

National Research Council, Mathematical Sciences Education Board. *Measuring What Counts: A Conceptual Guide for Mathematics Assessment.* Washington, D.C.: National Academy Press, 1993.

Pearson, Bethyl, and Cathy Berghoff. "London Bridge Is Not Falling Down: It's Supporting Alternative Assessment." *TESOL Journal* 5, no. 4 (summer, 1996): 28–31.

Shepard, Lorrie A. "Using Assessment to Improve Learning." *Educational Leadership* 52, no. 5 (February, 1995): 38–43.

Stenmark, Jean Kerr, ed. *Mathematics Assessment: Myths, Models, Good Questions, and Practical Suggestions.* Reston, Va.: National Council of Teachers of Mathematics, 1991.

Stiggens, Richard J. *Student-Centered Classroom Assessment.* Englewood Cliffs, N.J.: Prentice-Hall, 1997.

Webb, N. L., and A. F. Coxford, eds. *Assessment in the Mathematics Classroom: 1993 Yearbook.* Reston, Va.: National Council of Teachers of Mathematics, 1993.

http://everydaymath.uchicago.edu/

Everyday Mathematics GOALS

The following tables list the Grade-Level Goals organized by Content Strand and Program Goal.

Everyday Mathematics®

Content Strand: NUMBER AND NUMERATION

Program Goal: Understand the Meanings, Uses, and Representations of Numbers

Content	Kindergarten	First Grade	Second Grade	Third Grade	Fourth Grade	Fifth Grade	Sixth Grade
Rote counting	**Goal 1.** Count on by 1s to 100; count on by 2s, 5s, and 10s and count back by 1s with number grids, number lines, and calculators.	**Goal 1.** Count on by 1s, 2s, 5s, and 10s past 100 and back by 1s from any number less than 100 with and without number grids, number lines, and calculators.	**Goal 1.** Count on by 1s, 2s, 5s, 10s, 25s, and 100s past 1,000 and back by 1s from any number less than 1,000 with and without number grids, number lines, and calculators.				
Rational counting	**Goal 2.** Count 20 or more objects; estimate the number of objects in a collection.	**Goal 2.** Count collections of objects accurately and reliably; estimate the number of objects in a collection.					
Place value and notation	**Goal 3.** Model numbers with manipulatives; use manipulatives to exchange 1s for 10s and 10s for 100s; recognize that digits can be used and combined to read and write numbers; read numbers up to 30.	**Goal 3.** Read, write, and model with manipulatives whole numbers up to 1,000; identify places in such numbers and the values of the digits in those places.	**Goal 2.** Read, write, and model with manipulatives whole numbers up to 10,000; identify places in such numbers and the values of the digits in those places; read and write money amounts in dollars-and-cents notation.	**Goal 1.** Read and write whole numbers up to 1,000,000; read, write, and model with manipulatives decimals through hundredths; identify places in such numbers and the values of the digits in those places; translate between whole numbers and decimals represented in words, in base-10 notation, and with manipulatives.	**Goal 1.** Read and write whole numbers up to 1,000,000,000 and decimals through thousandths; identify places in such numbers and the values of the digits in those places; translate between whole numbers and decimals represented in words and in base-10 notation.	**Goal 1.** Read and write whole numbers and decimals; identify places in such numbers and the values of the digits in those places; use expanded notation to represent whole numbers and decimals.	**Goal 1.** Read and write whole numbers and decimals; identify places in such numbers and the values of the digits in those places; use expanded notation, number-and-word notation, exponential notation, and scientific notation to represent whole numbers and decimals.

Everyday Mathematics

Content Strand: NUMBER AND NUMERATION *cont.*

Program Goal: Understand the Meanings, Uses, and Representations of Numbers *cont.*

Content	Kindergarten	First Grade	Second Grade	Third Grade	Fourth Grade	Fifth Grade	Sixth Grade
Meanings and uses of fractions	**Goal 4.** Use manipulatives to model half of a region or a collection; describe the model.	**Goal 4.** Use manipulatives and drawings to model halves, thirds, and fourths as equal parts of a region or a collection; describe the model.	**Goal 3.** Use manipulatives and drawings to model fractions as equal parts of a region or a collection; describe the models and name the fractions.	**Goal 2.** Read, write, and model fractions; solve problems involving fractional parts of a region or a collection; describe strategies used.	**Goal 2.** Read, write, and model fractions; solve problems involving fractional parts of a region or a collection; describe and explain strategies used; given a fractional part of a region or a collection, identify the unit whole.	**Goal 2.** Solve problems involving percents and discounts; describe and explain strategies used; identify the unit whole in situations involving fractions.	**Goal 2.** Solve problems involving percents and discounts; explain strategies used; identify the unit whole in situations involving fractions, decimals, and percents.
Number theory		**Goal 5.** Use manipulatives to identify and model odd and even numbers.	**Goal 4.** Recognize numbers as odd or even.	**Goal 3.** Find multiples of 2, 5, and 10.	**Goal 3.** Find multiples of whole numbers less than 10; find whole-number factors of numbers.	**Goal 3.** Identify prime and composite numbers; factor numbers; find prime factorizations.	**Goal 3.** Use GCFs, LCMs, and divisibility rules to manipulate fractions.
Program Goal: Understand Equivalent Names for Numbers							
Equivalent names for whole numbers	**Goal 5.** Use manipulatives, drawings, and numerical expressions involving addition and subtraction of 1-digit numbers to give equivalent names for whole numbers up to 20.	**Goal 6.** Use manipulatives, drawings, tally marks, and numerical expressions involving addition and subtraction of 1- or 2-digit numbers to give equivalent names for whole numbers up to 100.	**Goal 5.** Use tally marks, arrays, and numerical expressions involving addition and subtraction to give equivalent names for whole numbers.	**Goal 4.** Use numerical expressions involving one or more of the basic four arithmetic operations to give equivalent names for whole numbers.	**Goal 4.** Use numerical expressions involving one or more of the basic four arithmetic operations and grouping symbols to give equivalent names for whole numbers.	**Goal 4.** Use numerical expressions involving one or more of the basic four arithmetic operations, grouping symbols, and exponents to give equivalent names for whole numbers; convert between base-10, exponential, and repeated-factor notations.	**Goal 4.** Apply the order of operations to numerical expressions to give equivalent names for rational numbers.

Everyday Mathematics

Content Strand: NUMBER AND NUMERATION *cont.*

Program Goal: Understand Equivalent Names for Numbers *cont.*

Content	Kindergarten	First Grade	Second Grade	Third Grade	Fourth Grade	Fifth Grade	Sixth Grade
Equivalent names for fractions, decimals, and percents			**Goal 6.** Use manipulatives and drawings to model equivalent names for $\frac{1}{2}$.	**Goal 5.** Use manipulatives and drawings to find and represent equivalent names for fractions; use manipulatives to generate equivalent fractions.	**Goal 5.** Use numerical expressions to find and represent equivalent names for fractions and decimals; use and explain a multiplication rule to find equivalent fractions; rename fourths, fifths, tenths, and hundredths as decimals and percents.	**Goal 5.** Use numerical expressions to find and represent equivalent names for fractions, decimals, and percents; use and explain multiplication and division rules to find equivalent fractions and fractions in simplest form; convert between fractions and mixed numbers; convert between fractions, decimals, and percents.	**Goal 5.** Find equivalent fractions and fractions in simplest form by applying multiplication and division rules and concepts from number theory; convert between fractions, mixed numbers, decimals, and percents.

Program Goal: Understand Common Numerical Relations

Content	Kindergarten	First Grade	Second Grade	Third Grade	Fourth Grade	Fifth Grade	Sixth Grade
Comparing and ordering numbers	**Goal 6.** Compare and order whole numbers up to 20.	**Goal 7.** Compare and order whole numbers up to 1,000.	**Goal 7.** Compare and order whole numbers up to 10,000; use area models to compare fractions.	**Goal 6.** Compare and order whole numbers up to 1,000,000; use manipulatives to order decimals through hundredths; use area models and benchmark fractions to compare and order fractions.	**Goal 6.** Compare and order whole numbers up to 1,000,000,000 and decimals through thousandths; compare and order integers between −100 and 0; use area models, benchmark fractions, and analyses of numerators and denominators to compare and order fractions.	**Goal 6.** Compare and order rational numbers; use area models, benchmark fractions, and analyses of numerators and denominators to compare and order fractions and mixed numbers; describe strategies used to compare fractions and mixed numbers.	**Goal 6.** Choose and apply strategies for comparing and ordering rational numbers; explain those choices and strategies.

Everyday Mathematics

Content Strand: OPERATIONS AND COMPUTATION

Program Goal: Compute Accurately

Content	Kindergarten	First Grade	Second Grade	Third Grade	Fourth Grade	Fifth Grade	Sixth Grade
Addition and subtraction facts		**Goal 1.** Demonstrate proficiency with +/− 0, +/− 1, doubles, and sum-equals-ten addition and subtraction facts such as 6 + 4 = 10 and 10 − 7 = 3.	**Goal 1.** Demonstrate automaticity with +/− 0, +/− 1, doubles, and sum-equals-ten facts, and proficiency with all addition and subtraction facts through 10 + 10.	**Goal 1.** Demonstrate automaticity with all addition and subtraction facts through 10 + 10; use basic facts to compute fact extensions such as 80 + 70.	**Goal 1.** Demonstrate automaticity with basic addition and subtraction facts and fact extensions.		
Addition and subtraction procedures	**Goal 1.** Use manipulatives, number lines, and mental arithmetic to solve problems involving the addition and subtraction of single-digit whole numbers.	**Goal 2.** Use manipulatives, number grids, tally marks, mental arithmetic, and calculators to solve problems involving the addition and subtraction of 1-digit whole numbers with 1- or 2-digit whole numbers; calculate and compare the values of combinations of coins.	**Goal 2.** Use manipulatives, number grids, tally marks, mental arithmetic, paper & pencil, and calculators to solve problems involving the addition and subtraction of 2-digit whole numbers; describe the strategies used; calculate and compare values of coin and bill combinations.	**Goal 2.** Use manipulatives, mental arithmetic, paper-and-pencil algorithms, and calculators to solve problems involving the addition and subtraction of whole numbers and decimals in a money context; describe the strategies used and explain how they work.	**Goal 2.** Use manipulatives, mental arithmetic, paper-and-pencil algorithms, and calculators to solve problems involving the addition and subtraction of whole numbers and decimals through hundredths; describe the strategies used and explain how they work.	**Goal 1.** Use mental arithmetic, paper-and-pencil algorithms, and calculators to solve problems involving the addition and subtraction of whole numbers, decimals, and signed numbers; describe the strategies used and explain how they work.	**Goal 1.** Use mental arithmetic, paper-and-pencil algorithms, and calculators to solve problems involving the addition and subtraction of whole numbers, decimals, and signed numbers; describe the strategies used and explain how they work.

Everyday Mathematics

Content Strand: OPERATIONS AND COMPUTATION *cont.*

Program Goal: Compute Accurately *cont.*

Content	Kindergarten	First Grade	Second Grade	Third Grade	Fourth Grade	Fifth Grade	Sixth Grade
Multiplication and division facts				**Goal 3.** Demonstrate automaticity with ×0, ×1, ×2, ×5, and ×10 multiplication facts; use strategies to compute remaining facts up to 10 × 10.	**Goal 3.** Demonstrate automaticity with multiplication facts through 10 * 10 and proficiency with related division facts; use basic facts to compute fact extensions such as 30 * 60.	**Goal 2.** Demonstrate automaticity with multiplication facts and proficiency with division facts and fact extensions.	
Multiplication and division procedures				**Goal 4.** Use arrays, mental arithmetic, paper-and-pencil algorithms, and calculators to solve problems involving the multiplication of 2- and 3-digit whole numbers by 1-digit whole numbers; describe the strategies used.	**Goal 4.** Use mental arithmetic, paper-and-pencil algorithms, and calculators to solve problems involving the multiplication of multidigit whole numbers by 2-digit whole numbers and the division of multidigit whole numbers by 1-digit whole numbers; describe the strategies used and explain how they work.	**Goal 3.** Use mental arithmetic, paper-and-pencil algorithms, and calculators to solve problems involving the multiplication of whole numbers and decimals and the division of multidigit whole numbers and decimals by whole numbers; express remainders as whole numbers or fractions as appropriate; describe the strategies used and explain how they work.	**Goal 2.** Use mental arithmetic, paper-and-pencil algorithms, and calculators to solve problems involving the multiplication and division of whole numbers, decimals, and signed numbers; describe the strategies used and explain how they work.

Everyday Mathematics

Content Strand: OPERATIONS AND COMPUTATION *cont.*

Program Goal: Compute Accurately *cont.*

Content	Kindergarten	First Grade	Second Grade	Third Grade	Fourth Grade	Fifth Grade	Sixth Grade
Procedures for addition and subtraction of fractions					**Goal 5.** Use manipulatives, mental arithmetic, and calculators to solve problems involving the addition and subtraction of fractions with like and unlike denominators; describe the strategies used.	**Goal 4.** Use mental arithmetic, paper-and-pencil algorithms, and calculators to solve problems involving the addition and subtraction of fractions and mixed numbers; describe the strategies used and explain how they work.	**Goal 3.** Use mental arithmetic, paper-and-pencil algorithms, and calculators to solve problems involving the addition and subtraction of fractions and mixed numbers; describe the strategies used and explain how they work.
Procedures for multiplication and division of fractions						**Goal 5.** Use area models, mental arithmetic, paper-and-pencil algorithms, and calculators to solve problems involving the multiplication of fractions and mixed numbers; use diagrams, a common-denominator method, and calculators to solve problems involving the division of fractions; describe the strategies used.	**Goal 4.** Use mental arithmetic, paper-and-pencil algorithms, and calculators to solve problems involving the multiplication and division of fractions and mixed numbers; describe the strategies used and explain how they work.

Everyday Mathematics

Content Strand: OPERATIONS AND COMPUTATION *cont.*

Program Goal: Make Reasonable Estimates

Content	Kindergarten	First Grade	Second Grade	Third Grade	Fourth Grade	Fifth Grade	Sixth Grade
Computational estimation		**Goal 3.** Estimate reasonableness of answers to basic fact problems (e.g., Will 7 + 8 be more or less than 10?).	**Goal 3.** Make reasonable estimates for whole number addition and subtraction problems; explain how the estimates were obtained.	**Goal 5.** Make reasonable estimates for whole number addition and subtraction problems; explain how the estimates were obtained.	**Goal 6.** Make reasonable estimates for whole number and decimal addition and subtraction problems and whole number multiplication and division problems; explain how the estimates were obtained.	**Goal 6.** Make reasonable estimates for whole number and decimal addition, subtraction, multiplication, and division problems and fraction and mixed number addition and subtraction problems; explain how the estimates were obtained.	**Goal 5.** Make reasonable estimates for whole number, decimal, fraction, and mixed number addition, subtraction, multi-plication, and division problems; explain how the estimates were obtained.

Program Goal: Understand Meanings of Operations

Content	Kindergarten	First Grade	Second Grade	Third Grade	Fourth Grade	Fifth Grade	Sixth Grade
Models for the operations	**Goal 2.** Identify join and take-away situations.	**Goal 4.** Identify change to more, change-to-less, comparison, and parts-and-total situations.	**Goal 4.** Identify and describe change, comparison, and parts-and-total situations; use repeated addition, arrays, and skip counting to model multiplication; use equal sharing and equal grouping to model division.	**Goal 6.** Recognize and describe change, comparison, and parts-and-total situations; use repeated addition, arrays, and skip counting to model multiplication; use equal sharing and equal grouping to model division.	**Goal 7.** Use repeated addition, skip counting, arrays, area, and scaling to model multiplication and division.	**Goal 7.** Use repeated addition, arrays, area, and scaling to model multiplication and division; use ratios expressed as words, fractions, percents, and with colons; solve problems involving ratios of parts of a set to the whole set.	**Goal 6.** Use ratios and scaling to model size changes and to solve size-change problems; represent ratios as fractions, percents, and decimals, and using a colon; model and solve problems involving part-to-whole and part-to-part ratios; model rate and ratio number stories with proportions; use and explain cross multiplication and other strategies to solve proportions.

Everyday Mathematics

Content Strand: DATA AND CHANCE

Program Goal: Select and Create Appropriate Graphical Representations of Collected or Given Data

Content	Kindergarten	First Grade	Second Grade	Third Grade	Fourth Grade	Fifth Grade	Sixth Grade
Data collection and representation	**Goal 1.** Collect and organize data to create class-constructed tally charts, tables, and bar graphs.	**Goal 1.** Collect and organize data to create tally charts, tables, bar graphs, and line plots.	**Goal 1.** Collect and organize data or use given data to create tally charts, tables, bar graphs, and line plots.	**Goal 1.** Collect and organize data or use given data to create charts, tables, bar graphs, and line plots.	**Goal 1.** Collect and organize data or use given data to create charts, tables, bar graphs, line plots, and line graphs.	**Goal 1.** Collect and organize data or use given data to create bar, line, and circle graphs with reasonable titles, labels, keys, and intervals.	**Goal 1.** Collect and organize data or use given data to create bar, line, circle, and stem-and-leaf graphs with reasonable titles, labels, keys, and intervals.

Program Goal: Analyze and Interpret Data

Content	Kindergarten	First Grade	Second Grade	Third Grade	Fourth Grade	Fifth Grade	Sixth Grade
Data analysis	**Goal 2.** Use graphs to answer simple questions.	**Goal 2.** Use graphs to answer simple questions and draw conclusions; find the maximum and minimum of a data set.	**Goal 2.** Use graphs to ask and answer simple questions and draw conclusions; find the maximum, minimum, mode, and median of a data set.	**Goal 2.** Use graphs to ask and answer simple questions and draw conclusions; find the maximum, minimum, range, mode, and median of a data set.	**Goal 2.** Use the maximum, minimum, range, median, mode, and graphs to ask and answer questions, draw conclusions, and make predictions.	**Goal 2.** Use the maximum, minimum, range, median, mode, and mean and graphs to ask and answer questions, draw conclusions, and make predictions.	**Goal 2.** Use the minimum, range, median, mode, and mean and graphs to ask and answer questions, draw conclusions, and make predictions; compare and contrast the median and mean of a data set.

Program Goal: Understand and Apply Basic Concepts of Probability

Content	Kindergarten	First Grade	Second Grade	Third Grade	Fourth Grade	Fifth Grade	Sixth Grade
Qualitative probability	**Goal 3.** Describe events using *certain, possible, impossible*, and other basic probability terms.	**Goal 3.** Describe events using *certain, likely, unlikely, impossible* and other basic probability terms.	**Goal 3.** Describe events using *certain, likely, unlikely, impossible* and other basic probability terms; explain the choice of language.	**Goal 3.** Describe events using *certain, very likely, likely, unlikely, very unlikely, impossible,* and other basic probability terms; explain the choice of language.	**Goal 3.** Describe events using *certain, very likely, likely, unlikely, very unlikely, impossible* and other basic probability terms; use *more likely, equally likely, same chance, 50–50, less likely*, and other basic probability terms to compare events; explain the choice of language.	**Goal 3.** Describe events using *certain, very likely, likely, unlikely, very unlikely, impossible* and other basic probability terms; use *more likely, equally likely, same chance, 50–50, less likely*, and other basic probability terms to compare events; explain the choice of language.	

Everyday Mathematics

Content Strand: DATA AND CHANCE *cont.*

Program Goal: Understand and Apply Basic Concepts of Probability *cont.*

Content	Kindergarten	First Grade	Second Grade	Third Grade	Fourth Grade	Fifth Grade	Sixth Grade
Quantitative probability				**Goal 4.** Predict the outcomes of simple experiments and test the predictions using manipulatives; express the probability of an event by using "__ out of __" language.	**Goal 4.** Predict the outcomes of experiments and test the predictions using manipulatives; summarize the results and use them to predict future events; express the probability of an event as a fraction.	**Goal 4.** Predict the outcomes of experiments, test the predictions using manipulatives, and summarize the results; compare predictions based on theoretical probability with experimental results; use summaries and comparisons to predict future events; express the probability of an event as a fraction, decimal, or percent.	**Goal 3.** Use the Multiplication Counting Principle, tree diagrams, and other counting strategies to identify all possible outcomes for a situation; predict results of experiments, test the predictions using manipulatives, and summarize the findings; compare predictions based on theoretical probability with experimental results; calculate probabilities and express them as fractions, decimals, and percents; explain how sample size affects results; use the results to predict future events.

Everyday Mathematics

Content Strand: MEASUREMENT AND REFERENCE FRAMES

Program Goal: Understand the Systems and Processes of Measurement; Use Appropriate Techniques, Tools, Units, and Formulas in Making Measurements

Content	Kindergarten	First Grade	Second Grade	Third Grade	Fourth Grade	Fifth Grade	Sixth Grade
Length, weight, and angles	**Goal 1.** Use nonstandard tools and techniques to estimate and compare weight and length; identify standard measuring tools.	**Goal 1.** Use nonstandard tools and techniques to estimate and compare weight and length; measure length with standard measuring tools.	**Goal 1.** Estimate length with and without tools; measure length to the nearest inch and centimeter; use standard and nonstandard tools to measure and estimate weight.	**Goal 1.** Estimate length with and without tools; measure length to the nearest $\frac{1}{2}$ inch and $\frac{1}{2}$ centimeter; draw and describe angles as records of rotations.	**Goal 1.** Estimate length with and without tools; measure length to the nearest $\frac{1}{4}$ inch and $\frac{1}{2}$ centimeter; estimate the size of angles without tools.	**Goal 1.** Estimate length with and without tools; measure length with tools to the nearest $\frac{1}{8}$ inch and millimeter; estimate the measure of angles with and without tools; use tools to draw angles with given measures.	**Goal 1.** Estimate length with and without tools; measure length with tools to the nearest $\frac{1}{16}$ inch and millimeter; estimate the measure of angles with and without tools; use tools to draw angles with given measures.
Area, perimeter, volume, and capacity			**Goal 2.** Count unit squares to find the area of rectangles.	**Goal 2.** Describe and use strategies to measure the perimeter of polygons; count unit squares to find the areas of rectangles.	**Goal 2.** Describe and use strategies to measure the perimeter and area of polygons, to estimate the area of irregular shapes, and to find the volume of rectangular prisms.	**Goal 2.** Describe and use strategies to find the perimeter of polygons and the area of circles; choose and use appropriate formulas to calculate the areas of rectangles, parallelograms, and triangles, and the volume of a prism; define *pi* as the ratio of a circle's circumference to its diameter.	**Goal 2.** Choose and use appropriate formulas to calculate the circumference of circles and to solve area, perimeter, and volume problems.
Units and systems of measurement			**Goal 3.** Describe relationships between days in a week and hours in a day.	**Goal 3.** Describe relationships among inches, feet, and yards; describe relationships between minutes in an hour, hours in a day, days in a week.	**Goal 3.** Describe relationships among U.S. customary units of length and among metric units of length.	**Goal 3.** Describe relationships among U.S. customary units of length; among metric units of length; and among U.S. customary units of capacity.	

Everyday Mathematics

Content Strand: MEASUREMENT AND REFERENCE FRAMES

Program Goal: Understand the Systems and Processes of Measurement; Use Appropriate Techniques, Tools, Units, and Formulas in Making Measurements *cont.*

Content	Kindergarten	First Grade	Second Grade	Third Grade	Fourth Grade	Fifth Grade	Sixth Grade
Money	**Goal 2.** Identify pennies, nickels, dimes, quarters, and dollar bills.	**Goal 2.** Know and compare the value of pennies, nickels, dimes, quarters, and dollar bills; make exchanges between coins.	**Goal 4.** Make exchanges between coins and bills.				
Program Goal: Use and Understand Reference Frames							
Temperature	**Goal 3.** Describe temperature using appropriate vocabulary, such as *hot, warm,* and *cold;* identify a thermometer as a tool for measuring temperature.	**Goal 3.** Identify a thermometer as a tool for measuring temperature; read temperatures on Fahrenheit and Celsius thermometers to the nearest 10°.	**Goal 5.** Read temperature on both the Fahrenheit and Celsius scales.				
Time	**Goal 4.** Describe and use measures of time periods relative to a day and week; identify tools that measure time.	**Goal 4.** Use a calendar to identify days, weeks, months, and dates; tell and show time to the nearest half and quarter hour on an analog clock.	**Goal 6.** Tell and show time to the nearest five minutes on an analog clock; tell and write time in digital notation.	**Goal 4.** Tell and show time to the nearest minute on an analog clock; tell and write time in digital notation.			
Coordinate systems					**Goal 4.** Use ordered pairs of numbers to name, locate, and plot points in the first quadrant of a coordinate grid.	**Goal 4.** Use ordered pairs of numbers to name, locate, and plot points in all four quadrants of a coordinate grid.	**Goal 3.** Use ordered pairs of numbers to name, locate, and plot points in all four quadrants of a coordinate grid.

Everyday Mathematics

Content Strand: GEOMETRY

Program Goal: Investigate Characteristics and Properties of Two- and Three-Dimensional Geometric Shapes

Content	Kindergarten	First Grade	Second Grade	Third Grade	Fourth Grade	Fifth Grade	Sixth Grade
Lines and angles			**Goal 1.** Draw line segments and identify parallel line segments.	**Goal 1.** Identify and draw points, intersecting and parallel line segments, and lines, rays, and right angles.	**Goal 1.** Identify, draw, and describe points, intersecting and parallel line segments and lines, rays, and right, acute, and obtuse angles.	**Goal 1.** Identify, describe, compare, name, and draw right, acute, obtuse, straight, and reflex angles; determine angle measures in vertical and supple-mentary angles and by applying properties of sums of angle measures in triangles and quadrangles.	**Goal 1.** Identify, describe, classify, name, and draw angles; determine angle measures by applying properties of orientations of angles and of sums of angle measures in triangles and quadrangles.
Plane and solid figures	**Goal 1.** Identify and describe plane and solid figures including circles, triangles, squares, rectangles, spheres, and cubes.	**Goal 1.** Identify and describe plane and solid figures including circles, triangles, squares, rectangles, spheres, cylinders, rectangular prisms, pyramids, cones, and cubes.	**Goal 2.** Identify, describe, and model plane and solid figures including circles, triangles, squares, rectangles, hexagons, trapezoids, rhombuses, spheres, cylinders, rectangular prisms, pyramids, cones, and cubes.	**Goal 2.** Identify, describe, model, and compare plane and solid figures including circles, polygons, spheres, cylinders, rectangular prisms, pyramids, cones, and cubes using appropriate geometric terms including the terms *face, edge, vertex*, and *base.*	**Goal 2.** Describe, compare, and classify plane and solid figures, including polygons, circles, spheres, cylinders, rectangular prisms, cones, cubes, and pyramids, using appropriate geometric terms including *vertex, base, face, edge,* and *congruent.*	**Goal 2.** Describe, compare, and classify plane and solid figures using appropriate geometric terms; identify congruent figures and describe their properties.	**Goal 2.** Identify and describe similar and congruent figures and describe their properties; construct a figure that is congruent to another figure using a compass and straightedge.

Program Goal: Apply Transformations and Symmetry in Geometric Situations

Content	Kindergarten	First Grade	Second Grade	Third Grade	Fourth Grade	Fifth Grade	Sixth Grade
Transformations and symmetry	**Goal 2.** Identify shapes having line symmetry.	**Goal 2.** Identify shapes having line symmetry; complete line-symmetric shapes or designs.	**Goal 3.** Create and complete two-dimensional symmetric shapes or designs.	**Goal 3.** Create and complete two-dimensional symmetric shapes or designs; locate multiple lines of symmetry in a two-dimensional shape.	**Goal 3.** Identify, describe, and sketch examples of reflections; identify and describe examples of translations and rotations.	**Goal 3.** Identify, describe, and sketch examples of reflections, translations, and rotations.	**Goal 3.** Identify, describe, and sketch (including plotting on the coordinate plane) instances of reflections, translations, and rotations.

Everyday Mathematics

Content Strand: PATTERNS, FUNCTIONS, AND ALGEBRA

Program Goal: Understand Patterns and Functions

Content	Kindergarten	First Grade	Second Grade	Third Grade	Fourth Grade	Fifth Grade	Sixth Grade
Patterns and functions	**Goal 1.** Extend, describe, and create visual, rhythmic, and movement patterns; use rules, which will lead to functions, to sort, make patterns, and play "What's My Rule?" and other games.	**Goal 1.** Extend, describe, and create numeric, visual, and concrete patterns; solve problems involving function machines, "What's My Rule?" tables, and Frames-and-Arrows diagrams.	**Goal 1.** Extend, describe, and create numeric, visual, and concrete patterns; describe rules for patterns and use them to solve problems; use words and symbols to describe and write rules for functions involving addition and subtraction and use those rules to solve problems.	**Goal 1.** Extend, describe, and create numeric patterns; describe rules for patterns and use them to solve problems; use words and symbols to describe and write rules for functions involving addition, subtraction, and multiplication and use those rules to solve problems.	**Goal 1.** Extend, describe, and create numeric patterns; describe rules for patterns and use them to solve problems; use words and symbols to describe and write rules for functions that involve the four basic arithmetic operations and use those rules to solve problems.	**Goal 1.** Extend, describe, and create numeric patterns; describe rules for patterns and use them to solve problems; write rules for functions involving the four basic arithmetic operations; represent functions using words, symbols, tables, and graphs and use those representations to solve problems.	**Goal 1.** Extend, describe, and create numeric patterns; describe rules for patterns and use them to solve problems; represent patterns and rules using algebraic notation; represent functions using words, algebraic notation, tables, and graphs; translate from one representation to another and use representations to solve problems involving functions.

Program Goal: Use Algebraic Notation to Represent and Analyze Situations and Structures

Content	Kindergarten	First Grade	Second Grade	Third Grade	Fourth Grade	Fifth Grade	Sixth Grade
Algebraic notation and solving number sentences	**Goal 2.** Read and write expressions and number sentences using the symbols +, −, and =.	**Goal 2.** Read, write, and explain expressions and number sentences using the symbols +, −, and = and the symbols > and < with cues; solve equations involving addition and subtraction.	**Goal 2.** Read, write, and explain expressions and number sentences using the symbols +, −, =, >, and <; solve number sentences involving addition and subtraction; write expressions and number sentences to model number stories.	**Goal 2.** Read, write, and explain number sentences using the symbols +, −, ×, ÷, =, >, and <; solve number sentences; write expressions and number sentences to model number stories.	**Goal 2.** Use conventional notation to write expressions and number sentences using the four basic arithmetic operations; determine whether number sentences are true or false; solve open sentences and explain the solutions; write expressions and number sentences to model number stories.	**Goal 2.** Determine whether number sentences are true or false; solve open number sentences and explain the solutions; use a letter variable to write an open sentence to model a number story; use a pan-balance model to solve linear equations in one unknown.	**Goal 2.** Determine whether equalities and inequalities are true or false; solve open number sentences and explain the solutions; use a pan-balance model to solve linear equations in one or two unknowns; use trial-and-error and equivalent equations strategies to solve linear equations in one unknown.

Everyday Mathematics

Content Strand: PATTERNS, FUNCTIONS, AND ALGEBRA *cont.*

Program Goal: Use Algebraic Notation to Represent and Analyze Situations and Structures *cont.*

Content	Kindergarten	First Grade	Second Grade	Third Grade	Fourth Grade	Fifth Grade	Sixth Grade
Order of operations				**Goal 3.** Recognize that numeric expressions can have different values depending on the order in which operations are carried out; understand that grouping symbols can be used to affect the order in which operations are carried out.	**Goal 3.** Evaluate numeric expressions containing grouping symbols; insert grouping symbols to make number sentences true.	**Goal 3.** Evaluate numeric expressions containing grouping symbols and nested grouping symbols; insert grouping symbols and nested grouping symbols to make number sentences true; describe and use the precedence of multiplication and division over addition and subtraction.	**Goal 3.** Describe and apply the conventional order of operations.
Properties of the arithmetic operations		**Goal 3.** Apply the Commutative Property of Addition and the Additive Identity to basic addition fact problems.	**Goal 3.** Describe the Commutative and Associative Properties of Addition and apply them to mental arithmetic problems.	**Goal 4.** Describe and apply the Commutative and Associative Properties of Addition, the Commutative Property of Multiplication, and the Multiplicative Identity.	**Goal 4.** Apply the Distributive Property of Multiplication over Addition to the partial-products multiplication algorithm.	**Goal 4.** Describe and apply properties of arithmetic.	**Goal 4.** Describe and apply properties of arithmetic and multiplicative and additive inverses.

Assessment Overviews

This section summarizes the assessment opportunities in each unit. Ongoing assessments, such as the Informing Instruction and Recognizing Student Achievement notes, are listed by lesson. Portfolio opportunities, paired or linked Math Boxes, and Writing/Reasoning prompts are also highlighted. You will find information on periodic assessments as well. Modifications for each unit's Progress Check Written Assessment, tips for implementing Open Response tasks (including rubrics for each task), and sample student responses for each rubric level are provided.

Contents

Unit 1 Naming and Constructing Geometric Figures . . . 52
Unit 2 Using Numbers and Organizing Data . . . 60
Unit 3 Multiplication and Division; Number Sentences and Algebra . . . 68
Unit 4 Decimals and Their Uses . . . 76
Unit 5 Big Numbers, Estimation, and Computation . . . 84
Unit 6 Division; Map Reference Frames; Measures of Angles . . . 92
Mid-Year Assessment Goals . . . 100
Unit 7 Fractions and Their Uses; Chance and Probability . . . 102
Unit 8 Perimeter and Area . . . 110
Unit 9 Fractions, Decimals, and Percents . . . 118
Unit 10 Reflections and Symmetry . . . 126
Unit 11 3-D Shapes, Weight, Volume, and Capacity . . . 134
Unit 12 Rates . . . 142
End-of-Year Assessment Goals . . . 150

Assessment Overview

In this unit, students describe, compare, and classify plane figures. Use the information in this section to develop your assessment plan for Unit 1.

Ongoing Assessment

Opportunities for using and collecting ongoing assessment information are highlighted in Informing Instruction and Recognizing Student Achievement notes. Student products, along with observations and suggested writing prompts, provide a range of useful assessment information.

Informing Instruction

The Informing Instruction notes highlight students' thinking and point out common misconceptions. Informing Instruction in Unit 1: Lessons 1-2, 1-3, 1-5, and 1-8.

Recognizing Student Achievement

The Recognizing Student Achievement notes highlight specific tasks from which teachers can collect assessment data to monitor and document student progress toward meeting Grade-Level Goals.

Lesson	Content Assessed	Where to Find It
1◆1	**Demonstrate automaticity with addition facts.** [Operations and Computation Goal 1]	*TLG,* p. 19
1◆2	**Describe a line segment and a line.** [Geometry Goal 1]	*TLG,* p. 27
1◆3	**Compare and contrast plane figures.** [Geometry Goal 2]	*TLG,* p. 32
1◆4	**Draw quadrangles with parallel line segments.** [Geometry Goal 1]	*TLG,* p. 38
1◆5	**Explain the properties of polygons.** [Geometry Goal 2]	*TLG,* p. 44
1◆6	**Draw a quadrangle with 1 right angle.** [Geometry Goal 1]	*TLG,* p. 50
1◆7	**Construct circles with a compass.** [Geometry Goal 2]	*TLG,* p. 54
1◆8	**Demonstrate automaticity with subtraction facts.** [Operations and Computation Goal 1]	*TLG,* p. 60

Math Boxes

Math Boxes, one of several types of tasks highlighted in the Recognizing Student Achievement notes, have an additional useful feature. Math Boxes in most lessons are paired or linked with Math Boxes in one or two other lessons that have similar problems. Paired or linked Math Boxes in Unit 1: 1-1 and 1-3; 1-2 and 1-4; 1-5 and 1-7; and 1-6 and 1-8.

Writing/Reasoning Prompts

In Unit 1, a variety of writing prompts encourage students to explain their strategies and thinking, to reflect on their learning, and to make connections to other mathematics or life experiences. Here are some of the Unit 1 suggestions:

Lesson	Writing/Reasoning Prompts	Where to Find It
1◆3	**Describe how you might solve the addition problem mentally.**	*TLG,* p. 33
1◆4	**Some students wrote that Mya sold $4\frac{1}{2}$ boxes of cookies. Explain the mistake they might have made when reading the graph.**	*TLG,* p. 39
1◆6	**Explain why the shapes you chose are not polygons.**	*TLG,* p. 50
1◆7	**How can you use a basic subtraction fact like 9 – 7 to solve an extended subtraction fact like 900 – 700?**	*TLG,* p. 55

Portfolio Opportunities

Portfolios are a versatile tool for assessment. They help students reflect on their mathematical growth and help teachers understand and document that growth. Each unit identifies several student products that can be selected and stored in a portfolio. Here are some of the Unit 1 suggestions:

Lesson	Portfolio Opportunities	Where to Find It
1◆3	**Students describe how to use mental math to solve a problem.**	*TLG,* p. 33
1◆5	**Students compare examples and nonexamples of kites and rhombuses.**	*TLG,* p. 46
1◆6	**Students create circle designs.**	*TLG,* p. 51
1◆7	**Students construct tangent circles.**	*TLG,* p. 56
1◆9	**Students sort polygons into groups based on the characteristics of the polygons.**	*TLG,* p. 65

Periodic Assessment

Every Progress Check lesson includes opportunities to observe student progress and to collect student products in a variety of ways—Self Assessment, Oral and Slate Assessment, Written Assessment, and an Open Response task. For more details, see the first page of Progress Check 1, Lesson 1-9, page 62, of the *Teacher's Lesson Guide*.

Progress Check Modifications

Written Assessments are one way students demonstrate what they know. The table below shows modifications for the Written Assessment in this unit. Use these to maximize opportunities for students to demonstrate what they know. Modifications can be given individually or written on the board for the class.

Problem(s)	Modifications for Written Assessment
5, 6	**For Problems 5 and 6, use *Student Reference Book* page 90 to help you name the line segments.**
7, 8	**For Problems 7 and 8, use *Student Reference Book* page 100 to help you name the figures.**
10, 11	**For Problems 10 and 11, use a number line or number grid to help you solve the problems.**
12	**For Problem 12, explain how you know which of the polygons is the regular hexagon.**

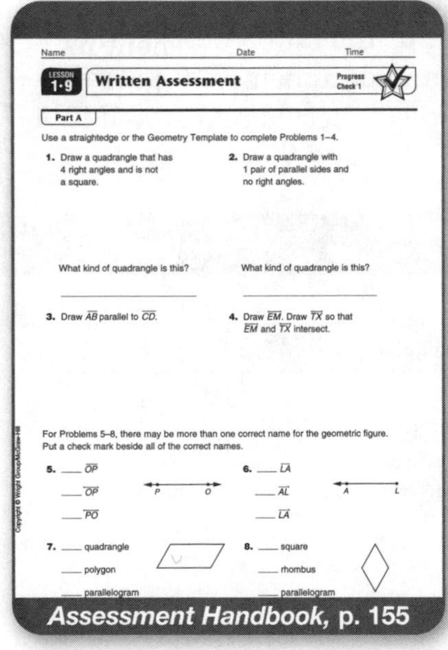

Name Date Time

LESSON 1·9 **Written Assessment** Progress Check 1

Part A

Use a straightedge or the Geometry Template to complete Problems 1–4.

1. Draw a quadrangle that has 4 right angles and is not a square.

   What kind of quadrangle is this? ______

2. Draw a quadrangle with 1 pair of parallel sides and no right angles.

   What kind of quadrangle is this? ______

3. Draw $\overline{AB}$ parallel to $\overline{CD}$.

4. Draw $\overline{EM}$. Draw $\overline{TX}$ so that $\overline{EM}$ and $\overline{TX}$ intersect.

For Problems 5–8, there may be more than one correct name for the geometric figure. Put a check mark beside all of the correct names.

5. ___ $\overline{OP}$ ___ $\overline{OP}$ ___ $\overline{PO}$

6. ___ $\overline{LA}$ ___ $\overline{AL}$ ___ $\overline{LA}$

7. ___ quadrangle ___ polygon ___ parallelogram

8. ___ square ___ rhombus ___ parallelogram

Assessment Handbook, p. 155

The Written Assessment for Unit 1 Progress Check is on pages 155–157.

Open Response, *Properties of Polygons*

Description

For this task, students sort polygons into groups according to polygon properties.

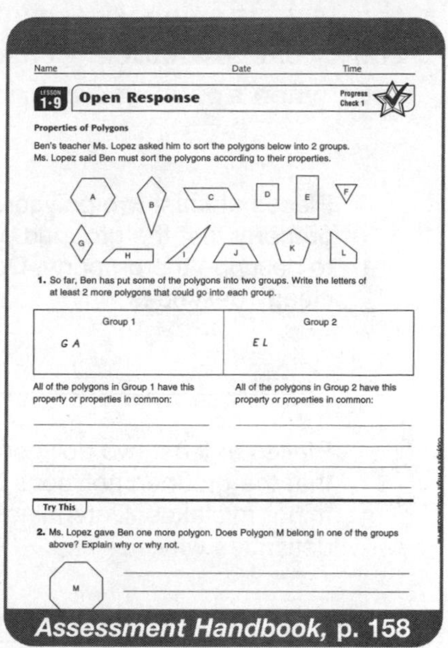

Name Date Time

LESSON 1·9 **Open Response** Progress Check 1

Properties of Polygons

Ben's teacher Ms. Lopez asked him to sort the polygons below into 2 groups. Ms. Lopez said Ben must sort the polygons according to their properties.

1. So far, Ben has put some of the polygons into two groups. Write the letters of at least 2 more polygons that could go into each group.

Group 1	Group 2
G A	E L

All of the polygons in Group 1 have this property or properties in common:

All of the polygons in Group 2 have this property or properties in common:

Try This

2. Ms. Lopez gave Ben one more polygon. Does Polygon M belong in one of the groups above? Explain why or why not.

Assessment Handbook, p. 158

Focus

- **Describe, compare, and classify polygons using appropriate geometric terms.** [Geometry Goal 2]

Implementation Tips

- Read through the task together. Ask students if they have questions.
- Remind students to record only the letters of the polygons in the two groups.

Modifications for Meeting Diverse Needs

- Make and cut out an enlarged version of each polygon on cardstock. Have students place the polygons into groups. Then ask them the rationale for their groupings before recording their thoughts on the paper.
- Have students make two distinct polygon groups. Emphasize that polygons placed in one group cannot have characteristics that allow for placement in the other group. Make it clear that all of the polygons must be sorted into one of the two groups.

Improving Open Response Skills

Before students begin the task, have them look over the problem and generate a list of vocabulary words that they might use in the explanation—for example, *parallel, right angles, sides, convex, concave, regular*.

Note: The wording and formatting of the text on the student samples that follow may vary slightly from the actual task your children will complete. These minor discrepancies will not affect the implementation of the task.

Rubric

This rubric is designed to help you assess levels of mathematical performance on this task. It emphasizes mathematical understanding with only a mention of clarity of explanation. Consider the expectations of standardized tests in your area when applying a rubric. Modify this sample rubric as appropriate.

4	Places at least two polygons in each group, and identifies and clearly describes a property that the grouped polygons have in common. Uses geometric terms correctly to describe the property. Determines that Polygon M will fit in one of the groups and clearly describes why.
3	Places at least two polygons in each group, and identifies and describes a property that the grouped polygons have in common. Might use geometric terms with minor mistakes. Determines that Polygon M will fit in one of the groups and describes why.
2	Places at least one polygon in each group, and attempts to identify and describe a property that the grouped polygons have in common. Might show evidence of misconceptions in applying geometric terms. Attempts to determine if Polygon M fits in one of the groups. Description might include errors or might be unclear.
1	Places at least one polygon in each group, but there might be no apparent common property among the polygons. Might use geometric terms incorrectly, or might not use them at all. Might attempt to determine if Polygon M fits in one of the groups. The description might not make sense in the context of the problem.
0	Does not attempt to solve the problem.

Sample Student Responses

This Level 4 paper illustrates the following features: The polygons placed in Group 1 are clearly described as having "at least one set of parallel sides," and in Group 2, described as "all are quadrilaterals." M is correctly placed in Group 1 because it has parallel sides.

Name ______________ Date ________ Time ________

LESSON 1·9 **Open Response** Progress Check 1

Ben's teacher Ms. Lopez asked him to sort the polygons below into two groups. Ms. Lopez said Ben must sort the polygons according to their properties.

A B C D E F G H I J K L

1. So far, Ben has put some of the polygons into two groups. Write the letters of at least 2 more polygons that could go into each group.

Group 1	Group 2
G ACH	E LDJ

All of the polygons in Group 1 have this property or properties in common: They all are polygons, and all have at least one set of parallel sides.

All of the polygons in Group 2 have this property or properties in common: They all are quadrilateral

Try This!

2. Ms. Lopez gave Ben one more polygon. Does Polygon M belong in one of the groups above? Explain why or why not.

M

Yes Because it could go in Group 1 with shapes that have at least one set of parallel sides.

This Level 4 paper illustrates the following features: The polygons placed in Group 1 are clearly described as having no right angles and in Group 2, as having at least two right angles. M is correctly placed in Group 1 because it does not have right angles.

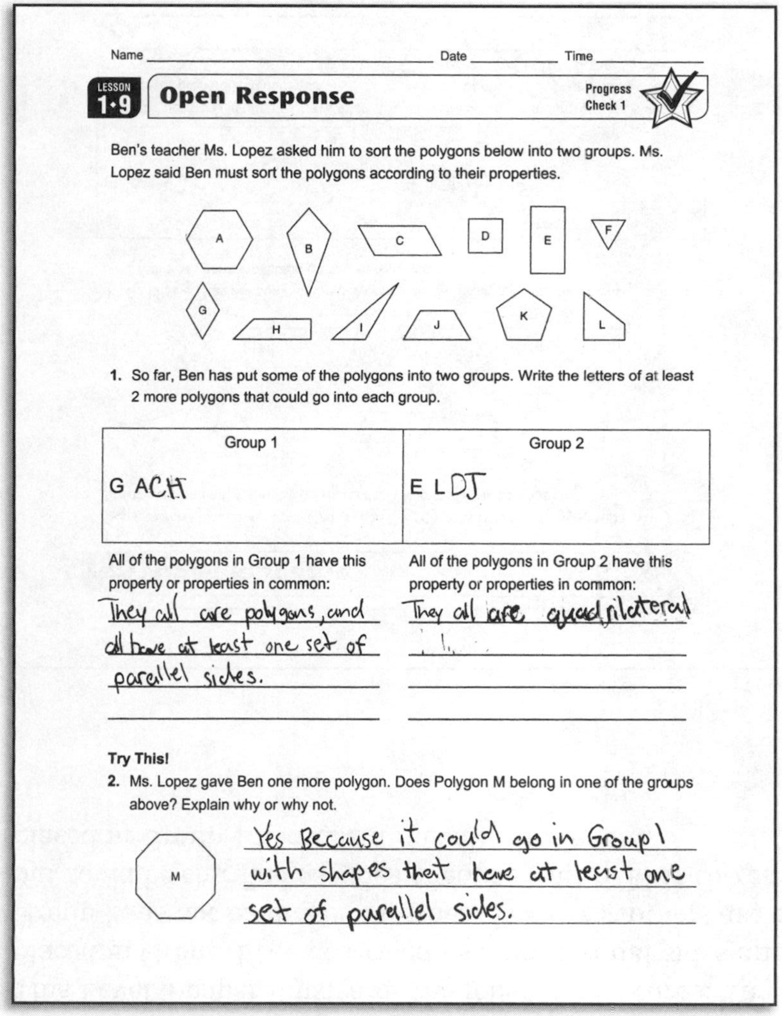

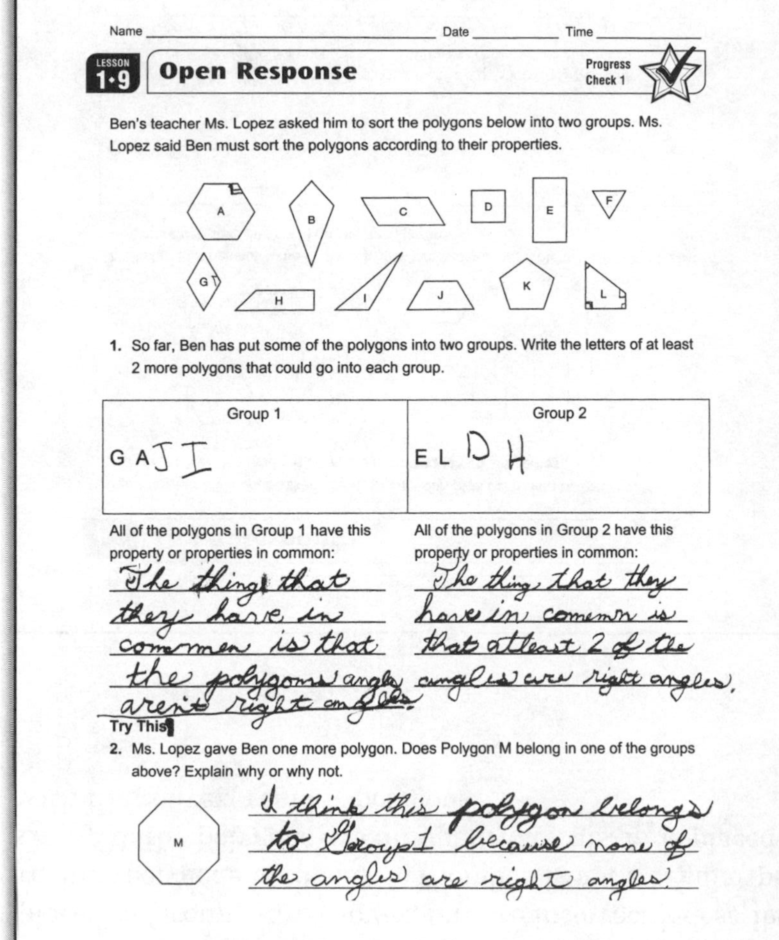

Name ______________ Date ________ Time ________

LESSON 1·9 **Open Response** Progress Check 1

Ben's teacher Ms. Lopez asked him to sort the polygons below into two groups. Ms. Lopez said Ben must sort the polygons according to their properties.

A B C D E F G H I J K L

1. So far, Ben has put some of the polygons into two groups. Write the letters of at least 2 more polygons that could go into each group.

Group 1	Group 2
G A J I	E L D H

All of the polygons in Group 1 have this property or properties in common: The thing that they have in commen is that the polygons angles aren't right angles

All of the polygons in Group 2 have this property or properties in common: The thing that they have in commen is that atleast 2 of the angles are right angles.

Try This!

2. Ms. Lopez gave Ben one more polygon. Does Polygon M belong in one of the groups above? Explain why or why not.

M

I think this polygon belongs to Group 1 because none of the angles are right angles.

This Level 3 paper illustrates the following features: The polygons placed in Group 1 are described as having equal sides and, in Group 2, as not having equal sides. The descriptions are complete but could be clarified as sides of equal length. M is correctly placed in Group 1 because it has all sides equal.

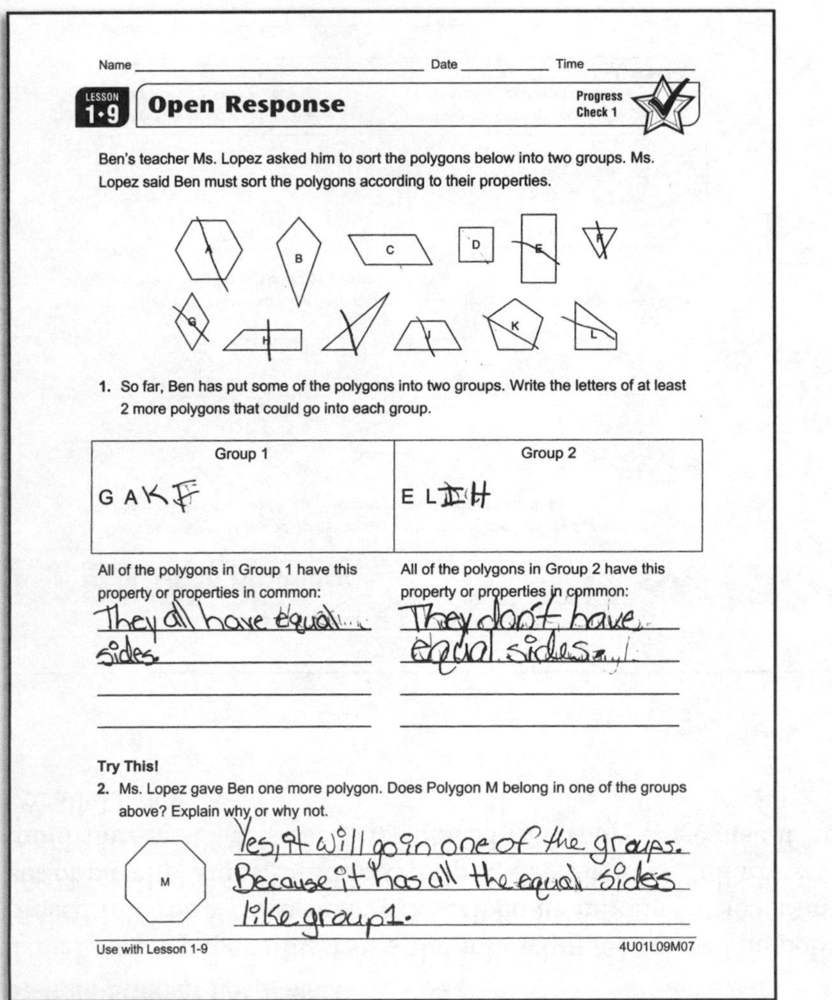

Name ______ Date ______ Time ______

LESSON 1·9 **Open Response** Progress Check 1

Ben's teacher Ms. Lopez asked him to sort the polygons below into two groups. Ms. Lopez said Ben must sort the polygons according to their properties.

1. So far, Ben has put some of the polygons into two groups. Write the letters of at least 2 more polygons that could go into each group.

Group 1	Group 2
G A K F	E L I H

All of the polygons in Group 1 have this property or properties in common: They all have equal sides.

All of the polygons in Group 2 have this property or properties in common: They don't have equal sides.

Try This!

2. Ms. Lopez gave Ben one more polygon. Does Polygon M belong in one of the groups above? Explain why or why not.

M

Yes, it will go in one of the groups. Because it has all the equal sides like group 1.

Use with Lesson 1-9 4U01L09M07

This Level 3 paper illustrates the following features: The polygons placed in Group 1 are convex, but are incorrectly described as regular polygons because the rhombus is not a regular polygon. In Group 2, the polygons are all quadrilaterals. M is placed correctly with the convex, regular polygons.

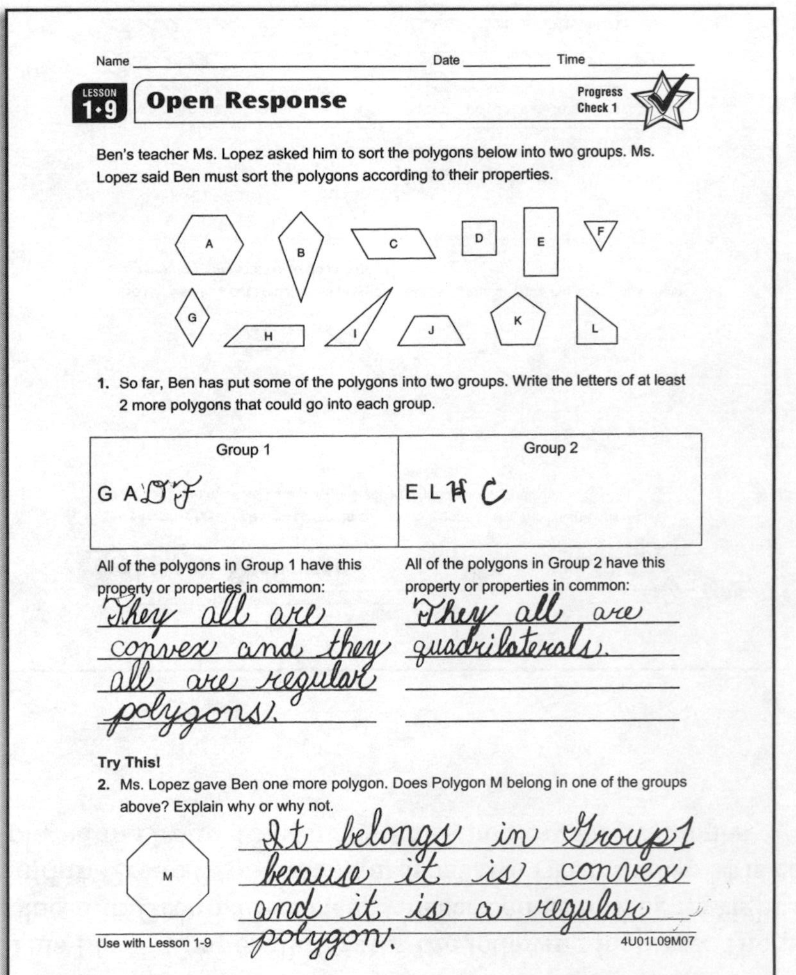

Name ______ Date ______ Time ______

LESSON 1·9 **Open Response** Progress Check 1

Ben's teacher Ms. Lopez asked him to sort the polygons below into two groups. Ms. Lopez said Ben must sort the polygons according to their properties.

1. So far, Ben has put some of the polygons into two groups. Write the letters of at least 2 more polygons that could go into each group.

Group 1	Group 2
G A D F	E L H C

All of the polygons in Group 1 have this property or properties in common: They all are convex and they all are regular polygons.

All of the polygons in Group 2 have this property or properties in common: They all are quadrilaterals.

Try This!

2. Ms. Lopez gave Ben one more polygon. Does Polygon M belong in one of the groups above? Explain why or why not.

M

It belongs in Group 1 because it is convex and it is a regular polygon.

Use with Lesson 1-9 4U01L09M07

This Level 2 paper illustrates the following features: The polygons placed in Group 1 are described as having no right angles and, in Group 2, as having right angles; but at least one polygon in both groups does not fit the stated rule. A new rule is written for M that is not related to the existing groups.

Name ______ Date ______ Time ______

LESSON 1·9 **Open Response** Progress Check 1

Ben's teacher Ms. Lopez asked him to sort the polygons below into two groups. Ms. Lopez said Ben must sort the polygons according to their properties.

A B C D E F G H I J K L

1. So far, Ben has put some of the polygons into two groups. Write the letters of at least 2 more polygons that could go into each group.

Group 1	Group 2
G A B H	E L K D

All of the polygons in Group 1 have this property or properties in common: They have in common they don't have right angles.

All of the polygons in Group 2 have this property or properties in common: They have in common they both have right angle's.

Try This!

2. Ms. Lopez gave Ben one more polygon. Does Polygon M belong in one of the groups above? Explain why or why not.

M

No, because none of the one's above do not have 8 sides so they do not have that many side's.

This Level 1 paper illustrates the following features: The descriptions of how the polygons are placed do not make mathematical sense. For example, "both B and H have a diagonal line on the left same size." A new rule is written for M that is not related to the existing groups.

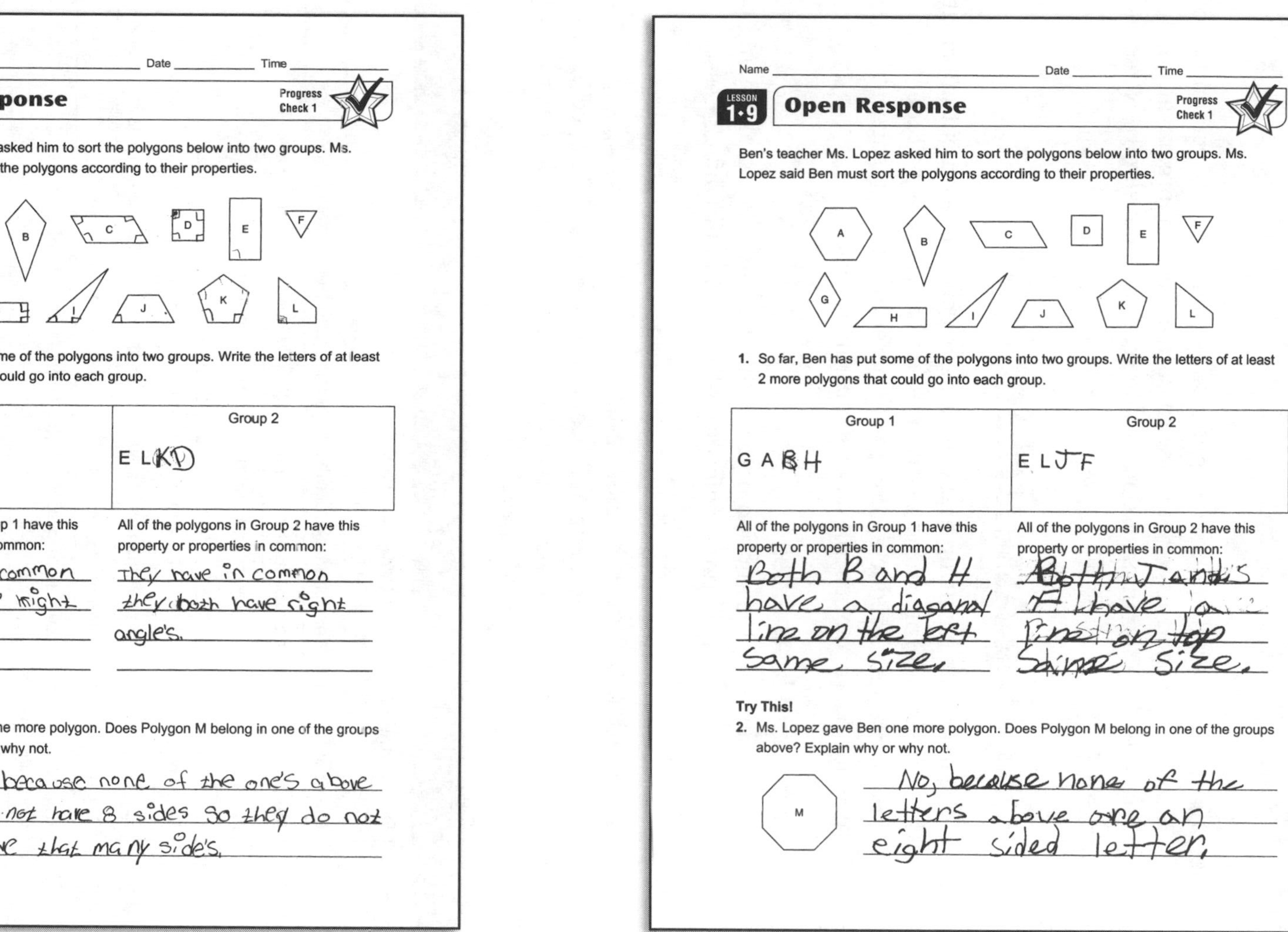

Name ______ Date ______ Time ______

LESSON 1·9 **Open Response** Progress Check 1

Ben's teacher Ms. Lopez asked him to sort the polygons below into two groups. Ms. Lopez said Ben must sort the polygons according to their properties.

A B C D E F G H I J K L

1. So far, Ben has put some of the polygons into two groups. Write the letters of at least 2 more polygons that could go into each group.

Group 1	Group 2
G A B H	E L J F

All of the polygons in Group 1 have this property or properties in common: Both B and H have a diagonal line on the left same size.

All of the polygons in Group 2 have this property or properties in common: Both J and F have a line on top same size.

Try This!

2. Ms. Lopez gave Ben one more polygon. Does Polygon M belong in one of the groups above? Explain why or why not.

M

No, because none of the letters above are an eight sided letter.

Assessment Overview

In this unit, students review place-value concepts and computation skills. They also expand their experiences with data collection, organization, display, and analysis. Use the information in this section to develop your assessment plan for Unit 2.

Ongoing Assessment

Opportunities for using and collecting ongoing assessment information are highlighted in Informing Instruction and Recognizing Student Achievement notes. Student products, along with observations and suggested writing prompts, provide a range of useful assessment information.

Informing Instruction

The Informing Instruction notes highlight students' thinking and point out common misconceptions. Informing Instruction in Unit 2: Lessons 2-1, 2-3, 2-5, 2-6, and 2-8.

Recognizing Student Achievement

The Recognizing Student Achievement notes highlight specific tasks from which teachers can collect assessment data to monitor and document student progress toward meeting Grade-Level Goals.

Lesson	Content Assessed	Where to Find It
2•1	**Demonstrate automaticity with extended addition facts.** [Operations and Computation Goal 1]	*TLG*, p. 83
2•2	**Give equivalent names for whole numbers.** [Number and Numeration Goal 4]	*TLG*, p. 91
2•3	**Identify the value of digits in whole numbers.** [Number and Numeration Goal 1]	*TLG*, p. 98
2•4	**Identify places in whole numbers and the values of the digits in those places.** [Number and Numeration Goal 1]	*TLG*, p. 103
2•5	**Demonstrate automaticity with basic addition facts.** [Operations and Computation Goal 1]	*TLG*, p. 109
2•6	**Identify the maximum, minimum, range, and mode of a data set.** [Data and Chance Goal 2]	*TLG*, p. 115
2•7	**Solve multidigit addition problems.** [Operations and Computation Goal 2]	*TLG*, p. 122
2•8	**Use data landmarks and a bar graph to draw conclusions about a data set.** [Data and Chance Goal 2]	*TLG*, p. 130
2•9	**Solve multidigit subtraction problems.** [Operations and Computation Goal 2]	*TLG*, p. 135

Math Boxes

Math Boxes, one of several types of tasks highlighted in the Recognizing Student Achievement notes, have an additional useful feature. Math Boxes in most lessons are paired or linked with Math Boxes in one or two other lessons that have similar problems. Paired or linked Math Boxes in Unit 2: 2-1 and 2-3; 2-2 and 2-4; 2-5, 2-7, and 2-9; and 2-6 and 2-8.

Writing/Reasoning Prompts

In Unit 2, a variety of writing prompts encourage students to explain their strategies and thinking, to reflect on their learning, and to make connections to other mathematics or life experiences. Here are some of the Unit 2 suggestions:

Lesson	Writing/Reasoning Prompts	Where to Find It
2◆2	Explain how you know that the polygon you drew is convex and not concave.	*TLG*, p. 92
2◆3	Explain how you know that the circles you drew are concentric.	*TLG*, p. 98
2◆5	Explain how you know that the pairs of sides you chose are parallel.	*TLG*, p. 110
2◆7	Shaneel said, "I can draw a rhombus, rectangle, square, or kite." Do you agree or disagree? Explain your answer.	*TLG*, p. 123
2◆8	Describe the patterns in number sentences.	*TLG*, p. 130

Portfolio Opportunities

Portfolios are a versatile tool for assessment. They help students reflect on their mathematical growth and help teachers understand and document that growth. Each unit identifies several student products that can be selected and stored in a portfolio. Here are some of the Unit 2 suggestions:

Lesson	Portfolio Opportunities	Where to Find It
2◆2	Students represent numbers in different ways.	*TLG*, p. 91
2◆4	Students apply their understanding of place value to decipher a packing-system code.	*TLG*, p. 105
2◆5	Students make a prediction based on a sample.	*TLG*, p. 111
2◆6	Students organize, summarize, and compare data sets and create displays.	*TLG*, p. 118
2◆9	Students apply their computation and estimation skills to find missing numbers in addition and subtraction problems.	*TLG*, p. 137

Periodic Assessment

Every Progress Check lesson includes opportunities to observe student progress and to collect student products in a variety of ways—Self Assessment, Oral and Slate Assessment, Written Assessment, and an Open Response task. For more details, see the first page of Progress Check 2, Lesson 2-10, page 138, of the *Teacher's Lesson Guide*.

Progress Check Modifications

Written Assessments are one way students demonstrate what they know. The table below shows modifications for the Written Assessment in this unit. Use these to maximize opportunities for students to demonstrate what they know. Modifications can be given individually or written on the board for the class.

Problem(s)	Modifications for Written Assessment
1–6	**For Problems 1–6, use base-10 blocks to model the problems. Use sheets of paper to represent the digits in the thousands place.**
7	**For Problem 7, draw a polygon that has exactly one right angle, two right angles, three right angles, and four right angles. Which of these was the hardest to draw? Why?**
10–14	**For Problems 10–14, for each student, write the number of rolls sold on a stick-on note. Arrange the stick-on notes in order, and use these to answer the questions.**
17, 18	**For Problems 17 and 18, use a ruler that has only centimeters and half-centimeters marked.**

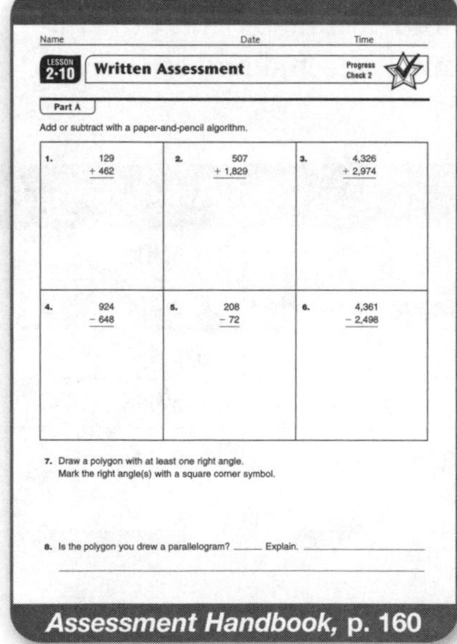

Name Date Time

LESSON 2·10 **Written Assessment** Progress Check 2

Part A

Add or subtract with a paper-and-pencil algorithm.

1. 129 + 462	2. 507 + 1,829	3. 4,326 + 2,974
4. 924 − 648	5. 208 − 72	6. 4,361 − 2,498

7. Draw a polygon with at least one right angle. Mark the right angle(s) with a square corner symbol.

8. Is the polygon you drew a parallelogram? ______ Explain. ____________

Assessment Handbook, p. 160

The Written Assessment for Unit 2 Progress Check is on pages 160–162.

Open Response, *Jelly Bean Data*

30-45 Min.

Description

For this task, students analyze data landmarks, create a matching data set, and make a graph.

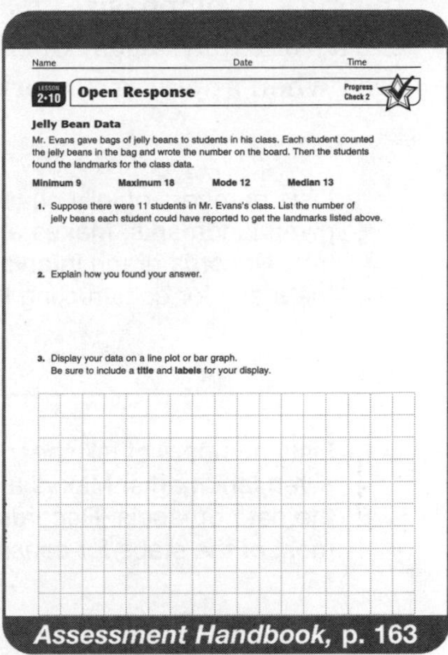

Name Date Time

LESSON 2·10 **Open Response** Progress Check 2

Jelly Bean Data

Mr. Evans gave bags of jelly beans to students in his class. Each student counted the jelly beans in the bag and wrote the number on the board. Then the students found the landmarks for the class data.

Minimum 9 **Maximum 18** **Mode 12** **Median 13**

1. Suppose there were 11 students in Mr. Evans's class. List the number of jelly beans each student could have reported to get the landmarks listed above.

2. Explain how you found your answer.

3. Display your data on a line plot or bar graph. Be sure to include a **title** and **labels** for your display.

Assessment Handbook, p. 163

Focus

- **Create a bar graph.** [Data and Chance Goal 1]
- **Use the maximum, minimum, range, median, and mode to answer questions.** [Data and Chance Goal 2]

Implementation Tips

- Review the data on journal page 40 with students. Highlight the way in which the line plot is labeled. Also, review the connection between the landmarks and the data.
- Review the definition for each landmark.

Modifications for Meeting Diverse Needs

- Have students write the landmarks on stick-on notes. Have them place the stick-on notes in a line plot. Ask how many more data points are needed. *(7 more)* They can place blank stick-on notes in the line plot to make the landmarks true. Once they have placed the blank stick-on notes, have them fill in the missing numbers.
- Ask students to predict how many jelly beans Mr. Evans would have if he also took a bag of jelly beans. Have them explain how they used landmarks to find the answer.

Improving Open Response Skills

Before students begin the task, read the problem together. Give students a few minutes to look at the problem. Display Level 4 of the rubric on the board or overhead and review it with students. Have them translate Level 4 of the rubric into their own words. Record the students' language on chart paper and display this during the task. Have students go back and check their work with the posted Level 4 description before turning in their papers.

Note: The wording and formatting of the text on the student samples that follow may vary slightly from the actual task your children will complete. These minor discrepancies will not affect the implementation of the task.

Rubric

This rubric is designed to help you assess levels of mathematical performance on this task. It emphasizes mathematical understanding with only a mention of clarity of explanation. Consider the expectations of standardized tests in your area when applying a rubric. Modify this sample rubric as appropriate.

4	Lists numbers of jelly beans for 11 students and constructs a data set that has the given landmarks. Makes a graph that matches the data set and labels the axes and title. Records graph intervals that make sense for the data set. Clearly explains all of the steps for constructing the data set based on the landmarks.
3	Lists numbers of jelly beans for 11 students and constructs a data set that has the given landmarks. Makes a graph that matches the data set with only minor errors in the data or labels. Records graph intervals that make sense for the data set. Explains most of the steps for constructing the data set based on the landmarks.
2	Lists numbers of jelly beans for 11 students and constructs a data set that has some of the landmarks. Attempts to make a graph that matches the data set, but there might be errors or missing labels. Attempts to describe some of the steps for constructing the data set, but some steps might be confusing or missing.
1	Constructs a data set that might have some of the landmarks, but others are incorrect. Attempts to make a graph, but there is little evidence of understanding the process. The explanation of the steps for constructing the data set might make no sense in the context of the problem.
0	Does not attempt to solve the problem.

Sample Student Responses

This Level 4 paper illustrates the following features: The data set is constructed with 11 students and the data has the correct landmarks. The explanation describes beginning with the maximum and minimum numbers, and figuring out where to place the median and the mode. The graph is complete and matches the data set exactly.

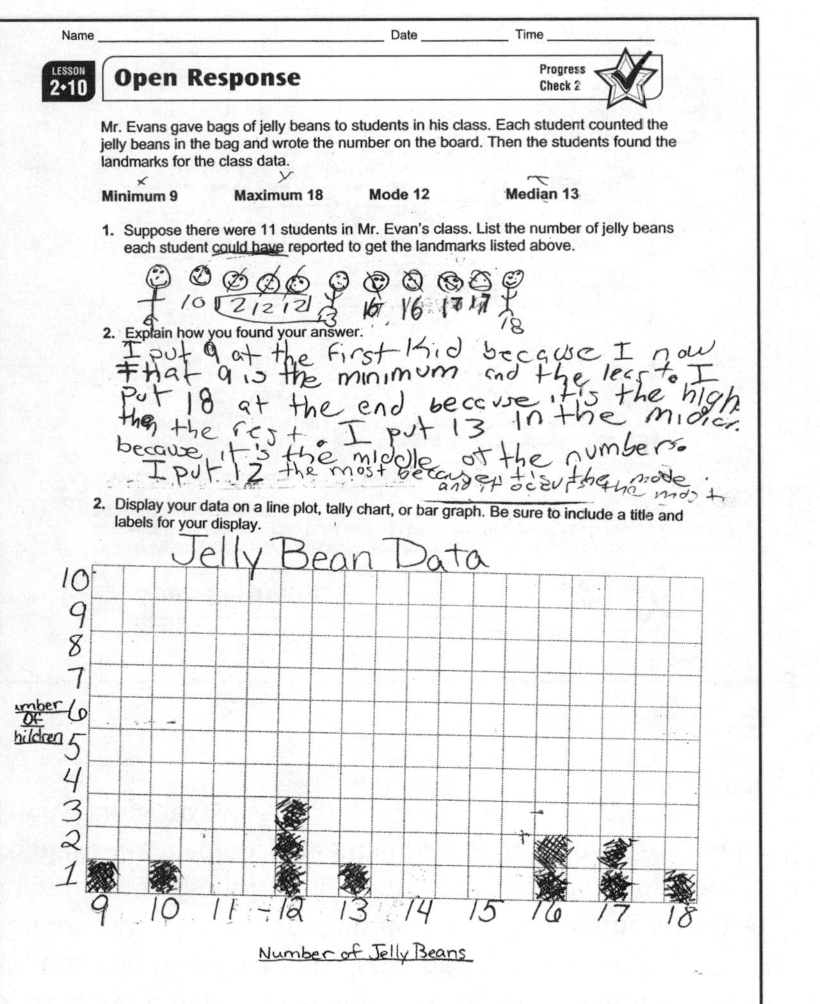

This Level 4 paper illustrates the following features: The data set is constructed with 11 students and the data has the correct landmarks. The explanation describes beginning with the maximum and minimum numbers, figuring out the mode, and then placing in the median. The graph is complete and matches the data set exactly.

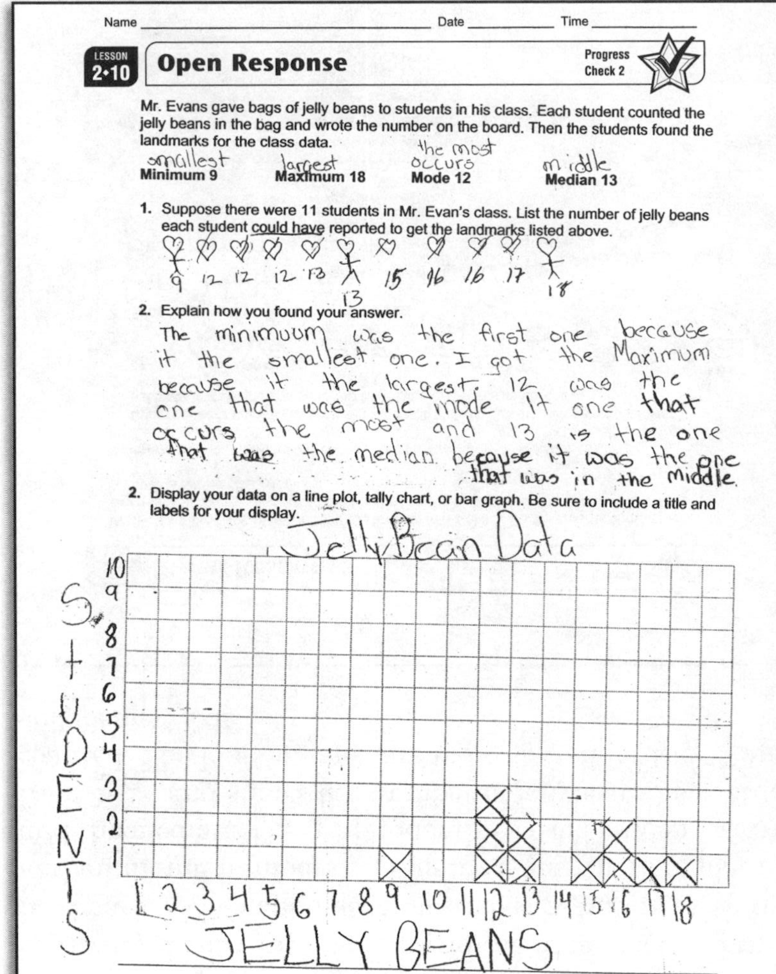

This Level 3 paper illustrates the following features: The data set is constructed with 11 students and the data has the correct landmarks. The explanation describes beginning with the maximum and minimum numbers and stops at figuring out where to place the median. The labeling appears to be shifted for the "Jellybeans" axis.

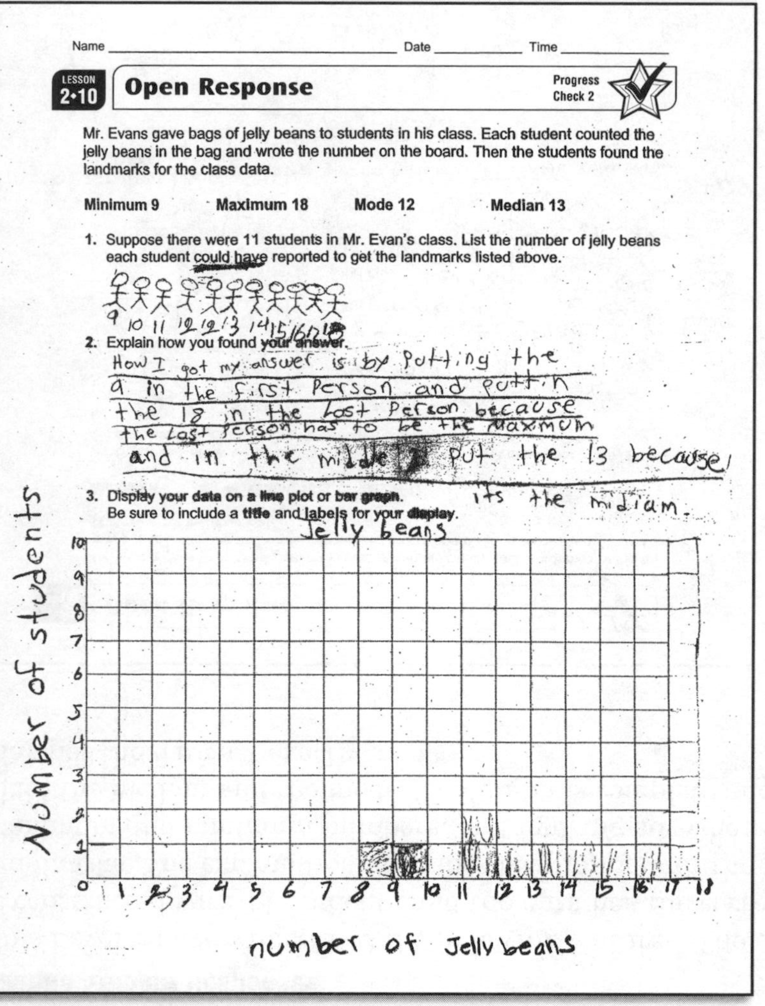

Name ______ Date ______ Time ______

LESSON 2·10 **Open Response** Progress Check 2

Mr. Evans gave bags of jelly beans to students in his class. Each student counted the jelly beans in the bag and wrote the number on the board. Then the students found the landmarks for the class data.

Minimum 9 **Maximum 18** **Mode 12** **Median 13**

1. Suppose there were 11 students in Mr. Evan's class. List the number of jelly beans each student could have reported to get the landmarks listed above.

9 10 11 12 12 13 14 15 16 17 18

2. Explain how you found your answer.

How I got my answer is by putting the 9 in the first person and puttin the 18 in the last person because the last person has to be the maxmum and in the middle put the 13 because its the midium.

3. Display your data on a line plot or bar graph. Be sure to include a title and labels for your display.

Jelly beans

Number of students

number of Jellybeans

This Level 3 paper illustrates the following features: The data set is constructed with 11 students and the data has the correct landmarks. The explanation describes beginning with the maximum and minimum numbers and figuring out where to place the mode and the median. The graph identifies each student with a number from 1–11 and shows the number of jellybeans each student counted. The labeling appears to be shifted for the "Number of Jellybeans" axis.

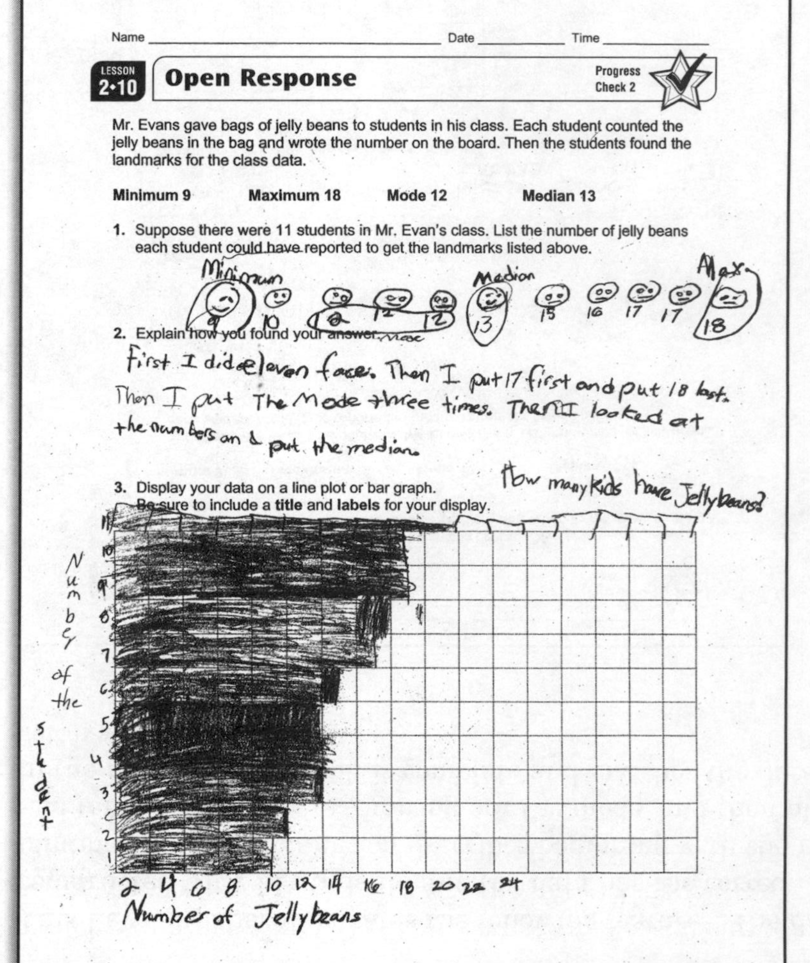

Name ______ Date ______ Time ______

LESSON 2·10 **Open Response** Progress Check 2

Mr. Evans gave bags of jelly beans to students in his class. Each student counted the jelly beans in the bag and wrote the number on the board. Then the students found the landmarks for the class data.

Minimum 9 **Maximum 18** **Mode 12** **Median 13**

1. Suppose there were 11 students in Mr. Evan's class. List the number of jelly beans each student could have reported to get the landmarks listed above.

Minimum 9 10 12 12 12 Median 13 15 16 17 17 Max 18

2. Explain how you found your answer.

First I did eleven faces. Then I put 17 first and put 18 last. Then I put The Mode three times. Then I looked at the numbers on & put the median.

3. Display your data on a line plot or bar graph. Be sure to include a title and labels for your display.

How many kids have Jellybeans?

Number of the student

Number of Jellybeans

This Level 2 paper illustrates the following features: The data set is constructed with 11 students and the data has the landmarks drawn at the correct spot in the illustration of the students, but the numbers do not work. The explanation describes placing the landmarks correctly in space but not relative to the set of numbers. The graph identifies each student with a number from 1–11 and shows the number of jellybeans each student counted.

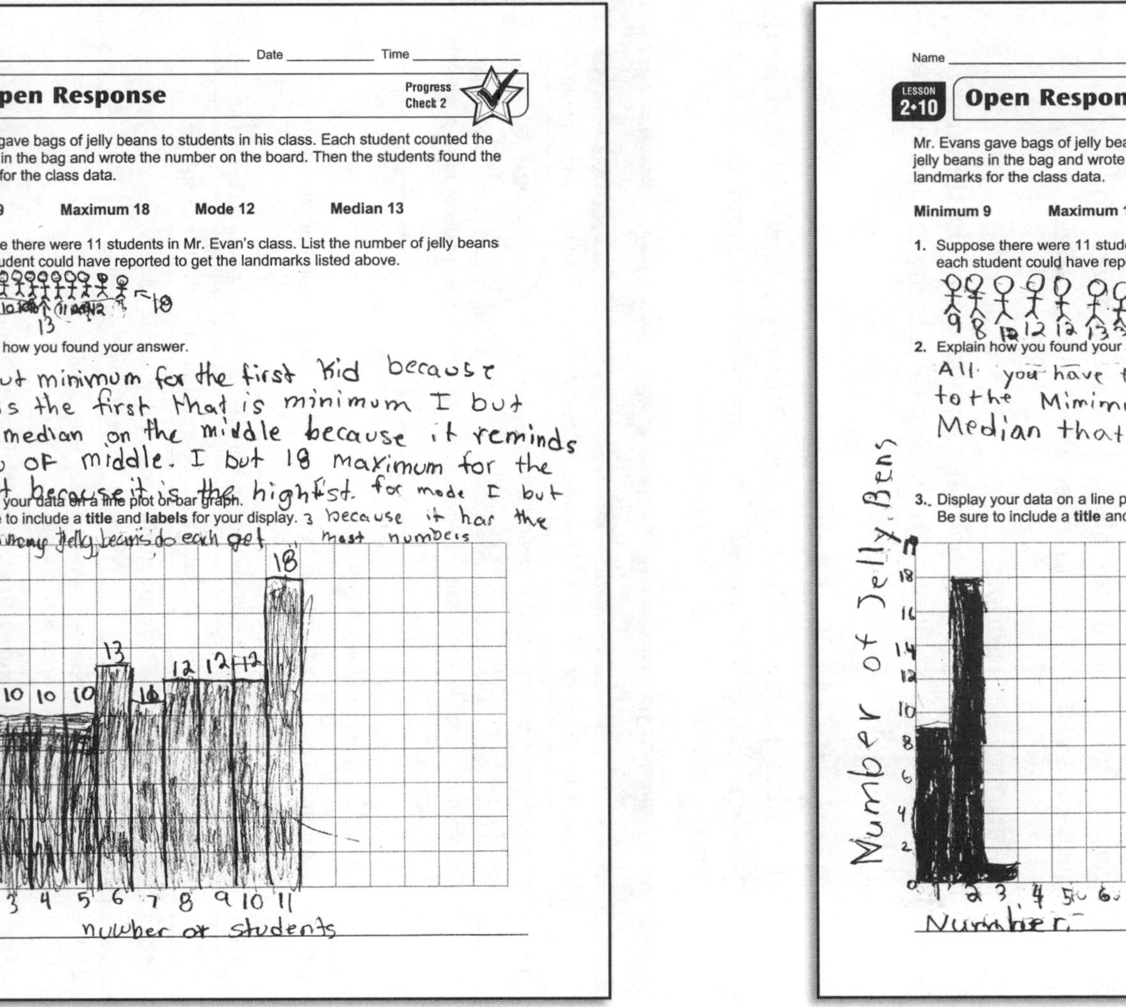

Name ________ Date ________ Time ________

LESSON 2·10 **Open Response** Progress Check 2

Mr. Evans gave bags of jelly beans to students in his class. Each student counted the jelly beans in the bag and wrote the number on the board. Then the students found the landmarks for the class data.

Minimum 9 **Maximum 18** **Mode 12** **Median 13**

1. Suppose there were 11 students in Mr. Evan's class. List the number of jelly beans each student could have reported to get the landmarks listed above.
2. Explain how you found your answer.
3. Display your data on a line plot or bar graph. Be sure to include a **title** and **labels** for your display.

This Level 1 paper illustrates the following features: The data set appears to be correct except that some numbers labeling the data set are recorded incorrectly. The explanation provides no information about a solution strategy. The graph is incomplete.

Name ________ Date ________ Time ________

LESSON 2·10 **Open Response** Progress Check 2

Mr. Evans gave bags of jelly beans to students in his class. Each student counted the jelly beans in the bag and wrote the number on the board. Then the students found the landmarks for the class data.

Minimum 9 **Maximum 18** **Mode 12** **Median 13**

1. Suppose there were 11 students in Mr. Evan's class. List the number of jelly beans each student could have reported to get the landmarks listed above.
2. Explain how you found your answer.
3. Display your data on a line plot or bar graph. Be sure to include a **title** and **labels** for your display.

Unit 3

Assessment Overview

In this unit, students practice multiplication facts, and extend their work with number sentences and variables. Use the information in this section to develop your assessment plan for Unit 3.

Ongoing Assessment

Opportunities for using and collecting ongoing assessment information are highlighted in Informing Instruction and Recognizing Student Achievement notes. Student products, along with observations and suggested writing prompts, provide a range of useful assessment information.

Informing Instruction

The Informing Instruction notes highlight student thinking and point out common misconceptions. Informing Instruction in Unit 3: Lessons 3-6, 3-7, 3-9, 3-10, and 3-11.

Recognizing Student Achievement

The Recognizing Student Achievement notes highlight specific tasks from which teachers can collect assessment data to monitor and document student progress toward meeting Grade-Level Goals.

Lesson	Content Assessed	Where to Find It
3•1	**Use rules to complete "What's My Rule?" tables.** [Patterns, Functions, and Algebra Goal 1]	*TLG*, p. 160
3•2	**Use numerical expressions involving one or more of the basic four operations to give equivalent names for whole numbers.** [Number and Numeration Goal 4]	*TLG*, p. 167
3•3	**Estimate reasonable solutions for whole-number addition and subtraction problems.** [Operations and Computation Goal 6]	*TLG*, p. 173
3•4	**Demonstrate automaticity with multiplication facts through 10 * 10.** [Operations and Computation Goal 3]	*TLG*, p. 177
3•5	**Use conventional notation to write multiplication and division number sentences.** [Patterns, Functions, and Algebra Goal 2]	*TLG*, p. 182
3•6	**Solve multidigit addition and subtraction problems.** [Operations and Computation Goal 2]	*TLG*, p. 190
3•7	**Use a map scale to estimate distances.** [Operations and Computation Goal 7]	*TLG*, p. 195
3•8	**Use and explain a strategy for solving an addition number story.** [Operations and Computation Goal 2]	*TLG*, p. 200
3•9	**Determine whether number sentences are true or false.** [Patterns, Functions, and Algebra Goal 2]	*TLG*, p. 206
3•10	**Demonstrate proficiency with basic division facts.** [Operations and Computation Goal 3]	*TLG*, p. 209
3•11	**Use and explain a strategy for solving open number sentences.** [Patterns, Functions, and Algebra Goal 2]	*TLG*, p. 217

Math Boxes

Math Boxes, one of several types of tasks highlighted in the Recognizing Student Achievement notes, have an additional useful feature. Math Boxes in most lessons are paired or linked with Math Boxes in one or two other lessons that have similar problems. Paired or linked Math Boxes in Unit 3: 3-1, 3-3 and 3-5; 3-2 and 3-4; 3-6 and 3-8; 3-7 and 3-9; and 3-10 and 3-11.

Writing/Reasoning Prompts

In Unit 3, a variety of writing prompts encourage students to explain their strategies and thinking, to reflect on their learning, and to make connections to other mathematics or life experiences. Here are some of the Unit 3 suggestions:

Lesson	Writing/Reasoning Prompts	Where to Find It
3•1	Explain how you found the range of the data set.	*TLG*, p. 161
3•4	Explain how you compared the data.	*TLG*, p. 178
3•7	Is the polygon a regular polygon? Explain why or why not.	*TLG*, p. 196
3•8	Explain why you chose the measurement that you did.	*TLG*, p. 201
3•10	Explain how you could use the bar graph to find the total number of books read by the students.	*TLG*, p. 212

Portfolio Opportunities

Portfolios are a versatile tool for assessment. They help students reflect on their mathematical growth and help teachers understand and document that growth. Each unit identifies several student products that can be selected and stored in a portfolio. Here are some of the Unit 3 suggestions:

Lesson	Portfolio Opportunities	Where to Find It
3•1	Students explore the relationships between pairs of numbers in "What's My Rule?" tables using a concrete model.	*TLG*, p. 162
3•1	Students explain the rule for finding the perimeter of shapes created by placing hexagon pattern blocks side by side.	*TLG*, p. 162
3•2	Students construct as many arrays as possible for a set of given numbers and use them to develop a definition for prime numbers.	*TLG*, p. 168
3•3	Students color skip-count patterns on a number grid.	*TLG*, p. 174
3•12	Students use order of operations to identify and correct number sentences.	*TLG*, p. 223

Periodic Assessment

Every Progress Check lesson includes opportunities to observe student progress and to collect student products in a variety of ways—Self Assessment, Oral and Slate Assessment, Written Assessment, and an Open Response task. For more details, see the first page of Progress Check 3, Lesson 3-12, page 220, of the *Teacher's Lesson Guide*.

Progress Check Modifications

Written Assessments are one way students demonstrate what they know. The table below shows modifications for the Written Assessment in this unit. Use these to maximize opportunities for students to demonstrate what they know. Modifications can be given individually or written on the board for the class.

Problem(s)	Modifications for Written Assessment
4–9	**For Problems 4–9, record the value for each side of the number sentence before deciding whether each number sentence is true or false.**
10–13	**For Problems 10–13, find the value of the expression in the parentheses first and write it above the expression. Then find the missing number.**
18	**For Problem 18, determine the mean number of apples picked. *(17.3)* How does the mean compare to the median? Why is it different?**
23–28	**For Problems 23–28, think of an empty box where the letter is. Use counters or pictures to help you find the missing numbers.**

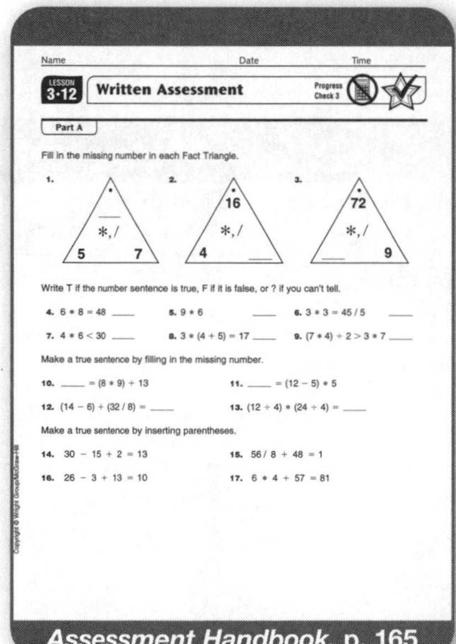

Name Date Time

LESSON 3·12 **Written Assessment** Progress Check 3

Part A

Fill in the missing number in each Fact Triangle.

1. Fact Triangle: ___ ; *,/ ; 5, 7
2. Fact Triangle: 16 ; *,/ ; 4, ___
3. Fact Triangle: 72 ; *,/ ; ___, 9

Write T if the number sentence is true, F if it is false, or ? if you can't tell.

4. 6 * 8 = 48 ___
5. 9 * 6 ___
6. 3 * 3 = 45 / 5 ___
7. 4 * 6 < 30 ___
8. 3 * (4 + 5) = 17 ___
9. (7 * 4) ÷ 2 > 3 * 7 ___

Make a true sentence by filling in the missing number.

10. ___ = (8 * 9) + 13
11. ___ = (12 − 5) * 5
12. (14 − 6) + (32 / 8) = ___
13. (12 ÷ 4) * (24 ÷ 4) = ___

Make a true sentence by inserting parentheses.

14. 30 − 15 + 2 = 13
15. 56 / 8 + 48 = 1
16. 26 − 3 + 13 = 10
17. 6 * 4 + 57 = 81

Assessment Handbook, p. 165

The Written Assessment for Unit 3 Progress Check is on pages 165–167.

Open Response, *Name That Number*

Description

For this task, students apply their knowledge of number sentences and computation skills to analyze a set of solutions to *Name That Number*.

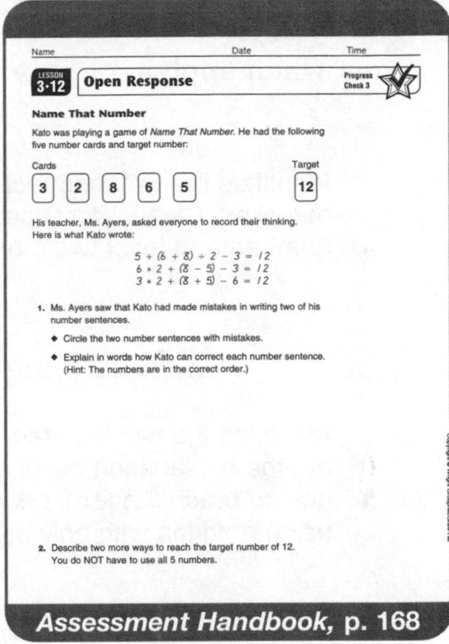

Name Date Time

LESSON 3·12 **Open Response** Progress Check 3

Name That Number

Kato was playing a game of *Name That Number*. He had the following five number cards and target number:

Cards: 3 2 8 6 5 Target: 12

His teacher, Ms. Ayers, asked everyone to record their thinking. Here is what Kato wrote:

$5 + (6 + 8) \div 2 - 3 = 12$
$6 * 2 + (8 - 5) - 3 = 12$
$3 * 2 + (8 + 5) - 6 = 12$

1. Ms. Ayers saw that Kato had made mistakes in writing two of his number sentences.
   - Circle the two number sentences with mistakes.
   - Explain in words how Kato can correct each number sentence. (Hint: The numbers are in the correct order.)

2. Describe two more ways to reach the target number of 12. You do NOT have to use all 5 numbers.

Assessment Handbook, p. 168

Focus

- **Use numerical expressions involving one or more of the basic four arithmetic operations to give equivalent names for whole numbers.**
  [Number and Numeration Goal 4]
- **Use conventional notation to write expressions and number sentences using the four basic arithmetic operations.**
  [Patterns, Functions, and Algebra Goal 2]
- **Evaluate numeric expressions containing grouping symbols.**
  [Patterns, Functions, and Algebra Goal 3]

Implementation Tips

- Make sure students have played *Name That Number*.
- Review the use of parentheses.
- Remind students to write their explanations in words.

Modifications for Meeting Diverse Needs

- Provide number cards, parentheses cards, and operation symbol cards for students to model the problems. Encourage students to use a calculator to check the number sentences and their work.
- Encourage students to use all five cards in a different way for their two solutions. Suggest that they use multiplication and division in both solutions.

Improving Open Response Skills

After students complete the task, have them reflect on, and write about what was easy and what was difficult about the task. Have them include what they think they could improve. When they have finished, have them share their reflections in small groups. After the discussion, return their papers and have them improve their work.

Note: The wording and formatting of the text on the student samples that follow may vary slightly from the actual task your children will complete. These minor discrepancies will not affect the implementation of the task.

Rubric

This rubric is designed to help you assess levels of mathematical performance on this task. It emphasizes mathematical understanding with only a mention of clarity of explanation. Consider the expectations of standardized tests in your area when applying a rubric. Modify this sample rubric as appropriate.

4	Identifies the two incorrect number sentences and clearly explains how to fix the mistakes. Clearly describes in words or shows with numbers how to reach the target number in at least two more ways. Writes number sentences using notation correctly.
3	Identifies the two incorrect number sentences and explains how to fix the mistakes, but the explanation might be incomplete. Describes in words or shows with numbers how to reach the target number in at least two more ways. Writes number sentences using notation with only minor errors.
2	Identifies the two incorrect number sentences and attempts to explain how to fix the mistakes, but the explanation might be unclear or confusing. Describes in words or shows with numbers how to reach the target number in at least one more way. Might write number sentences using incorrect notation.
1	Attempts to identify the two incorrect number sentences. Might attempt to explain the mistakes, but the explanation might be incorrect. Might describe one way to reach the target number, but there might be errors. Might write number sentences with mistakes.
0	Does not attempt to solve the problem.

Sample Student Responses

This Level 4 paper illustrates the following features: The incorrect number sentences are identified and rewritten correctly by moving parentheses and changing operations. There is an explanation of the changes in words. Two number sentences that equal 12 are recorded and written correctly.

Name ______ Date ______ Time ______

LESSON 3·12 **Open Response** Progress Check 3

Kato was playing a game of *Name That Number*. He had the following five number cards and target number:

Cards: 3 2 8 6 5 Target: 12

His teacher Ms. Dillard asked everyone to record their thinking. Here is what Kato wrote:

5 + (6 + 8) ÷ 2 − 3 = 12
6 * 2 + (8 − 5) − 3 = 12
3 * 2 + (8 + 5) − 6 = 12

1. Ms. Dillard saw that Kato's had made mistakes in writing two of his number sentences.
   - Circle the two number sentences with mistakes.
   - Explain in words how Kato can correct each number sentence. [Hint: The numbers are in the correct order.]

(3 X 2) X (8 − 5) − 6 = 12 I put parenies on 3x2 and 8-5 they I srchdach 6 and I got 12.

(5+6) + (8 ÷ 2) + 3 = 12

I put a purericson 5+6 and 8 ÷ 2 then I srchetced 3 and I got 12.

2. Describe two more ways to reach the target number of 12. You do NOT have to use all 5 numbers.

(6 + 5) + 3 − 2 = 12 sit + five in purinies + 3 srchated 2 = 12

(2 X 3) + 6 = 12 tuox three in purinies + 6 = 12

Use with Lesson 3-12 4U03L12M05

This Level 4 paper illustrates the following features: The incorrect number sentences are identified and rewritten correctly by moving parentheses and changing operations one step at a time. There is an explanation of the changes in words. Two number sentences that equal 12 are recorded and written correctly.

Name ______ Date ______ Time ______

LESSON 3·12 **Open Response** Progress Check 3

Kato was playing a game of *Name That Number*. He had the following five number cards and target number:

Cards: 3 2 8 6 5 Target: 12

His teacher Ms. Dillard asked everyone to record their thinking. Here is what Kato wrote:

5 + (6 + 8) ÷ 2 − 3 = 12
6 * 2 + (8 − 5) − 3 = 12
3 * 2 + (8 + 5) − 6 = 12

1. Ms. Dillard saw that Kato's had made mistakes in writing two of his number sentences.
   - Circle the two number sentences with mistakes.
   - Explain in words how Kato can correct each number sentence. [Hint: The numbers are in the correct order.]

The parthess is on 5+6, I added 5+6 it equal 11 then 8 ÷ 2 which equaled 4, 11 + 4 = 15 and 15 − 3 = 12. (5+6) + 8 ÷ 2 − 3 = 12. I changed 3x2 to 3+2, 3+2 = 5, 5+5 = 10 and 10 + 8 = 18, 18 − 6 = 12.

2. Describe two more ways to reach the target number of 12. You do NOT have to use all 5 numbers.

I added 8+6 which equal 14, 14 − 2 = 12.

I multiplied 6x2 which equal 12.

Use with Lesson 3-12 4U03L12M05

This Level 3 paper illustrates the following features: The incorrect number sentences are identified and corrected by moving parentheses in one and changing the operations in the other. There is an explanation in words, but the number sentences are not rewritten. There are two more solutions totaling the target number of 12, but the second one uses the number 2 twice.

Name ______________ Date ________ Time ________

LESSON 3·12 **Open Response** Progress Check 3

Kato was playing a game of *Name That Number*. He had the following five number cards and target number:

Cards: 3 2 8 6 5 Target: 12

His teacher Ms. Dillard asked everyone to record their thinking. Here is what Kato wrote:

1. 5 + (6 + 8) ÷ 2 – 3 = 12
2. 6 * 2 + (8 – 5) – 3 = 12
3. 3 * 2 + (8 + 5) – 6 = 12

1. Ms. Dillard saw that Kato's had made mistakes in writing two of his number sentences.
   - Circle the two number sentences with mistakes.
   - Explain in words how Kato can correct each number sentence. [Hint: The numbers are in the correct order.]

Kato should correct his mistakes by putting the 8 ÷ 2 in perrenthisis in #1.

In #3 Kato should put 3 × 2 not [illegible] perrenthisis 3 × 2.

2. Describe two more ways to reach the target number of 12. You do NOT have to use all 5 numbers.

(8+6) – 2 = 12 — You should put 8+6 in perrenthisis and put –2 equals 12.

(3+2)+5+2 = 12 — You should put 3+2 in () then put +5+2 equals 12.

This Level 3 paper illustrates the following features: The incorrect number sentences are identified and corrected by moving parentheses in one and changing the operations in the other. There is an explanation in words, but the number sentences are not rewritten. There are two more solutions totaling the target number of 12, but the notation used for recording is incorrect.

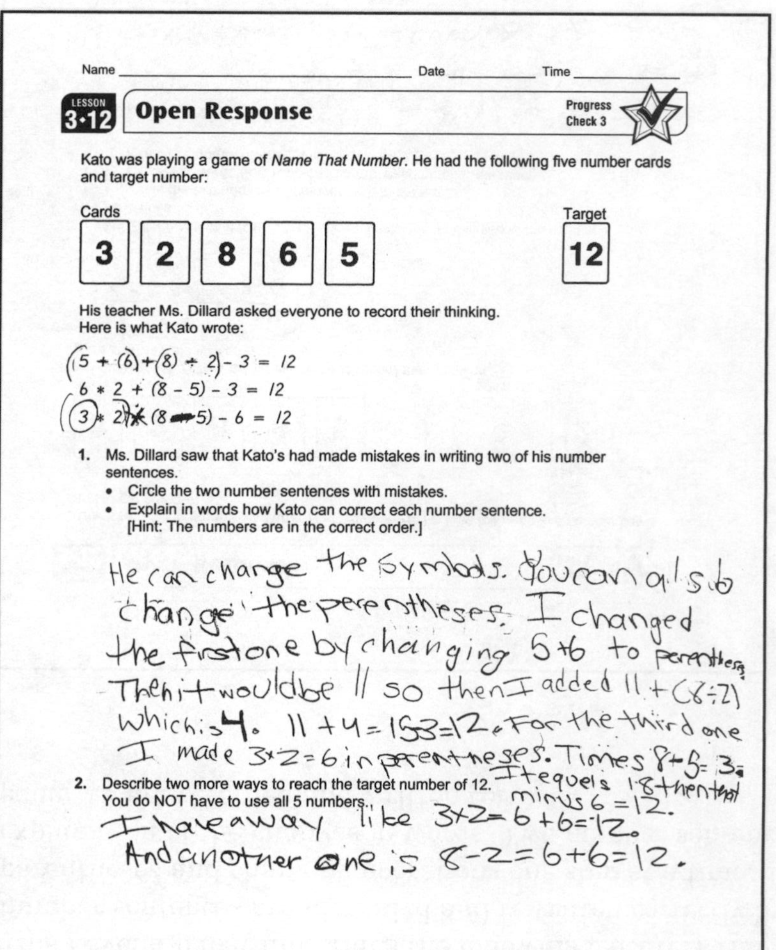

Name ______________ Date ________ Time ________

LESSON 3·12 **Open Response** Progress Check 3

Kato was playing a game of *Name That Number*. He had the following five number cards and target number:

Cards: 3 2 8 6 5 Target: 12

His teacher Ms. Dillard asked everyone to record their thinking. Here is what Kato wrote:

5 + (6 + 8) ÷ 2 – 3 = 12
6 * 2 + (8 – 5) – 3 = 12
3 * 2 + (8 + 5) – 6 = 12

1. Ms. Dillard saw that Kato's had made mistakes in writing two of his number sentences.
   - Circle the two number sentences with mistakes.
   - Explain in words how Kato can correct each number sentence. [Hint: The numbers are in the correct order.]

He can change the symbols. You can also change the perentheses. I changed the first one by changing 5+6 to perentheses. Then it would be 11 so then I added 11 + (8 ÷ 2) which is 4. 11 + 4 = 15 – 3 = 12. For the third one I made 3×2 = 6 in perentheses. Times 8+5 – 3 = 18 then that minus 6 = 12.

2. Describe two more ways to reach the target number of 12. You do NOT have to use all 5 numbers.

I have a way like 3×2 = 6 + 6 = 12.
And another one is 8 – 2 = 6 + 6 = 12.

This Level 2 paper illustrates the following features: The incorrect number sentences are identified and corrected by deleting numbers. There is an explanation in words. There are two more solutions totaling the target number of 12.

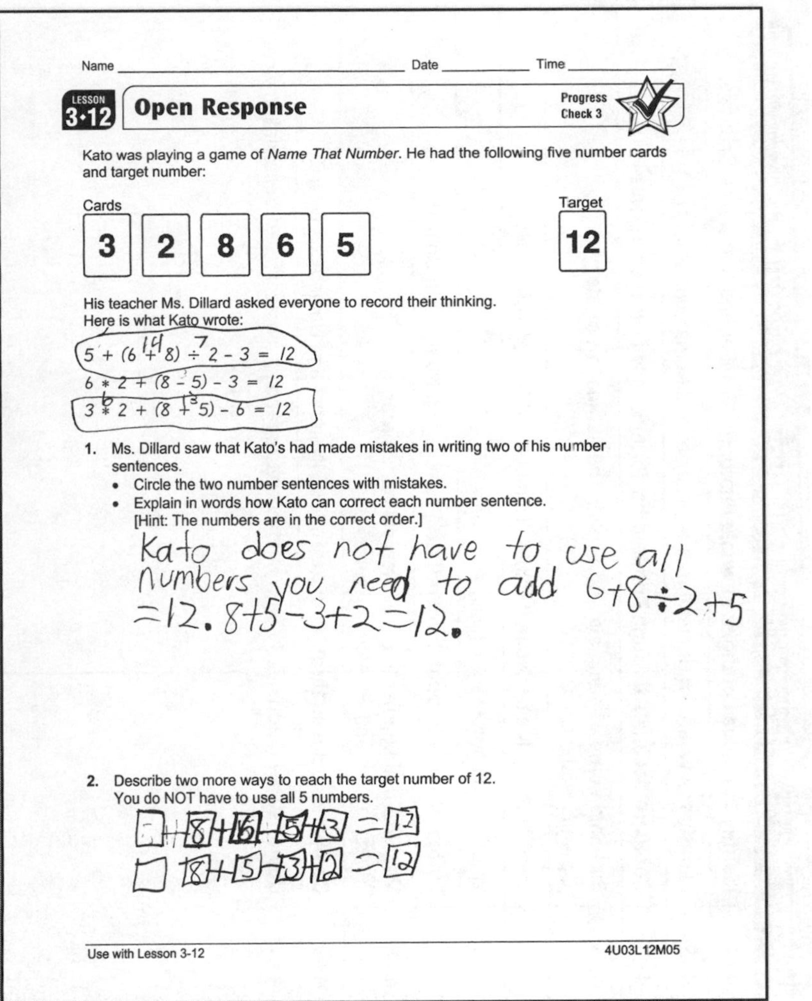

Name ________ Date ________ Time ________

LESSON 3·12 **Open Response** Progress Check 3

Kato was playing a game of *Name That Number*. He had the following five number cards and target number:

Cards: 3 2 8 6 5 — Target: 12

His teacher Ms. Dillard asked everyone to record their thinking. Here is what Kato wrote:

5 + (6 + 8) ÷ 2 − 3 = 12

6 ∗ 2 + (8 − 5) − 3 = 12

3 ∗ 2 + (8 + 5) − 6 = 12

1. Ms. Dillard saw that Kato's had made mistakes in writing two of his number sentences.
   - Circle the two number sentences with mistakes.
   - Explain in words how Kato can correct each number sentence. [Hint: The numbers are in the correct order.]

Kato does not have to use all numbers you need to add 6+8÷2+5 =12. 8+5−3+2=12.

2. Describe two more ways to reach the target number of 12. You do NOT have to use all 5 numbers.

Use with Lesson 3-12 4U03L12M05

This Level 1 paper illustrates the following features: The incorrect number sentences are identified, but the corrections do not make sense. There is a confusing explanation in words. There are three more solutions totaling the target number of 12, but only two are correct because the third one uses the number 3 twice.

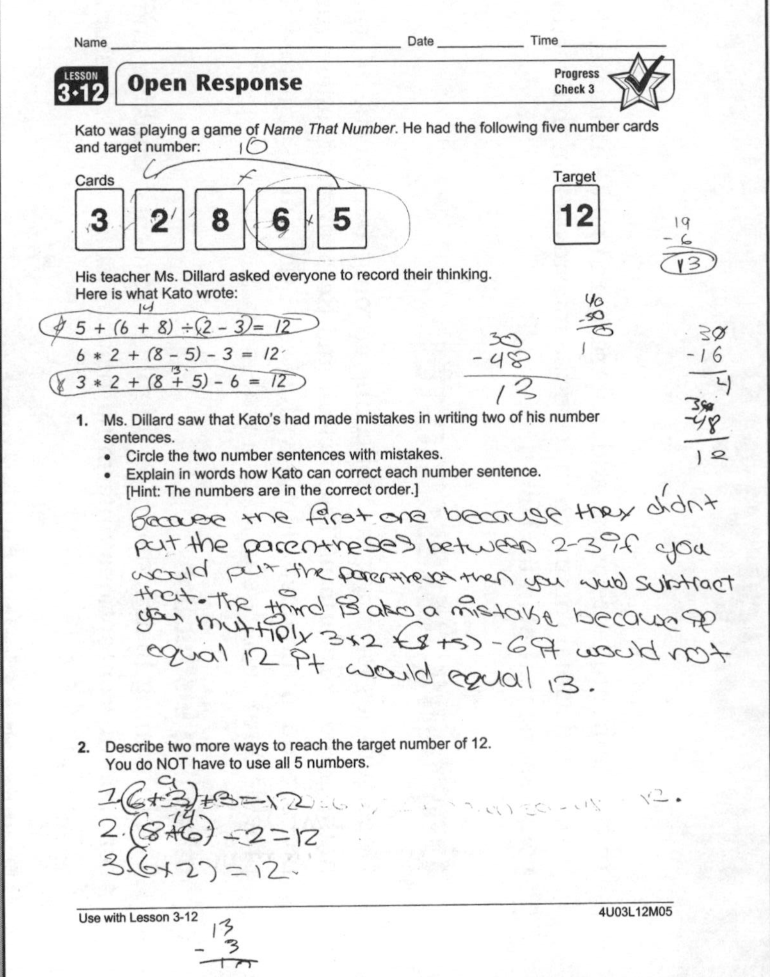

Name ________ Date ________ Time ________

LESSON 3·12 **Open Response** Progress Check 3

Kato was playing a game of *Name That Number*. He had the following five number cards and target number:

Cards: 3 2 8 6 5 — Target: 12

His teacher Ms. Dillard asked everyone to record their thinking. Here is what Kato wrote:

5 + (6 + 8) ÷ (2 − 3) = 12

6 ∗ 2 + (8 − 5) − 3 = 12

3 ∗ 2 + (8 + 5) − 6 = 12

1. Ms. Dillard saw that Kato's had made mistakes in writing two of his number sentences.
   - Circle the two number sentences with mistakes.
   - Explain in words how Kato can correct each number sentence. [Hint: The numbers are in the correct order.]

Because the first one because they didn't put the parentheses between 2−3 if you would put the parentheses then you would subtract that. The third is also a mistake because if you multiply 3×2 (8+5) − 6 it would not equal 12 it would equal 13.

2. Describe two more ways to reach the target number of 12. You do NOT have to use all 5 numbers.

1. (6+3)+3=12
2. (8+6)−2=12
3. (6×2)=12.

Use with Lesson 3-12 4U03L12M05

Unit 4 Assessment Overview

In this unit, students order, add, subtract, and make estimates for problems involving decimal computation. Use the information in this section to develop your assessment plan for Unit 4.

Ongoing Assessment

Opportunities for using and collecting ongoing assessment information are highlighted in Informing Instruction and Recognizing Student Achievement notes. Student products, along with observations and suggested writing prompts, provide a range of useful assessment information.

Informing Instruction

The Informing Instruction notes highlight students' thinking and point out common misconceptions. Informing Instruction in Unit 4: Lessons 4-2, 4-3, 4-4, 4-5, 4-7, and 4-8.

Recognizing Student Achievement

The Recognizing Student Achievement notes highlight specific tasks from which teachers can collect assessment data to monitor and document student progress toward meeting Grade-Level Goals.

Lesson	Content Assessed	Where to Find It
4•1	**Identify the values of digits in whole numbers.** [Number and Numeration Goal 1]	*TLG*, p. 242
4•2	**Identify the values of decimal digits.** [Number and Numeration Goal 1]	*TLG*, p. 248
4•3	**Compare decimals through hundredths.** [Number and Numeration Goal 6]	*TLG*, p. 252
4•4	**Estimate sums of decimals and explain the estimation strategy.** [Operations and Computation Goal 6]	*TLG*, p. 258
4•5	**Identify the value of decimal digits.** [Number and Numeration Goal 1]	*TLG*, p. 262
4•6	**Identify data landmarks.** [Data and Chance Goal 2]	*TLG*, p. 269
4•7	**Write decimals through hundredths.** [Number and Numeration Goal 1]	*TLG*, p. 272
4•8	**Measure line segments to the nearest centimeter.** [Measurement and Reference Frames Goal 1]	*TLG*, p. 280
4•9	**Compare decimals through thousandths.** [Number and Numeration Goal 6]	*TLG*, p. 287
4•10	**Demonstrate automaticity with multiplication facts.** [Operations and Computation Goal 3]	*TLG*, p. 290

Math Boxes

Math Boxes, one of several types of tasks highlighted in the Recognizing Student Achievement notes, have an additional useful feature. Math Boxes in most lessons are paired or linked with Math Boxes in one or two other lessons that have similar problems. Paired or linked Math Boxes in Unit 4: 4-1 and 4-3; 4-2 and 4-4; 4-5 and 4-7; 4-6 and 4-9; and 4-8 and 4-10.

Writing/Reasoning Prompts

In Unit 4, a variety of writing prompts encourage students to explain their strategies and thinking, to reflect on their learning, and to make connections to other mathematics or life experiences. Here are some of the Unit 4 suggestions:

Lesson	Writing/Reasoning Prompts	Where to Find It
4•2	Explain the strategy you used to convert 10 quarters and 7 dimes into dollars and cents.	*TLG*, p. 248
4•3	Is $\overrightarrow{TC}$ another name for $\overrightarrow{CT}$? Explain why or why not.	*TLG*, p. 252
4•5	Explain how you found the value of *S*.	*TLG*, p. 264
4•8	Explain how you knew which number was closer to 47.	*TLG*, p. 281
4•9	Explain the strategy you used to order the decimals.	*TLG*, p. 287

Portfolio Opportunities

Portfolios are a versatile tool for assessment. They help students reflect on their mathematical growth and help teachers understand and document that growth. Each unit identifies several student products that can be selected and stored in a portfolio. Here are some of the Unit 4 suggestions:

Lesson	Portfolio Opportunities	Where to Find It
4•1	Students create place-value puzzles.	*TLG*, p. 243
4•2	Students explain the difference between 0.9 and 0.09.	*TLG*, p. 248
4•3	Students write and solve decimal riddles.	*TLG*, p. 254
4•6	Students solve "Goodie Bag" problems with decimal computation skills.	*TLG*, p. 270
4•9	Students use metric units of linear measure to create a scavenger hunt.	*TLG*, p. 288

Periodic Assessment

Every Progress Check lesson includes opportunities to observe students' progress and to collect student products in a variety of ways—Self Assessment, Oral and Slate Assessment, Written Assessment, and an Open Response task. For more details, see the first page of Progress Check 4, Lesson 4-11, page 294, of the *Teacher's Lesson Guide*.

Progress Check Modifications

Written Assessments are one way students demonstrate what they know. The table below shows modifications for the Written Assessment in this unit. Use these to maximize opportunities for students to demonstrate what they know. Modifications can be given individually or written on the board for the class.

Problem(s)	Modifications for Written Assessment
1–4	**For Problems 1–4, build each number or model each sum or difference with base-10 blocks before filling in the missing symbol.**
7	**For Problem 7, explain how many numbers there are between 1 and 2 and how you know.**
9 and 10	**For Problems 9 and 10, use a ruler that is divided into centimeters and half-centimeters only.**
13–18	**For Problems 13–18, rewrite each of the decimals as a decimal to the hundredths place. Use bills and coins to model the problems.**

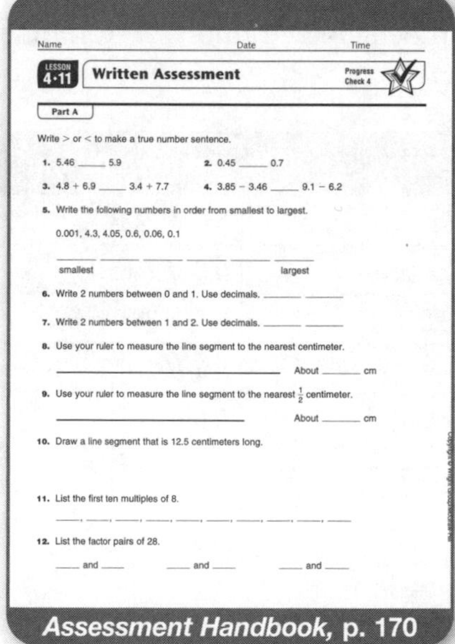
Name Date Time

LESSON 4·11 Written Assessment Progress Check 4

Part A

Write > or < to make a true number sentence.

1. 5.46 ____ 5.9
2. 0.45 ____ 0.7
3. 4.8 + 6.9 ____ 3.4 + 7.7
4. 3.85 − 3.46 ____ 9.1 − 6.2
5. Write the following numbers in order from smallest to largest.
   0.001, 4.3, 4.05, 0.6, 0.06, 0.1
   ____ ____ ____ ____ ____ ____
   smallest largest
6. Write 2 numbers between 0 and 1. Use decimals. ____ ____
7. Write 2 numbers between 1 and 2. Use decimals. ____ ____
8. Use your ruler to measure the line segment to the nearest centimeter.
   About ____ cm
9. Use your ruler to measure the line segment to the nearest $\frac{1}{2}$ centimeter.
   About ____ cm
10. Draw a line segment that is 12.5 centimeters long.
11. List the first ten multiples of 8.
   ____, ____, ____, ____, ____, ____, ____, ____, ____, ____
12. List the factor pairs of 28.
   ____ and ____ ____ and ____ ____ and ____

Assessment Handbook, p. 170

The Written Assessment for Unit 4 Progress Check is on pages 170–172.

Open Response, *Forming a Relay Team*

Description

For this task, students create evenly matched relay teams using estimated running times to the nearest tenth of a second.

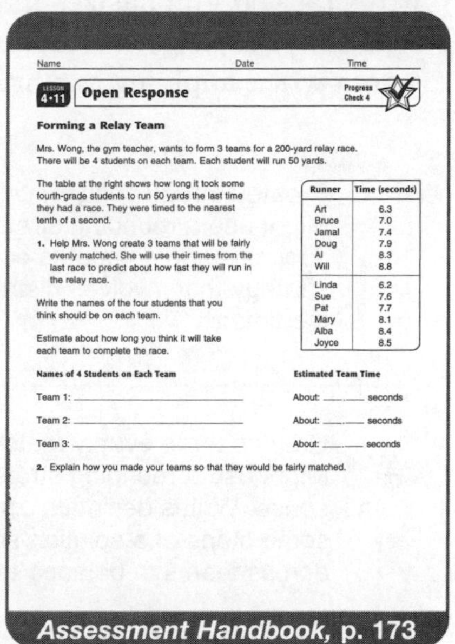

Name ______ Date ______ Time ______

LESSON 4•11 **Open Response** Progress Check 4

Forming a Relay Team

Mrs. Wong, the gym teacher, wants to form 3 teams for a 200-yard relay race. There will be 4 students on each team. Each student will run 50 yards.

The table at the right shows how long it took some fourth-grade students to run 50 yards the last time they had a race. They were timed to the nearest tenth of a second.

Runner	Time (seconds)
Art	6.3
Bruce	7.0
Jamal	7.4
Doug	7.9
Al	8.3
Will	8.8
Linda	6.2
Sue	7.6
Pat	7.7
Mary	8.1
Alba	8.4
Joyce	8.5

1. Help Mrs. Wong create 3 teams that will be fairly evenly matched. She will use their times from the last race to predict about how fast they will run in the relay race.

Write the names of the four students that you think should be on each team.

Estimate about how long you think it will take each team to complete the race.

Names of 4 Students on Each Team | **Estimated Team Time**

Team 1: ______ About: ___.___ seconds

Team 2: ______ About: ___.___ seconds

Team 3: ______ About: ___.___ seconds

2. Explain how you made your teams so that they would be fairly matched.

Assessment Handbook, p. 173

Focus

- **Compare and order decimals through tenths.**
  [Number and Numeration Goal 6]
- **Make reasonable estimates for whole-number and decimal computations.**
  [Operations and Computation Goal 6]

Implementation Tips

- Explain what *fairly matched* means.
- Have students record number models for how they find each team total.

Modifications for Meeting Diverse Needs

- Provide 3-in. by 5-in. cards and have students record the name and time for each student. To help them make their estimates, have students record the seconds in red and the tenths of a second in blue. Students can move the cards to form teams and use a calculator to check their estimates.
- Have students predict what the total race time for an average team might be. Have them explain how they arrived at their answers.

Improving Open Response Skills

Before students begin the task, have them read it together. Give students a minute or two to think about how they will solve the problem. In small groups, have students share ideas for how they plan to organize their work.

Note: The wording and formatting of the text on the student samples that follow may vary slightly from the actual task your children will complete. These minor discrepancies will not affect the implementation of the task.

Rubric

This rubric is designed to help you assess levels of mathematical performance on this task. It emphasizes mathematical understanding with only a mention of clarity of explanation. Consider the expectations of standardized tests in your area when applying a rubric. Modify this sample rubric as appropriate.

4	Creates three evenly matched teams with total times between 29 and 32 seconds. Might use a rounding strategy, and it is consistent throughout the work. Writes decimals and computes correctly. Clearly describes all of the steps of a solution strategy that involves distributing fast and slow runners across teams to balance the times.
3	Creates three evenly matched teams with total times between 29 and 32 seconds. Might use a rounding strategy. The strategy might vary but the variance makes sense. Writes decimals correctly. Might make minor errors in computation. Describes some steps of a solution strategy that involves distributing fast and slow runners across teams to balance the times.
2	Creates three teams organized with some strategy. Might make rounding mistakes. Writes decimals correctly. Might make computation errors. Attempts to describe some steps of a solution strategy that is related to the context of the problem.
1	Attempts to create teams, but there is no apparent strategy. Might make rounding mistakes and computation errors. Might make errors in decimal notation. Might attempt to write an explanation, but it might not make sense in the context of the problem.
0	Does not attempt to solve the problem.

Sample Student Responses

This Level 4 paper illustrates the following features: There are three evenly matched teams. A rounding strategy is used consistently before finding team totals. The explanation describes exactly how the runners are distributed according to their times.

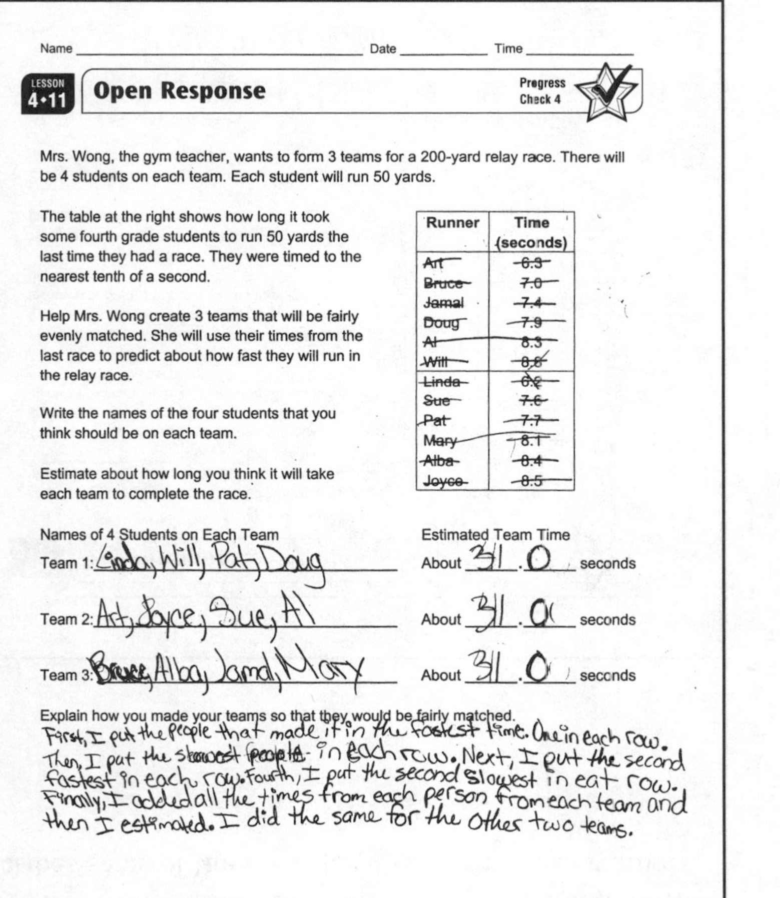

Name ______ Date ______ Time ______

LESSON 4•11 **Open Response** Progress Check 4

Mrs. Wong, the gym teacher, wants to form 3 teams for a 200-yard relay race. There will be 4 students on each team. Each student will run 50 yards.

The table at the right shows how long it took some fourth grade students to run 50 yards the last time they had a race. They were timed to the nearest tenth of a second.

Help Mrs. Wong create 3 teams that will be fairly evenly matched. She will use their times from the last race to predict about how fast they will run in the relay race.

Write the names of the four students that you think should be on each team.

Estimate about how long you think it will take each team to complete the race.

Runner	Time (seconds)
Art	6.3
Bruce	7.0
Jamal	7.4
Doug	7.9
Al	8.3
Will	8.8
Linda	6.2
Sue	7.6
Pat	7.7
Mary	8.1
Alba	8.4
Joyce	8.5

Names of 4 Students on Each Team	Estimated Team Time
Team 1: Linda, Will, Pat, Doug	About 31.0 seconds
Team 2: Art, Joyce, Sue, Al	About 31.0 seconds
Team 3: Bruce, Alba, Jamal, Mary	About 31.0 seconds

Explain how you made your teams so that they would be fairly matched.
First, I put the people that made it in the fastest time. One in each row. Then, I put the slowest people in each row. Next, I put the second fastest in each row. Fourth, I put the second slowest in eat row. Finally, I added all the times from each person from each team and then I estimated. I did the same for the other two teams.

This Level 4 paper illustrates the following features: There are three evenly matched teams. A rounding strategy is used consistently to find subtotals for every two runners. The explanation is sparsely worded, but the necessary information is provided in the form of notes made on the data table.

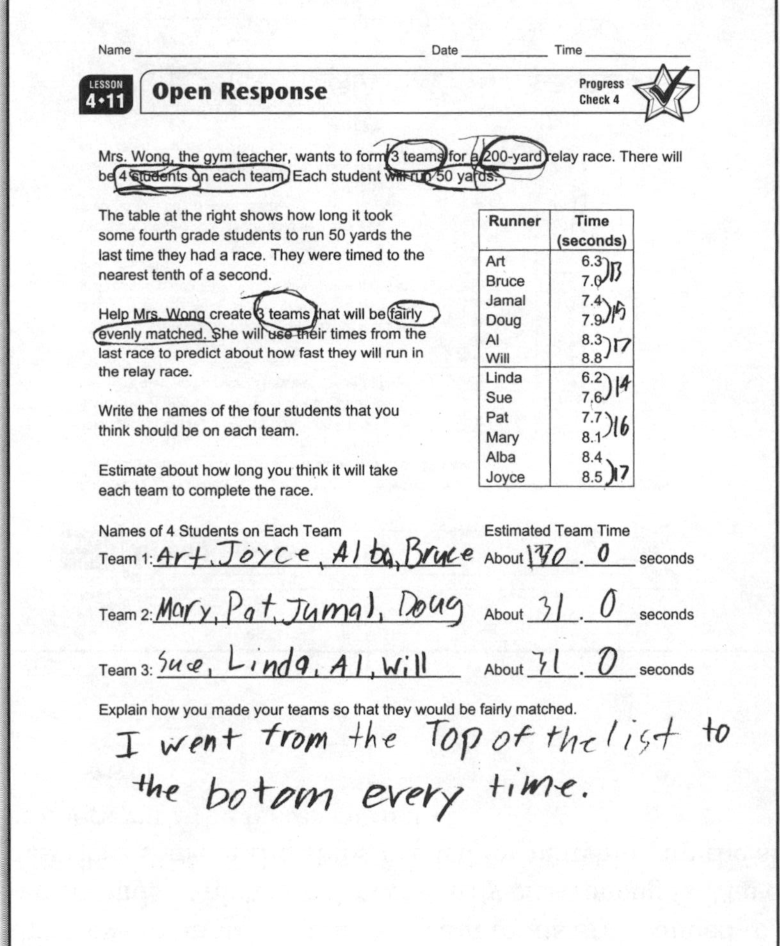

Name ______ Date ______ Time ______

LESSON 4•11 **Open Response** Progress Check 4

Mrs. Wong, the gym teacher, wants to form 3 teams for a 200-yard relay race. There will be 4 students on each team. Each student will run 50 yards.

The table at the right shows how long it took some fourth grade students to run 50 yards the last time they had a race. They were timed to the nearest tenth of a second.

Help Mrs. Wong create 3 teams that will be fairly evenly matched. She will use their times from the last race to predict about how fast they will run in the relay race.

Write the names of the four students that you think should be on each team.

Estimate about how long you think it will take each team to complete the race.

Runner	Time (seconds)
Art	6.3
Bruce	7.0
Jamal	7.4
Doug	7.9
Al	8.3
Will	8.8
Linda	6.2
Sue	7.6
Pat	7.7
Mary	8.1
Alba	8.4
Joyce	8.5

Names of 4 Students on Each Team	Estimated Team Time
Team 1: Art, Joyce, Alba, Bruce	About 30.0 seconds
Team 2: Mary, Pat, Jumal, Doug	About 31.0 seconds
Team 3: Sue, Linda, Al, Will	About 31.0 seconds

Explain how you made your teams so that they would be fairly matched.
I went from the Top of the list to the botom every time.

This Level 3 paper illustrates the following features: There are three evenly matched teams. Team totals are calculated exactly. There is a computation error on Team 3. The explanation describes some of the steps for distributing the runners.

Name ______ Date ______ Time ______

LESSON 4•11 **Open Response** Progress Check 4

Mrs. Wong, the gym teacher, wants to form 3 teams for a 200-yard relay race. There will be 4 students on each team. Each student will run 50 yards.

The table at the right shows how long it took some fourth grade students to run 50 yards the last time they had a race. They were timed to the nearest tenth of a second.

Help Mrs. Wong create 3 teams that will be fairly evenly matched. She will use their times from the last race to predict about how fast they will run in the relay race.

Write the names of the four students that you think should be on each team.

Estimate about how long you think it will take each team to complete the race.

Runner	Time (seconds)
Art	6.3
Bruce	7.0
Jamal	7.4
Doug	7.9
Al	8.3
Will	8.8
Linda	6.2
Sue	7.6
Pat	7.7
Mary	8.1
Alba	8.4
Joyce	8.5

Names of 4 Students on Each Team — Estimated Team Time

Team 1: Art, Bruce, Doug, and Al — About 29.5 seconds

Team 2: Jamal, Sue, Joyce, and Pat — About 31.2 seconds

Team 3: Mary, Alba, Linda, and Will — About 31.9 seconds

Explain how you made your teams so that they would be fairly matched.

I picked one fast person on each team. Then I would pick the slow/fast people. Last I would pick the slow people.

This Level 3 paper illustrates the following features: There are three evenly matched teams. Team totals are rounded to the nearest ten seconds (which is not necessarily close enough). The explanation describes some of the steps needed for matching up the slower runners with the faster runners.

Name ______ Date ______ Time ______

LESSON 4•11 **Open Response** Progress Check 4

Mrs. Wong, the gym teacher, wants to form 3 teams for a 200-yard relay race. There will be 4 students on each team. Each student will run 50 yards.

The table at the right shows how long it took some fourth grade students to run 50 yards the last time they had a race. They were timed to the nearest tenth of a second.

Help Mrs. Wong create 3 teams that will be fairly evenly matched. She will use their times from the last race to predict about how fast they will run in the relay race.

Write the names of the four students that you think should be on each team.

Estimate about how long you think it will take each team to complete the race.

Runner	Time (seconds)
Art	6.3
Bruce	7.0
Jamal	7.4
Doug	7.9
Al	8.3
Will	8.8
Linda	6.2
Sue	7.6
Pat	7.7
Mary	8.1
Alba	8.4
Joyce	8.5

Names of 4 Students on Each Team — Estimated Team Time

Team 1: Art, Joyce, Bruce, Alba — About 30.00 seconds

Team 2: Mary, Jamal, Pat, Doug — About 30.00 seconds

Team 3: Al, Sue, Will, Linda — About 30.00 seconds

Explain how you made your teams so that they would be fairly matched.

First I thought on how to put them. Second I seperated the fastest and slowest, and put the slowest with the fastest.

This Level 2 paper illustrates the following features: There are three teams. A rounding strategy is used before finding team totals. There is an error in the rounding for Team 1. The explanation states that the teams should be equally matched but does not explain how.

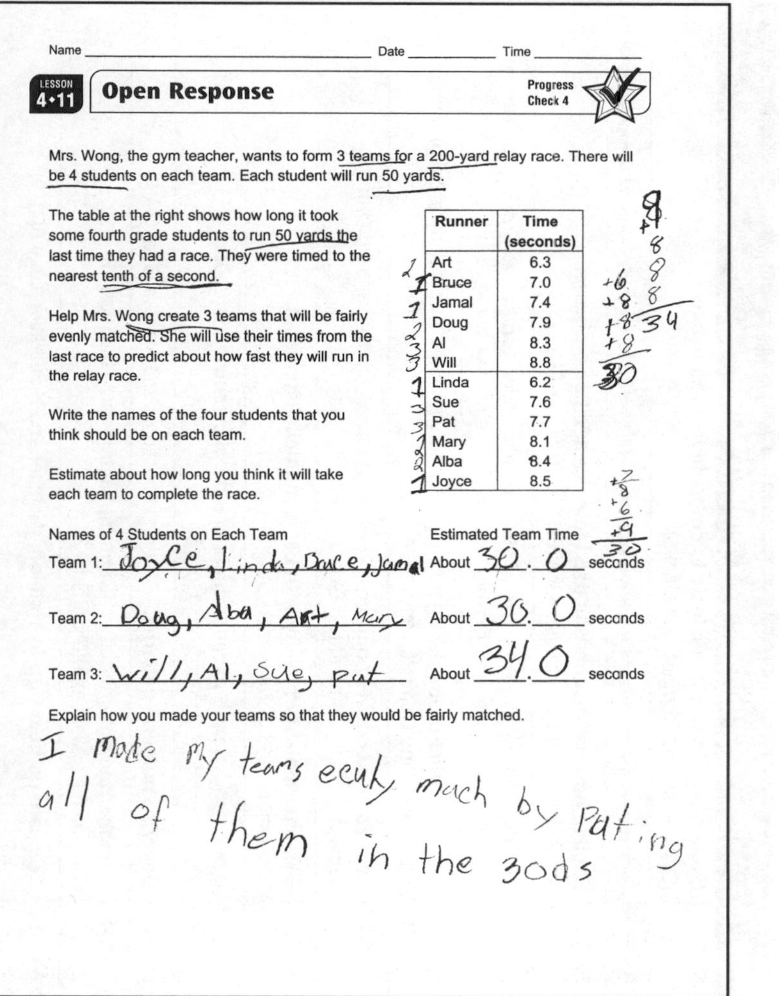

Name ______ Date ______ Time ______

LESSON 4•11 **Open Response** Progress Check 4

Mrs. Wong, the gym teacher, wants to form 3 teams for a 200-yard relay race. There will be 4 students on each team. Each student will run 50 yards.

The table at the right shows how long it took some fourth grade students to run 50 yards the last time they had a race. They were timed to the nearest tenth of a second.

Help Mrs. Wong create 3 teams that will be fairly evenly matched. She will use their times from the last race to predict about how fast they will run in the relay race.

Write the names of the four students that you think should be on each team.

Estimate about how long you think it will take each team to complete the race.

Runner	Time (seconds)
Art	6.3
Bruce	7.0
Jamal	7.4
Doug	7.9
Al	8.3
Will	8.8
Linda	6.2
Sue	7.6
Pat	7.7
Mary	8.1
Alba	8.4
Joyce	8.5

Names of 4 Students on Each Team — Estimated Team Time

Team 1: Joyce, Linda, Bruce, Jamal — About 30.0 seconds

Team 2: Doug, Aba, Art, Mary — About 30.0 seconds

Team 3: will, Al, Sue, put — About 34.0 seconds

Explain how you made your teams so that they would be fairly matched.

I Make my teams ecuk much by Pating all of them in the 30ds

This Level 1 paper illustrates the following features: There are three teams. A rounding strategy appears to have been used. The explanation describes a strategy, which will result in the formation of teams that would be least fairly matched. It has all the fastest runners on one team and the slowest on another.

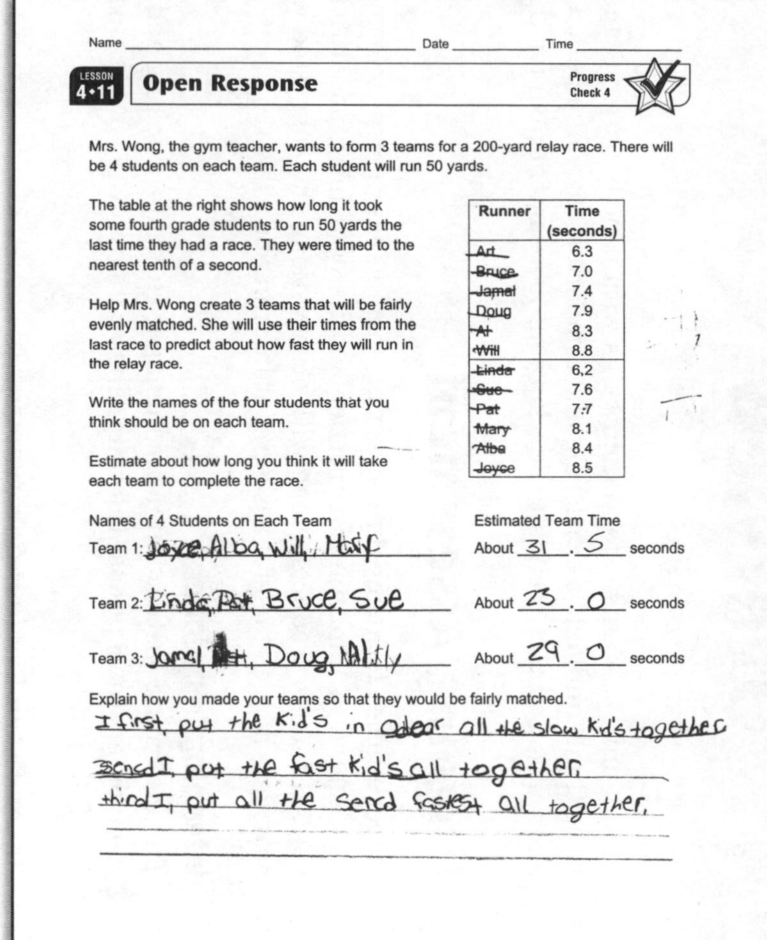

Name ______ Date ______ Time ______

LESSON 4•11 **Open Response** Progress Check 4

Mrs. Wong, the gym teacher, wants to form 3 teams for a 200-yard relay race. There will be 4 students on each team. Each student will run 50 yards.

The table at the right shows how long it took some fourth grade students to run 50 yards the last time they had a race. They were timed to the nearest tenth of a second.

Help Mrs. Wong create 3 teams that will be fairly evenly matched. She will use their times from the last race to predict about how fast they will run in the relay race.

Write the names of the four students that you think should be on each team.

Estimate about how long you think it will take each team to complete the race.

Runner	Time (seconds)
Art	6.3
Bruce	7.0
Jamal	7.4
Doug	7.9
Al	8.3
Will	8.8
Linda	6.2
Sue	7.6
Pat	7.7
Mary	8.1
Alba	8.4
Joyce	8.5

Names of 4 Students on Each Team — Estimated Team Time

Team 1: Joyce, Alba, Will, Mary — About 31.5 seconds

Team 2: Linda, Pat, Bruce, Sue — About 25.0 seconds

Team 3: Jamal, Art, Doug, Al — About 29.0 seconds

Explain how you made your teams so that they would be fairly matched.

I first put the kid's in odear all the slow kid's together

Second I put the fast kid's all together.

third I put all the Secnd fastest all together.

Unit 5

Assessment Overview

In this unit, students extend their skills with pencil-and-paper multiplication algorithms, and explore ordering and comparing large numbers. Use the information in this section to develop your assessment plan for Unit 5.

Ongoing Assessment

Opportunities for using and collecting ongoing assessment information are highlighted in Informing Instruction and Recognizing Student Achievement notes. Student products, along with observations and suggested writing prompts, provide a range of useful assessment information.

Informing Instruction

The Informing Instruction notes highlight students' thinking and point out common misconceptions. Informing Instruction in Unit 5: Lessons 5-1, 5-2, 5-3, 5-5, 5-6, and 5-8.

Recognizing Student Achievement

The Recognizing Student Achievement notes highlight specific tasks from which teachers can collect assessment data to monitor and document students progress toward meeting Grade-Level Goals.

Lesson	Content Assessed	Where to Find It
5◆1	**Explain how to use basic facts to compute fact extensions.** [Operations and Computation Goal 3]	*TLG*, p. 317
5◆2	**Determine if a number sentence is true or false.** [Patterns, Functions, and Algebra Goal 2]	*TLG*, p. 323
5◆3	**Explain how estimation was used to solve addition problems.** [Operations and Computation Goal 6]	*TLG*, p. 329
5◆4	**Use the Distributive Property of Multiplication over Addition to find partial-products.** [Patterns, Functions, and Algebra Goal 4]	*TLG*, p. 334
5◆5	**Use the partial-products algorithm to multiply a 1-digit number by a 2-digit number.** [Operations and Computation Goal 4]	*TLG*, p. 340
5◆6	**Estimate reasonable solutions to whole-number multiplication problems.** [Operations and Computation Goal 6]	*TLG*, p. 344
5◆7	**Demonstrate automaticity with basic multiplication facts.** [Operations and Computation Goal 3]	*TLG*, p. 353
5◆8	**Use extended multiplication facts in a problem solving situation.** [Operations and Computation Goal 3]	*TLG*, p. 358
5◆9	**Describe numeric patterns.** [Patterns, Functions, and Algebra Goal 1]	*TLG*, p. 365
5◆10	**Demonstrate automaticity with multiplication facts through 10 * 10.** [Operations and Computation Goal 3]	*TLG*, p. 370
5◆11	**Compare numbers up to 1 billion.** [Number and Numeration Goal 6]	*TLG*, p. 376

Math Boxes

Math Boxes, one of several types of tasks highlighted in the Recognizing Student Achievement notes, have an additional useful feature. Math Boxes in most lessons are paired or linked with Math Boxes in one or two other lessons that have similar problems. Paired or linked Math Boxes in Unit 5: 5-1 and 5-3; 5-2 and 5-4; 5-5 and 5-7; 5-6, 5-8, and 5-10; and 5-9 and 5-11.

Writing/Reasoning Prompts

In Unit 5, a variety of writing prompts encourage students to explain their strategies and thinking, to reflect on their learning, and to make connections to other mathematics or life experiences. Here are some of the Unit 5 suggestions:

Lesson	Writing/Reasoning Prompts	Where to Find It
5•4	Explain a shortcut you might use to solve the division problems.	*TLG*, p. 335
5•5	Donato said there is more than one correct answer for each of the estimates. Do you agree or disagree? Explain.	*TLG*, p. 341
5•6	Devon wrote 342,000 for three hundred forty-two thousandths. Explain the error he might have made.	*TLG*, p. 346
5•8	Explain how you determined the number of pies that could be made with 75 apples.	*TLG*, p. 359
5•9	Explain if intersecting lines can be perpendicular lines.	*TLG*, p. 365

Portfolio Opportunities

Portfolios are a versatile tool for assessment. They help students reflect on their mathematical growth and help teachers understand and document that growth. Each unit identifies several student products that can be selected and stored in a portfolio. Here are some of the Unit 5 suggestions:

Lesson	Portfolio Opportunities	Where to Find It
5•2	Students judge a *Multiplication Wrestling* competition.	*TLG*, p. 324
5•3	Students plan a route connecting four cities.	*TLG*, p. 330
5•8	Students devise a strategy to see how many dots would fill a classroom.	*TLG*, p. 360
5•12	Students estimate if one million dollars will fit in a suitcase that will hold the equivalent of one carton of paper.	*TLG*, p. 381

Periodic Assessment

Every Progress Check lesson includes opportunities to observe students' progress and to collect student products in a variety of ways—Self Assessment, Oral and Slate Assessment, Written Assessment, and an Open Response task. For more details, see the first page of Progress Check 5, Lesson 5-12, page 378, of the *Teacher's Lesson Guide*.

Progress Check Modifications

Written Assessments are one way students demonstrate what they know. The table below shows modifications for the Written Assessment in this unit. Use these to maximize opportunities for students to demonstrate what they know. Modifications can be given individually or written on the board for the class.

Problem(s)	Modifications for Written Assessment
6	**For Problem 6, Maria said that 32 * 50 is the same as 32 * 5 * 10. Do you agree or disagree? Explain.**
7–10	**For Problems 7–10, build each number with base-10 blocks, and find the sum or difference.**
16, 17	**For Problems 16 and 17, round each of the numbers in the problem up to the nearest 10 to find your estimate.**
19	**For Problem 19, record the total for one week on a quarter-sheet of paper. Repeat 4 times for a month and find the total.**

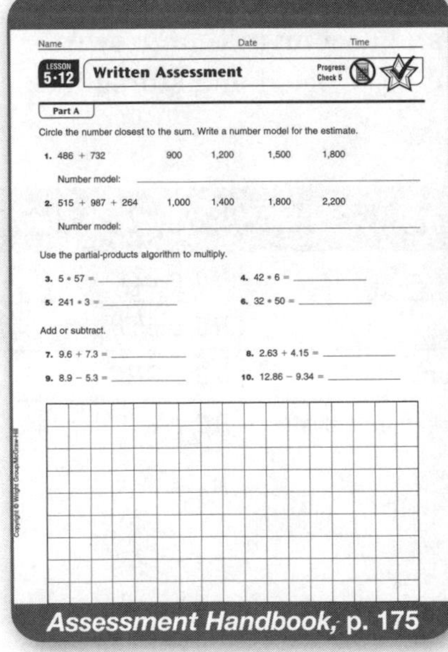
Name Date Time

LESSON 5·12 **Written Assessment** Progress Check 5

Part A

Circle the number closest to the sum. Write a number model for the estimate.

1. 486 + 732 900 1,200 1,500 1,800

 Number model: ______

2. 515 + 987 + 264 1,000 1,400 1,800 2,200

 Number model: ______

Use the partial-products algorithm to multiply.

3. 5 * 57 = ______
4. 42 * 6 = ______
5. 241 * 3 = ______
6. 32 * 50 = ______

Add or subtract.

7. 9.6 + 7.3 = ______
8. 2.63 + 4.15 = ______
9. 8.9 − 5.3 = ______
10. 12.86 − 9.34 = ______

Assessment Handbook, p. 175

The Written Assessment for Unit 5 Progress Check is on pages 175–177.

Open Response, *Walking Away with a Million Dollars*

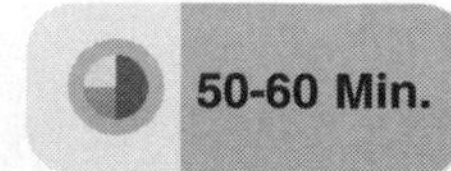

Description

For this task, students estimate if one million dollars will fit in a suitcase that will hold the equivalent of one carton of paper.

Name Date Time

LESSON 5·12 **Open Response** Progress Check 5

Walking Away with a Million Dollars

You will need the following information to solve the problem below:

You can cover a **sheet** of paper with about six $100 bills.

There are 500 sheets in one **ream** of paper.

There are 10 reams in one **carton.**

Imagine that you have inherited one million dollars. The bank has only $700,000 in $100 bills. The bank gives you the rest of the money in $20 bills and $10 bills. Your suitcase will hold as much as 1 carton of paper.

Will one million dollars fit in your suitcase? Show all of your work. Explain what you did to solve the problem.

Assessment Handbook, p. 178

Focus

- ◆ **Read and write whole numbers up to 1,000,000.** [Number and Numeration Goal 1]
- ◆ **Use paper-and-pencil algorithms to solve problems involving the multiplication of multidigit whole numbers.** [Operations and Computation Goal 4]
- ◆ **Give reasonable estimates for whole number multiplication problems.** [Operations and Computation Goal 6]

Implementation Tips

- ◆ Emphasize that the suitcase will hold the same number of bills as the carton. Remind students that they already know how much money they can take in $100 bills.

Modifications for Meeting Diverse Needs

- ◆ Have students break the problem into simpler steps. Provide students with pictures, and ask them to label each with its total value in $100s, $20s, and $10s. For example, a sheet is worth $600, $120, or $60; a ream is worth..., and so on. Oncc they have determined the value of a sheet and a ream of each bill, have them work together to find a combination with a total value of one million dollars. Encourage students to use a calculator to check their calculations. Have them record a number sentence for each step.
- ◆ Have students solve the problem by determining which denominations to use to come as close as possible to one million dollars. *(Sample answer: With full reams of each kind of bill—2 reams of $100 bills, 5 reams of $20 bills, and 3 reams of $10 bills—the total is 10 reams (1 carton) and the amount of money is $990,000.)*

Improving Open Response Skills

Before students begin the task, have them read the problem individually. As they read, they can record questions they need to answer in order to solve the problem. Have them share their questions in small groups. Students can then pool the questions to make a class list that they can refer to during the task. For example, *How much money is in 1 ream of $100 bills? How many bills does a ream hold? How much money do I still need in $20 bills and $10 bills? How many $10 bills do I want to include?*

Note: The wording and formatting of the text on the student samples that follow may vary slightly from the actual task your children will complete. These minor discrepancies will not affect the implementation of the task.

Rubric

This rubric is designed to help you assess levels of mathematical performance on this task. It emphasizes mathematical understanding with only a mention of clarity of explanation. Consider the expectations of standardized tests in your area when applying a rubric. Modify this sample rubric as appropriate.

4	Determines that $1,000,000 will fit in the suitcase and describes in numbers or words the number of dollars or number of bills required for each kind of bill. Shows all computation and provides clear justification in numbers or words for why $1,000,000 will fit in the suitcase. Clearly explains how the estimate is calculated.
3	Determines that $1,000,000 will fit in the suitcase and describes in numbers or words the number of dollars or number of bills required for each kind of bill. Shows computation steps, but there might be some errors. Provides some justification for why $1,000,000 will fit in the suitcase. Explains how the estimate is calculated.
2	Might determine that $1,000,000 will fit in the suitcase, but there might be errors in calculating the number of dollars or number of bills required. Shows computation steps, but there might be errors or steps might be missing.
1	Might restate some of the facts and perform some of the computation, but there might be errors. There might be evidence of major misunderstandings in interpreting the problem.
0	Does not attempt to solve the problem.

Sample Student Responses

This Level 4 paper illustrates the following features: Calculations show that a carton will hold 30,000 bills and that $700,000 in $100 bills takes 7,000 bills and $300,000 in $20 bills takes 15,000 bills. At the end, there is a trade of one $20 bill for two $10 bills, and an explanation that this will still fit because a total of 30,000 bills will fit in a carton and so far there are only 22,000 in $100 bills and $20 bills. The steps are clearly described.

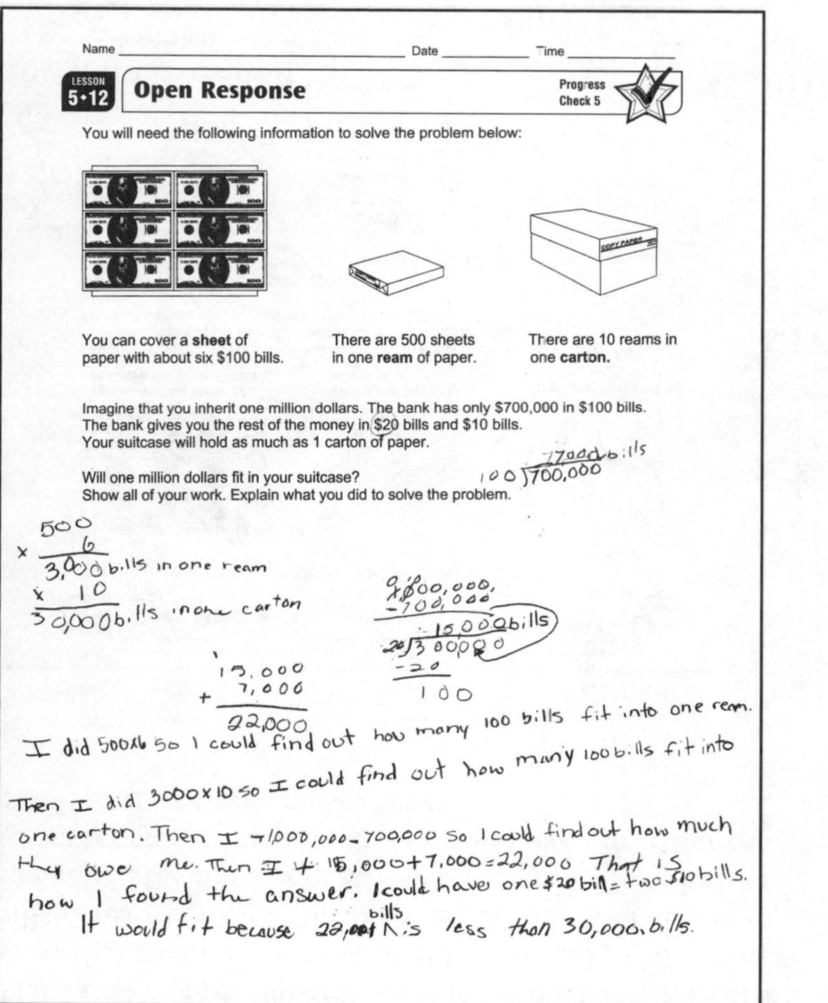

Name ____________ Date ________ Time ________

LESSON 5•12 **Open Response** Progress Check 5

You will need the following information to solve the problem below:

You can cover a **sheet** of paper with about six $100 bills.

There are 500 sheets in one **ream** of paper.

There are 10 reams in one **carton.**

Imagine that you inherit one million dollars. The bank has only $700,000 in $100 bills. The bank gives you the rest of the money in $20 bills and $10 bills. Your suitcase will hold as much as 1 carton of paper.

Will one million dollars fit in your suitcase?
Show all of your work. Explain what you did to solve the problem.

500 × 6 = 3,000 bills in one ream
× 10 = 30,000 bills in one carton

100) 700,000 = 7000 bills

1,000,000 − 700,000 = 300,000
20) 300,000 = 15,000 bills

15,000 + 7,000 = 22,000

I did 500×6 so I could find out how many 100 bills fit into one ream.
Then I did 3000×10 so I could find out how many 100 bills fit into one carton. Then I ÷1,000,000−700,000 so I could find out how much they owe me. Then I + 15,000+7,000=22,000 That is how I found the answer. I could have one $20 bill = two $10 bills.
It would fit because 22,000 bills is less than 30,000 bills.

This Level 4 paper illustrates the following features: Calculations show that $700,000 in $100 bills is just over 2 reams and $300,000 in $20 bills is 5 reams. At the end, there is a trade of one $20 bill for two $10 bills, and an explanation that this will still fit because a total of 10 reams will fit in a carton, and so far there are only about seven reams. The explanation clearly describes all of the steps.

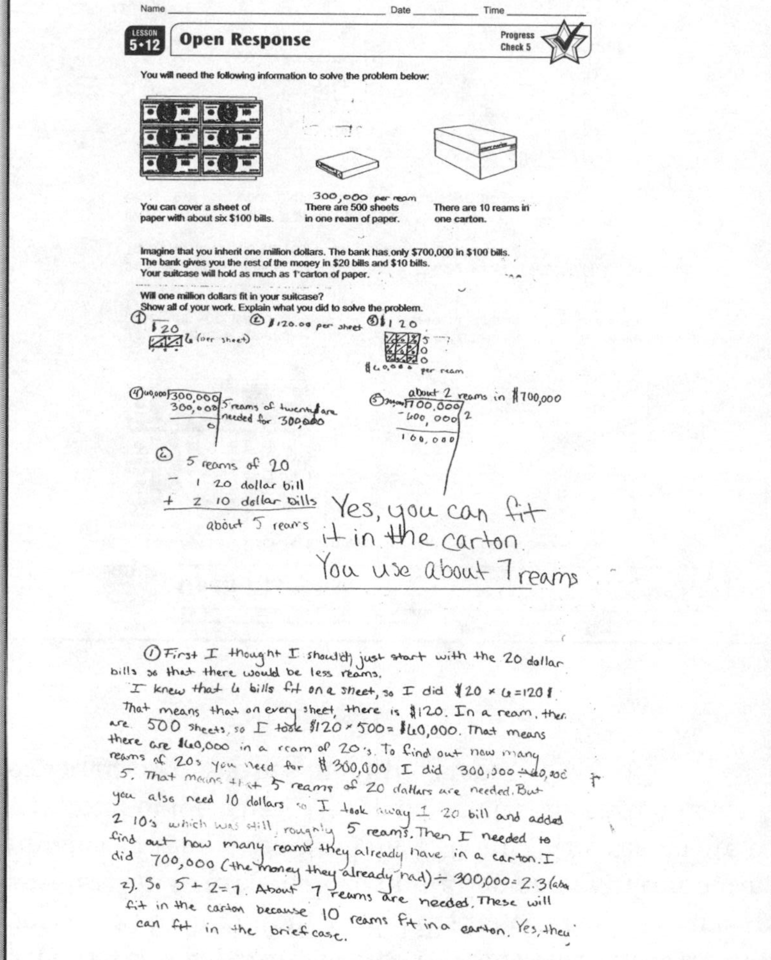

Name ____________ Date ________ Time ________

LESSON 5•12 **Open Response** Progress Check 5

You will need the following information to solve the problem below:

You can cover a sheet of paper with about six $100 bills.

There are 500 sheets in one ream of paper. (300,000 per ream)

There are 10 reams in one carton.

Imagine that you inherit one million dollars. The bank has only $700,000 in $100 bills. The bank gives you the rest of the money in $20 bills and $10 bills. Your suitcase will hold as much as 1 carton of paper.

Will one million dollars fit in your suitcase?
Show all of your work. Explain what you did to solve the problem.

① $20 × 6 (per sheet) ② $120.00 per sheet ③ $120 × 500 = $60,000 per ream

④ 60,000) 300,000 — 5 reams of twenties are needed for 300,000

⑤ 300,000) 700,000 — about 2 reams in $700,000

⑥ 5 reams of 20
− 1 20 dollar bill
+ 2 10 dollar bills
about 5 reams

Yes, you can fit it in the carton.
You use about 7 reams

① First I thought I should just start with the 20 dollar bills so that there would be less reams.
I knew that 6 bills fit on a sheet, so I did $20 × 6 = 120$. That means that on every sheet, there is $120. In a ream, there are 500 sheets, so I took $120 × 500 = $60,000. That means there are $60,000 in a ream of 20's. To find out how many reams of 20's you need for $300,000 I did 300,000 ÷ 60,000 = 5. That means that 5 reams of 20 dollars are needed. But you also need 10 dollars so I took away 1 20 bill and added 2 10's which was still roughly 5 reams. Then I needed to find out how many reams they already have in a carton. I did 700,000 (the money they already had) ÷ 300,000 = 2.3 (about 2). So 5 + 2 = 7. About 7 reams are needed. These will fit in the carton because 10 reams fit in a carton. Yes, they can fit in the brief case.

This Level 3 paper illustrates the following features: Calculations show that a carton will hold 30,000 bills and $700,000 in $100 bills takes 7,000 bills, but there are computation errors in computing the number of $20 bills required. There are some computations on the page that do not make sense, but the explanation in words makes sense.

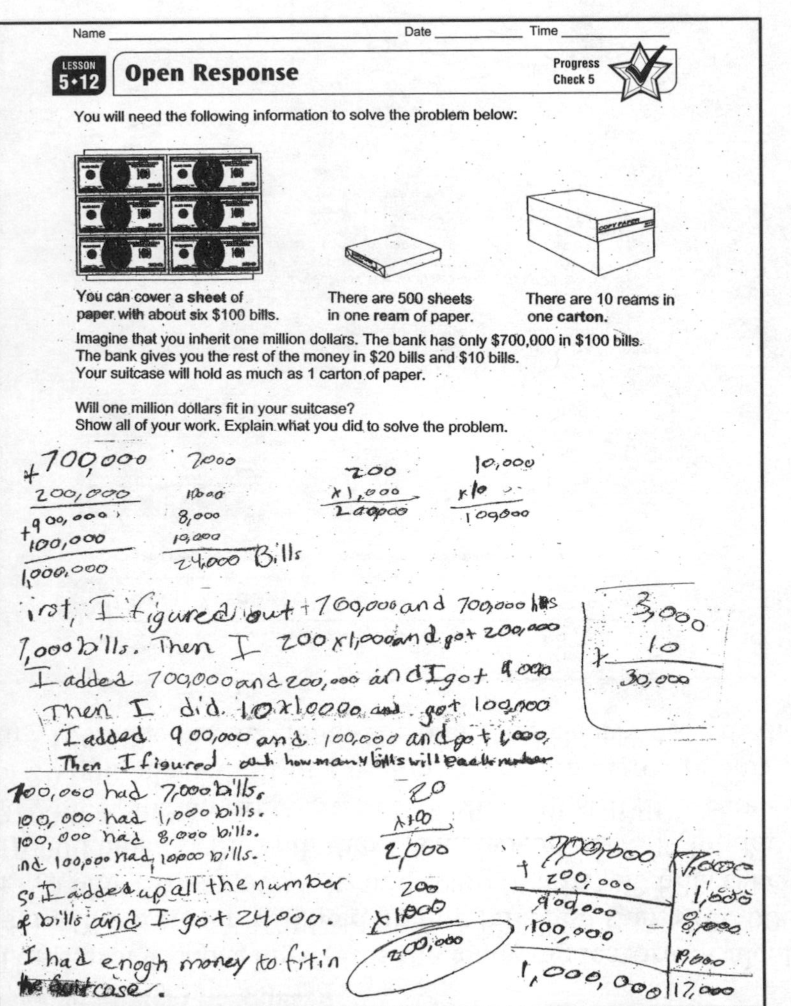

Name ______ Date ______ Time ______

LESSON 5•12 **Open Response** Progress Check 5

You will need the following information to solve the problem below:

You can cover a **sheet** of paper with about six $100 bills.

There are 500 sheets in one **ream** of paper.

There are 10 reams in one **carton.**

Imagine that you inherit one million dollars. The bank has only $700,000 in $100 bills. The bank gives you the rest of the money in $20 bills and $10 bills. Your suitcase will hold as much as 1 carton of paper.

Will one million dollars fit in your suitcase?
Show all of your work. Explain what you did to solve the problem.

This Level 3 paper illustrates the following features: Calculations show that $700,000 in $100 bills takes about 2 reams (plus 166 sheets). There are small computation errors in computing the number of reams required for $20 bills. The reams are counted up to a total of less than 10 reams, which the carton holds. The explanation describes all of the steps.

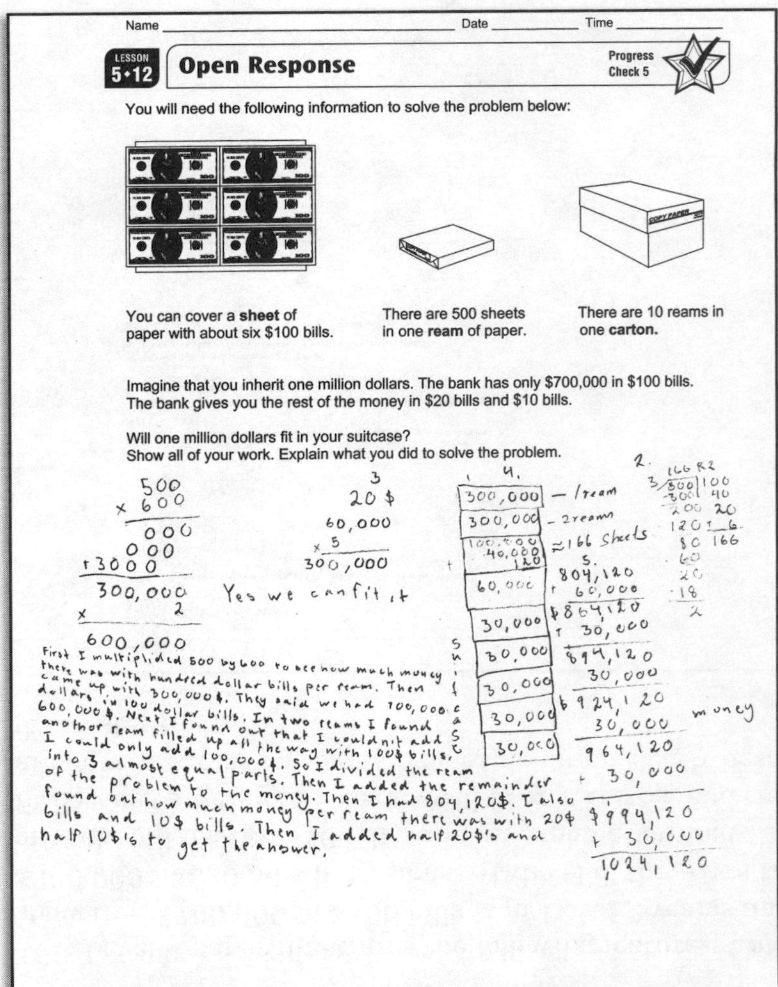

Name ______ Date ______ Time ______

LESSON 5•12 **Open Response** Progress Check 5

You will need the following information to solve the problem below:

You can cover a **sheet** of paper with about six $100 bills.

There are 500 sheets in one **ream** of paper.

There are 10 reams in one **carton.**

Imagine that you inherit one million dollars. The bank has only $700,000 in $100 bills. The bank gives you the rest of the money in $20 bills and $10 bills.

Will one million dollars fit in your suitcase?
Show all of your work. Explain what you did to solve the problem.

This Level 2 paper illustrates the following features: There is a multiplication pattern with extended facts to find the number of $20 bills needed to make $100,000. The total of 5,000 bills is tripled to find the number for $300,000. There is no connection made between this and a step explaining that in $100 bills, the suitcase can hold $3,000,000.

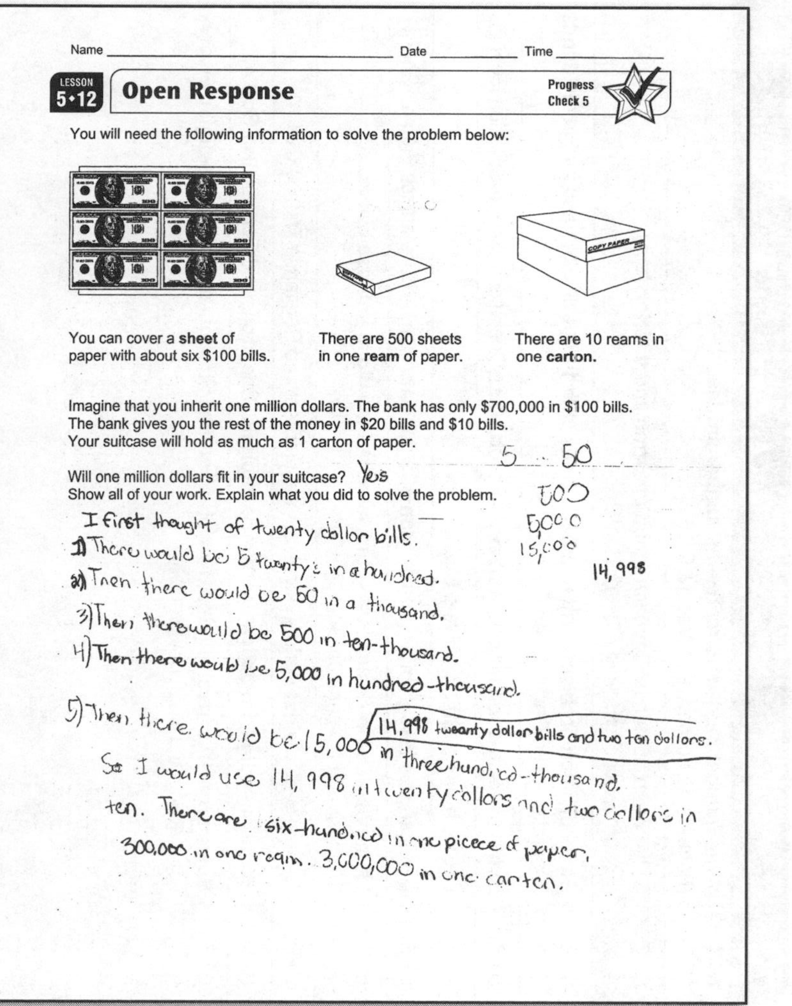

Name ______ Date ______ Time ______

LESSON 5•12 **Open Response** Progress Check 5

You will need the following information to solve the problem below:

You can cover a **sheet** of paper with about six $100 bills.

There are 500 sheets in one **ream** of paper.

There are 10 reams in one **carton.**

Imagine that you inherit one million dollars. The bank has only $700,000 in $100 bills. The bank gives you the rest of the money in $20 bills and $10 bills. Your suitcase will hold as much as 1 carton of paper.

Will one million dollars fit in your suitcase? Yes
Show all of your work. Explain what you did to solve the problem.

I first thought of twenty dollar bills.
1) There would be 5 twenty's in a hundred.
2) Then there would be 50 in a thousand.
3) Then there would be 500 in ten-thousand.
4) Then there would be 5,000 in hundred-thousand.
5) Then there would be 15,000 in three hundred-thousand.
14,998 twenty dollar bills and two ten dollars.
So I would use 14,998 in twenty dollars and two dollars in ten. There are six-hundred in one piece of paper, 300,000 in one ream. 3,000,000 in one carton.

This Level 1 paper illustrates the following features: The only computations or notes on the page show that $700,000 in $100 bills will take 7,000 bills. No answer is given.

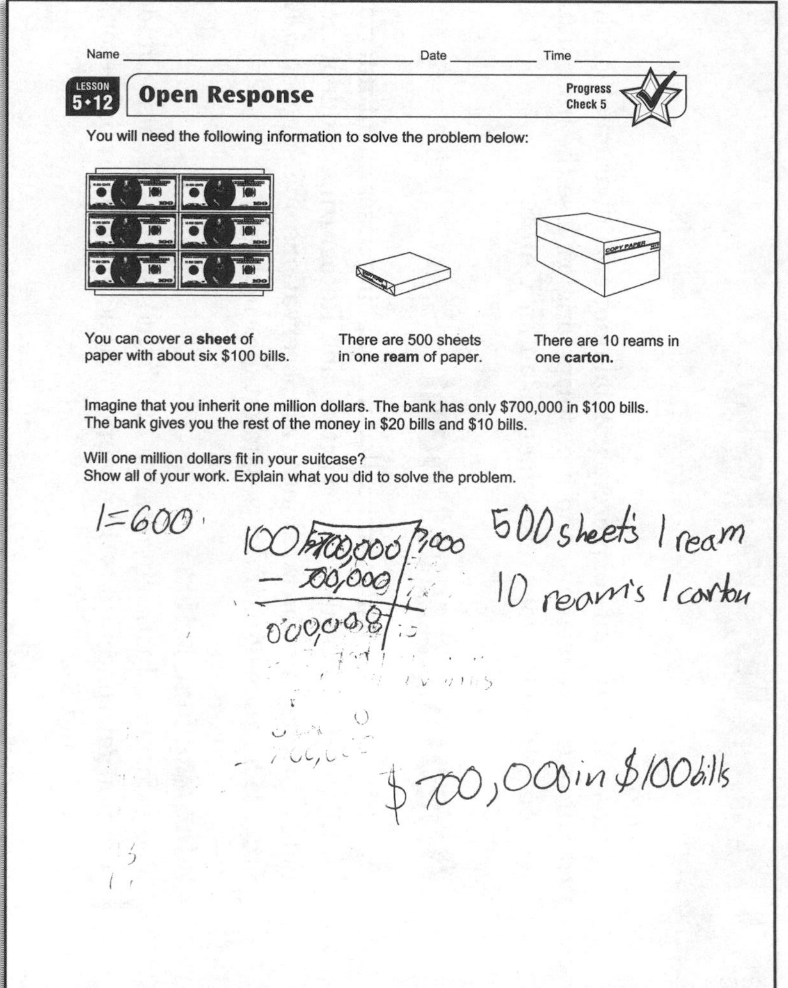

Name ______ Date ______ Time ______

LESSON 5•12 **Open Response** Progress Check 5

You will need the following information to solve the problem below:

You can cover a **sheet** of paper with about six $100 bills.

There are 500 sheets in one **ream** of paper.

There are 10 reams in one **carton.**

Imagine that you inherit one million dollars. The bank has only $700,000 in $100 bills. The bank gives you the rest of the money in $20 bills and $10 bills.

Will one million dollars fit in your suitcase?
Show all of your work. Explain what you did to solve the problem.

1=600
500 sheets 1 ream
10 ream's 1 carton
$700,000 in $100 bills

Unit 6

Assessment Overview

In this unit, students explore a partial-quotients division algorithm, coordinate-grid systems, and measuring angles. Use the information in this section to develop your assessment plan for Unit 6.

Ongoing Assessment

Opportunities for using and collecting ongoing assessment information are highlighted in Informing Instruction and Recognizing Student Achievement notes. Student products, along with observations and suggested writing prompts, provide a range of useful assessment information.

Informing Instruction

The Informing Instruction notes highlight students' thinking and point out common misconceptions. Informing Instruction in Unit 6: Lessons 6-1, 6-3, 6-5, 6-6, 6-7, and 6-9.

Recognizing Student Achievement

The Recognizing Student Achievement notes highlight specific tasks from which teachers can collect assessment data to monitor and document student progress toward meeting Grade-Level Goals.

Lesson	Content Assessed	Where to Find It
6◆1	**Write number models to represent number stories.** [Patterns, Functions, and Algebra Goal 2]	*TLG*, p. 404
6◆2	**Solve open sentences involving multiplication and division facts.** [Patterns, Functions, and Algebra Goal 2]	*TLG*, p. 411
6◆3	**Solve division problems and number stories with 1-digit divisors and 2-digit dividends.** [Operations and Computation Goal 4]	*TLG*, p. 416
6◆4	**Solve decimal addition and subtraction problems.** [Operations and Computation Goal 2]	*TLG*, p. 423
6◆5	**Create a bar graph.** [Data and Chance Goal 1]	*TLG*, p. 429
6◆6	**Draw angles less than or greater than 90°.** [Measurement and Reference Frames Goal 1]	*TLG*, p. 435
6◆7	**Identify places in decimals and the values of the digits in those places.** [Number and Numeration Goal 1]	*TLG*, p. 438
6◆8	**Compare coordinate grid systems.** [Measurement and Reference Frames Goal 4]	*TLG*, p. 445
6◆9	**Solve multidigit multiplication number stories.** [Operations and Computation Goal 4]	*TLG*, p. 453
6◆10	**Solve problems involving the division of multidigit whole numbers by 1-digit divisors.** [Operations and Computation Goal 4]	*TLG*, p. 458

Math Boxes

Math Boxes, one of several types of tasks highlighted in the Recognizing Student Achievement notes, have an additional useful feature. Math Boxes in most lessons are paired or linked with Math Boxes in one or two other lessons that have similar problems. Paired or linked Math Boxes in Unit 6: 6-1 and 6-3; 6-2 and 6-4; 6-5 and 6-7; 6-6 and 6-9; and 6-8 and 6-10.

Writing/Reasoning Prompts

In Unit 6, a variety of writing prompts encourage students to explain their strategies and thinking, to reflect on their learning, and to make connections to other mathematics or life experiences. Here are some of the Unit 6 suggestions:

Lesson	Writing/Reasoning Prompts	Where to Find It
6◆1	Explain how you rounded the number to the nearest ten million.	*TLG*, p. 404
6◆3	Explain how the exponent changes the value of 10.	*TLG*, p. 417
6◆6	Winnona said there isn't enough information provided to answer the question. Do you agree or disagree? Explain your answer.	*TLG*, p. 435
6◆7	Wei said that both squares have $\frac{1}{3}$ shaded. Do you agree or disagree? Explain your answer.	*TLG*, p. 441
6◆10	True or false? (5,0) and (0,5) are both ordered number pairs that can be used to describe the location of point *A*. Explain your answer.	*TLG*, p. 459

Portfolio Opportunities

Portfolios are a versatile tool for assessment. They help students reflect on their mathematical growth and help teachers understand and document that growth. Each unit identifies several student products that can be selected and stored in a portfolio. Here are some of the Unit 6 suggestions:

Lesson	Portfolio Opportunities	Where to Find It
6◆4	Students apply their understanding of multiples, factors, and division and remainders to solve a marble-sharing number story.	*TLG*, p. 424
6◆7	Students draw two triangles, measure the angles, and find the sum of the angle measures for each triangle.	*TLG*, p. 442
6◆8	Students explain how to use the *in* and *out* numbers to determine the rule.	*TLG*, p. 447
6◆10	Students apply their understanding of coordinates to explain why ordered pairs can be used to describe location.	*TLG*, p. 459

Periodic Assessment

Every Progress Check lesson includes opportunities to observe students' progress and to collect student products in a variety of ways—Self Assessment, Oral and Slate Assessment, Written Assessment, and an Open Response task. For more details, see the first page of Progress Check 6, Lesson 6-11 on page 460, of the *Teacher's Lesson Guide*.

Progress Check Modifications

Written Assessments are one way students demonstrate what they know. The table below shows modifications for the Written Assessment in this unit. Use these to maximize opportunities for students to demonstrate what they know. Modifications can be given individually or written on the board for the class.

Problem(s)	Modifications for Written Assessment
1, 2	For Problems 1 and 2, draw pictures to help you solve the problems.
6, 7	For Problems 6 and 7, use page 93 in your *Student Reference Book* to help you identify the types of angles.
8	For Problem 8, list the three points that are at the same horizontal location, and explain how you can tell from the coordinates which points to list.
14, 15	For Problems 14 and 15, list several multiples for 12 and 26 before solving the problems. Suggested multiples: 2 times, 10 times, 5 times, and 20 times each number.

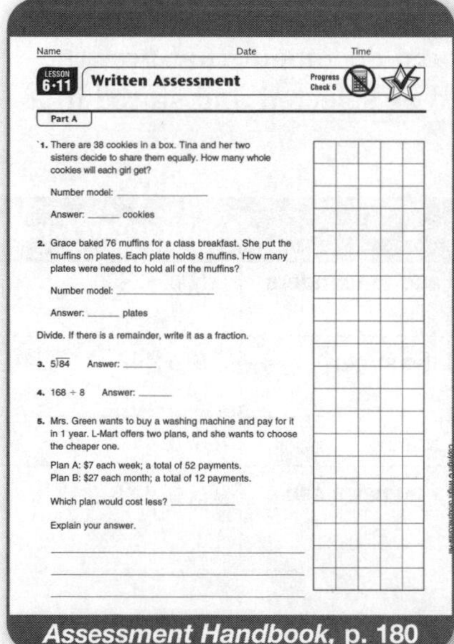

Name Date Time

LESSON 6·11 **Written Assessment** Progress Check 6

Part A

1. There are 38 cookies in a box. Tina and her two sisters decide to share them equally. How many whole cookies will each girl get?

   Number model: ______

   Answer: ______ cookies

2. Grace baked 76 muffins for a class breakfast. She put the muffins on plates. Each plate holds 8 muffins. How many plates were needed to hold all of the muffins?

   Number model: ______

   Answer: ______ plates

Divide. If there is a remainder, write it as a fraction.

3. $5\overline{)84}$ Answer: ______

4. $168 \div 8$ Answer: ______

5. Mrs. Green wants to buy a washing machine and pay for it in 1 year. L-Mart offers two plans, and she wants to choose the cheaper one.

   Plan A: $7 each week; a total of 52 payments.
   Plan B: $27 each month; a total of 12 payments.

   Which plan would cost less? ______

   Explain your answer.

Assessment Handbook, p. 180

The Written Assessment for Unit 6 Progress Check is on pages 180–182.

Open Response, *A Trip to Adventure Land*

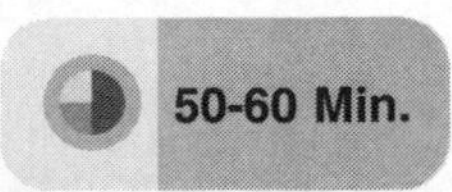

Description

For this task, students calculate the cost per student for a field trip.

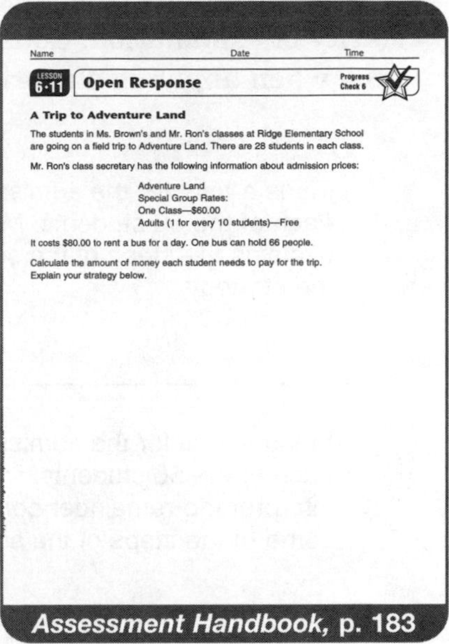

Name Date Time

LESSON 6·11 **Open Response** Progress Check 6

A Trip to Adventure Land

The students in Ms. Brown's and Mr. Ron's classes at Ridge Elementary School are going on a field trip to Adventure Land. There are 28 students in each class.

Mr. Ron's class secretary has the following information about admission prices:

Adventure Land
Special Group Rates:
One Class—$60.00
Adults (1 for every 10 students)—Free

It costs $80.00 to rent a bus for a day. One bus can hold 66 people.

Calculate the amount of money each student needs to pay for the trip.
Explain your strategy below.

Assessment Handbook, p. 183

Focus

- **Use paper-and-pencil algorithms to solve problems involving the division of multidigit whole numbers by 1-digit whole numbers; describe the strategies used and explain how they work.**
  [Operations and Computation Goal 4]
- **Make reasonable estimates for whole number multiplication and division problems, and explain how the estimates were obtained.**
  [Operations and Computation Goal 6]

Implementation Tips

- Encourage students to use a calculator to perform division to the hundredths place.
- Have students determine if they have collected enough money to pay for the trip. They can check their work by multiplying the cost per student times the number of students.

Modifications for Meeting Diverse Needs

- Provide an organizer divided into three sections. Label the sections—Section 1: Total Number of Students, Section 2: Total Cost of the Trip (for both classes), and Section 3: Cost per Student. Include unit labels and a prompt to explain their thinking for each section.
- Have students calculate the problem with a 5% tax added to the price of admission and the bus.

Improving Open Response Skills

Before students begin the task, have them read it independently. Have students share ideas about and record a list of the important numbers that they need to use in order to solve the problem. Record the list on the board and keep it posted during the task.

Note: The wording and formatting of the text on the student samples that follow may vary slightly from the actual task your children will complete. These minor discrepancies will not affect the implementation of the task.

Rubric

This rubric is designed to help you assess levels of mathematical performance on this task. It emphasizes mathematical understanding with only a mention of clarity of explanation. Consider the expectations of standardized tests in your area when applying a rubric. Modify this sample rubric as appropriate.

4	Finds a total for the admission price for 2 classes and the bus. Finds the cost for each of the 56 students. Might round up to figure out the cost per student. Clearly explains the steps of the solution strategy and might include some justification for the strategy.
3	Finds a total for the admission price for 2 classes and the bus. Finds the cost for each of the 56 students. Might use division to solve the problem, but might not interpret the remainder correctly. There might be minor computation errors. Explains some of the steps of the solution strategy, but the explanation might be confusing.
2	Appears to calculate the total cost by totaling the admission price for 2 classes and a bus, and might be aware this total is shared among the total number of students. There might be computation errors. The explanation of the solution strategy might be missing, incomplete, or might not match the other work on the paper.
1	There might be evidence of some understanding of the problem, but might make computation errors. The explanation of the solution strategy might be missing or makes no sense in the context of the problem.
0	Does not attempt to solve the problem.

Sample Student Responses

This Level 4 paper illustrates the following features: The computation for finding the total cost of the admission for 2 classes and a bus is clearly labeled. It is estimated that each of the 56 students must pay $4, followed by a labeled step to verify that enough money will be collected.

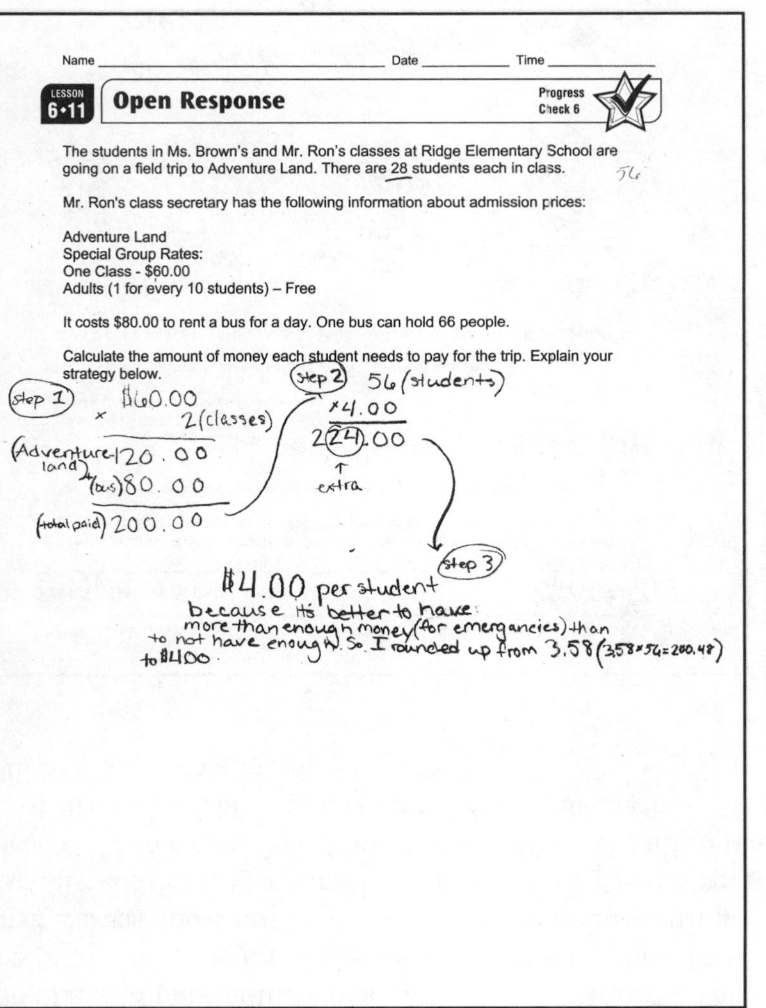

Name ______________ Date ________ Time ________

LESSON 6•11 **Open Response** Progress Check 6

The students in Ms. Brown's and Mr. Ron's classes at Ridge Elementary School are going on a field trip to Adventure Land. There are 28 students each in class.

Mr. Ron's class secretary has the following information about admission prices:

Adventure Land
Special Group Rates:
One Class - $60.00
Adults (1 for every 10 students) – Free

It costs $80.00 to rent a bus for a day. One bus can hold 66 people.

Calculate the amount of money each student needs to pay for the trip. Explain your strategy below.

This Level 4 paper illustrates the following features: The computation is embedded in the explanation. The total for the 2 classes and a bus is divided by 56 students (with a calculator) to get a decimal in the thousandths place. This figure is rounded up to the nearest dime as the cost for each student.

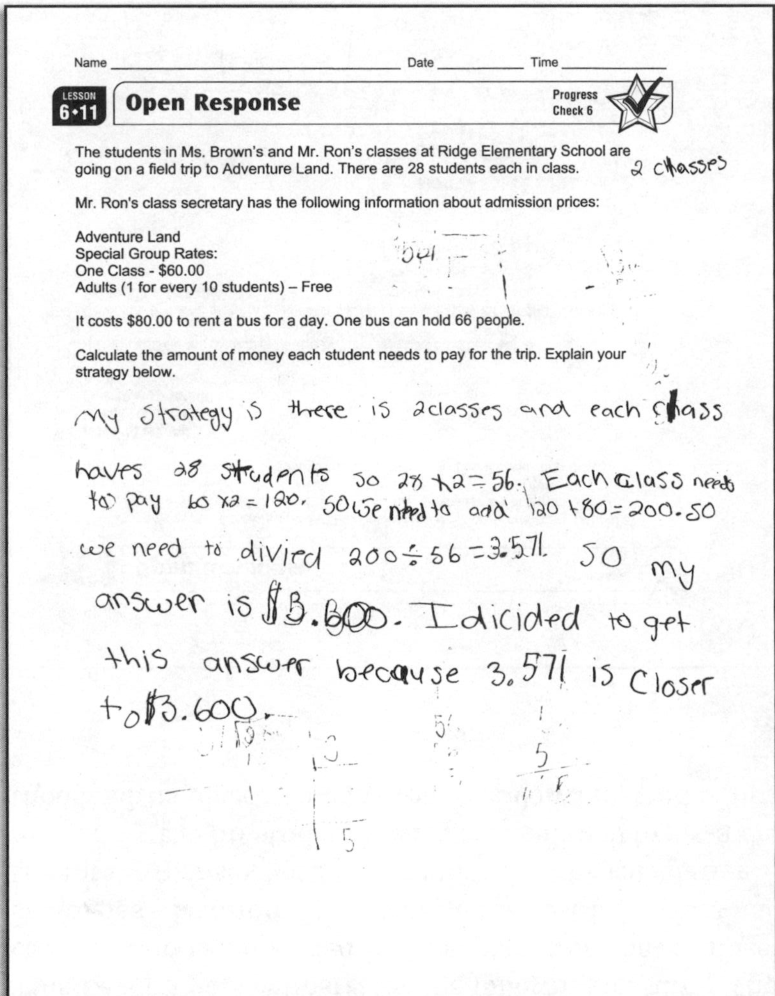

Name ______________ Date ________ Time ________

LESSON 6•11 **Open Response** Progress Check 6

The students in Ms. Brown's and Mr. Ron's classes at Ridge Elementary School are going on a field trip to Adventure Land. There are 28 students each in class.

Mr. Ron's class secretary has the following information about admission prices:

Adventure Land
Special Group Rates:
One Class - $60.00
Adults (1 for every 10 students) – Free

It costs $80.00 to rent a bus for a day. One bus can hold 66 people.

Calculate the amount of money each student needs to pay for the trip. Explain your strategy below.

This Level 3 paper illustrates the following features: The computation at the top of the page has small errors. The total for 2 classes and a bus is divided by 56 students (with a partial-quotients algorithm) but the remainder is interpreted incorrectly as cents. The steps of the strategy are all in place until the division of decimals, and there is no check to see if there will be enough money.

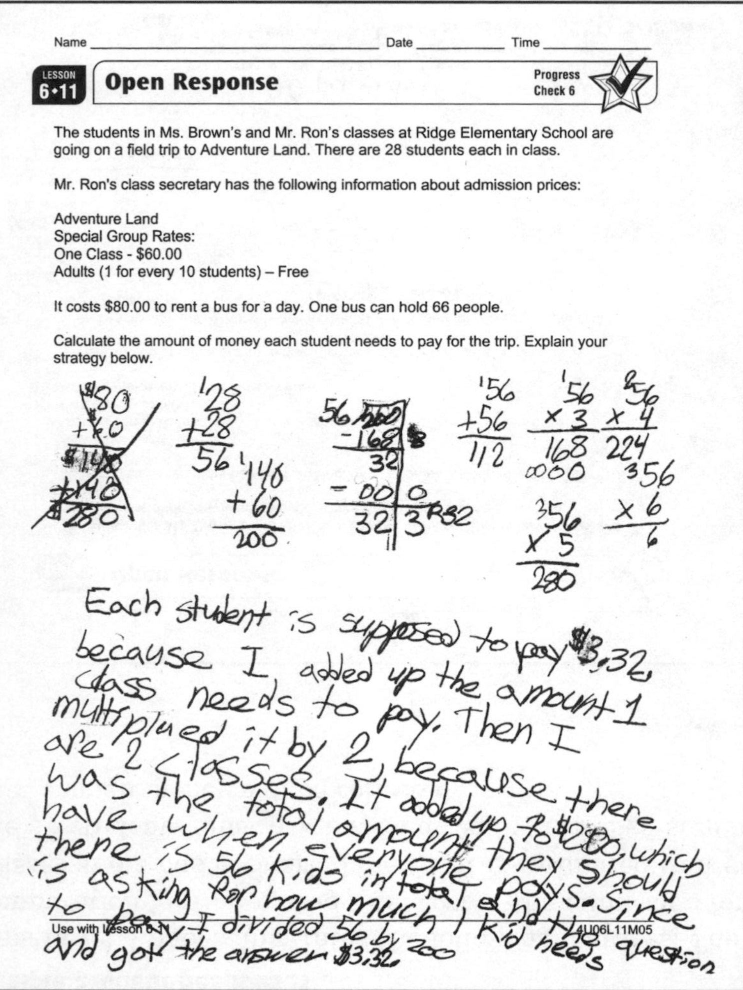

Name ______ Date ______ Time ______

LESSON 6•11 **Open Response** Progress Check 6

The students in Ms. Brown's and Mr. Ron's classes at Ridge Elementary School are going on a field trip to Adventure Land. There are 28 students each in class.

Mr. Ron's class secretary has the following information about admission prices:

Adventure Land
Special Group Rates:
One Class - $60.00
Adults (1 for every 10 students) – Free

It costs $80.00 to rent a bus for a day. One bus can hold 66 people.

Calculate the amount of money each student needs to pay for the trip. Explain your strategy below.

Each student is supposed to pay $3.32 because I added up the amount 1 class needs to pay. Then I multiplied it by 2, because there are 2 classes. It added up to $280, which was the total amount they should have when everyone pays. Since there is 56 kids in total and the question is asking for how much 1 kid needs to pay, I divided 56 by 200 and got the answer $3.32

Use with Lesson 6-11 4U06L11M05

This Level 3 paper illustrates the following features: The computation is embedded in an explanation that confuses 2 strategies—beginning to calculate the cost for 1 class and then using the total expenses for 2 classes to finish the calculation. The total is divided by the 56 students (with a calculator) to get a decimal in the thousandths place, which is rounded down instead of up.

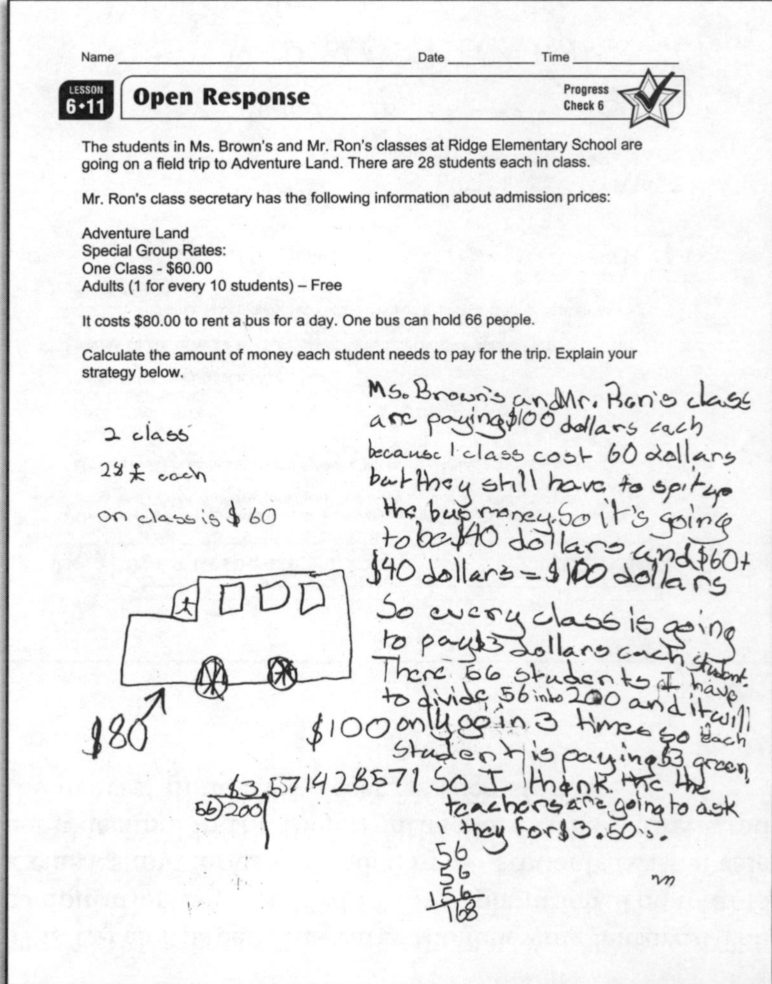

Name ______ Date ______ Time ______

LESSON 6•11 **Open Response** Progress Check 6

The students in Ms. Brown's and Mr. Ron's classes at Ridge Elementary School are going on a field trip to Adventure Land. There are 28 students each in class.

Mr. Ron's class secretary has the following information about admission prices:

Adventure Land
Special Group Rates:
One Class - $60.00
Adults (1 for every 10 students) – Free

It costs $80.00 to rent a bus for a day. One bus can hold 66 people.

Calculate the amount of money each student needs to pay for the trip. Explain your strategy below.

Ms. Brown's and Mr. Ron's class are paying $100 dollars each because 1 class cost 60 dollars but they still have to spit up the bus money. So it's going to be $40 dollars and $60 + $40 dollars = $100 dollars. So every class is going to pay $3 dollars each student. There 56 students. I have to divide 56 into 200 and it will only go in 3 times so each student is paying $3 green, $3.571428571 So I think the teachers are going to ask they for $3.50.

This Level 2 paper illustrates the following features: Some computation steps are explained on the page—how to find the total cost of admission and the number of students. The steps described in the explanation are correct, but steps are missing, and the answer presented has no connection to the work.

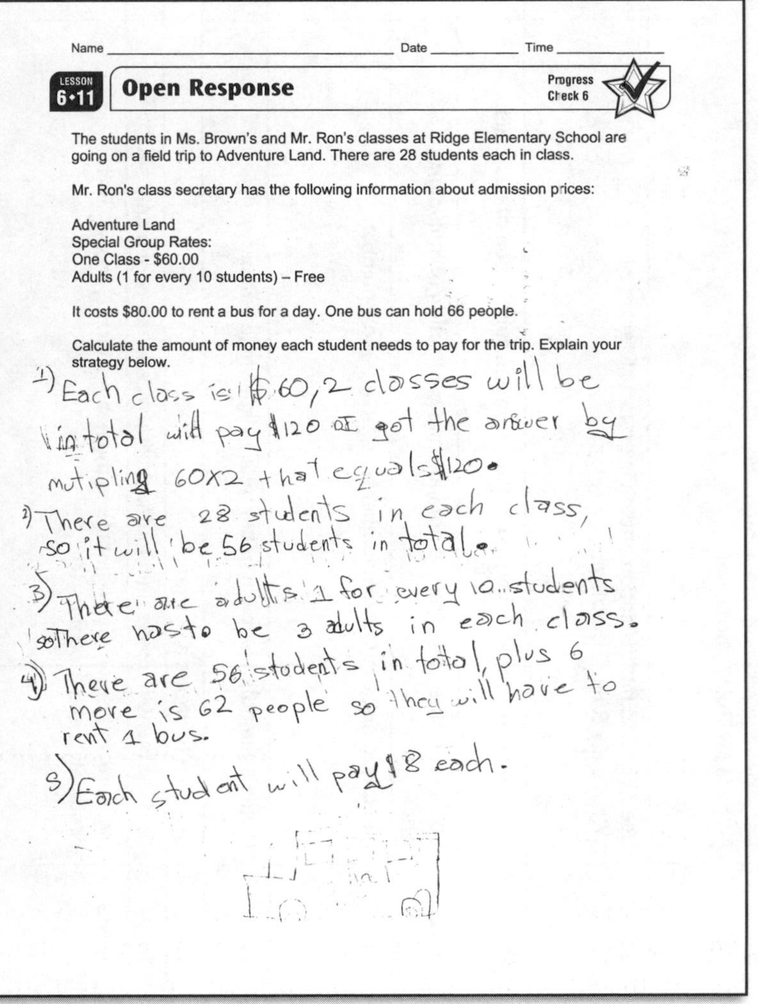

Name ______ Date ______ Time ______

LESSON 6•11 **Open Response** Progress Check 6

The students in Ms. Brown's and Mr. Ron's classes at Ridge Elementary School are going on a field trip to Adventure Land. There are 28 students each in class.

Mr. Ron's class secretary has the following information about admission prices:

Adventure Land
Special Group Rates:
One Class - $60.00
Adults (1 for every 10 students) – Free

It costs $80.00 to rent a bus for a day. One bus can hold 66 people.

Calculate the amount of money each student needs to pay for the trip. Explain your strategy below.

1) Each class is $60, 2 classes will be in total will pay $120 I got the answer by mutipling 60x2 that equals $120.
2) There are 28 students in each class, so it will be 56 students in total.
3) There are adults 1 for every 10 students so there has to be 3 adults in each class.
4) There are 56 students in total, plus 6 more is 62 people so they will have to rent 1 bus.
5) Each student will pay $8 each.

This Level 1 paper illustrates the following features: There is evidence of some understanding of the problem, but the statements made in the explanation are not supported by the work on the page. The answer is given, but there is no work shown to justify it.

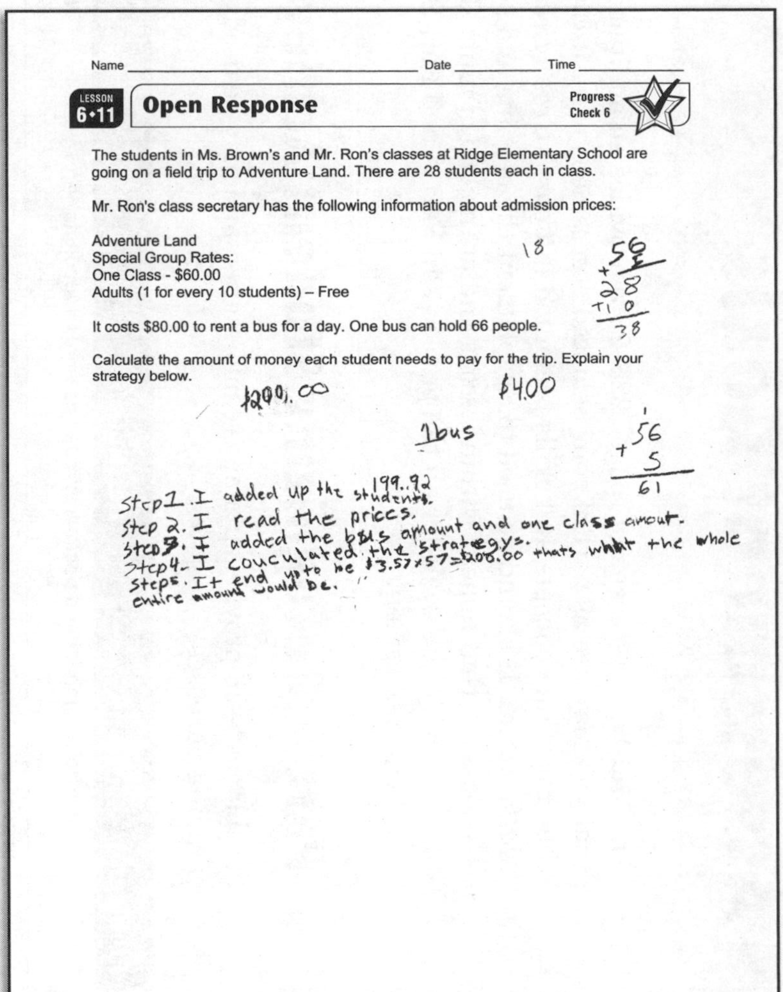

Name ______ Date ______ Time ______

LESSON 6•11 **Open Response** Progress Check 6

The students in Ms. Brown's and Mr. Ron's classes at Ridge Elementary School are going on a field trip to Adventure Land. There are 28 students each in class.

Mr. Ron's class secretary has the following information about admission prices:

Adventure Land
Special Group Rates:
One Class - $60.00
Adults (1 for every 10 students) – Free

It costs $80.00 to rent a bus for a day. One bus can hold 66 people.

Calculate the amount of money each student needs to pay for the trip. Explain your strategy below.

$200.00 $400

1bus

56 + 5 = 61

Step1. I added up the students. 199.92
Step 2. I read the prices.
Step 3. I added the bus amount and one class amout.
Step 4. I couculated the strategys.
Step 5. It end up to be $3.57x57=$200.00 thats what the whole entire amount would be.

Mid-Year Assessment Goals

The Mid-Year Assessment (pages 228–233) provides an additional opportunity that you may use as part of your balanced assessment plan. It covers some of the important concepts and skills presented in *Fourth Grade Everyday Mathematics.* It should be used to complement the ongoing and periodic assessments that appear within lessons and at the end of units. The following tables provide the goals for all the problems in Part A and Part B of the Mid-Year Assessment.

Part A Recognizing Student Achievement

Problems 1–26 provide summative information and may be used for grading purposes.

Problem(s)	Description	Grade-Level Goal
1	Write whole numbers and decimals written as words with digits.	Number and Numeration Goal 1
2	List factor pairs.	Number and Numeration Goal 3
3	Name the first 10 multiples of a number.	Number and Numeration Goal 3
4	Give equivalent names for a number.	Number and Numeration Goal 4
5	Use extended addition and subtraction facts to solve a "What's My Rule?" problem.	Operations and Computation Goal 1; Patterns, Functions, and Algebra Goal 1
6	Use extended multiplication and division facts to solve a "What's My Rule?" problem.	Operations and Computation Goal 3; Patterns, Functions, and Algebra Goal 1
7, 8	Solve number stories involving the addition and subtraction of decimals.	Operations and Computation Goal 2
9, 10	Solve problems involving the addition and subtraction of multidigit whole numbers.	Operations and Computation Goal 2
11	Multiply a multidigit whole number by a 1-digit whole number.	Operations and Computation Goal 4; Patterns, Functions, and Algebra Goal 4
12	Divide a multidigit whole number by a 1-digit whole number divisor.	Operations and Computation Goal 4
13	Use data to create a bar graph.	Data and Chance Goal 1
14	Find the median, mode, minimum, maximum, and range of a data set.	Data and Chance Goal 2
15–19	Measure and draw line segments to the nearest inch, $\frac{1}{2}$ inch, $\frac{1}{4}$ inch, centimeter, and $\frac{1}{2}$ centimeter.	Measurement and Reference Frames Goal 1

Problem(s)	Description *continued*	Grade-Level Goal
20	Draw a ray parallel to a given line. Draw a line segment that intersects a given ray and line.	Geometry Goal 1
21	Draw a quadrangle.	Geometry Goal 2
22	Draw a regular polygon.	Geometry Goal 2
23	Draw a trapezoid.	Geometry Goal 2
24	Draw a shape that is not a polygon.	Geometry Goal 2
25	Solve open sentences involving multiplication and division facts.	Operations and Computation Goal 3; Patterns, Functions, and Algebra Goal 2
26	Determine whether number sentences are true or false.	Patterns, Functions, and Algebra Goal 2

Part B Informing Instruction

Problems 27–33 provide formative information that can be useful in planning future instruction.

Problem(s)	Description	Grade-Level Goal
27	Compare whole numbers and whole numbers represented in exponential notation.	Number and Numeration Goal 6
28	Rename decimals as fractions.	Number and Numeration Goal 5
29, 30	Multiply a multidigit whole number by a 2-digit whole number.	Operations and Computation Goal 4; Patterns, Functions, and Algebra Goal 4
31	Divide a multidigit whole number by a 2-digit divisor.	Operations and Computation Goal 4
32	Create a data set with a given mean.	Data and Chance Goal 2
33	Describe relationships among U.S. customary and metric units of length.	Measurement and Reference Frames Goal 3

Unit 7

Assessment Overview

In this unit, students review fraction ideas introduced earlier, further develop an understanding of equivalent fractions, and explore probability through informal activities. Use the information in this section to develop your assessment plan for Unit 7.

Ongoing Assessment

Opportunities for using and collecting ongoing assessment information are highlighted in Informing Instruction and Recognizing Student Achievement notes. Student products, along with observations and suggested writing prompts, provide a range of useful assessment information.

Informing Instruction

The Informing Instruction notes highlight students' thinking and point out common misconceptions. Informing Instruction in Unit 7: Lessons 7-2, 7-4, 7-6, 7-7, 7-9, 7-11 and 7-12.

Recognizing Student Achievement

The Recognizing Student Achievement notes highlight specific tasks from which teachers can collect assessment data to monitor and document student's progress toward meeting Grade-Level Goals.

Lesson	Content Assessed	Where to Find It
7◆1	**Explain that fractions are equal parts of a whole.** [Number and Numeration Goal 2]	*TLG,* p. 572
7◆2	**Solve "fraction-of" problems** [Number and Numeration Goal 2]	*TLG,* p. 578
7◆3	**Use a basic probability term to describe the likelihood of an event.** [Data and Chance Goal 3]	*TLG,* p. 585
7◆4	**Explain the relationship between a whole and its fractional parts.** [Number and Numeration Goal 2]	*TLG,* p. 590
7◆5	**Use pattern blocks to solve fraction addition problems.** [Operations and Computation Goal 5]	*TLG,* p. 596
7◆6	**Estimate the measure of an angle.** [Measurement and Reference Frames Goal 1]	*TLG,* p. 601
7◆7	**Describe a method for determining fraction equivalency.** [Number and Numeration Goal 5]	*TLG,* p. 606
7◆8	**Rename tenths and hundredths as decimals.** [Number and Numeration Goal 5]	*TLG,* p. 611
7◆9	**Compare fractions and explain strategies.** [Number and Numeration Goal 6]	*TLG,* p. 618
7◆10	**Compare fractions.** [Number and Numeration Goal 6]	*TLG,* p. 624
7◆11	**Express the probability of an event as a fraction.** [Data and Chance Goal 4]	*TLG,* p. 627
7◆12	**Predict the outcome of an experiment and test the predictions using manipulatives.** [Data and Chance Goal 4]	*TLG,* p. 635

Math Boxes

Math Boxes, one of several types of tasks highlighted in the Recognizing Student Achievement notes, have an additional useful feature. Math Boxes in most lessons are paired or linked with Math Boxes in one or two other lessons that have similar problems. Paired or linked Math Boxes in Unit 7: 7-1 and 7-3; 7-2 and 7-4; 7-5 and 7-7; 7-6 and 7-8; 7-9 and 7-11; and 7-10 and 7-12.

Writing/Reasoning Prompts

In Unit 7, a variety of writing prompts encourage students to explain their strategies and thinking, to reflect on their learning, and to make connections to other mathematics or life experiences. Here are some of the Unit 7 suggestions:

Lesson	Writing/Reasoning Prompts	Where to Find It
7•1	How did you determine whether the angle was obtuse or acute?	*TLG,* p. 573
7•4	Explain how you determined the number of months in $\frac{5}{6}$ of a year.	*TLG,* p. 590
7•8	Explain how you determined the probability of drawing a red block.	*TLG,* p. 613
7•9	Explain why $\frac{2}{2}$ inch was given as a possible answer.	*TLG,* p. 619
7•12	Explain the strategy used to decide which fraction was greater.	*TLG,* p. 636

Portfolio Opportunities

Portfolios are a versatile tool for assessment. They help students reflect on their mathematical growth and help teachers understand and document that growth. Each unit identifies several student products that can be selected and stored in a portfolio. Here are some of the Unit 7 suggestions:

Lesson	Portfolio Opportunities	Where to Find It
7•1	Students use pattern blocks to draw and color a design to understand the whole.	*TLG,* p. 575
7•4	Students explain why the same pattern blocks take on different fractional values for each of the Shapes A, B, and C.	*TLG,* p. 590
7•7	Students determine the number of squares in $\frac{3}{8}$ of the set.	*TLG,* p. 606
7•10	Students describe how a candy bar was divided.	*TLG,* p. 625
7•12	Students compare the predicted and actual results of a probability experiment.	*TLG,* p. 636

Periodic Assessment

Every Progress Check lesson includes opportunities to observe students' progress and to collect student products in a variety of ways—Self Assessment, Oral and Slate Assessment, Written Assessment, and an Open Response task. For more details, see the first page of Progress Check 7, Lesson 7-13 on page 638, of the *Teacher's Lesson Guide*.

Progress Check Modifications

Written Assessments are one way students demonstrate what they know. The table below shows modifications for the Written Assessment in this unit. Use these to maximize opportunities for students to demonstrate what they know. Modifications can be given individually or written on the board for the class.

Problem(s)	Modifications for Written Assessment
1–3	**For Problems 1–3, use your Everything Math Deck to help you find equivalent fractions.**
11	**For Problem 11, use counters or quarters to model the problem before recording your answers.**
12	**For Problem 12, explain how you determined what fraction of the time you would expect to get a yellow block.**
13	**For Problem 13, use a different color pencil for each point, and draw a horizontal line for the first coordinate and a vertical line for the second coordinate to locate the point.**

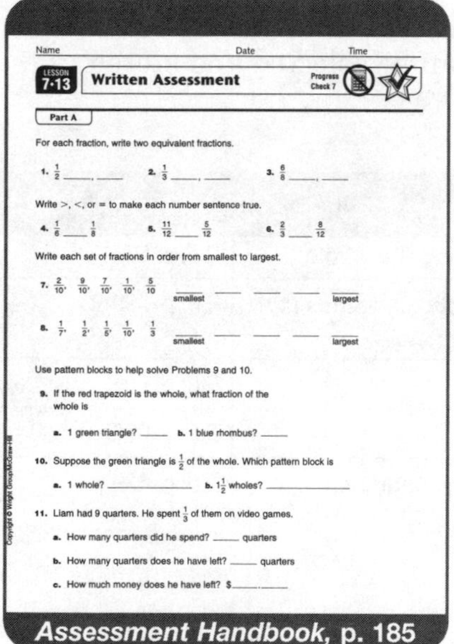
Name Date Time

LESSON 7·13 **Written Assessment** Progress Check 7

Part A

For each fraction, write two equivalent fractions.

1. $\frac{1}{2}$ ____, ____ 2. $\frac{1}{3}$ ____, ____ 3. $\frac{6}{8}$ ____, ____

Write >, <, or = to make each number sentence true.

4. $\frac{1}{6}$ ____ $\frac{1}{8}$ 5. $\frac{11}{12}$ ____ $\frac{5}{12}$ 6. $\frac{2}{3}$ ____ $\frac{8}{12}$

Write each set of fractions in order from smallest to largest.

7. $\frac{2}{10}$, $\frac{9}{10}$, $\frac{7}{10}$, $\frac{1}{10}$, $\frac{5}{10}$ ____ (smallest) ____ ____ ____ ____ (largest)

8. $\frac{1}{7}$, $\frac{1}{2}$, $\frac{1}{5}$, $\frac{1}{10}$, $\frac{1}{3}$ ____ (smallest) ____ ____ ____ ____ (largest)

Use pattern blocks to help solve Problems 9 and 10.

9. If the red trapezoid is the whole, what fraction of the whole is
   a. 1 green triangle? ____ b. 1 blue rhombus? ____

10. Suppose the green triangle is $\frac{1}{2}$ of the whole. Which pattern block is
    a. 1 whole? ____ b. $1\frac{1}{2}$ wholes? ____

11. Liam had 9 quarters. He spent $\frac{1}{3}$ of them on video games.
    a. How many quarters did he spend? ____ quarters
    b. How many quarters does he have left? ____ quarters
    c. How much money does he have left? $____.____

Assessment Handbook, p. 185

The Written Assessment for the Unit 7 Progress Check is on pages 185–187.

Open Response, *Queen Arlene's Dilemma*

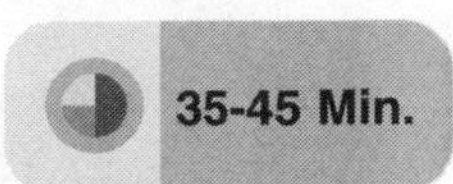

Description

For this task, students divide regions into fractional parts according to a number story.

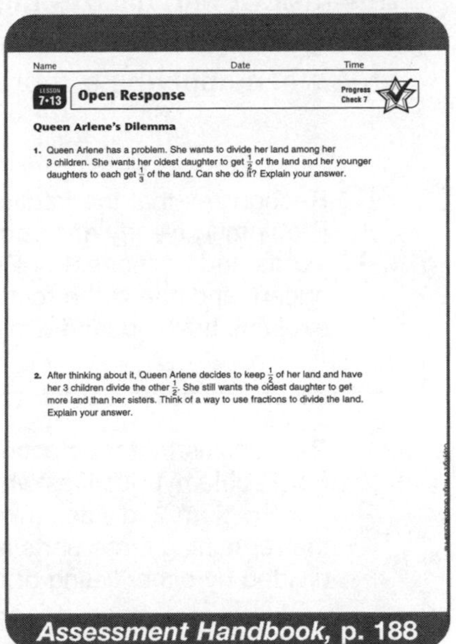

Name Date Time

LESSON 7•13 **Open Response** Progress Check 7

Queen Arlene's Dilemma

1. Queen Arlene has a problem. She wants to divide her land among her 3 children. She wants her oldest daughter to get $\frac{1}{2}$ of the land and her younger daughters to each get $\frac{1}{3}$ of the land. Can she do it? Explain your answer.

2. After thinking about it, Queen Arlene decides to keep $\frac{1}{2}$ of her land and have her 3 children divide the other $\frac{1}{2}$. She still wants the oldest daughter to get more land than her sisters. Think of a way to use fractions to divide the land. Explain your answer.

Assessment Handbook, p. 188

Focus

- **Read, write, and model fractions; solve problems involving fractional parts of a region; describe and explain strategies used.** [Number and Numeration Goal 2]
- **Use manipulatives and mental arithmetic to solve problems involving the addition of fractions with like and unlike denominators; describe the strategies used.** [Operations and Computation Goal 5]

Implementation Tips

- Review the meaning of the numerator and the denominator in fractions, and review comparing fractions.
- Encourage students to draw pictures to help them solve problems and explain the solutions.

Modifications for Meeting Diverse Needs

- Have students use pattern blocks. Review the relationship of each block to the hexagon (whole). Label each block with its fraction name. Have students model the problem situation using the pattern blocks. For Problem 2, 1 option would be to change the whole to 2 hexagons in order to model the problem with the blocks.
- Have students write number sentences that can be used to solve the problem.

Improving Open Response Skills

After students complete the task, have them model a variety of explanations for how they solved Problem 2. Have them compare their explanations and list the similarities and differences. What components are necessary for the explanations to be complete?

Note: The wording and formatting of the text on the student samples that follow may vary slightly from the actual task your students will complete. These minor discrepancies will not affect the implementation of the task.

Rubric

This rubric is designed to help you assess levels of mathematical performance on this task. It emphasizes mathematical understanding with only a mention of clarity of explanation. Consider the expectations of standardized tests in your area when applying a rubric. Modify this sample rubric as appropriate.

4	Recognizes that the fraction combination $\frac{1}{2}$, $\frac{1}{3}$, and $\frac{1}{3}$ will total more than a whole. For Problem 1, clearly and completely justifies why the total is more than the whole using words and fractions. For Problem 2, divides a whole into four parts including $\frac{1}{2}$ for the queen, and one of the remaining three parts is larger than the other two. Clearly explains how the land is divided by listing the fraction each daughter receives.
3	Recognizes that the fraction combination of $\frac{1}{2}$, $\frac{1}{3}$, and $\frac{1}{3}$ will total more than a whole. For Problem 1, justifies why the total is more than the whole using fractions or words. For Problem 2, divides a whole into four parts including $\frac{1}{2}$ for the queen, and one of the remaining three parts is larger than the other two. Explains how the land is divided by either listing or illustrating each fraction with only minor errors.
2	Recognizes that the fraction combination of $\frac{1}{2}$, $\frac{1}{3}$, and $\frac{1}{3}$ will total more than a whole. For Problem 1, attempts to justify why the total is more than the whole using fractions, words, or pictures. For Problem 2, explains and justifies with either words or pictures why one daughter will receive more land than the other two. There might be errors, but it is apparent one sister has more, and the solution makes sense.
1	Attempts to solve both problems but might have errors. Recognizes that fractions are used to solve the problems. Might recognize that the fractions in Problem 1 total more than a whole. For Problem 2, might demonstrate an understanding that all three daughters do not receive the same amount of land but might have errors in the explanations or illustrations for both problems.
0	Does not attempt to solve the problem.

Sample Student Responses

This Level 4 paper illustrates the following features: A rectangle is divided to solve Problem 1. The rectangle is divided into $\frac{1}{2}$ for the older daughter and into thirds for the younger daughters. The overlap of $\frac{1}{2}$ and $\frac{2}{3}$ is clearly indicated and the explanation states that $\frac{1}{2}$ cannot be divided evenly into thirds. For Problem 2, the illustration shows a rectangle divided into eighths and shared correctly among the queen and the daughters.

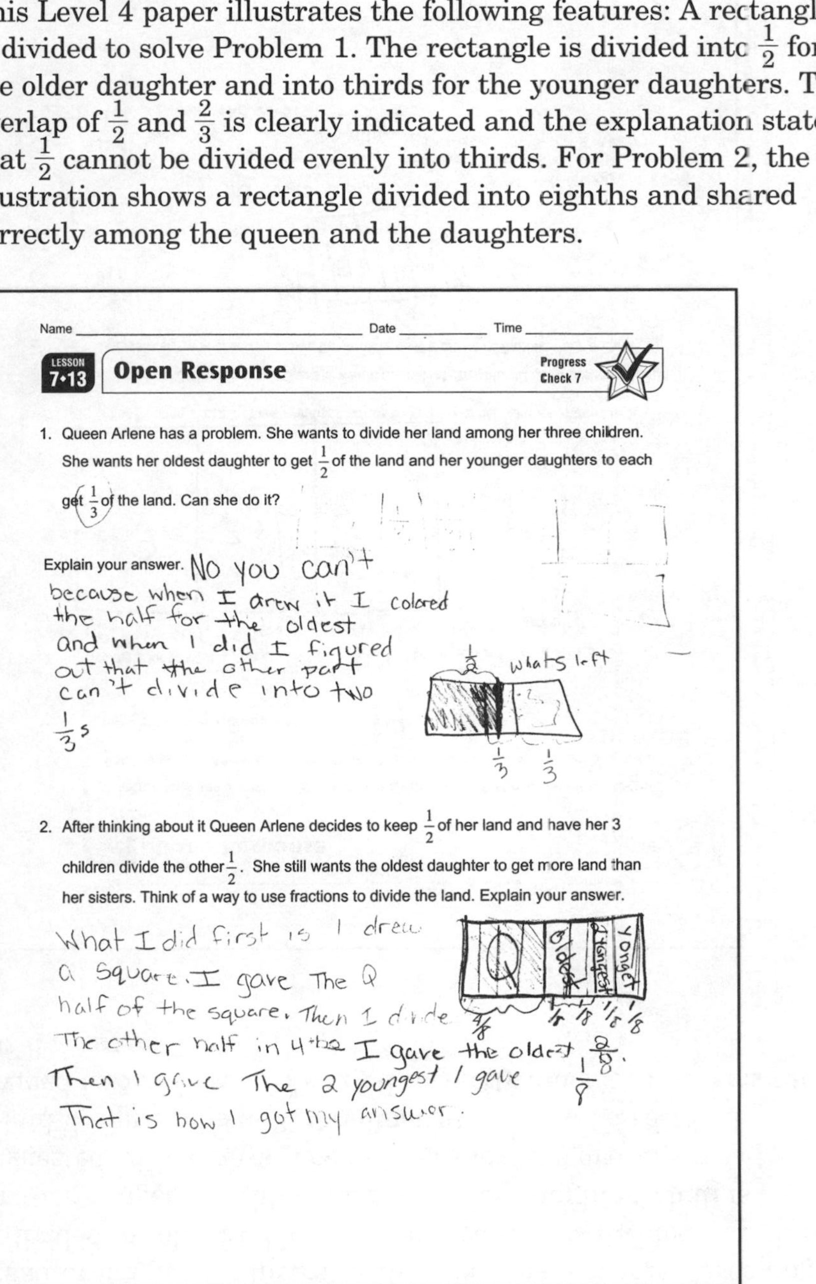

Name ______ Date ______ Time ______

LESSON 7•13 **Open Response** Progress Check 7

1. Queen Arlene has a problem. She wants to divide her land among her three children. She wants her oldest daughter to get $\frac{1}{2}$ of the land and her younger daughters to each get $\frac{1}{3}$ of the land. Can she do it?

Explain your answer. No you can't because when I drew it I colored the half for the oldest and when I did I figured out that the other part can't divide into two $\frac{1}{3}$s

2. After thinking about it Queen Arlene decides to keep $\frac{1}{2}$ of her land and have her 3 children divide the other $\frac{1}{2}$. She still wants the oldest daughter to get more land than her sisters. Think of a way to use fractions to divide the land. Explain your answer.

What I did first is I drew a square. I gave The Q half of the square. Then I divide The other half in 4ths I gave the oldest $\frac{2}{8}$. Then I gave The 2 youngest I gave $\frac{1}{8}$ That is how I got my answer.

This Level 4 paper illustrates the following features: Pattern blocks represent Problem 1. If the hexagon is assumed to be the whole, the illustration shows more than a whole when all of the daughters' shares are assembled. The explanation states that the queen needs more land for her plan. For Problem 2, the illustration shows pattern-block shapes divided and a list of the fractional parts each daughter receives.

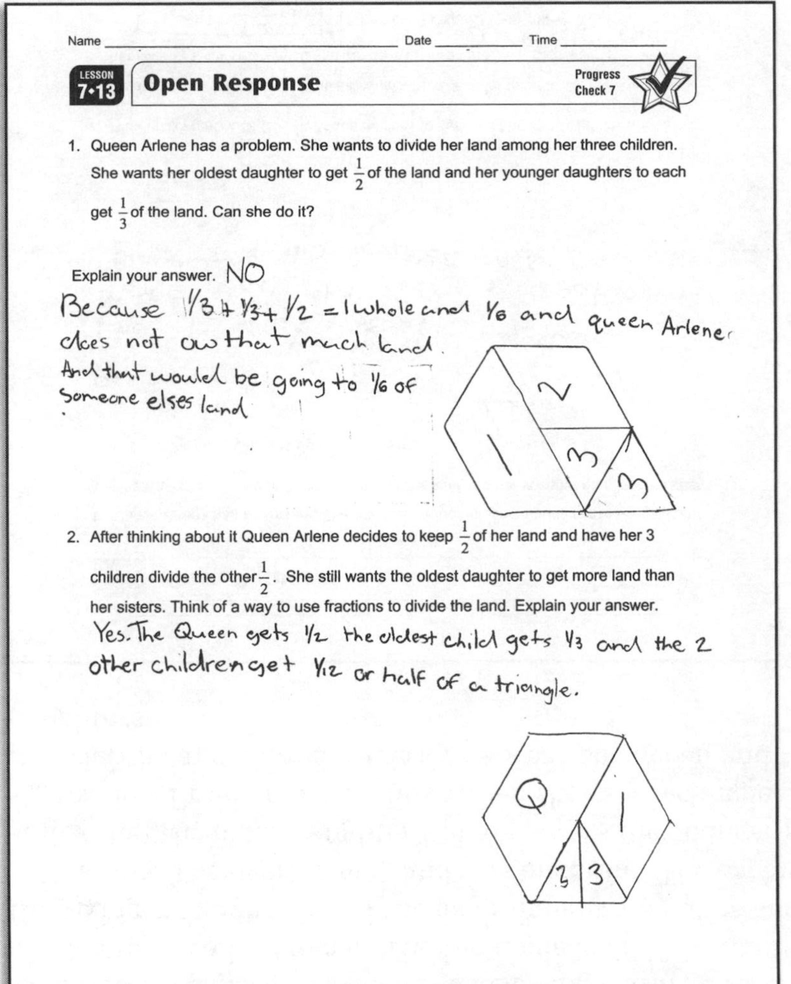

Name ______ Date ______ Time ______

LESSON 7•13 **Open Response** Progress Check 7

1. Queen Arlene has a problem. She wants to divide her land among her three children. She wants her oldest daughter to get $\frac{1}{2}$ of the land and her younger daughters to each get $\frac{1}{3}$ of the land. Can she do it?

Explain your answer. NO Because 1/3 + 1/3 + 1/2 = 1 whole and 1/6 and queen Arlene does not ow that much land. And that would be going to 1/6 of someone elses land

2. After thinking about it Queen Arlene decides to keep $\frac{1}{2}$ of her land and have her 3 children divide the other $\frac{1}{2}$. She still wants the oldest daughter to get more land than her sisters. Think of a way to use fractions to divide the land. Explain your answer.

Yes. The Queen gets 1/2 the oldest child gets 1/3 and the 2 other children get 1/12 or half of a triangle.

This Level 3 paper illustrates the following features: A rectangle is divided to solve Problem 1. The rectangle is divided into thirds for the younger daughters and the older daughter's half is suggested with arrows. The arrows show the overlap of $\frac{1}{2}$ and $\frac{2}{3}$. For Problem 2, the illustration shows a rectangle divided into eighths and shared correctly among the queen and the daughters.

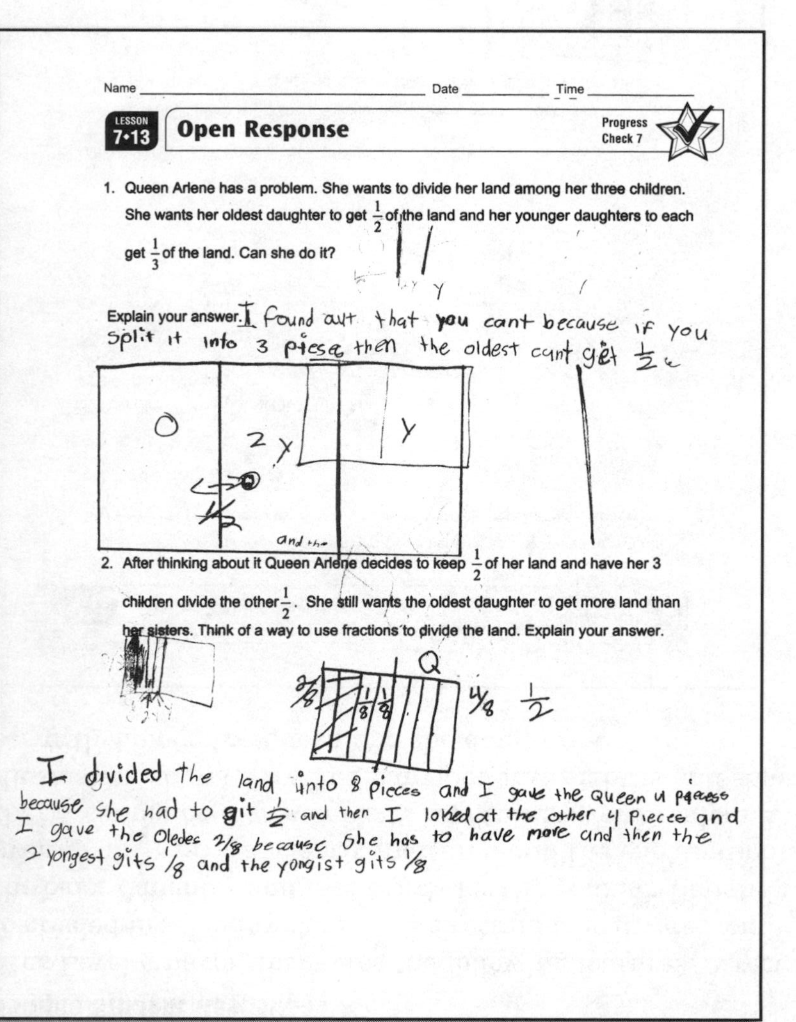

Name ______ Date ______ Time ______

LESSON 7•13 **Open Response** Progress Check 7

1. Queen Arlene has a problem. She wants to divide her land among her three children. She wants her oldest daughter to get $\frac{1}{2}$ of the land and her younger daughters to each get $\frac{1}{3}$ of the land. Can she do it?

Explain your answer. I found out that you cant because if you split it into 3 piese then the oldest cant get $\frac{1}{2}$

2. After thinking about it Queen Arlene decides to keep $\frac{1}{2}$ of her land and have her 3 children divide the other $\frac{1}{2}$. She still wants the oldest daughter to get more land than her sisters. Think of a way to use fractions to divide the land. Explain your answer.

I divided the land into 8 pieces and I gave the queen 4 pieces because she had to git $\frac{1}{2}$ and then I loked at the other 4 pieces and I gave the Oldes 2/8 because she has to have more and then the 2 yongest gits 1/8 and the yongist gits 1/8

This Level 3 paper illustrates the following features: A rectangle is divided to solve Problem 1. The rectangle is divided into thirds for the younger daughters and the older daughter's half is suggested with a line. The overlap of $\frac{1}{2}$ and $\frac{2}{3}$ is apparent. The explanation states that the older daughter's share covers the younger sisters' shares. For Problem 2, the illustration shows a rectangle divided into eighths and shared correctly between the queen and the daughters.

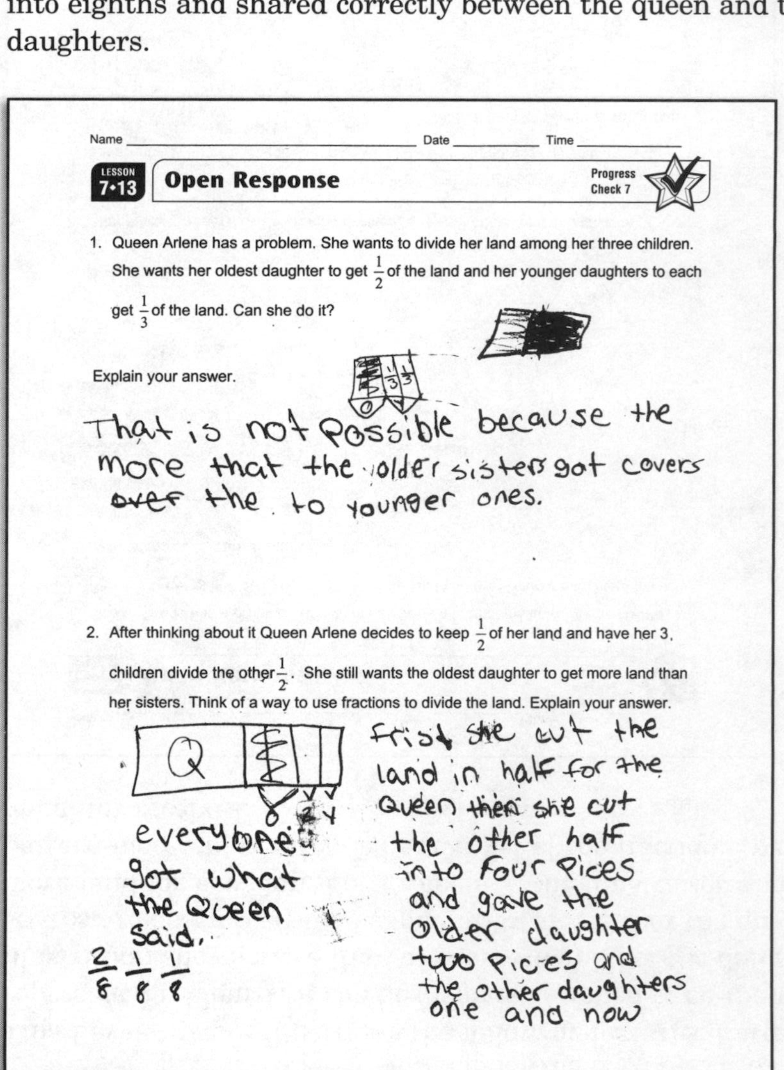

Name ______ Date ______ Time ______

LESSON 7•13 **Open Response** Progress Check 7

1. Queen Arlene has a problem. She wants to divide her land among her three children. She wants her oldest daughter to get $\frac{1}{2}$ of the land and her younger daughters to each get $\frac{1}{3}$ of the land. Can she do it?

Explain your answer.

That is not possible because the more that the older sisters got covers ~~over~~ the to younger ones.

2. After thinking about it Queen Arlene decides to keep $\frac{1}{2}$ of her land and have her 3 children divide the other $\frac{1}{2}$. She still wants the oldest daughter to get more land than her sisters. Think of a way to use fractions to divide the land. Explain your answer.

Frist she cut the land in half for the Queen then she cut the other half into four pices and gave the older daughter two pices and the other daughters one and now everyone got what the Queen said.

$\frac{2}{8}$ $\frac{1}{8}$ $\frac{1}{8}$

This Level 2 paper illustrates the following features: A rectangle is divided to solve Problem 1. It appears to be divided into thirds for the younger daughters and $\frac{1}{2}$ for the older daughter. The explanation indicates that there is enough for only one daughter after giving the first $\frac{1}{2}$ away. For Problem 2, the illustration appears to be divided according to the problem, but the explanation describes dividing the rectangle into sevenths, which are distributed incorrectly.

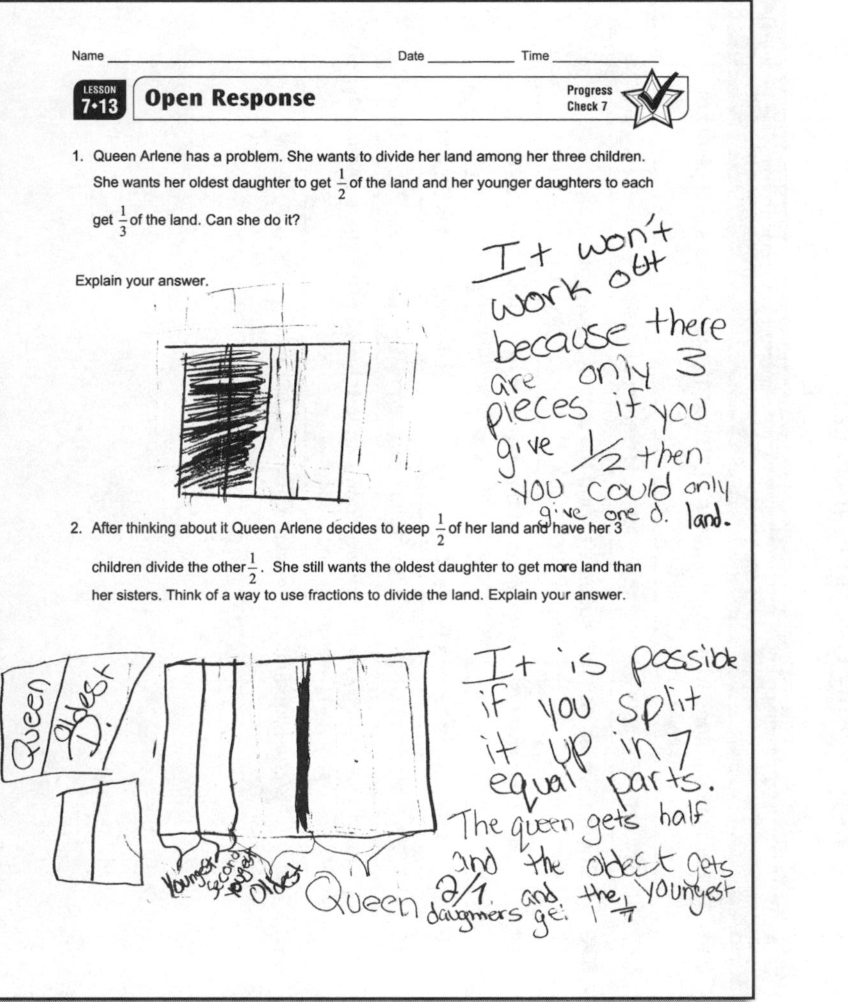

Name _______ Date _______ Time _______

LESSON 7•13 **Open Response** Progress Check 7

1. Queen Arlene has a problem. She wants to divide her land among her three children. She wants her oldest daughter to get $\frac{1}{2}$ of the land and her younger daughters to each get $\frac{1}{3}$ of the land. Can she do it?

Explain your answer.

It won't work out because there are only 3 pieces if you give 1/2 then you could only give one d. land.

2. After thinking about it Queen Arlene decides to keep $\frac{1}{2}$ of her land and have her 3 children divide the other $\frac{1}{2}$. She still wants the oldest daughter to get more land than her sisters. Think of a way to use fractions to divide the land. Explain your answer.

It is possible if you split it up in 7 equal parts. The queen gets half and the oldest gets 2/1 and the youngest daughters get 1 1/7

This Level 1 paper illustrates the following features: Provides several illustrations that relate to Problem 1. There is no evidence of understanding the problem. For Problem 2, the illustration appears to be correct, but the explanation does not relate to the information in the illustration.

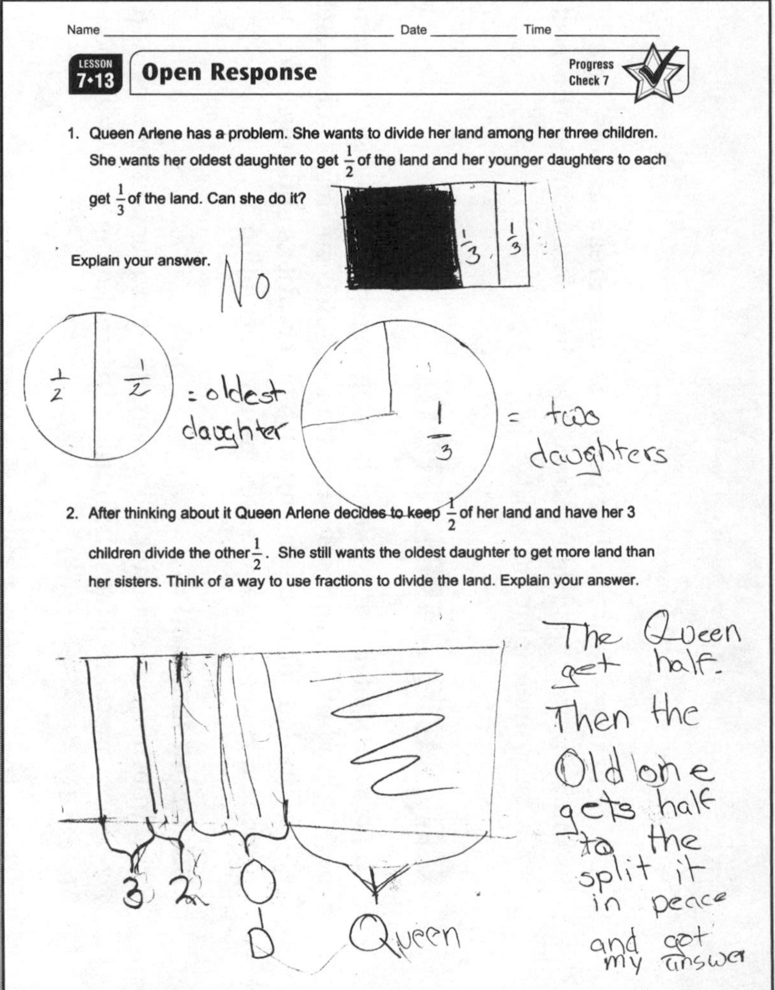

Name _______ Date _______ Time _______

LESSON 7•13 **Open Response** Progress Check 7

1. Queen Arlene has a problem. She wants to divide her land among her three children. She wants her oldest daughter to get $\frac{1}{2}$ of the land and her younger daughters to each get $\frac{1}{3}$ of the land. Can she do it?

Explain your answer. No

$\frac{1}{2}$ $\frac{1}{2}$ = oldest daughter $\frac{1}{3}$ = two daughters

2. After thinking about it Queen Arlene decides to keep $\frac{1}{2}$ of her land and have her 3 children divide the other $\frac{1}{2}$. She still wants the oldest daughter to get more land than her sisters. Think of a way to use fractions to divide the land. Explain your answer.

The Queen get half. Then the Old one gets half to the split it in peace and get my answer

Unit 8 Assessment Overview

In this unit, students review perimeter and area concepts, and develop formulas as mathematical models for area. Use the information in this section to develop your assessment plan for Unit 8.

Ongoing Assessment

Opportunities for using and collecting ongoing assessment information are highlighted in Informing Instruction and Recognizing Student Achievement notes. Student products, along with observations and suggested writing prompts, provide a range of useful assessment information.

Informing Instruction

The Informing Instruction notes highlight students' thinking and point out common misconceptions. Informing Instruction in Unit 8: Lessons 8-2, 8-3, 8-5, and 8-6.

Recognizing Student Achievement

The Recognizing Student Achievement notes highlight specific tasks from which teachers can collect assessment data to monitor and document student's progress toward meeting Grade-Level Goals.

Lesson	Content Assessed	Where to Find It
8•1	**Rename fractions with denominators of 10 and 100 as decimals and percents.** [Number and Numeration Goal 5]	*TLG,* p. 659
8•2	**Use data to create a line graph.** [Data and Chance Goal 1]	*TLG,* p. 667
8•3	**Count squares and half squares to find the area of a polygon.** [Measurement and Reference Frames Goal 2]	*TLG,* p. 672
8•4	**Count unit squares and fractions of unit squares to estimate the area of an irregular figure.** [Measurement and Reference Frames Goal 2]	*TLG,* p. 677
8•5	**Find the perimeter of a figure.** [Measurement and Reference Frames Goal 2]	*TLG,* p. 684
8•6	**Solve fraction addition and subtraction problems.** [Operations and Computation Goal 5]	*TLG,* p. 691
8•7	**Describe a strategy for finding and comparing the area of a square and a polygon.** [Measurement and Reference Frames Goal 2]	*TLG,* p. 696
8•8	**Calculate the probability of an event.** [Data and Chance Goal 4]	*TLG,* p. 702

Math Boxes

Math Boxes, one of several types of tasks highlighted in the Recognizing Student Achievement notes, have an additional useful feature. Math Boxes in most lessons are paired or linked with Math Boxes in one or two other lessons that have similar problems. Paired or linked Math Boxes in Unit 8: 8-1 and 8-3; 8-2 and 8-4; 8-5 and 8-7; and 8-6 and 8-8.

Writing/Reasoning Prompts

In Unit 8, a variety of writing prompts encourage students to explain their strategies and thinking, to reflect on their learning, and to make connections to other mathematics or life experiences. Here are some of the Unit 8 suggestions:

Lesson	Writing/Reasoning Prompts	Where to Find It
8◆1	Explain how you made your spinner predictions.	*TLG*, p. 662
8◆3	Describe the strategy you used to decide which fraction, $\frac{4}{8}$ or $\frac{7}{15}$, is greater.	*TLG*, p. 673
8◆4	Describe the strategy you used to estimate the product.	*TLG*, p. 679
8◆7	Write 2 probability questions about rolling a die for which the correct answer would be 210 times.	*TLG*, p. 697
8◆8	Explain the strategy you used to solve the fraction subtraction problem.	*TLG*, p. 702

Portfolio Opportunities

Portfolios are a versatile tool for assessment. They help students reflect on their mathematical growth and help teachers understand and document that growth. Each unit identifies several student products that can be selected and stored in a portfolio. Here are some of the Unit 8 suggestions:

Lesson	Portfolio Opportunities	Where to Find It
8◆1	Students use a set of pattern blocks to create polygons with as many different perimeters as possible.	*TLG*, p. 663
8◆2	Students make scale drawings of their bedrooms.	*TLG*, p. 668
8◆3	Students use geoboards to find polygons with an area of four square units.	*TLG*, p. 674
8◆6	Students construct parallelograms and perpendicular line segments.	*TLG*, p. 692
8◆7	Students find the area and perimeter of a non-regular hexagon.	*TLG*, p. 698

Periodic Assessment

Every Progress Check lesson includes opportunities to observe students' progress and to collect student products in a variety of ways—Self Assessment, Oral and Slate Assessment, Written Assessment, and an Open Response task. For more details, see the first page of Progress Check 8, Lesson 8-9 on page 704, of the *Teacher's Lesson Guide*.

Progress Check Modifications

Written Assessments are one way students demonstrate what they know. The table below shows modifications for the Written Assessment in this unit. Use these to maximize opportunities for students to demonstrate what they know. Modifications can be given individually or written on the board for the class.

Problem(s)	Modifications for Written Assessment
1, 2	For Problems 1 and 2, draw the figures on centimeter grid paper so that 1 cm represents 1 m.
3, 4	For Problems 3 and 4, label the dimensions of the polygon. Divide the polygon into rectangles, triangles, or parallelograms to find the area.
6	For Problem 6, draw the room on centimeter grid paper so that 1 cm represents 1 ft.
12	For Problem 12, explain how you made your prediction for how many times you would expect to land on white, and write the number sentence you used to solve the problem.

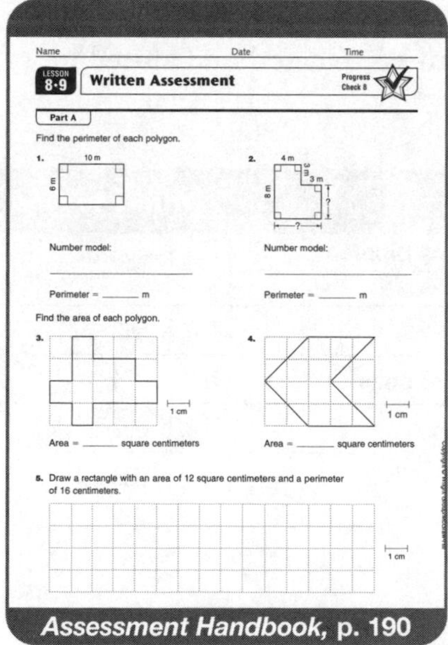
Name Date Time

LESSON 8·9 **Written Assessment** Progress Check 8

Part A

Find the perimeter of each polygon.

Number model: ______ Perimeter = ______ m

Number model: ______ Perimeter = ______ m

Find the area of each polygon.

Area = ______ square centimeters

Area = ______ square centimeters

5. Draw a rectangle with an area of 12 square centimeters and a perimeter of 16 centimeters.

Assessment Handbook, p. 190

The Written Assessment for the Unit 8 Progress Check is on pages 190–192.

Open Response, *Comparing Areas*

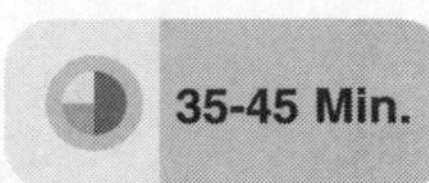

Description

For this task, students compare the areas of several 2-dimensional shapes.

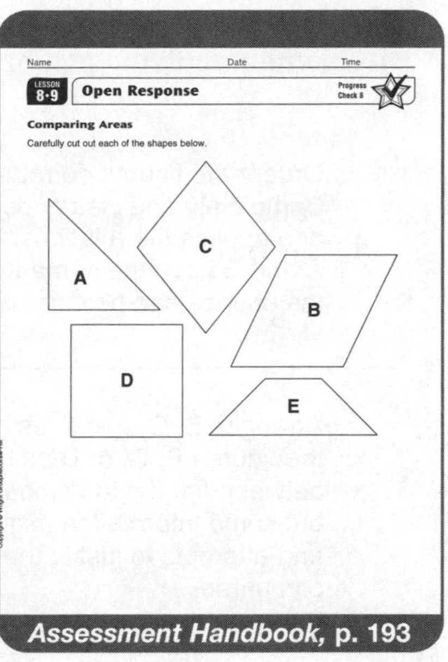
Name Date Time

LESSON 8·9 **Open Response** Progress Check 8

Comparing Areas

Carefully cut out each of the shapes below.

Assessment Handbook, p. 193

Focus

- **Describe and use strategies to measure the area of polygons.**
  [Measurement and Reference Frames Goal 2]
- **Describe and compare plane figures using appropriate geometric terms.**
  [Geometry Goal 2]

Implementation Tips

- Review the concept of area and the names of the figures in the *Assessment Handbook,* page 193.
- Remind students that since they are not measuring the dimensions of any of the figures, they have to use what they know about the relationships between the areas of the figures to solve the problem.

Modifications for Meeting Diverse Needs

- Provide additional copies of the figures so that students can cut them apart in different ways to compare the areas. Provide tag board versions of the figures so they can be traced to facilitate recording their work.
- Have students describe how they can find the area of the trapezoid (Shape E) based on the area formulas they know.

Improving Open Response Skills

After students complete the task, have them analyze several samples of written explanations for Problem 3 (without the number sentences). Consider using some of the explanations included in the Sample Student Responses beginning on page 115 of this book. Copy each explanation on a piece of chart paper and give one to each group. Have students determine and record what information is missing from the explanation. Have them work together to write a clearer and more complete explanation.

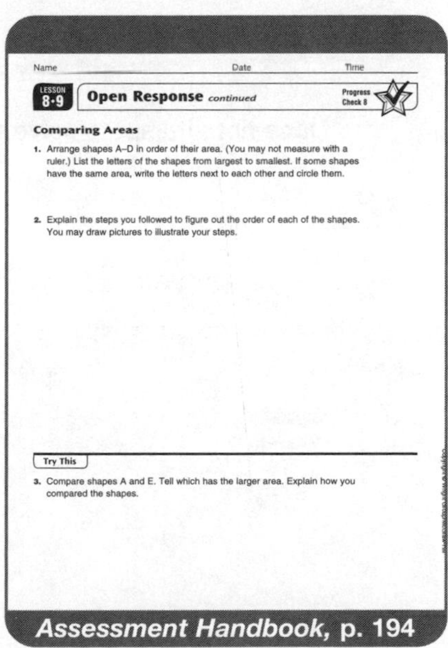
Name Date Time

LESSON 8·9 **Open Response** *continued* Progress Check 8

Comparing Areas

1. Arrange shapes A–D in order of their area. (You may not measure with a ruler.) List the letters of the shapes from largest to smallest. If some shapes have the same area, write the letters next to each other and circle them.

2. Explain the steps you followed to figure out the order of each of the shapes. You may draw pictures to illustrate your steps.

Try This

3. Compare shapes A and E. Tell which has the larger area. Explain how you compared the shapes.

Assessment Handbook, p. 194

Note: The wording and formatting of the text on the student samples that follow may vary slightly from the actual task your students will complete. These minor discrepancies will not affect the implementation of the task.

Rubric

This rubric is designed to help you assess levels of mathematical performance on this task. It emphasizes mathematical understanding with only a mention of clarity of explanation. Consider the expectations of standardized tests in your area when applying a rubric. Modify this sample rubric as appropriate.

4	Orders the figures correctly. Identifies B, C, and D as having the same area. Completely and clearly describes the steps for comparing all four figures. Recognizes and applies the relationships between the figures to compare areas. Concludes that A and E have the same area, and justifies the conclusion by clearly describing how the shapes can be compared using relationships among them.
3	Arranges B, C, and D as the first three in some order. Identifies at least one pair from the figures B, C, or D as having the same area. Recognizes and applies relationships between figures to compare areas. Describes some steps for comparing the figures, but some information might be missing. Concludes that A and E have the same area, and attempts to justify the conclusion by describing how the shapes can be compared.
2	Arranges B, C, and D as the first three in some order. Describes some steps for comparing the figures, but might have omissions or minor errors. Compares A and E and attempts to justify the conclusion by describing how the shapes can be compared.
1	Attempts to order some of the figures in Problem 1, and explains some reasoning in either words or pictures for how comparisons are made. There might be errors. Compares A and E and describes how these figures are compared, but might show little evidence of understanding the relationships among figures.
0	Does not attempt to solve the problem.

Sample Student Responses

This Level 4 paper illustrates the following features: B, C, and D are identified as being the same size and A is listed as the smallest. The illustration and explanation describe how B and D can be compared by cutting B and rearranging the pieces. A is described as being half of C. A and E are compared by rearranging sections of A to get a figure that looks like E. The explanation includes an illustration of the process.

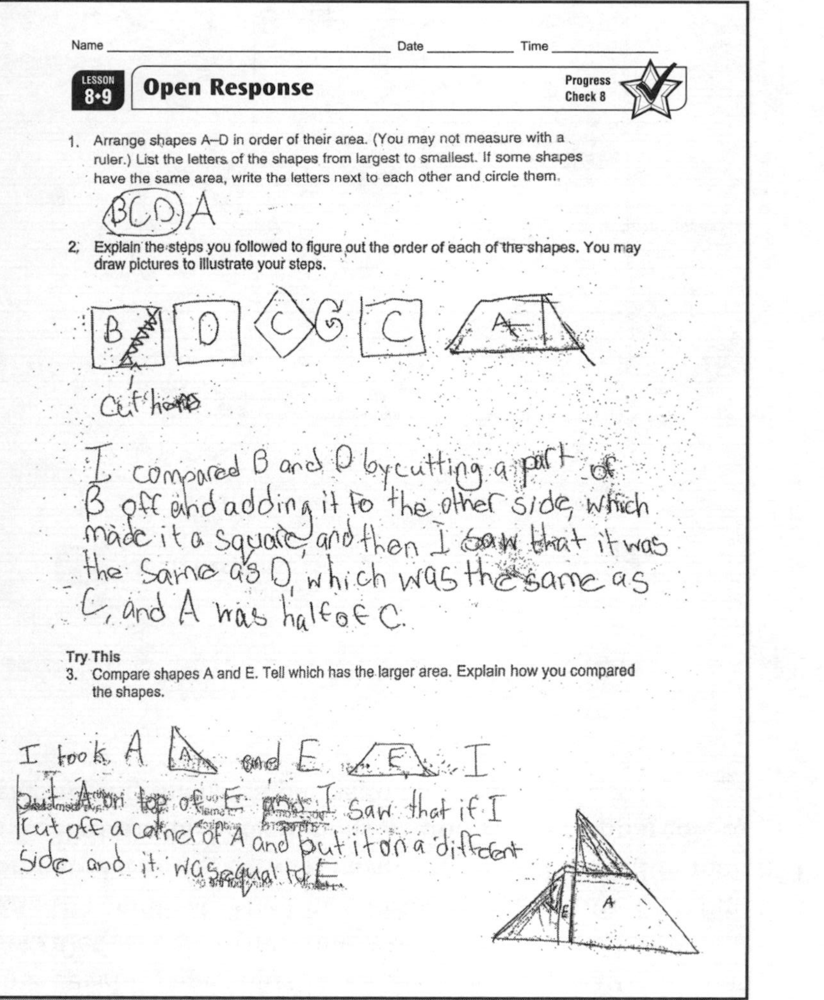

Name ______________ Date ________ Time ________

LESSON 8•9 **Open Response** Progress Check 8

1. Arrange shapes A–D in order of their area. (You may not measure with a ruler.) List the letters of the shapes from largest to smallest. If some shapes have the same area, write the letters next to each other and circle them.

(BCD) A

2. Explain the steps you followed to figure out the order of each of the shapes. You may draw pictures to illustrate your steps.

I compared B and D by cutting a part of B off and adding it to the other side, which made it a square, and then I saw that it was the Same as D, which was the same as C, and A was half of C.

Try This

3. Compare shapes A and E. Tell which has the larger area. Explain how you compared the shapes.

I took A and E. I put A on top of E. I saw that if I cut off a corner of A and put it on a different side and it was equal to E.

This Level 4 paper illustrates the following features: B, C, and D are identified as being the same size and A is listed as the smallest. The explanation describes how figures are compared with parts cut off and moved to match. There is an illustration showing how the figures are manipulated to compare them. A and E are compared by covering E with A, cutting off the section of A that does not fit inside, and inserting that section so that the rearranged sections of A cover E exactly.

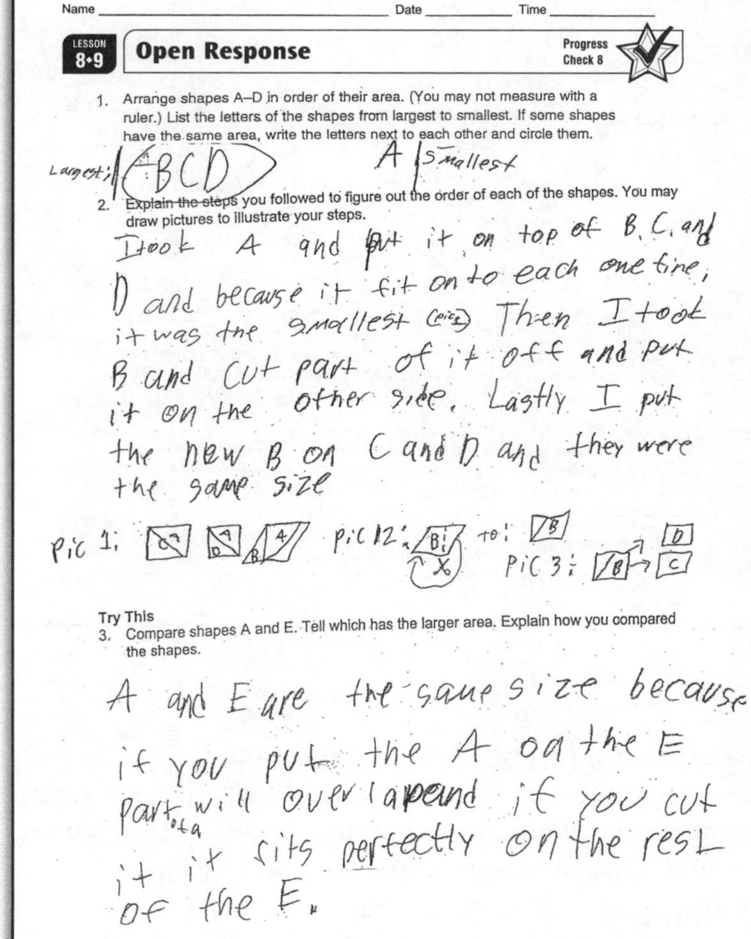

Name ______________ Date ________ Time ________

LESSON 8•9 **Open Response** Progress Check 8

1. Arrange shapes A–D in order of their area. (You may not measure with a ruler.) List the letters of the shapes from largest to smallest. If some shapes have the same area, write the letters next to each other and circle them.

Largest: (BCD) A smallest

2. Explain the steps you followed to figure out the order of each of the shapes. You may draw pictures to illustrate your steps.

I took A and put it on top of B, C, and D and because it fit on to each one time, it was the smallest. Then I took B and cut part of it off and put it on the other side. Lastly I put the new B on C and D and they were the same size

Pic 1: Pic 2: to: Pic 3:

Try This

3. Compare shapes A and E. Tell which has the larger area. Explain how you compared the shapes.

A and E are the same size because if you put the A on the E part will over lap and if you cut it it sits perfectly on the rest of the E.

This Level 3 paper illustrates the following features: B and D are identified as being the same size, listing C as slightly smaller, and A as the smallest. The illustrations demonstrate how figures are compared directly or with parts cut off and moved to match. There is an illustration showing how A and E are compared—by rearranging the extra pieces to match the areas.

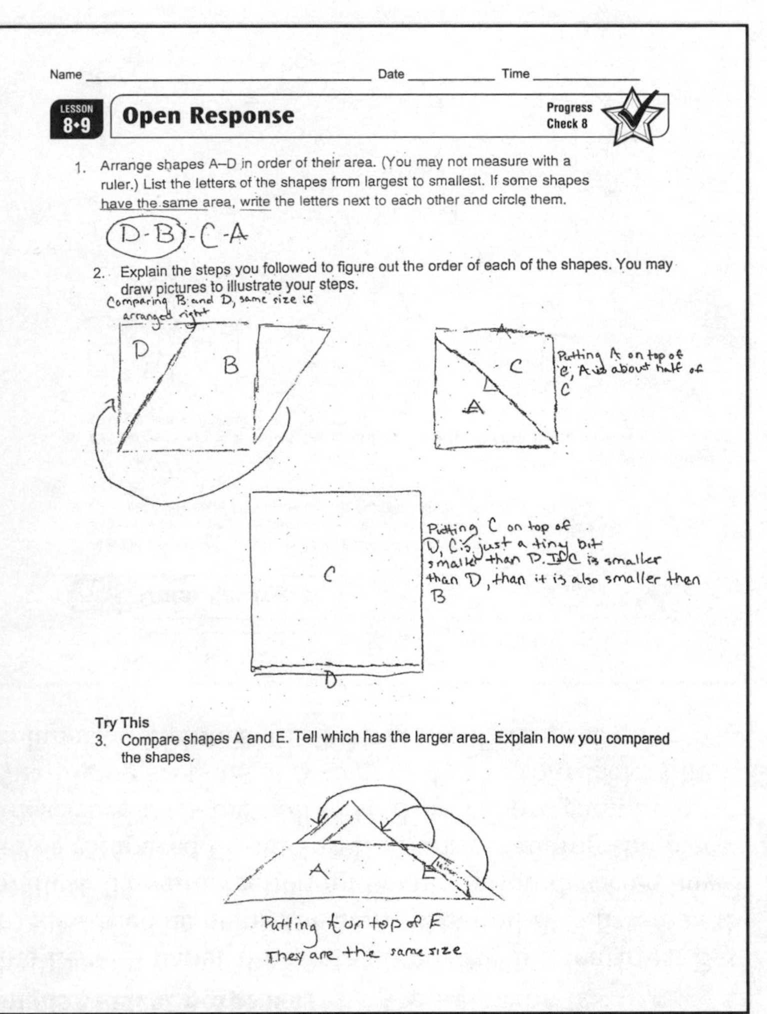
Name ______ Date ______ Time ______

LESSON 8•9 **Open Response** Progress Check 8

1. Arrange shapes A–D in order of their area. (You may not measure with a ruler.) List the letters of the shapes from largest to smallest. If some shapes have the same area, write the letters next to each other and circle them.

(D-B)-C-A

2. Explain the steps you followed to figure out the order of each of the shapes. You may draw pictures to illustrate your steps.

Comparing B and D, same size if arranged right

Putting A on top of C, A is about half of C

Putting C on top of D, C is just a tiny bit smaller than D. If C is smaller than D, than it is also smaller then B

Try This

3. Compare shapes A and E. Tell which has the larger area. Explain how you compared the shapes.

Putting A on top of E
They are the same size

This Level 3 paper illustrates the following features: B and D are identified as being the same size, listing C as slightly smaller, and A as the smallest. The explanation describes folding pieces of the figures that do not match and then comparing the folded pieces. The explanation points out that the unmatched areas are equal for B and D. Using the same folding strategy, A and E are described as being equal.

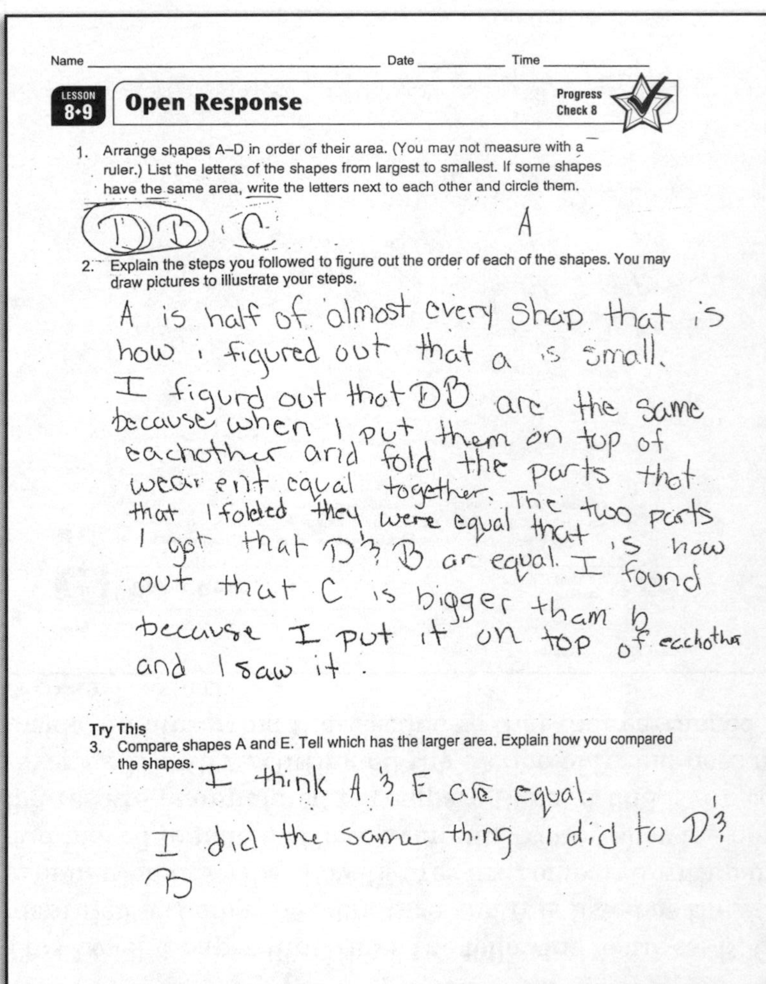
Name ______ Date ______ Time ______

LESSON 8•9 **Open Response** Progress Check 8

1. Arrange shapes A–D in order of their area. (You may not measure with a ruler.) List the letters of the shapes from largest to smallest. If some shapes have the same area, write the letters next to each other and circle them.

(D B) C A

2. Explain the steps you followed to figure out the order of each of the shapes. You may draw pictures to illustrate your steps.

A is half of almost every Shap that is how i figured out that a is small. I figurd out that DB are the same because when I put them on top of eachother and fold the parts that wearent equal together. The two parts that I folded they were equal that is how I got that D & B ar equal. I found out that C is bigger tham b because I put it on top of eachother and I saw it.

Try This

3. Compare shapes A and E. Tell which has the larger area. Explain how you compared the shapes.

I think A & E are equal.
I did the same thing i did to D & B

This Level 2 paper illustrates the following features: B and D are identified as being the same size and being the largest. C is listed as being slightly smaller and A as the smallest, and the explanation does not provide additional information. A and E are described as being equal, and the illustration clearly shows how this conclusion is reached.

Name ______________ Date ________ Time ________

LESSON 8•9 **Open Response** Progress Check 8

1. Arrange shapes A–D in order of their area. (You may not measure with a ruler.) List the letters of the shapes from largest to smallest. If some shapes have the same area, write the letters next to each other and circle them.

(DB) C A

2. Explain the steps you followed to figure out the order of each of the shapes. You may draw pictures to illustrate your steps.

I first compared D and C together and D was the Bigest by a little. So I but D for biggest then C for smallest. Then I compared D and B they were the same size I but them together and circled them. Thired I compared C and A A was smaller So I but it for last so I got (D,B),C,A.

Try This

3. Compare shapes A and E. Tell which has the larger area. Explain how you compared the shapes.

first I but them together the I figured that tha is going to be the hard way so I turned it and cut it they were the same size.

This Level 1 paper illustrates the following features: The answer to Problem 1 makes no sense in the context of the problem. The illustrations and explanations in Problem 2 do not provide any information. A and E are described as being the same, but the illustrated strategy appears to involve counting dots the student has drawn around the perimeters of the figures.

Name ______________ Date ________ Time ________

LESSON 8•9 **Open Response** Progress Check 8

1. Arrange shapes A–D in order of their area. (You may not measure with a ruler.) List the letters of the shapes from largest to smallest. If some shapes have the same area, write the letters next to each other and circle them.

AD (CD) CB AB CB

2. Explain the steps you followed to figure out the order of each of the shapes. You may draw pictures to illustrate your steps.

A is half of D. So it is kind of diffrent. If I had

C and D have the same area. But they aren't the same size.

Try This

3. Compare shapes A and E. Tell which has the larger area. Explain how you compared the shapes.

area = 15

I think they are both the same.

area = 15

Unit 9

Assessment Overview

In this unit, students explore the relationship among and convert between fractions, decimals, and percents with a special emphasis on percents. Use the information in this section to develop your assessment plan for Unit 9.

Ongoing Assessment

Opportunities for using and collecting ongoing assessment information are highlighted in Informing Instruction and Recognizing Student Achievement notes. Student products, along with observations and suggested writing prompts, provide a range of useful assessment information.

Informing Instruction

The Informing Instruction notes highlight students' thinking and point out common misconceptions. Informing Instruction in Unit 9: Lessons 9-1, 9-4, 9-5, and 9-7.

Recognizing Student Achievement

The Recognizing Student Achievement notes highlight specific tasks from which teachers can collect assessment data to monitor and document student's progress toward meeting Grade-Level Goals.

Lesson	Content Assessed	Where to Find It
9♦1	**Find equivalent fractions.** [Number and Numeration Goal 5]	*TLG*, p. 726
9♦2	**Rename fourths, fifths, tenths, and hundredths as decimals and percents.** [Number and Numeration Goal 5]	*TLG*, p. 730
9♦3	**Rename fourths, fifths, tenths, and hundredths as decimals and percents.** [Number and Numeration Goal 5]	*TLG*, p. 735
9♦4	**Solve "fraction-of" problems.** [Number and Numeration Goal 2]	*TLG*, p. 742
9♦5	**Divide a multidigit whole number by a 1-digit divisor.** [Operations and Computation Goal 4]	*TLG*, p. 748
9♦6	**Interpret a map scale.** [Operations and Computation Goal 7]	*TLG*, p. 754
9♦7	**Draw conclusions from a data representation.** [Data and Chance Goal 2]	*TLG*, p. 760
9♦8	**Estimate the product of a whole number and a decimal.** [Operations and Computation Goal 6]	*TLG*, p. 765
9♦9	**Estimate the quotient of a decimal divided by a whole number.** [Operations and Computation Goal 6]	*TLG*, p. 771

Math Boxes

Math Boxes, one of several types of tasks highlighted in the Recognizing Student Achievement notes, have an additional useful feature. Math Boxes in most lessons are paired or linked with Math Boxes in one or two other lessons that have similar problems. Paired or linked Math Boxes in Unit 9: 9-1 and 9-3; 9-2 and 9-4; 9-5, 9-7, and 9-9; and 9-6 and 9-8.

Writing/Reasoning Prompts

In Unit 9, a variety of writing prompts encourage students to explain their strategies and thinking, to reflect on their learning, and to make connections to other mathematics or life experiences. Here are some of the Unit 9 suggestions:

Lesson	Writing/Reasoning Prompts	Where to Find It
9•2	Explain how you found the opposite of 5.	*TLG*, p. 732
9•3	Explain how to estimate the measure of an angle.	*TLG*, p. 737
9•7	Use a drawing and number models to explain how you determined what percent 6 is of 24.	*TLG*, p. 761
9•8	Explain how you found a percent value between $\frac{3}{4}$ and $\frac{3}{5}$.	*TLG*, p. 766
9•9	Draw another parallelogram that has the same area as the given parallelogram. Do the parallelogram you drew and the original have the same perimeter? Explain your answer.	*TLG*, p. 772

Portfolio Opportunities

Portfolios are a versatile tool for assessment. They help students reflect on their mathematical growth and help teachers understand and document that growth. Each unit identifies several student products that can be selected and stored in a portfolio. Here are some of the Unit 9 suggestions:

Lesson	Portfolio Opportunities	Where to Find It
9•2	Students write, illustrate, and solve "percent of" number stories.	*TLG*, p. 733
9•4	Students solve number stories in which they compare the discounts of two items.	*TLG*, p. 743
9•6	Students graph the results of a class survey.	*TLG*, p. 755
9•7	Students rank countries and color a map to show literacy data, and use this information to draw conclusions.	*TLG*, p. 761
9•9	Students write and solve number stories involving the division of a decimal by a whole number.	*TLG*, p. 773

Periodic Assessment

Every Progress Check lesson includes opportunities to observe students' progress and to collect student products in a variety of ways—Self Assessment, Oral and Slate Assessment, Written Assessment, and an Open Response task. For more details, see the first page of Progress Check 9, Lesson 9-10 on page 774, of the Teacher's Lesson Guide.

Progress Check Modifications

Written Assessments are one way students demonstrate what they know. The table below shows modifications for the Written Assessment in this unit. Use these to maximize opportunities for students to demonstrate what they know. Modifications can be given individually or written on the board for the class.

Problem(s)	Modifications for Written Assessment
3	**For Problem 3, use base-10 blocks with the flat as the whole to model the fractions, decimals, and percents.**
5c	**For Problem 5c, record the steps for renaming $\frac{3}{96}$ as a percent. Explain how you could estimate the percent without using a calculator.**
10	**For Problem 10, record each number sentence on another sheet of paper so there is space between the numbers and symbols. Use craft sticks or strips of paper to model the parentheses. Move the parentheses around in each number sentence until you find the position that will make the sentence true.**
13–16	**For Problems 13–16, use a calculator to check your placement of the decimal.**

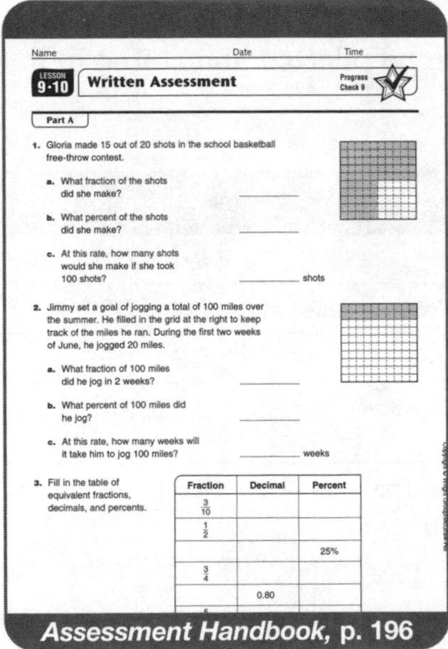
Name Date Time

LESSON 9·10 **Written Assessment** Progress Check 9

Part A

1. Gloria made 15 out of 20 shots in the school basketball free-throw contest.
   a. What fraction of the shots did she make? ________
   b. What percent of the shots did she make? ________
   c. At this rate, how many shots would she make if she took 100 shots? ________ shots
2. Jimmy set a goal of jogging a total of 100 miles over the summer. He filled in the grid at the right to keep track of the miles he ran. During the first two weeks of June, he jogged 20 miles.
   a. What fraction of 100 miles did he jog in 2 weeks? ________
   b. What percent of 100 miles did he jog? ________
   c. At this rate, how many weeks will it take him to jog 100 miles? ________ weeks
3. Fill in the table of equivalent fractions, decimals, and percents.

Fraction	Decimal	Percent
$\frac{3}{10}$		
$\frac{1}{2}$		
		25%
$\frac{3}{4}$		
	0.80	

Assessment Handbook, p. 196

The Written Assessment for the Unit 9 Progress Check is on pages 196–198.

Open Response, *Designing a Floor*

45-55 Min.

Description

For this task, students find the number of tiles of each color used to cover a floor based on a total number of tiles and percents given for each color.

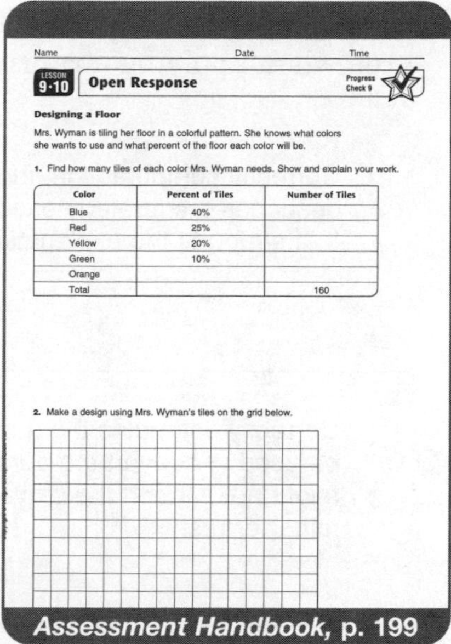

Name Date Time

LESSON 9·10 **Open Response** Progress Check 9

Designing a Floor

Mrs. Wyman is tiling her floor in a colorful pattern. She knows what colors she wants to use and what percent of the floor each color will be.

1. Find how many tiles of each color Mrs. Wyman needs. Show and explain your work.

Color	Percent of Tiles	Number of Tiles
Blue	40%	
Red	25%	
Yellow	20%	
Green	10%	
Orange		
Total		160

2. Make a design using Mrs. Wyman's tiles on the grid below.

Assessment Handbook, p. 199

Focus

- **Solve problems involving fractional parts of a collection; describe and explain strategies used.** [Number and Numeration Goal 2]
- **Use numerical expressions to find equivalent names for fractions and percents.** [Number and Numeration Goal 5]

Implementation Tips

- Review how to rewrite a percent as a fraction. Remind students that, in this problem, the total number of tiles is 160, not 100.

Modifications for Meeting Diverse Needs

- Provide extra copies of the 16 × 10 grid at the bottom of the page. Have students discuss how they know that each **row** of the grid is worth 10%. Have students make a visual model for each of the percents listed in the problem by shading a separate grid for each step of the problem. Have them use the visual model to figure out the number of tiles.
- Have students compare working with a hundred-grid to working with the grid given in the problem. How are the two models alike and how they are different when solving problems?

Improving Open Response Skills

After students complete the task, have them reorganize their answers into two columns on a separate sheet of paper—*What* each step is and *Why* each step is required. For example, *What* could be, "Multiplied 0.4 times 160"; *Why* could be, "to find 40% of 160." Remind students that when they explain their answers, the explanation should include both of these components.

Note: The wording and formatting of the text on the student samples that follow may vary slightly from the actual task your students will complete. These minor discrepancies will not affect the implementation of the task.

Rubric

This rubric is designed to help you assess levels of mathematical performance on this task. It emphasizes mathematical understanding with only a mention of clarity of explanation. Consider the expectations of standardized tests in your area when applying a rubric. Modify this sample rubric as appropriate.

4	Correctly computes the number of tiles for each color. Clearly and completely describes the strategy used to convert the percent to the number of tiles. Shows work that supports the explanation. Colors the correct number of tiles in Problem 2.
3	Correctly computes the number of tiles for each color. Describes a strategy that can be used to convert the percent to the number of tiles. Shows some work, but this might not support the explanation. Colors the tiles in Problem 2, but might have minor errors.
2	Might correctly compute the number of tiles for each color. Describes some steps of a strategy that makes sense, but the explanation might be incomplete. Shows some work, but this might not support the explanation. Problem 2 might have errors or be incomplete.
1	Attempts to compute the number of tiles for each color. Might attempt to describe some steps of a strategy, but there is little evidence of an understanding of the problem.
0	Does not attempt to solve the problem.

Sample Student Responses

This Level 4 paper illustrates the following features: The numbers of tiles are calculated correctly in the table. The explanation clearly describes converting the percents into fractions; dividing 160 (the total number of tiles) by the denominator of the fraction; and then multiplying the results by the numerator of the fraction. The work on the page does not contradict the explanation. The grid is colored correctly.

Name ______ Date ______ Time ______

LESSON 9•10 **Open Response** Progress Check 9

Mrs. Wyman is tiling her floor in a colorful pattern. She knows what colors she wants to use and what percent of the floor each color will be.

1. Find how many tiles of each color Mrs. Wyman needs. Show and explain your work.

Color	Percent of Tiles	Number of Tiles
Blue	40%	64
Red	25%	40
Yellow	20%	32
Green	10%	16
Orange	5%	8
Total	100%	160

40% of 160 = 64
$\frac{40}{100}$
25% of 160 = 40
$\frac{1}{4}$
20% of 160 = 32
$\frac{1}{5}$

10% of 160 =
$\frac{10}{100}$

I divided 160 from how much percent but I made the perce into a fraction then I divided 160 to the denomanato and then timesed it by the numerator.

2. Make a design using Mrs. Wyman's tiles on the grid below.

This Level 4 paper illustrates the following features: The numbers of tiles are calculated correctly in the table. The explanation clearly describes converting the percents into fractions; dividing 160 by the denominator of the fraction; and then multiplying the results by the numerator of the fraction. The work supports the explanation and includes a description of how the number of orange tiles is calculated. The grid is colored correctly.

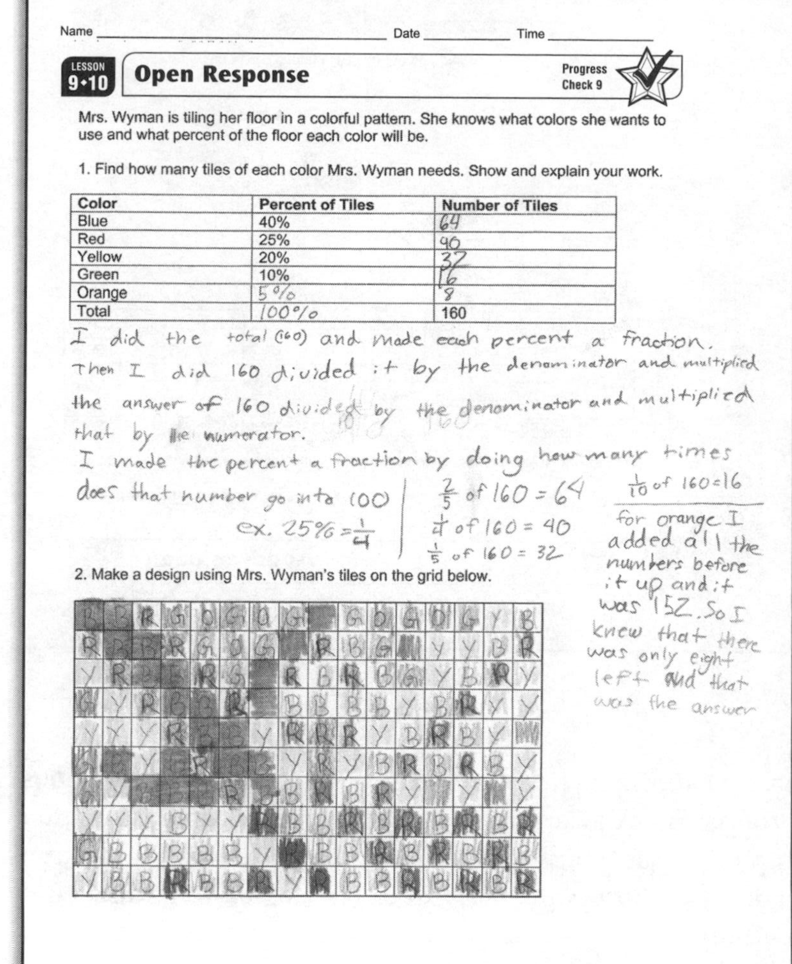

Name ______ Date ______ Time ______

LESSON 9•10 **Open Response** Progress Check 9

Mrs. Wyman is tiling her floor in a colorful pattern. She knows what colors she wants to use and what percent of the floor each color will be.

1. Find how many tiles of each color Mrs. Wyman needs. Show and explain your work.

Color	Percent of Tiles	Number of Tiles
Blue	40%	64
Red	25%	40
Yellow	20%	32
Green	10%	16
Orange	5%	8
Total	100%	160

I did the total (160) and made each percent a fraction. Then I did 160 divided it by the denominator and multiplied the answer of 160 divided by the denominator and multiplied that by the numerator.
I made the percent a fraction by doing how many times does that number go into 100 ex. 25% = $\frac{1}{4}$

$\frac{2}{5}$ of 160 = 64
$\frac{1}{4}$ of 160 = 40
$\frac{1}{5}$ of 160 = 32
$\frac{1}{10}$ of 160 = 16

for orange I added all the numbers before it up and it was 152. So I knew that there was only eight left and that was the answer

2. Make a design using Mrs. Wyman's tiles on the grid below.

This Level 3 paper illustrates the following features: The numbers of tiles are calculated correctly in the table. The subtotal of the percents is listed instead of the percent for the orange tiles. The explanation describes converting the percents into fractions, and then doing some division. The work on the page supports the explanation. The grid is correct except that 4 tiles need to be switched from yellow to orange.

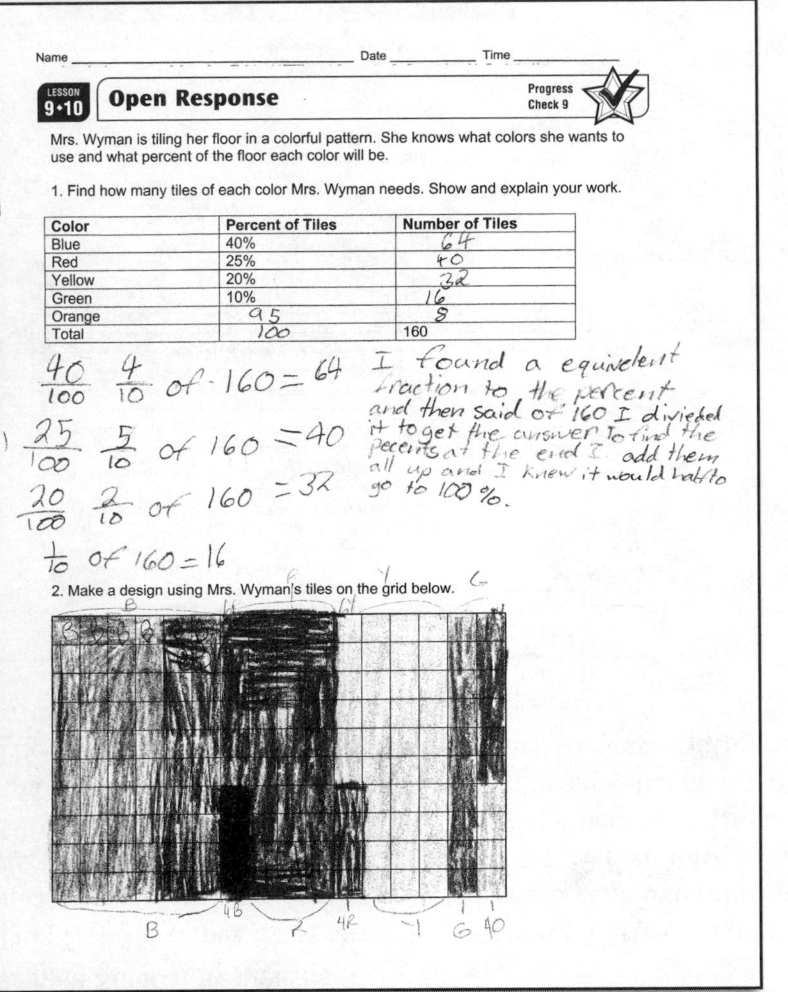

Name ________ Date ________ Time ________

LESSON 9•10 **Open Response** Progress Check 9

Mrs. Wyman is tiling her floor in a colorful pattern. She knows what colors she wants to use and what percent of the floor each color will be.

1. Find how many tiles of each color Mrs. Wyman needs. Show and explain your work.

Color	Percent of Tiles	Number of Tiles
Blue	40%	64
Red	25%	40
Yellow	20%	32
Green	10%	16
Orange	95/100	8
Total		160

$\frac{40}{100}$ $\frac{4}{10}$ of 160 = 64

$\frac{25}{100}$ $\frac{5}{10}$ of 160 = 40

$\frac{20}{100}$ $\frac{2}{10}$ of 160 = 32

$\frac{1}{10}$ of 160 = 16

I found a equivelent fraction to the percent and then said of 160 I divided it to get the answer to find the percents at the end I add them all up and I knew it would hafto go to 100%.

2. Make a design using Mrs. Wyman's tiles on the grid below.

This Level 3 paper illustrates the following features: The numbers of tiles are calculated correctly in the table. The explanation describes converting the percents into fractions; dividing 160 (the total number of tiles) by the denominator of the fraction; and then multiplying the results by the numerator of the fraction. The work shown does not match the explanation. The grid is colored correctly.

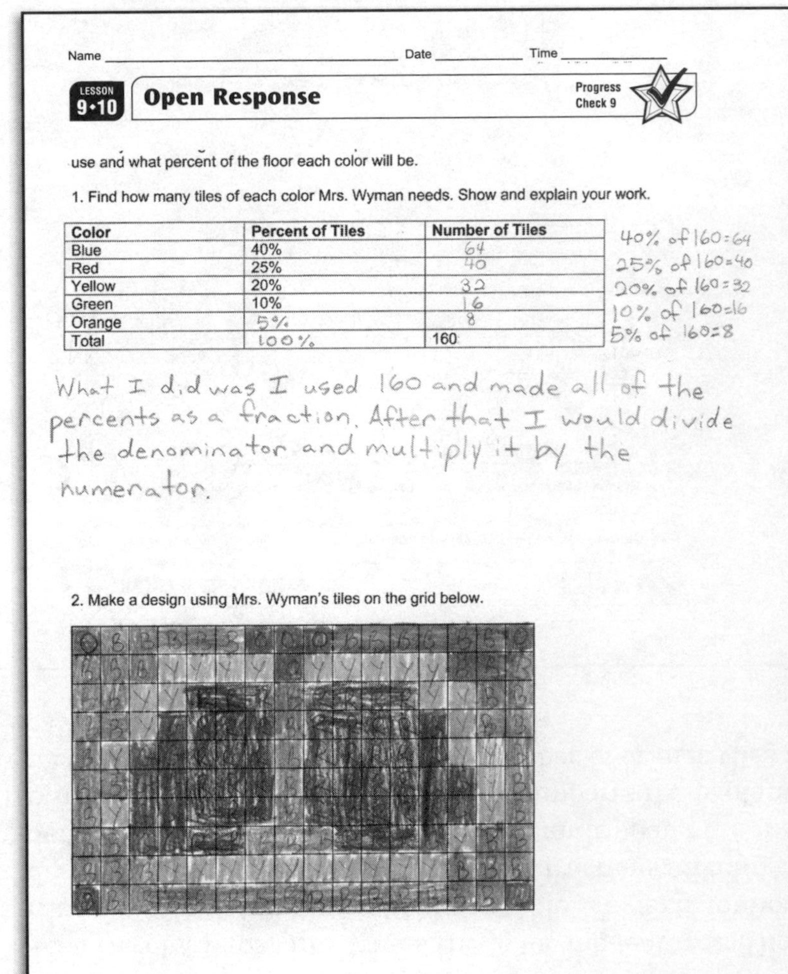

Name ________ Date ________ Time ________

LESSON 9•10 **Open Response** Progress Check 9

use and what percent of the floor each color will be.

1. Find how many tiles of each color Mrs. Wyman needs. Show and explain your work.

Color	Percent of Tiles	Number of Tiles
Blue	40%	64
Red	25%	40
Yellow	20%	32
Green	10%	16
Orange	5%	8
Total	100%	160

40% of 160 = 64
25% of 160 = 40
20% of 160 = 32
10% of 160 = 16
5% of 160 = 8

What I did was I used 160 and made all of the percents as a fraction. After that I would divide the denominator and multiply it by the numerator.

2. Make a design using Mrs. Wyman's tiles on the grid below.

This Level 2 paper illustrates the following features: The numbers of tiles are calculated correctly in the table. The explanation only describes adding up to find the answer and requires further clarification. The grid is colored incorrectly.

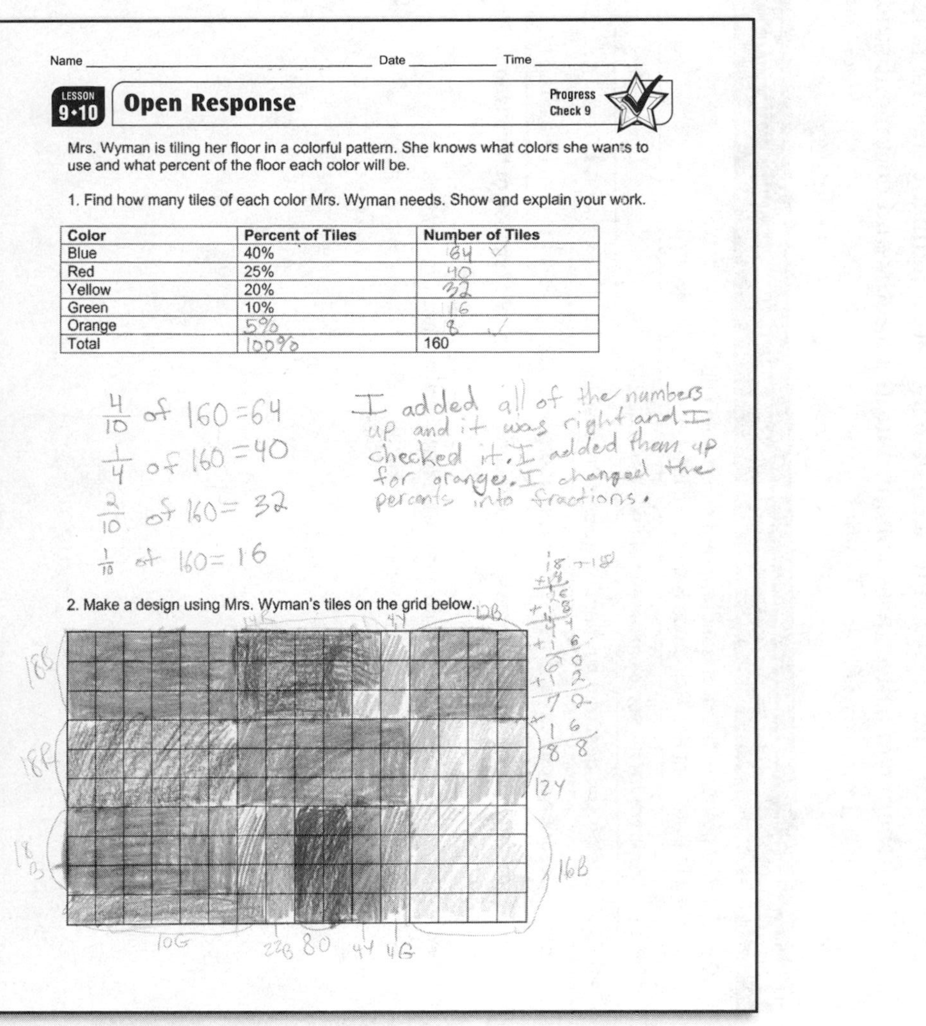

Name ______ Date ______ Time ______

LESSON 9•10 **Open Response** Progress Check 9

Mrs. Wyman is tiling her floor in a colorful pattern. She knows what colors she wants to use and what percent of the floor each color will be.

1. Find how many tiles of each color Mrs. Wyman needs. Show and explain your work.

Color	Percent of Tiles	Number of Tiles
Blue	40%	64
Red	25%	40
Yellow	20%	32
Green	10%	16
Orange	5%	8
Total	100%	160

$\frac{4}{10}$ of 160 = 64
$\frac{1}{4}$ of 160 = 40
$\frac{2}{10}$ of 160 = 32
$\frac{1}{10}$ of 160 = 16

I added all of the numbers up and it was right and I checked it. I added them up for orange. I changed the percents into fractions.

2. Make a design using Mrs. Wyman's tiles on the grid below.

This Level 1 paper illustrates the following features: The numbers of tiles are calculated correctly in the table. The explanation and work shown describe dividing each percent by 160. Although the correct answers are listed, these answers are not the result of the described division.

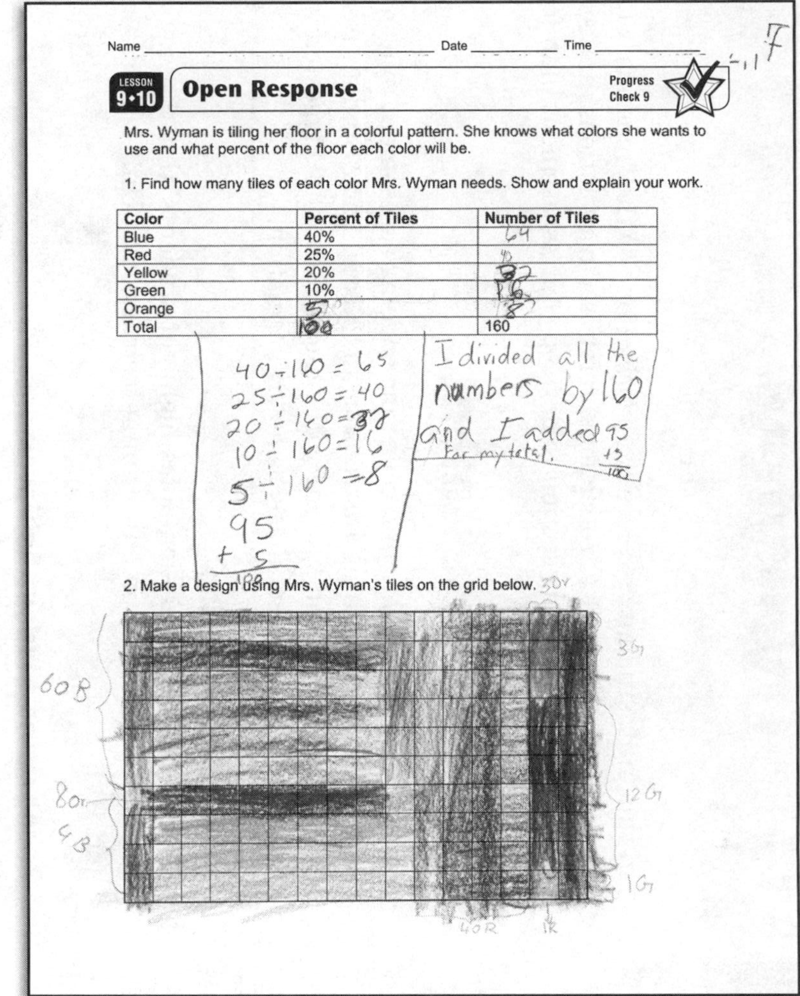

Name ______ Date ______ Time ______

LESSON 9•10 **Open Response** Progress Check 9

Mrs. Wyman is tiling her floor in a colorful pattern. She knows what colors she wants to use and what percent of the floor each color will be.

1. Find how many tiles of each color Mrs. Wyman needs. Show and explain your work.

Color	Percent of Tiles	Number of Tiles
Blue	40%	64
Red	25%	40
Yellow	20%	32
Green	10%	16
Orange	5	8
Total	100	160

40 ÷ 160 = 65
25 ÷ 160 = 40
20 ÷ 160 = 32
10 ÷ 160 = 16
5 ÷ 160 = 8

I divided all the numbers by 160 and I added 95 + 5 = 100 for my total.

2. Make a design using Mrs. Wyman's tiles on the grid below.

Assessment Overview

In this unit, students explore *transformations* or the "motions" of geometric figures in the context of reflections, rotations, translations, and similarity. Use the information in this section to develop your assessment plan for Unit 10.

Ongoing Assessment

Opportunities for using and collecting ongoing assessment information are highlighted in Informing Instruction and Recognizing Student Achievement notes. Student products, along with observations and suggested writing prompts, provide a range of useful assessment information.

Informing Instruction

The Informing Instruction notes highlight students' thinking and point out common misconceptions. Informing Instruction in Unit 10: Lessons 10-2, 10-4, and 10-6.

Recognizing Student Achievement

The Recognizing Student Achievement notes highlight specific tasks from which teachers can collect assessment data to monitor and document students' progress toward meeting Grade-Level Goals.

Lesson	Content Assessed	Where to Find It
10◆1	**Plot points in the first quadrant of a coordinate grid.** [Measurement and Reference Frames Goal 4]	*TLG,* p. 797
10◆2	**Compare fractions.** [Number and Numeration Goal 6]	*TLG,* p. 800
10◆3	**Sketch and describe a reflection.** [Geometry Goal 3]	*TLG,* p. 807
10◆4	**Describe a pattern and use it to solve problems.** [Patterns, Functions, and Algebra Goal 1]	*TLG,* p. 813
10◆5	**Identify and sketch an example of a reflection and identify examples of translations and rotations.** [Geometry Goal 3]	*TLG,* p. 818
10◆6	**Express the probability of an event as a fraction.** [Data and Chance Goal 4]	*TLG,* p. 826

Math Boxes

Math Boxes, one of several types of tasks highlighted in the Recognizing Student Achievement notes, have an additional useful feature. Math Boxes in most lessons are paired or linked with Math Boxes in one or two other lessons that have similar problems. Paired or linked Math Boxes in Unit 10: 10-1 and 10-4; 10-2 and 10-5; and 10-3 and 10-6.

Writing/Reasoning Prompts

In Unit 10, a variety of writing prompts encourage students to explain their strategies and thinking, to reflect on their learning, and to make connections to other mathematics or life experiences. Here are some of the Unit 10 suggestions:

Lesson	Writing/Reasoning Prompts	Where to Find It
10•1	Explain the strategy you used to insert the decimal point.	*TLG*, p. 797
10•3	Explain how you chose the weight for the cat.	*TLG*, p. 808
10•5	Explain your strategy for calculating the mean number of hours Julia babysat last week.	*TLG*, p. 819

Portfolio Opportunities

Portfolios are a versatile tool for assessment. They help students reflect on their mathematical growth and help teachers understand and document that growth. Each unit identifies several student products that can be selected and stored in a portfolio. Here are some of the Unit 10 suggestions:

Lesson	Portfolio Opportunities	Where to Find It
10•2	Students create a paint reflection, write answers to questions about their design, and then describe a reflection.	*TLG*, p. 803
10•4	Students apply their understanding of line symmetry by interpreting a cartoon.	*TLG*, p. 814
10•5	Students make frieze patterns and then describe any reflections, translations, or rotations they used.	*TLG*, p. 821
10•7	Students solve problems involving pentominoes.	*TLG*, p. 831

Periodic Assessment

Every Progress Check lesson includes opportunities to observe students' progress and to collect student products in a variety of ways—Self Assessment, Oral and Slate Assessment, Written Assessment, and an Open Response task. For more details, see the first page of Progress Check 10, Lesson 10-7 on page 828, of the *Teacher's Lesson Guide*.

Progress Check Modifications

Written Assessments are one way students demonstrate what they know. The table below shows modifications for the Written Assessment in this unit. Use these to maximize opportunities for students to demonstrate what they know. Modifications can be given individually or written on the board for the class.

Problem(s)	Modifications for Written Assessment
1–4	**For Problems 1–4, test for symmetry by drawing your shape on a quarter-sheet of paper and folding it to identify lines of symmetry.**
6	**For Problem 6, cut out a copy of the shape and rotate it.**
7	**For Problem 7, explain what you are doing when you draw a reflection of a figure.**
11	**For Problem 11, use a number line to add the signed numbers.**

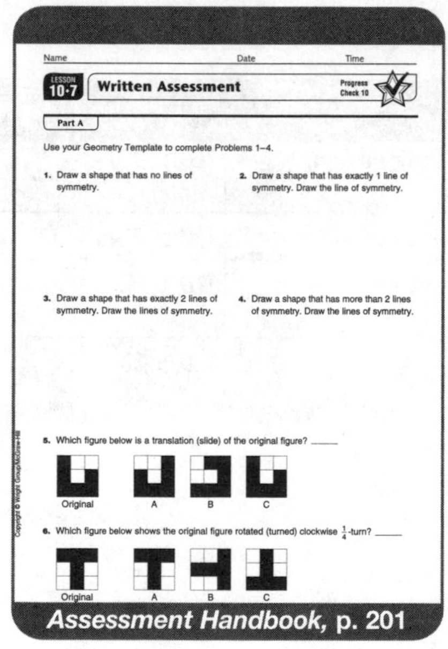
Name Date Time

LESSON 10·7 **Written Assessment** Progress Check 10

Part A

Use your Geometry Template to complete Problems 1–4.

1. Draw a shape that has no lines of symmetry.
2. Draw a shape that has exactly 1 line of symmetry. Draw the line of symmetry.
3. Draw a shape that has exactly 2 lines of symmetry. Draw the lines of symmetry.
4. Draw a shape that has more than 2 lines of symmetry. Draw the lines of symmetry.
5. Which figure below is a translation (slide) of the original figure? _____

Original A B C

6. Which figure below shows the original figure rotated (turned) clockwise $\frac{1}{4}$-turn? _____

Original A B C

Assessment Handbook, p. 201

The Written Assessment for the Unit 10 Progress Check is on pages 201–203.

Open Response, *Pentominoes*

Description

For this task, students use reflections, rotations, and translations to solve a pentomino puzzle.

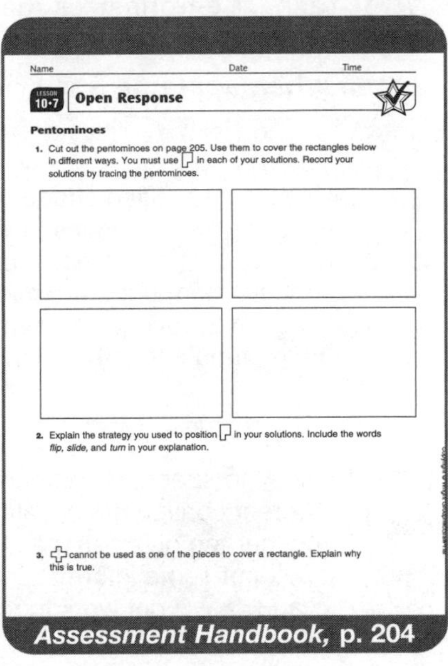

Name Date Time

LESSON 10•7 **Open Response**

Pentominoes

1. Cut out the pentominoes on page 205. Use them to cover the rectangles below in different ways. You must use [P pentomino] in each of your solutions. Record your solutions by tracing the pentominoes.

2. Explain the strategy you used to position [P pentomino] in your solutions. Include the words *flip, slide,* and *turn* in your explanation.

3. [X pentomino] cannot be used as one of the pieces to cover a rectangle. Explain why this is true.

Assessment Handbook, p. 204

Focus

- **Identify, describe, and sketch examples of reflections; identify and describe examples of translations and rotations.** [Geometry Goal 3]

Implementation Tips

- Review the definition of *flips, slides,* and *turns*. Illustrate each of these terms, and leave the illustration displayed during the task.
- Copy the pentominoes on tagboard to make tracing easier.

Modifications for Meeting Diverse Needs

- Provide extra copies of the pentomino page (*Asessment Handbook,* page 205). Consider making the outlines heavier so that they still appear when students cut the pentominoes apart. Have students tape or glue the pentominoes for each solution.
- Have students use both the required pentomino and the 'C' pentomino in each configuration. The third block in each case should be different.

Improving Open Response Skills

Before students begin the task, have them read it together and make a list of its necessary components. Post this list during the task implementation. For example, the rectangles should each include one 'P' pentomino; each rectangle should have a different set of three shapes; the explanation should describe all of the steps for how the 'P' is translated from one rectangle to the next; it should be clear which rectangle goes with which description; and so on.

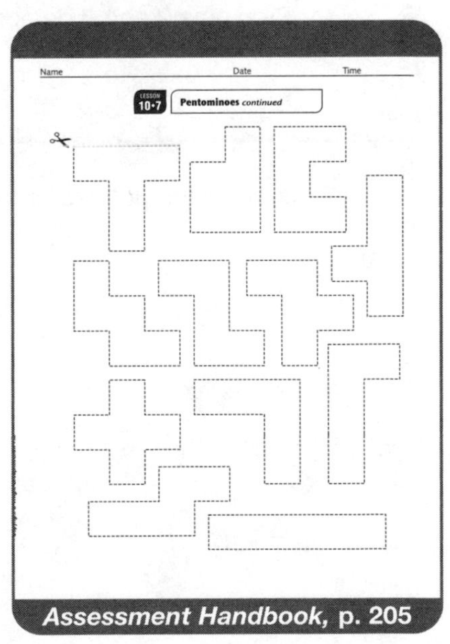

Name Date Time

LESSON 10•7 **Pentominoes** *continued*

Assessment Handbook, p. 205

Note: The wording and formatting of the text on the student samples that follow may vary slightly from the actual task your students will complete. These minor discrepancies will not affect the implementation of the task.

Rubric

This rubric is designed to help you assess levels of mathematical performance on this task. It emphasizes mathematical understanding with only a mention of clarity of explanation. Consider the expectations of standardized tests in your area when applying a rubric. Modify this sample rubric as appropriate.

Score	Description
4	Uses the specified shape in each rectangle. Completes the four rectangles with different configurations, although the same pentominoes might be used. Clearly describes whether the given shape is flipped, turned, or slid for each new configuration, but there might be omissions. Uses vocabulary correctly. For Problem 3, recognizes that and will not work together because they cannot fit in the rectangle together without leaving squares open.
3	Uses the specified figure in each rectangle. Completes the four rectangles with different configurations, although the same pentominoes might be used. Describes whether the given shape is flipped, turned, or slid for each new configuration. Might leave out some information about the translations. For Problem 3, recognizes that and will not work together.
2	Uses the specified figure in each rectangle. Attempts to complete the four rectangles with different configurations, but there might be some errors. The explanation makes sense in the context of the problem, but there might be errors or steps might be omitted. For Problem 3, might not describe why and will not work together.
1	Might use the specified figure in each rectangle. Might attempt to complete the four rectangles with different configurations, but there might be errors. The explanations for Problems 2 and 3 demonstrate little evidence of understanding translations.
0	Does not attempt to solve the problem.

Sample Student Responses

This Level 4 paper illustrates the following features: The four rectangles are completed and each one contains the required pentomino. The explanation in Problem 2 describes how the original figure is translated to get to the first rectangle, and then how it is flipped, slid, and turned for each subsequent rectangle. The explanation in Problem 3 includes a reference to the "little squares" that result when ✚ is used.

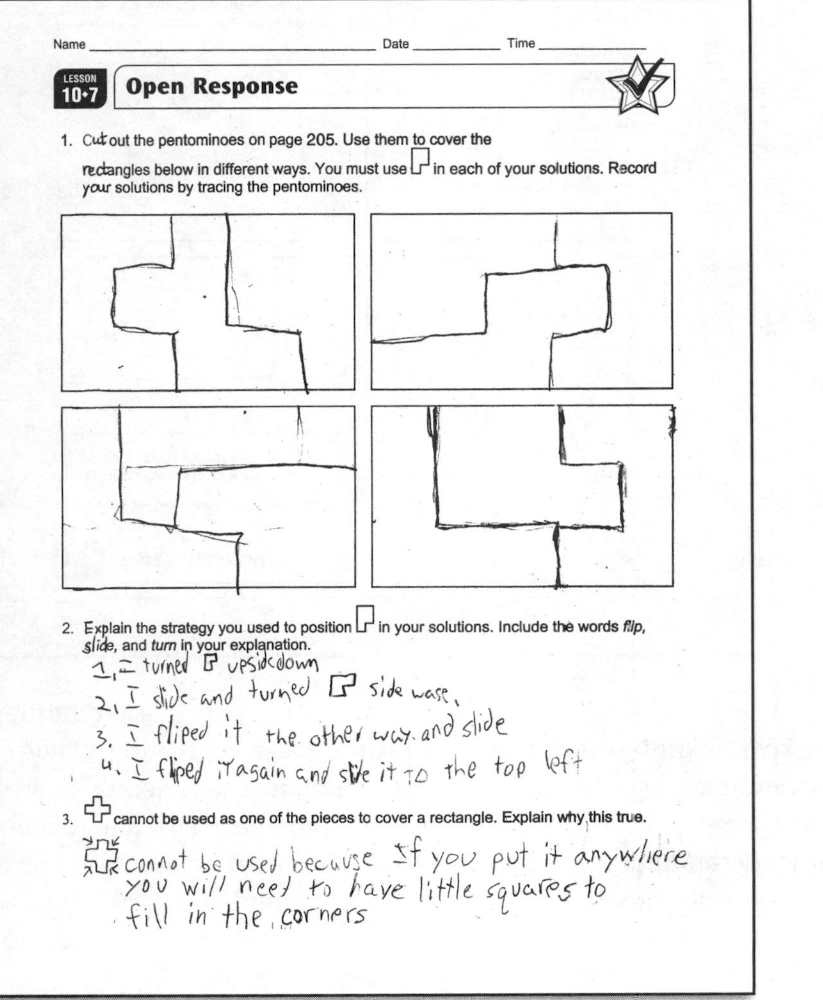

Name ______ Date ______ Time ______

LESSON 10•7 **Open Response**

1. Cut out the pentominoes on page 205. Use them to cover the rectangles below in different ways. You must use ⌐ in each of your solutions. Record your solutions by tracing the pentominoes.

2. Explain the strategy you used to position ⌐ in your solutions. Include the words *flip*, *slide*, and *turn* in your explanation.

1, I turned ⌐ upsidedown
2, I slide and turned ⌐ side wase,
3. I fliped it the other way. and slide
4. I fliped it again and slide it to the top left

3. ✚ cannot be used as one of the pieces to cover a rectangle. Explain why this true.

✚ connot be used becuase If you put it anywhere you will need to have little squares to fill in the corners

This Level 4 paper illustrates the following features: The four rectangles are completed and each one contains the required pentomino. The explanation in Problem 2 describes how the original figure is translated to get to the first rectangle, and then how it is flipped, slid, and turned for each subsequent rectangle. The explanation in Problem 3 includes a reference to the "open spaces" that result when ✚ is used.

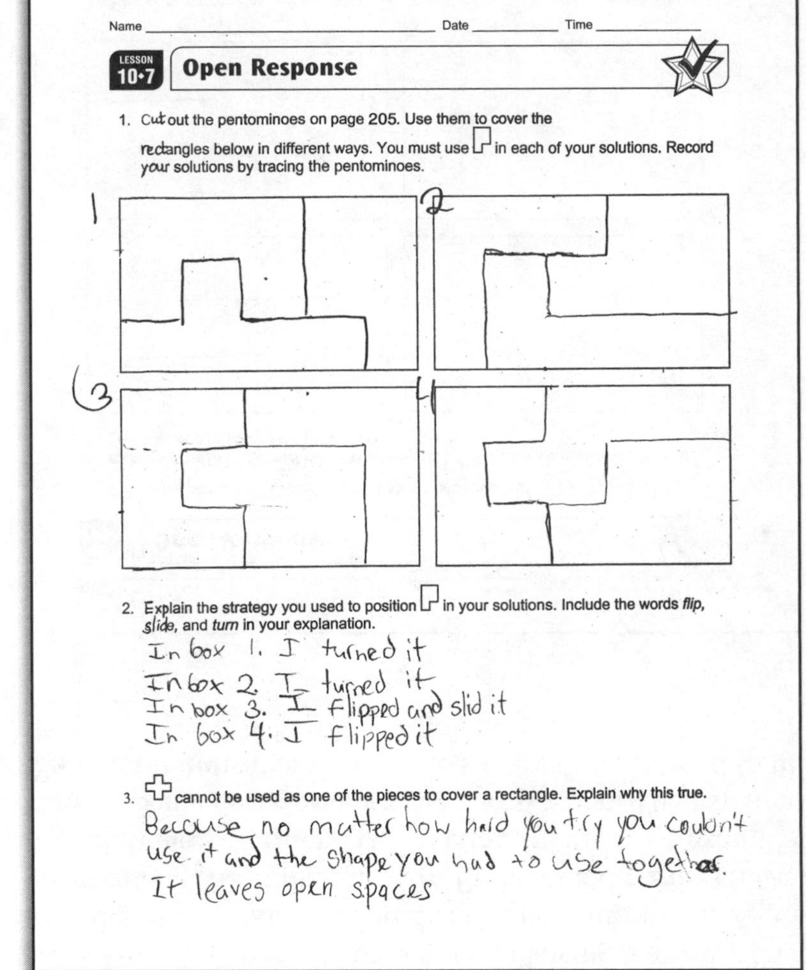

Name ______ Date ______ Time ______

LESSON 10•7 **Open Response**

1. Cut out the pentominoes on page 205. Use them to cover the rectangles below in different ways. You must use ⌐ in each of your solutions. Record your solutions by tracing the pentominoes.

2. Explain the strategy you used to position ⌐ in your solutions. Include the words *flip*, *slide*, and *turn* in your explanation.

In box 1. I turned it
In box 2. I turned it
In box 3. I flipped and slid it
In box 4. I flipped it

3. ✚ cannot be used as one of the pieces to cover a rectangle. Explain why this true.

Because no matter how hard you try you couldn't use it and the shape you had to use together. It leaves open spaces

This Level 3 paper illustrates the following features: The four rectangles are completed and each one contains the required pentomino. The explanation in Problem 2 describes how the original figure is translated to get to the first rectangle. Most of the translations are listed, but the descriptions only include one type of translation when more than one occurs. The explanation in Problem 3 includes a reference to the solution requiring two 'C' pentominoes.

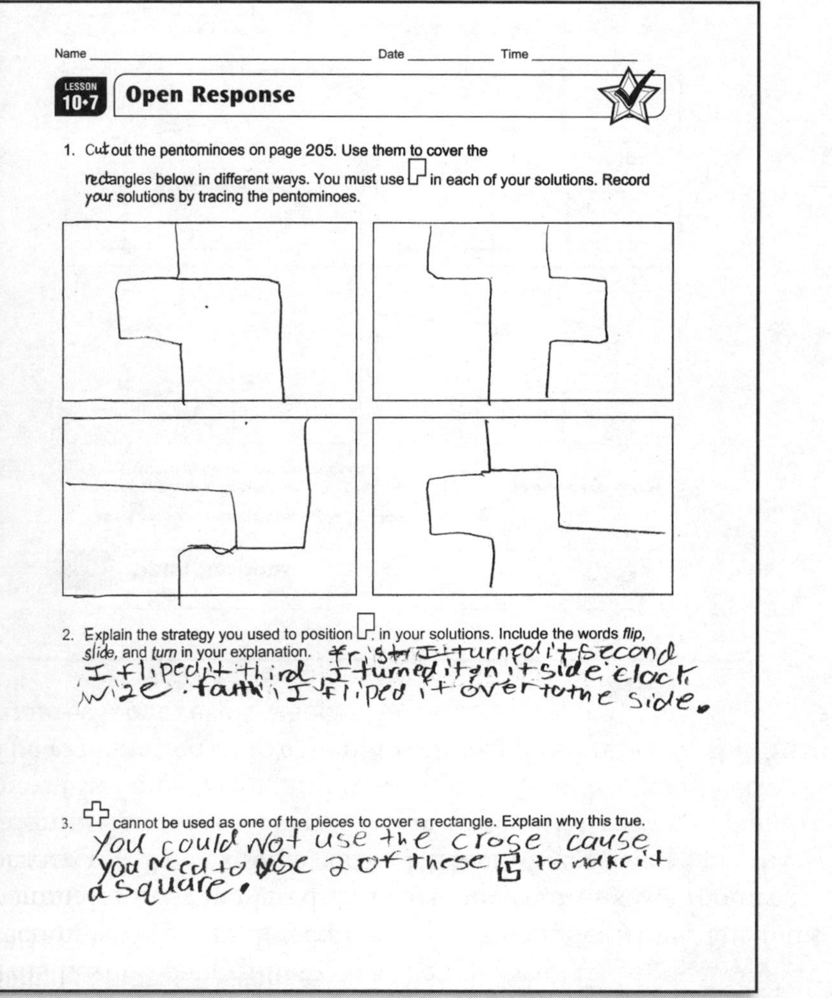

Name ______ Date ______ Time ______

LESSON 10•7 **Open Response**

1. Cut out the pentominoes on page 205. Use them to cover the rectangles below in different ways. You must use [pentomino] in each of your solutions. Record your solutions by tracing the pentominoes.

2. Explain the strategy you used to position [pentomino] in your solutions. Include the words *flip*, *slide*, and *turn* in your explanation.
frist I turned it second I fliped it third I turned it on it side clock wize forth I fliped it over to the side.

3. [cross pentomino] cannot be used as one of the pieces to cover a rectangle. Explain why this true.
You could not use the crose cause you need to use 2 of these [pentomino] to make it a square.

This Level 3 paper illustrates the following features: The four rectangles are completed and each one contains the required pentomino. The explanation in Problem 2 describes most of the translations, but imprecise language is used, for example, "upside down." Some descriptions need clarification. The explanation in Problem 3 indicates that "little squares" are needed to fill the space.

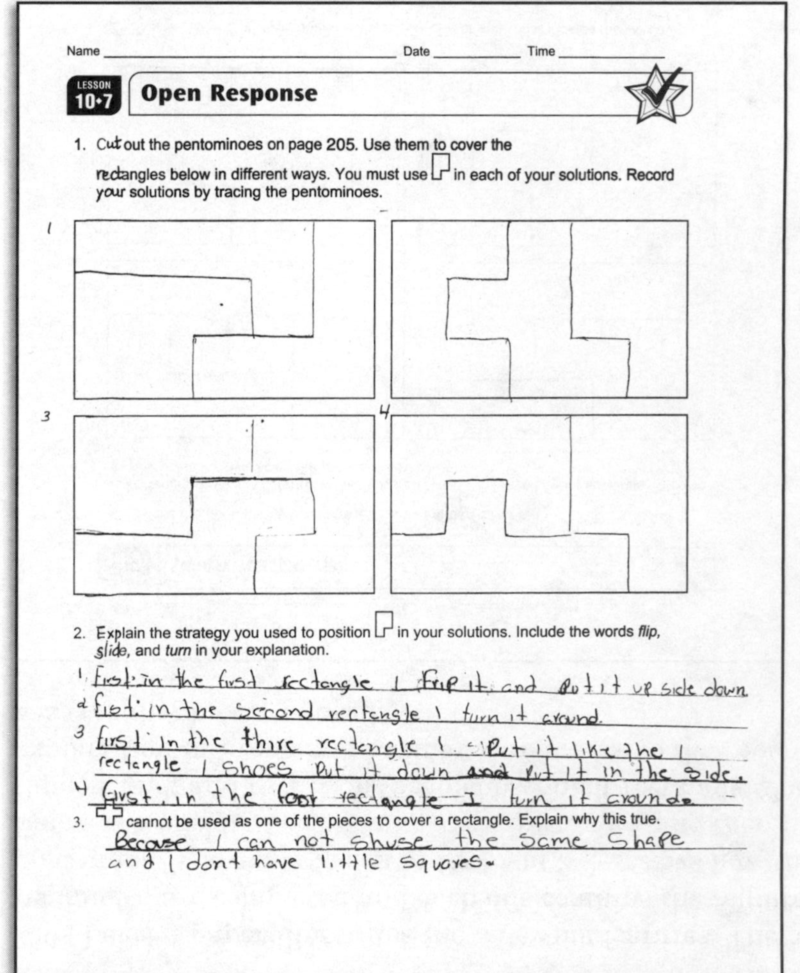

Name ______ Date ______ Time ______

LESSON 10•7 **Open Response**

1. Cut out the pentominoes on page 205. Use them to cover the rectangles below in different ways. You must use [pentomino] in each of your solutions. Record your solutions by tracing the pentominoes.

2. Explain the strategy you used to position [pentomino] in your solutions. Include the words *flip*, *slide*, and *turn* in your explanation.
1 First: in the fust rectangle I flip it and put it up side down
2 fist: in the second rectangle I turn it around.
3 first in the thire rectangle I put it like the 1 rectangle I shoes put it down and put it in the side.
4 First: in the foot rectangle I turn it around.

3. [cross pentomino] cannot be used as one of the pieces to cover a rectangle. Explain why this true.
Because I can not shuse the same shape and I dont have little squares.

This Level 2 paper illustrates the following features: The four rectangles are completed and each one contains the required pentomino. The explanation in Problem 2 describes how the original figure is translated to get each rectangle. The descriptions for the first and fourth rectangles do not include mathematical language. The explanation in Problem 3 attempts to describe various aspects of using ✚, explaining why this shape will not fit in a corner of the rectangle.

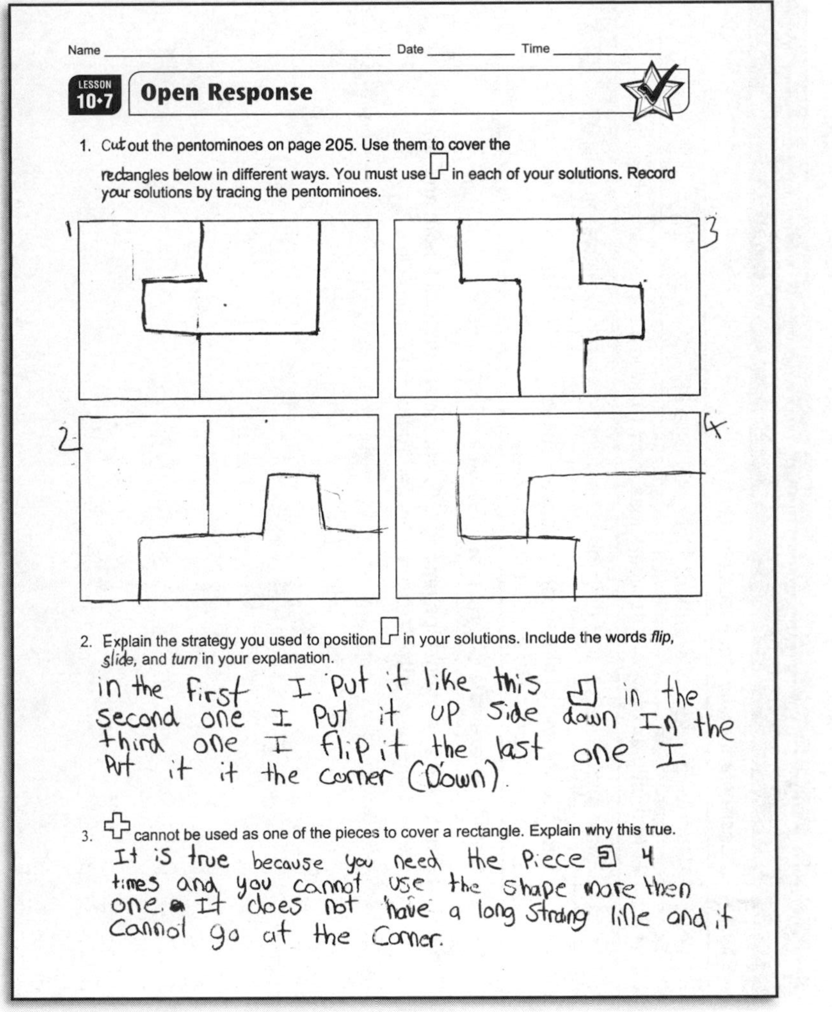

Name ______ Date ______ Time ______

LESSON 10·7 **Open Response**

1. Cut out the pentominoes on page 205. Use them to cover the rectangles below in different ways. You must use ⌐ in each of your solutions. Record your solutions by tracing the pentominoes.

2. Explain the strategy you used to position ⌐ in your solutions. Include the words *flip, slide,* and *turn* in your explanation.
in the First I put it like this in the second one I put it up side down In the third one I flip it the last one I put it it the corner (Down).

3. ✚ cannot be used as one of the pieces to cover a rectangle. Explain why this true.
It is true because you need the piece 4 times and you cannot use the shape more then one. It does not have a long straing line and it cannot go at the corner.

This Level 1 paper illustrates the following features: The four rectangles are completed and each one contains the required pentomino. The explanation seems to describe the relationship between two of the specified shapes that are contained in both Rectangles 1 and 2. The description listed for Rectangle 4 is incorrect. The explanation in Problem 3 includes a reference indicating that "little squares" are needed.

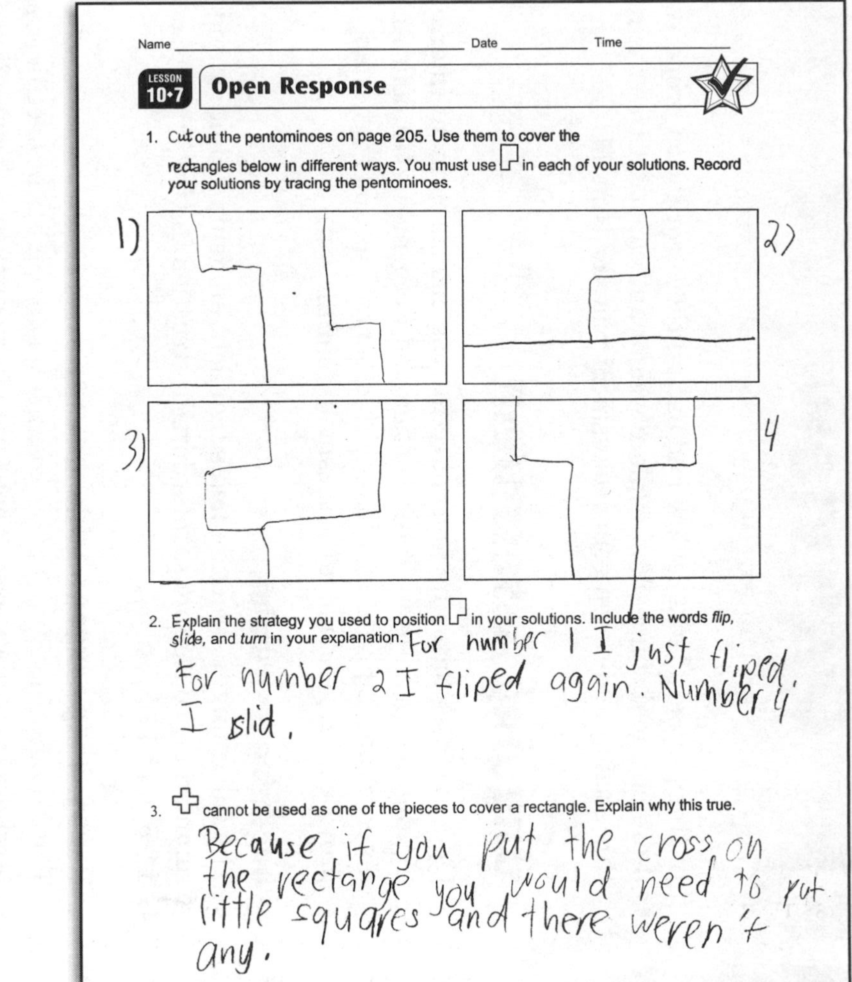

Name ______ Date ______ Time ______

LESSON 10·7 **Open Response**

1. Cut out the pentominoes on page 205. Use them to cover the rectangles below in different ways. You must use ⌐ in each of your solutions. Record your solutions by tracing the pentominoes.

2. Explain the strategy you used to position ⌐ in your solutions. Include the words *flip, slide,* and *turn* in your explanation.
For number 1 I just fliped. For number 2 I fliped again. Number 4 I slid.

3. ✚ cannot be used as one of the pieces to cover a rectangle. Explain why this true.
Because if you put the cross on the rectange you would need to put little squares and there weren't any.

Unit 11 Assessment Overview

In this unit, students review and extend their work with properties of 3-dimensional shapes and explore weight and capacity. Use the information in this section to develop your assessment plan for Unit 11.

Ongoing Assessment

Opportunities for using and collecting ongoing assessment information are highlighted in Informing Instruction and Recognizing Student Achievement notes. Student products, along with observations and suggested writing prompts, provide a range of useful assessment information.

Informing Instruction

The Informing Instruction notes highlight students' thinking and point out common misconceptions. Informing Instruction in Unit 11: Lessons 11-1, 11-5, 11-6, and 11-7.

Recognizing Student Achievement

The Recognizing Student Achievement notes highlight specific tasks from which teachers can collect assessment data to monitor and document students' progress toward meeting Grade-Level Goals.

Lesson	Content Assessed	Where to Find It
11◆1	**Describe a translation.** [Geometry Goal 3]	*TLG*, p. 852
11◆2	**Describe a rectangular prism.** [Geometry Goal 2]	*TLG*, p. 857
11◆3	**Find multiples of whole numbers less than 10.** [Number and Numeration Goal 3]	*TLG*, p. 864
11◆4	**Solve multiplication and division facts.** [Operations and Computation Goal 3]	*TLG*, p. 867
11◆5	**Find the volume of stacks of centimeter cubes.** [Measurement and Reference Frames Goal 2]	*TLG*, p. 876
11◆6	**Identify an example of a rotation.** [Geometry Goal 3]	*TLG*, p. 881
11◆7	**Describe the relationships among U.S. customary units of length and among metric units of length.** [Measurement and Reference Frames Goal 3]	*TLG*, p. 887

Math Boxes

Math Boxes, one of several types of tasks highlighted in the Recognizing Student Achievement notes, have an additional useful feature. Math Boxes in most lessons are paired or linked with Math Boxes in one or two other lessons that have similar problems. Paired or linked Math Boxes in Unit 11: 11-1 and 11-3; 11-2, 11-4, and 11-6; and 11-5 and 11-7.

Writing/Reasoning Prompts

In Unit 11, a variety of writing prompts encourage students to explain their strategies and thinking, to reflect on their learning, and to make connections to other mathematics or life experiences. Here are some of the Unit 11 suggestions:

Lesson	Writing/Reasoning Prompts	Where to Find It
11•2	Explain how you would determine the number of calories in $3\frac{1}{2}$ bagels.	*TLG*, p. 858
11•4	Explain how you rounded each number to the nearest tenth.	*TLG*, p. 870
11•5	Explain the likelihood of each of the events using probability terms.	*TLG*, p. 876

Portfolio Opportunities

Portfolios are a versatile tool for assessment. They help students reflect on their mathematical growth and help teachers understand and document that growth. Each unit identifies several student products that can be selected and stored in a portfolio. Here are some of the Unit 11 suggestions.

Lesson	Portfolio Opportunities	Where to Find It
11•3	Students create cube nets.	*TLG*, p. 865
11•4	Students build penticubes and describe surface areas.	*TLG*, p. 871
11•5	Students estimate the volume of a sheet of paper.	*TLG*, p. 877
11•7	Students model the capacity of annual rice consumption for a Thai family of 4.	*TLG*, p. 888
11•8	Students solve a record rainfall problem.	*TLG*, p. 893

Periodic Assessment

Every Progress Check lesson includes opportunities to observe students' progress and to collect student products in a variety of ways—Self Assessment, Oral and Slate Assessment, Written Assessment, and an Open Response task. For more details, see the first page of Progress Check 11, Lesson 11-8 on page 890, of the *Teacher's Lesson Guide*.

Progress Check Modifications

Written Assessments are one way students demonstrate what they know. The table below shows modifications for the Written Assessment in this unit. Use these to maximize opportunities for students to demonstrate what they know. Modifications can be given individually or written on the board for the class.

Problem(s)	Modifications for Written Assessment
2–5	For Problems 2–5, use a set of geometric solids to help you answer the questions.
9	For Problem 9, describe two different ways you can find the volume for the stacked cubes.
13, 14	For Problems 13 and 14, build the figures with centimeter cubes before finding the volume.
15–22	For Problems 15–22, use a number line to add and subtract the signed numbers.

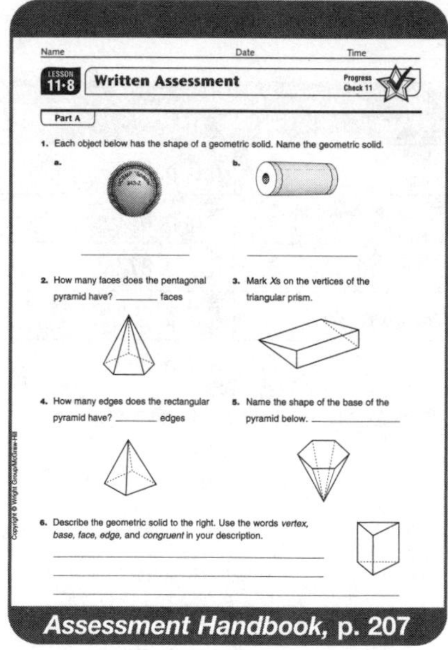

Name ______ Date ______ Time ______

LESSON 11·8 **Written Assessment** Progress Check 11

Part A

1. Each object below has the shape of a geometric solid. Name the geometric solid.

   a. ______

   b. ______

2. How many faces does the pentagonal pyramid have? ______ faces

3. Mark *X*s on the vertices of the triangular prism.

4. How many edges does the rectangular pyramid have? ______ edges

5. Name the shape of the base of the pyramid below. ______

6. Describe the geometric solid to the right. Use the words *vertex, base, face, edge,* and *congruent* in your description.

Assessment Handbook, p. 207

The Written Assessment for the Unit 11 Progress Check is on pages 207–209.

Open Response, *Record Rainfall*

Description

For this task, students develop and implement an estimation strategy for figuring out how much 42 inches of rainfall in a classroom would weigh.

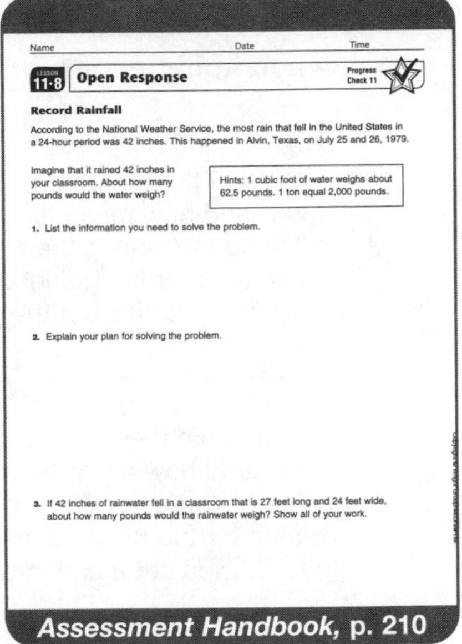

Name Date Time

LESSON 11·8 **Open Response** Progress Check 11

Record Rainfall

According to the National Weather Service, the most rain that fell in the United States in a 24-hour period was 42 inches. This happened in Alvin, Texas, on July 25 and 26, 1979.

Imagine that it rained 42 inches in your classroom. About how many pounds would the water weigh?

Hints: 1 cubic foot of water weighs about 62.5 pounds. 1 ton equal 2,000 pounds.

1. List the information you need to solve the problem.

2. Explain your plan for solving the problem.

3. If 42 inches of rainwater fell in a classroom that is 27 feet long and 24 feet wide, about how many pounds would the rainwater weigh? Show all of your work.

Assessment Handbook, p. 210

Focus

- **Make reasonable estimates for whole number and decimal multiplication problems.** [Operations and Computation Goal 6]
- **Explain how estimates for multiplication problems are obtained.** [Operations and Computation Goal 6]
- **Describe and use strategies to estimate the volume of rectangular prisms.** [Measurement and Reference Frames Goal 2]
- **Describe relationships among U.S. customary units of length and among metric units of length.** [Measurement and Reference Frames Goal 3]

Implementation Tips

- Review formulas for finding the area of a rectangle and the volume of a rectangular prism.
- Remind students that they have to convert all of their linear measurements to the same unit.
- Provide calculators for students to perform the computations.

Modifications for Meeting Diverse Needs

- Draw a rectangular prism and have students work together to label it with the dimensions for the problem they are solving—length is 27 feet, width is 24 feet, and height is 42 inches.
- Have students figure out how many tons the water would weigh.

Improving Open Response Skills

Before students begin the task, have them discuss what it means to make a plan and why it may be useful to plan before solving the problem. Have students share some of their ideas with the whole group before working independently. You might want to record and display some of their ideas about what a plan is.

Note: The wording and formatting of the text on the student samples that follow may vary slightly from the actual task your students will complete. These minor discrepancies will not affect the implementation of the task.

Rubric

This rubric is designed to help you assess levels of mathematical performance on this task. It emphasizes mathematical understanding with only a mention of clarity of explanation. Consider the expectations of standardized tests in your area when applying a rubric. Modify this sample rubric as appropriate.

4	Lists all of the required information—the dimensions of the room, the height of the water, and how much the water weighs. Clearly describes each step of the plan including measuring the classroom, converting linear units to the same unit, finding the volume for the height of the water, and multiplying the volume by the weight per cubic foot. Carries out the plan with correct computation.
3	Lists most of the required information—the dimensions of the room, the height of the water, and how much the water weighs. Describes some steps of a plan that might include measuring the classroom, converting linear units to the same unit, finding the volume for the height of the water, and multiplying the volume by the weight per cubic foot. Carries out the plan with only minor errors.
2	Lists some of the required information—the dimensions of the room, the height of the water, and how much the water weighs. Describes some steps of a plan that might include measuring the classroom, finding the volume for the height of the water, and multiplying the volume by the weight per cubic foot. Might convert linear measures to the same unit. Might carry out some of the plan but might have errors.
1	Lists some information that might relate to the problem. Describes the steps of a plan, some of which might relate to solving the problem. Might attempt to carry out some of the plan, but might make errors or demonstrate little evidence of understanding the problem.
0	Does not attempt to solve the problem.

Sample Student Responses

This Level 4 paper illustrates the following features: The important information is listed, including the dimensions of the room, height, and weight of the water. The plan clearly describes finding the dimensions, finding the volume after converting units, and calculating the total weight by multiplying the volume by the weight per cubic foot. Each step of the plan is shown and explained, and all computations are correct.

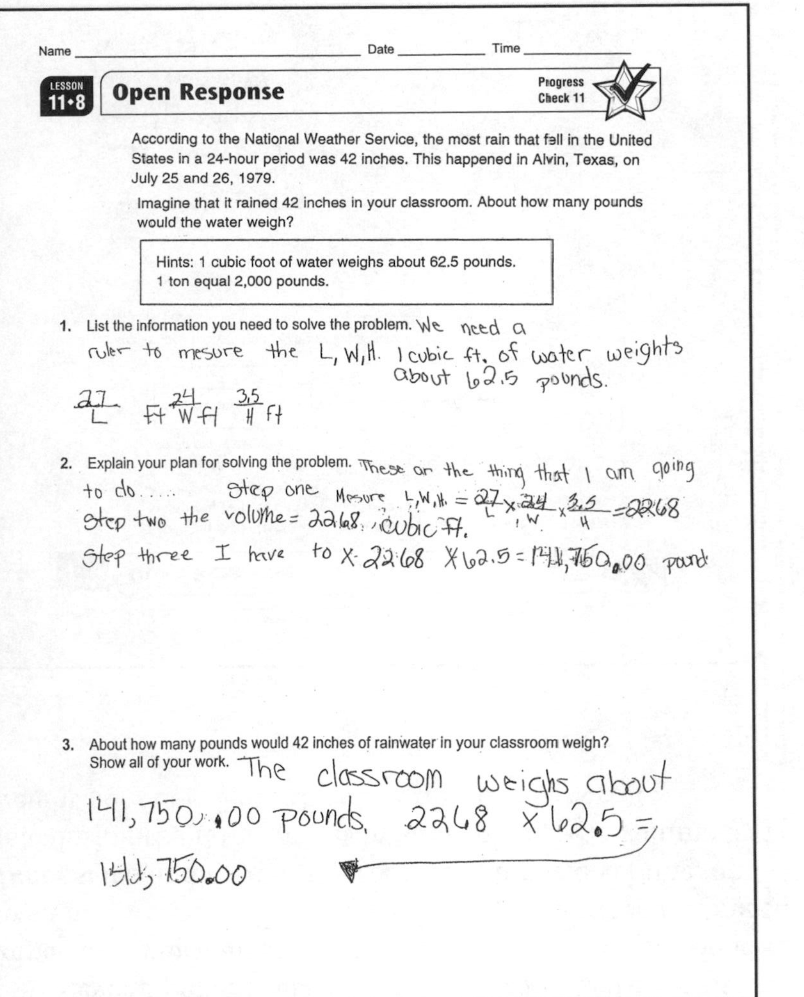

Name ______ Date ______ Time ______

LESSON 11•8 **Open Response** Progress Check 11

According to the National Weather Service, the most rain that fell in the United States in a 24-hour period was 42 inches. This happened in Alvin, Texas, on July 25 and 26, 1979.

Imagine that it rained 42 inches in your classroom. About how many pounds would the water weigh?

Hints: 1 cubic foot of water weighs about 62.5 pounds.
1 ton equal 2,000 pounds.

1. List the information you need to solve the problem. We need a ruler to mesure the L, W, H. 1 cubic ft. of water weights about 62.5 pounds.
27 L Ft 24 W ft 3.5 H ft

2. Explain your plan for solving the problem. These or the thing that I am going to do..... Step one Mesure L,W,H. = 27 L x 24 W x 3.5 H = 2268
Step two the volume = 2268, cubic ft.
Step three I have to x 2268 x 62.5 = 141,750.00 pound

3. About how many pounds would 42 inches of rainwater in your classroom weigh? Show all of your work. The classroom weighs about 141,750.00 pounds. 2268 x 62.5 =
141,750.00

This Level 4 paper illustrates the following features: The important information is listed, including the dimensions of the room, height, and weight of the water. The plan clearly describes finding the dimensions, converting the height of the water to the same unit, finding the volume with a formula, and calculating the total weight. Each step of the plan is shown and completely explained, and all computations are correct.

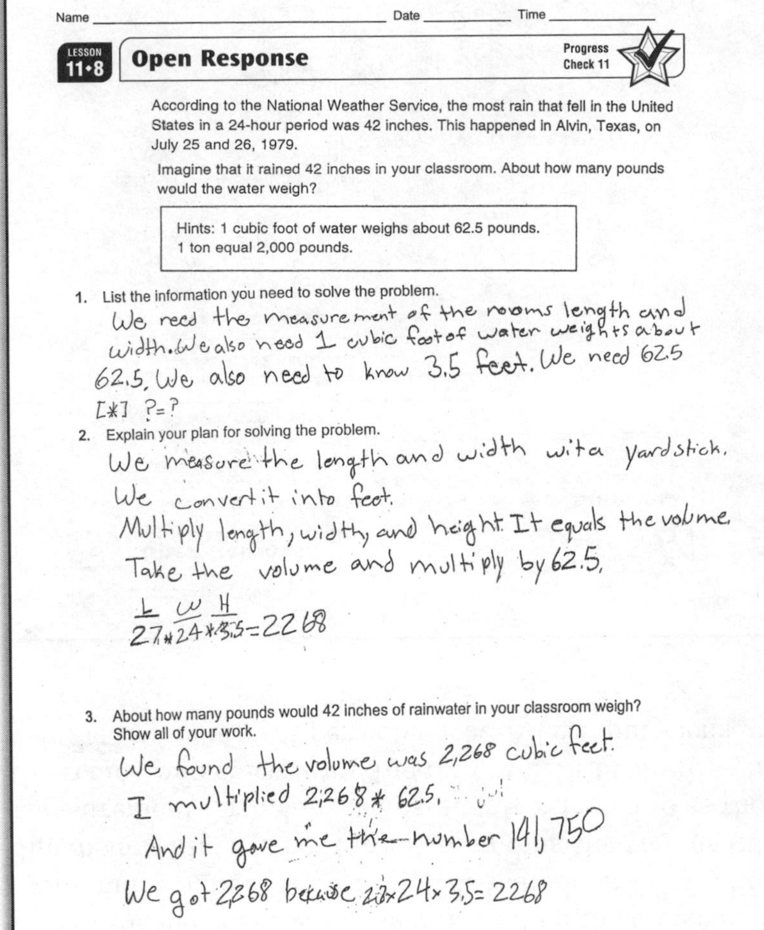

Name ______ Date ______ Time ______

LESSON 11•8 **Open Response** Progress Check 11

According to the National Weather Service, the most rain that fell in the United States in a 24-hour period was 42 inches. This happened in Alvin, Texas, on July 25 and 26, 1979.

Imagine that it rained 42 inches in your classroom. About how many pounds would the water weigh?

Hints: 1 cubic foot of water weighs about 62.5 pounds.
1 ton equal 2,000 pounds.

1. List the information you need to solve the problem.
We need the measurement of the rooms length and width. We also need 1 cubic foot of water weights about 62.5. We also need to know 3.5 feet. We need 62.5 [*] ?=?

2. Explain your plan for solving the problem.
We measure the length and width with a yardstick.
We convert it into feet.
Multiply length, width, and height. It equals the volume.
Take the volume and multiply by 62.5.
L W H
27 * 24 * 3.5 = 2268

3. About how many pounds would 42 inches of rainwater in your classroom weigh? Show all of your work.
We found the volume was 2,268 cubic feet.
I multiplied 2,268 * 62.5.
And it gave me the number 141,750
We got 2268 because 27x24x3.5 = 2268

This Level 3 paper illustrates the following features: Some of the important information is listed, including the dimensions of the room and weight of the water. The plan describes finding the dimensions and area of the room, finding the volume, and calculating the total weight by multiplying the volume by the weight per cubic foot. All computations are correct.

Name ______ Date ______ Time ______

LESSON 11•8 **Open Response** Progress Check 11

According to the National Weather Service, the most rain that fell in the United States in a 24-hour period was 42 inches. This happened in Alvin, Texas, on July 25 and 26, 1979.

Imagine that it rained 42 inches in your classroom. About how many pounds would the water weigh?

Hints: 1 cubic foot of water weighs about 62.5 pounds.
1 ton equal 2,000 pounds.

1. List the information you need to solve the problem.
Measurment of length & width of classroom.
62.5 * ? = ?

2. Explain your plan for solving the problem.
1. Measure length and width
2. Convert meachurments into feet
3. Multiply length * width * height
4. multiply volume by 62.5
5. Multiply 27 feet by 24 feet by 3.5 feet, width = 27 ft length = 24 ft = 648

3. About how many pounds would 42 inches of rainwater in your classroom weigh? Show all of your work.
The volume was 2268 cubic feet
I multiplied 62.5 by 2268 = 141,750 pounds.

This Level 3 paper illustrates the following features: Some of the important information is listed, including the dimensions of the room and weight of the water. The plan describes finding the dimensions and area of the room, finding the volume (although the measurement for height is mistakenly referred to as the height of the room), and calculating the total weight by multiplying the volume by the weight per cubic foot. All computations are correct.

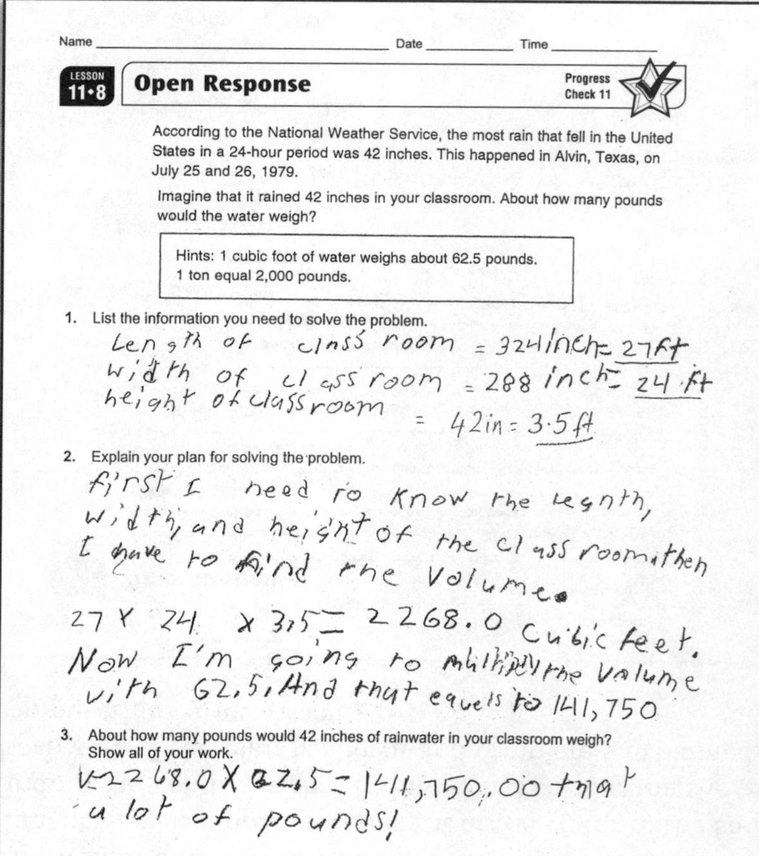

Name ______ Date ______ Time ______

LESSON 11•8 **Open Response** Progress Check 11

According to the National Weather Service, the most rain that fell in the United States in a 24-hour period was 42 inches. This happened in Alvin, Texas, on July 25 and 26, 1979.

Imagine that it rained 42 inches in your classroom. About how many pounds would the water weigh?

Hints: 1 cubic foot of water weighs about 62.5 pounds.
1 ton equal 2,000 pounds.

1. List the information you need to solve the problem.
Length of class room = 324 inch = 27 ft
width of classroom = 288 inch = 24 ft
height of classroom = 42 in = 3.5 ft

2. Explain your plan for solving the problem.
first I need to know the length, width, and height of the classroom then I have to find the volume.
27 X 24 X 3.5 = 2268.0 Cubic feet.
Now I'm going to multiply the volume with 62.5, And that equels to 141,750

3. About how many pounds would 42 inches of rainwater in your classroom weigh? Show all of your work.
V = 2268.0 X 62.5 = 141,750.00 that a lot of pounds!

This Level 2 paper illustrates the following features: The important information referred to is the height of the rain and dimensions of the room. The plan describes finding the dimensions of the room multiplied by the height. The computation shown does not make sense. There is no evidence that the plan was followed.

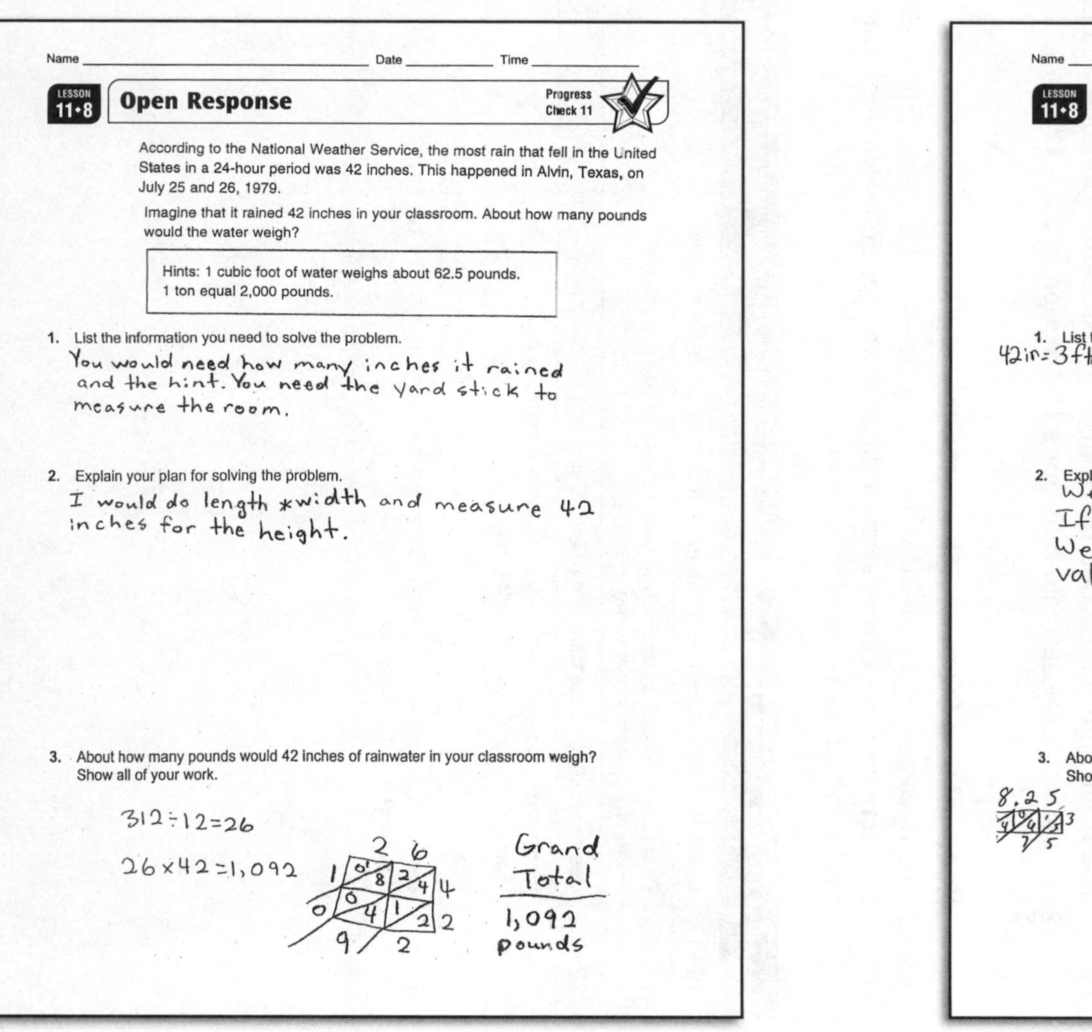

Name ______ Date ______ Time ______

LESSON 11•8 **Open Response** Progress Check 11

According to the National Weather Service, the most rain that fell in the United States in a 24-hour period was 42 inches. This happened in Alvin, Texas, on July 25 and 26, 1979.

Imagine that it rained 42 inches in your classroom. About how many pounds would the water weigh?

Hints: 1 cubic foot of water weighs about 62.5 pounds.
1 ton equal 2,000 pounds.

1. List the information you need to solve the problem.
   You would need how many inches it rained and the hint. You need the yard stick to measure the room.

2. Explain your plan for solving the problem.
   I would do length *width and measure 42 inches for the height.

3. About how many pounds would 42 inches of rainwater in your classroom weigh? Show all of your work.
   312÷12=26
   26×42=1,092
   Grand Total 1,092 pounds

This Level 1 paper illustrates the following features: The important information referred to shows converting the height of rain from inches to feet. The plan describes multiplying the height in inches by the weight per cubic foot. The work provides no evidence of understanding the problem.

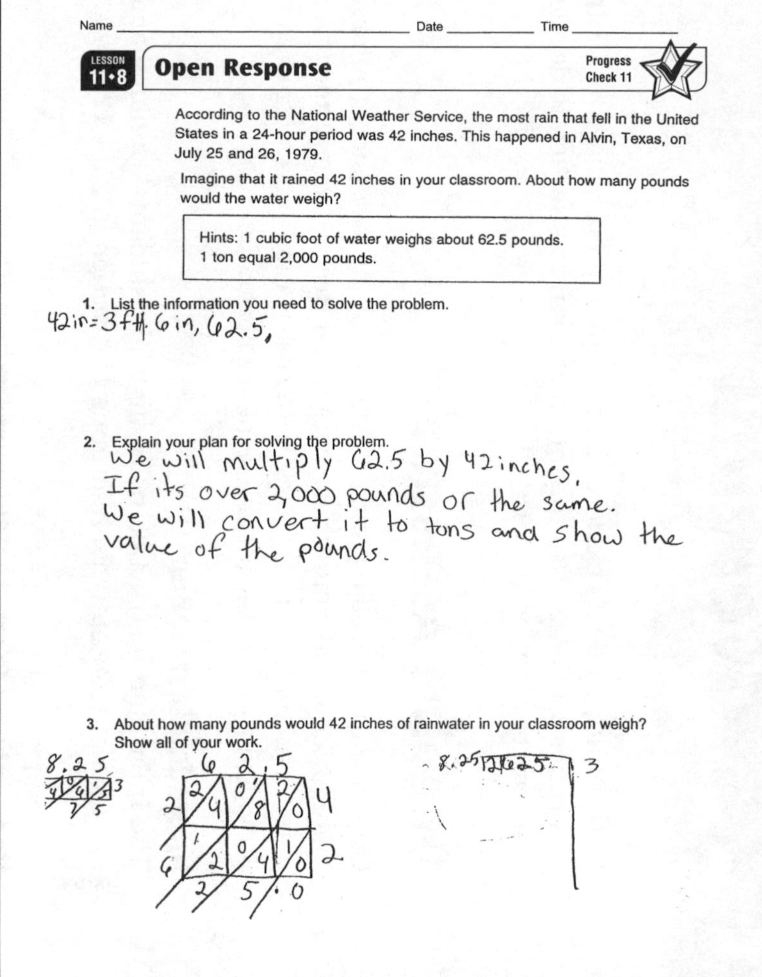

Name ______ Date ______ Time ______

LESSON 11•8 **Open Response** Progress Check 11

According to the National Weather Service, the most rain that fell in the United States in a 24-hour period was 42 inches. This happened in Alvin, Texas, on July 25 and 26, 1979.

Imagine that it rained 42 inches in your classroom. About how many pounds would the water weigh?

Hints: 1 cubic foot of water weighs about 62.5 pounds.
1 ton equal 2,000 pounds.

1. List the information you need to solve the problem.
   42in=3ft 6in, 62.5,

2. Explain your plan for solving the problem.
   We will multiply 62.5 by 42inches. If its over 2,000 pounds or the same. We will convert it to tons and show the value of the pounds.

3. About how many pounds would 42 inches of rainwater in your classroom weigh? Show all of your work.
   8.25
   62.5 × 42 = 2,625.0
   8.25)2625 3

Assessment Overview

In this unit, students explore the concept of proportional reasoning through rates and ratios problems. Use the information in this section to develop your assessment plan for Unit 12.

Ongoing Assessment

Opportunities for using and collecting ongoing assessment information are highlighted in Informing Instruction and Recognizing Student Achievement notes. Student products, along with observations and suggested writing prompts, provide a range of useful assessment information.

Informing Instruction

The Informing Instruction notes highlight students' thinking and point out common misconceptions. Informing Instruction in Unit 12: Lessons 12-2, 12-3, and 12-4.

Recognizing Student Achievement

The Recognizing Student Achievement notes highlight specific tasks from which teachers can collect assessment data to monitor and document students' progress toward meeting Grade-Level Goals.

Lesson	Content Assessed	Where to Find It
12•1	**Compare integers between 100 and −100.** [Number and Numeration Goal 6]	*TLG,* p. 912
12•2	**Describe a rule for a pattern and use the rule to solve problems.** [Patterns, Functions, and Algebra Goal 1]	*TLG,* p. 918
12•3	**Use given data to create a line graph.** [Data and Chance Goal 1]	*TLG,* p. 924
12•4	**Insert grouping symbols to make number sentences true.** [Patterns, Functions, and Algebra Goal 3]	*TLG,* p. 929
12•5	**Use scaling to model multiplication and division.** [Operations and Computation Goal 7]	*TLG,* p. 933
12•6	**Demonstrate automaticity with multiplication facts through 10 * 10.** [Operations and Computation Goal 3]	*TLG,* p. 938

Math Boxes

Math Boxes, one of several types of tasks highlighted in the Recognizing Student Achievement notes, have an additional useful feature. Math Boxes in most lessons are paired or linked with Math Boxes in one or two other lessons that have similar problems. Paired or linked Math Boxes in Unit 12: 12-1 and 12-3; 12-2, 12-4, and 12-6; and 12-5 and 12-7.

Writing/Reasoning Prompts

In Unit 12, a variety of writing prompts encourage students to explain their strategies and thinking, to reflect on their learning, and to make connections to other mathematics or life experiences. Here are some of the Unit 12 suggestions:

Lesson	Writing/Reasoning Prompts	Where to Find It
12•2	Describe two events that are equally likely and express the probability of each event as a fraction.	*TLG*, p. 918
12•3	Explain how you knew that you had listed all of the factors of a number.	*TLG*, p. 924
12•5	Describe how you can find the number of cups in $5\frac{3}{4}$ gallons and check your answer.	*TLG*, p. 934

Portfolio Opportunities

Portfolios are a versatile tool for assessment. They help students reflect on their mathematical growth and help teachers understand and document that growth. Each unit identifies several student products that can be selected and stored in a portfolio. Here are some of the Unit 12 suggestions:

Lesson	Portfolio Opportunities	Where to Find It
12•1	Students create a side-by-side bar graph to display eye-blinking data.	*TLG*, p. 913
12•2	Students use values found in a rate table to make a line graph.	*TLG*, p. 919
12•7	Students use rates to solve a cookie-buying problem.	*TLG*, p. 945

Periodic Assessment

Every Progress Check lesson includes opportunities to observe students' progress and to collect student products in a variety of ways—Self Assessment, Oral and Slate Assessment, Written Assessment, and an Open Response task. For more details, see the first page of Progress Check 12, Lesson 12-7, page 941, of the *Teacher's Lesson Guide*.

Progress Check Modifications

Written Assessments are one way students demonstrate what they know. The table below shows modifications for the Written Assessment in this unit. Use these to maximize opportunities for students to demonstrate what they know. Modifications can be given individually or written on the board for the class.

Problem(s)	Modifications for Written Assessment
2	**For Problem 2, explain how you found the rate for 5 lawns. Record number sentences you can use to solve the problem.**
5	**For Problem 5, build arrays with 64 counters to help you find the factors.**
6, 7	**For Problems 6 and 7, use a number line to help you compare and order the signed numbers.**
9	**For Problem 9, build each prism with centimeter cubes before finding the volume.**

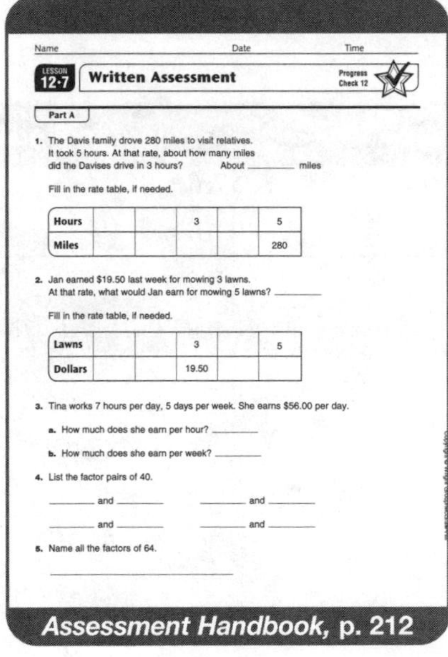

Name Date Time

LESSON 12·7 **Written Assessment** Progress Check 12

Part A

1. The Davis family drove 280 miles to visit relatives. It took 5 hours. At that rate, about how many miles did the Davises drive in 3 hours? About ______ miles

Fill in the rate table, if needed.

Hours			3		5
Miles					280

2. Jan earned $19.50 last week for mowing 3 lawns. At that rate, what would Jan earn for mowing 5 lawns? ______

Fill in the rate table, if needed.

Lawns			3		5
Dollars			19.50		

3. Tina works 7 hours per day, 5 days per week. She earns $56.00 per day.

a. How much does she earn per hour? ______

b. How much does she earn per week? ______

4. List the factor pairs of 40.

______ and ______ ______ and ______

______ and ______ ______ and ______

5. Name all the factors of 64.

______

Assessment Handbook, p. 212

The Written Assessment for the Unit 12 Progress Check is on pages 212–214.

Open Response, *Buying Cookies*

Description

For this task, students find the best buy for a variety of cookies.

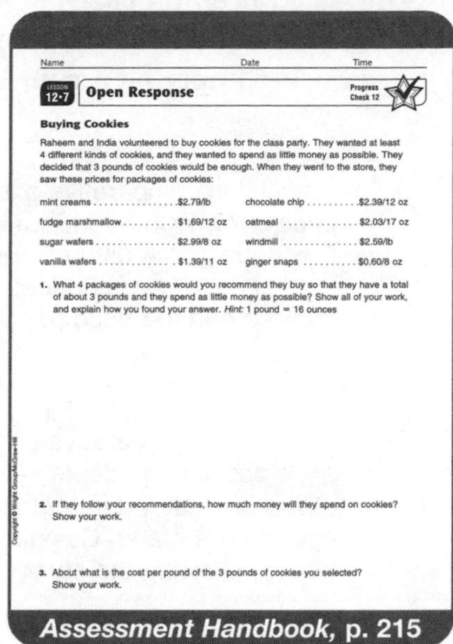

Name Date Time

LESSON 12•7 **Open Response** Progress Check 12

Buying Cookies

Raheem and India volunteered to buy cookies for the class party. They wanted at least 4 different kinds of cookies, and they wanted to spend as little money as possible. They decided that 3 pounds of cookies would be enough. When they went to the store, they saw these prices for packages of cookies:

mint creams . . . .$2.79/lb — chocolate chip . . . .$2.39/12 oz
fudge marshmallow . . . . $1.69/12 oz — oatmeal . . . . $2.03/17 oz
sugar wafers . . . . $2.99/8 oz — windmill $2.59/lb
vanilla wafers . . . . $1.39/11 oz — ginger snaps . . . . $0.60/8 oz

1. What 4 packages of cookies would you recommend they buy so that they have a total of about 3 pounds and they spend as little money as possible? Show all of your work, and explain how you found your answer. *Hint:* 1 pound = 16 ounces

2. If they follow your recommendations, how much money will they spend on cookies? Show your work.

3. About what is the cost per pound of the 3 pounds of cookies you selected? Show your work.

Assessment Handbook, p. 215

Focus

- **Use mental arithmetic and paper-and-pencil algorithms to solve problems involving the addition of decimals through hundredths. Describe the strategies used and explain how they work.** [Operations and Computation Goal 2]
- **Use mental arithmetic, paper-and-pencil algorithms, and a calculator to solve problems involving division. Describe the strategies used and explain how they work.** [Operations and Computation Goal 4]
- **Use scaling to model multiplication and division.** [Operations and Computation Goal 7]

Implementation Tips

- Review how to compare rates to calculate best buys. Scaling the rates of all packages to the unit price is one way to make this comparison.
- Provide calculators for computing unit prices.

Modifications for Meeting Diverse Needs

- Change pounds to ounces for the cookie packages. Create a chart for all cookies like the one below. Have students work together to calculate price per ounce and to complete the chart.

Cookie	Price at the Store	Price per Ounce
Mint Creams	$2.79/16 oz	17¢
Fudge Marshmallow	$1.69/12 oz	

- Have students write instructions on how to determine the best buy in any situation.

Improving Open Response Skills

After students complete the task, have them translate Level 4 of the rubric into their own words, record it on chart paper, and post it. Have students discuss the meaning of the statements in the rubric in small groups. After the discussion, have students take their own papers and try to improve or enhance their explanations according to the rubric.

Rubric

This rubric is designed to help you assess levels of mathematical performance on this task. It emphasizes mathematical understanding with only a mention of clarity of explanation. Consider the expectations of standardized tests in your area when applying a rubric. Modify this sample rubric as appropriate.

4	Calculates comparative prices by computing the price per ounce or the price per pound. Identifies the best buys and the cheapest combination for exactly 3 pounds with 4 different kinds of cookies. Clearly explains how cookie choices are made based on unit prices and weight. Calculates the total cost of the chosen cookies and the price per pound by explaining or showing the computation used.
3	Calculates comparative prices by computing the price per ounce or the price per pound. Identifies the best buys and the cheapest combination for exactly 3 pounds with 4 different kinds of cookies. Explains some steps for how cookie choices are made. Calculates the total cost of the chosen cookies and the price per pound, showing the computation used, but there might be minor errors.
2	Identifies 4 cookie choices, and explains some steps of how cookie choices are made. The explanation might refer to cost or the target weight of 3 pounds. Attempts to calculate the total cost for the chosen cookies and the price per pound. Might show the operations and numbers used, but there might be computation errors.
1	Identifies 4 cookie choices and might explain some steps for how the cookie choices are made. The explanation might not make sense in the context of the problem. Might attempt to calculate the total cost for the chosen cookies and the price per pound, but might demonstrate little evidence of understanding the problem.
0	Does not attempt to solve the problem.

Sample Student Responses

This Level 4 paper illustrates the following features: Prices per ounce are calculated and used to compare the cookie prices. The answer is recorded. The steps for choosing the cookie combination are clearly explained, beginning with finding the unit price and ending with checking the weight for a total of 3 pounds. The computation for finding the total cost and price per pound is recorded.

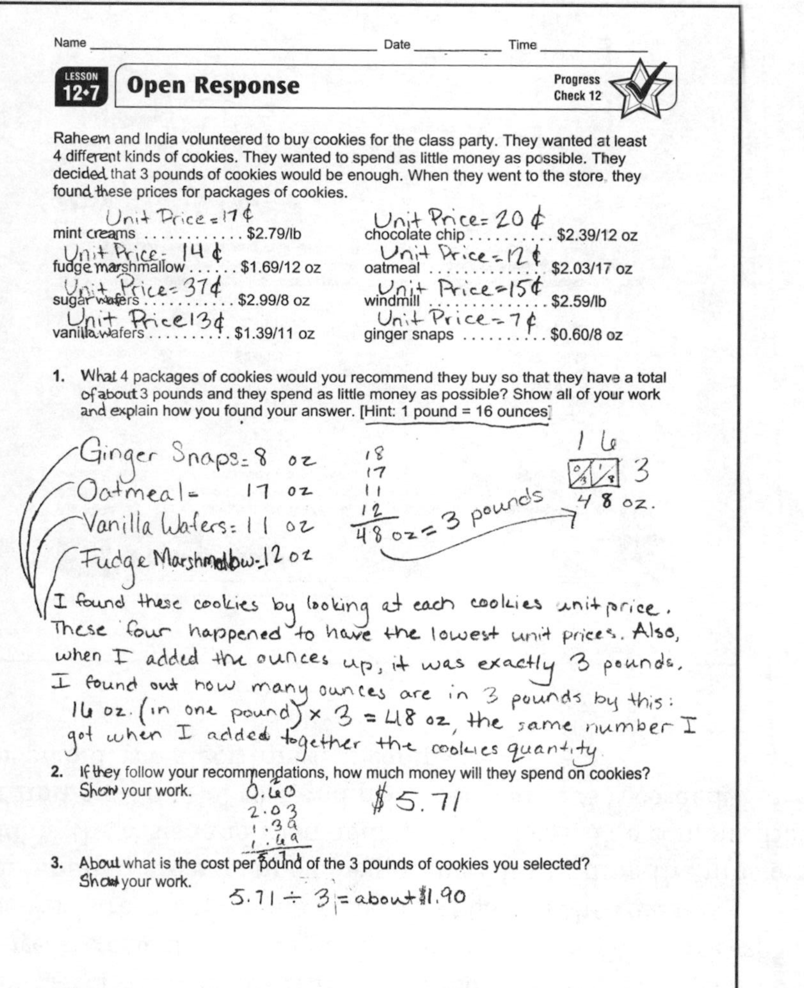

Name ______ Date ______ Time ______

LESSON 12•7 **Open Response** Progress Check 12

Raheem and India volunteered to buy cookies for the class party. They wanted at least 4 different kinds of cookies. They wanted to spend as little money as possible. They decided that 3 pounds of cookies would be enough. When they went to the store, they found these prices for packages of cookies.

Unit Price = 17¢ mint creams $2.79/lb	Unit Price = 20¢ chocolate chip .... $2.39/12 oz
Unit Price: 14¢ fudge marshmallow ...... $1.69/12 oz	Unit Price = 12¢ oatmeal .... $2.03/17 oz
Unit Price = 37¢ sugar wafers .... $2.99/8 oz	Unit Price = 15¢ windmill $2.59/lb
Unit Price 13¢ vanilla wafers .... $1.39/11 oz	Unit Price = 7¢ ginger snaps .... $0.60/8 oz

1. What 4 packages of cookies would you recommend they buy so that they have a total of about 3 pounds and they spend as little money as possible? Show all of your work and explain how you found your answer. [Hint: 1 pound = 16 ounces]

Ginger Snaps = 8 oz
Oatmeal = 17 oz
Vanilla Wafers: 11 oz
Fudge Marshmallow: 12 oz

18 + 17 + 11 + 12 = 48 oz = 3 pounds

16 × 3 = 48 oz.

I found these cookies by looking at each cookies unit price. These four happened to have the lowest unit prices. Also, when I added the ounces up, it was exactly 3 pounds. I found out how many ounces are in 3 pounds by this: 16 oz. (in one pound) × 3 = 48 oz, the same number I got when I added together the cookies quantity.

2. If they follow your recommendations, how much money will they spend on cookies? Show your work.

0.60 + 2.03 + 1.39 + 1.69 $5.71

3. About what is the cost per pound of the 3 pounds of cookies you selected? Show your work.

5.71 ÷ 3 = about $1.90

This Level 4 paper illustrates the following features: Prices per ounce are calculated and labeled and used to compare the cookie prices. The answer is recorded. In addition to listing the steps for finding the cookie combination, there are clear explanations for how to find the unit price, the total cost, and the price per pound. The number sentences for finding the total cost and price per pound are recorded.

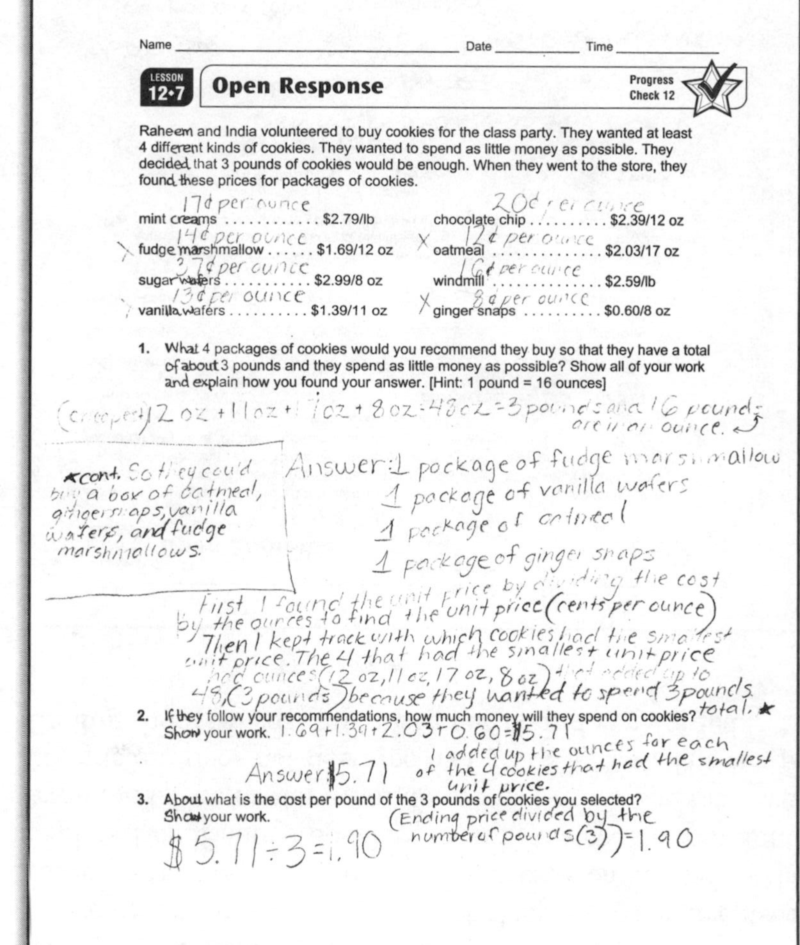

Name ______ Date ______ Time ______

LESSON 12•7 **Open Response** Progress Check 12

Raheem and India volunteered to buy cookies for the class party. They wanted at least 4 different kinds of cookies. They wanted to spend as little money as possible. They decided that 3 pounds of cookies would be enough. When they went to the store, they found these prices for packages of cookies.

17¢ per ounce mint creams $2.79/lb	20¢ per ounce chocolate chip .... $2.39/12 oz
14¢ per ounce ✓ fudge marshmallow ...... $1.69/12 oz	12¢ per ounce X oatmeal .... $2.03/17 oz
37¢ per ounce sugar wafers .... $2.99/8 oz	16¢ per ounce windmill $2.59/lb
13¢ per ounce ✓ vanilla wafers .... $1.39/11 oz	8¢ per ounce X ginger snaps .... $0.60/8 oz

1. What 4 packages of cookies would you recommend they buy so that they have a total of about 3 pounds and they spend as little money as possible? Show all of your work and explain how you found your answer. [Hint: 1 pound = 16 ounces]

(cheapest) 12 oz + 11 oz + 17 oz + 8 oz = 48 oz = 3 pounds and 16 pounds are in an ounce.

Answer: 1 package of fudge marshmallow
1 package of vanilla wafers
1 package of oatmeal
1 package of ginger snaps

*cont. So they could buy a box of oatmeal, ginger snaps, vanilla wafers, and fudge marshmallows.

First I found the unit price by dividing the cost by the ounces to find the unit price (cents per ounce). Then I kept track with which cookies had the smallest unit price. The 4 that had the smallest unit price had ounces (12 oz, 11 oz, 17 oz, 8 oz) that added up to 48 (3 pounds) because they wanted to spend 3 pounds total. ★

2. If they follow your recommendations, how much money will they spend on cookies? Show your work. 1.69 + 1.39 + 2.03 + 0.60 = $5.71

Answer $5.71   I added up the ounces for each of the 4 cookies that had the smallest unit price.

3. About what is the cost per pound of the 3 pounds of cookies you selected? Show your work.

$5.71 ÷ 3 = 1.90   (Ending price divided by the number of pounds (3)) = 1.90

This Level 3 paper illustrates the following features: Prices per ounce are calculated and used to compare the cookie prices. The answer is recorded. Some steps for choosing the cookie combination are explained, beginning with finding the unit price, adding the costs, and then adding the ounces. The computation for finding the total cost and price per pound is recorded. For price per pound, the algorithm is incomplete.

Name ______ Date ______ Time ______

LESSON 12•7 **Open Response** Progress Check 12

Raheem and India volunteered to buy cookies for the class party. They wanted at least 4 different kinds of cookies. They wanted to spend as little money as possible. They decided that 3 pounds of cookies would be enough. When they went to the store, they found these prices for packages of cookies.

mint creams	$2.79/lb	chocolate chip	$2.39/12 oz
fudge marshmallow	$1.69/12 oz	oatmeal	$2.03/17 oz
sugar wafers	$2.99/8 oz	windmill	$2.59/lb
vanilla wafers	$1.39/11 oz	ginger snaps	$0.60/8 oz

1. What 4 packages of cookies would you recommend they buy so that they have a total of about 3 pounds and they spend as little money as possible? Show all of your work and explain how you found your answer. [Hint: 1 pound = 16 ounces]

oatmeal 11¢ 17 oz
ginger snap 7¢ 8 oz
vinalla wafers 12¢ 11 oz
fudge marshmallow 14¢ 12 oz
48 oz

The first thing I did was that I found unit price. Then I found the 4 cheapest cookies and then I added the ounces. I added the cost and I found the 4 cookies

2. If they follow your recommendations, how much money will they spend on cookies? Show your work.

$5.71

3. About what is the cost per pound of the 3 pounds of cookies you selected? Show your work.

This Level 3 paper illustrates the following features: Prices per ounce are calculated, but it is not clear how they are used to compare the cookie prices. The answer is embedded in the explanation. Some steps for choosing the cookie combination are explained. The explanation describes finding the total weight of 3 pounds but does not describe using unit prices. The computation for finding the total cost and price per pound is recorded.

Name ______ Date ______ Time ______

LESSON 12•7 **Open Response** Progress Check 12

Raheem and India volunteered to buy cookies for the class party. They wanted at least 4 different kinds of cookies. They wanted to spend as little money as possible. They decided that 3 pounds of cookies would be enough. When they went to the store, they found these prices for packages of cookies.

mint creams	$2.79/lb	chocolate chip	$2.39/12 oz
fudge marshmallow	$1.69/12 oz	oatmeal	$2.03/17 oz
sugar wafers	$2.99/8 oz	windmill	$2.59/lb
vanilla wafers	$1.39/11 oz	ginger snaps	$0.60/8 oz

1. What 4 packages of cookies would you recommend they buy so that they have a total of about 3 pounds and they spend as little money as possible? Show all of your work and explain how you found your answer. [Hint: 1 pound = 16 ounces]

First I multipy 3 x 16 which equal 48oz. then I divide the weight and the money for each cookie then I looked at the lowest amount of cookies to equal 48oz so it was ginger snaps, oatmeal, vanilla wafers and fudge marshmallow.

2. If they follow your recommendations, how much money will they spend on cookies? Show your work.

5.71

3. About what is the cost per pound of the 3 pounds of cookies you selected? Show your work.

1.90

This Level 2 paper illustrates the following features: Cookies are selected based on finding a total weight of 3 pounds with 4 types of cookies. The work for this is shown and explained, and the answer is recorded. The computation for finding the total cost is correct. There is no computation for finding the price per pound.

This Level 1 paper illustrates the following features: The explanation describes using the cookies with the least number of ounces and adding their prices to find the total. The statement for price per pound refers only to totaling ounces, but it incorrectly describes 48 ounces as equivalent to 4 pounds.

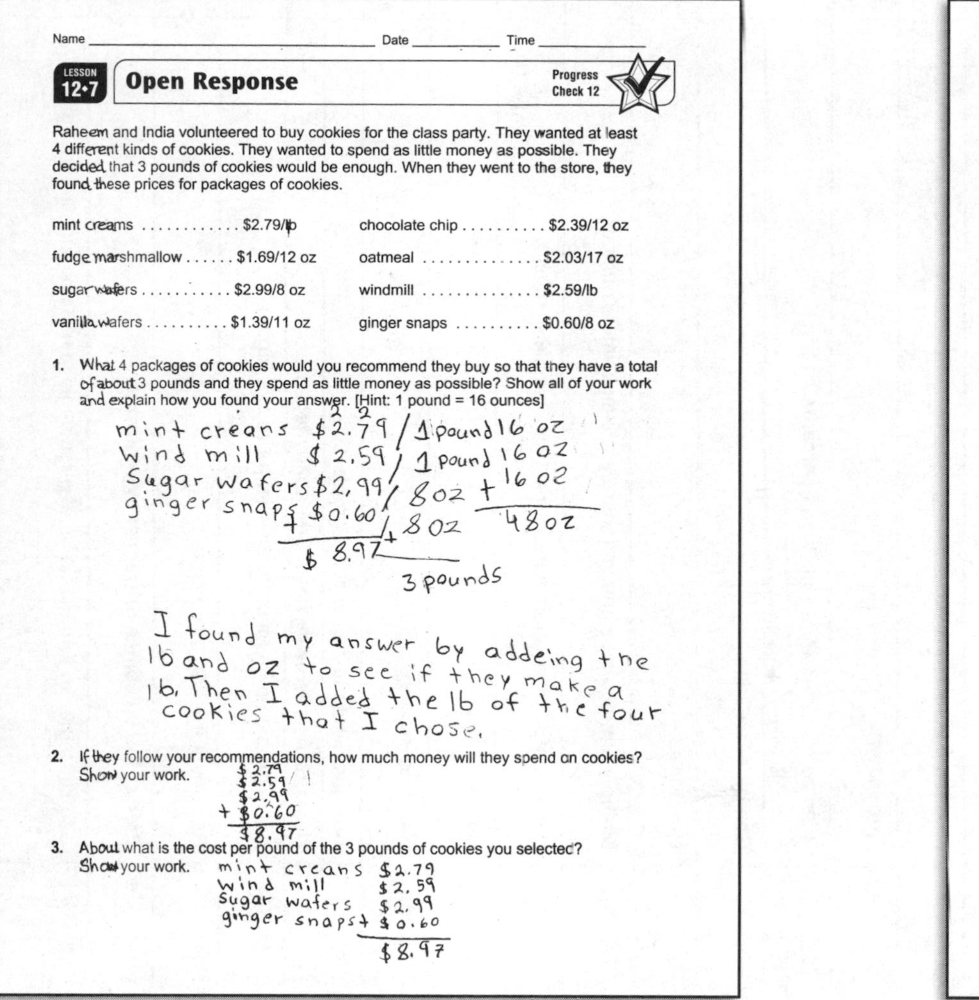

Name ______ Date ______ Time ______

LESSON 12•7 **Open Response** Progress Check 12

Raheem and India volunteered to buy cookies for the class party. They wanted at least 4 different kinds of cookies. They wanted to spend as little money as possible. They decided that 3 pounds of cookies would be enough. When they went to the store, they found these prices for packages of cookies.

mint creams	$2.79/lb	chocolate chip	$2.39/12 oz
fudge marshmallow	$1.69/12 oz	oatmeal	$2.03/17 oz
sugar wafers	$2.99/8 oz	windmill	$2.59/lb
vanilla wafers	$1.39/11 oz	ginger snaps	$0.60/8 oz

1. What 4 packages of cookies would you recommend they buy so that they have a total of about 3 pounds and they spend as little money as possible? Show all of your work and explain how you found your answer. [Hint: 1 pound = 16 ounces]

mint creans $2.79 / 1 pound 16 oz
wind mill $2.59 / 1 pound 16 oz
Sugar wafers $2.99 / 8 oz + 16 oz
ginger snaps + $0.60 / 8 oz 48 oz
$8.97 3 pounds

I found my answer by addeing the lb and oz to see if they make a lb. Then I added the lb of the four cookies that I chose.

2. If they follow your recommendations, how much money will they spend on cookies? Show your work.

$2.79
$2.59
$2.99
+ $0.60
$8.97

3. About what is the cost per pound of the 3 pounds of cookies you selected? Show your work.

mint creans $2.79
wind mill $2.59
Sugar wafers $2.99
ginger snaps + $0.60
$8.97

Name ______ Date ______ Time ______

LESSON 12•7 **Open Response** Progress Check 12

Raheem and India volunteered to buy cookies for the class party. They wanted at least 4 different kinds of cookies. They wanted to spend as little money as possible. They decided that 3 pounds of cookies would be enough. When they went to the store, they found these prices for packages of cookies.

mint creams	$2.79/lb ✓	chocolate chip	$2.39/12 oz
fudge marshmallow	$1.69/12 oz	oatmeal	$2.03/17 oz
sugar wafers	$2.99/8 oz ✓	windmill	$2.59/lb ✓
vanilla wafers	$1.39/11 oz	ginger snaps	$0.60/8 oz ✓

1. What 4 packages of cookies would you recommend they buy so that they have a total of about 3 pounds and they spend as little money as possible? Show all of your work and explain how you found your answer. [Hint: 1 pound = 16 ounces]

I found my answer by adding the four less oz and I add the money and it was $8.94 but that is not to much money.

$2.76
$2.99
$2.59
$0.60
$8.94

16
+16
16
48

2. If they follow your recommendations, how much money will they spend on cookies? Show your work. They will spend $8.94 because I add: 2.76 + 2.99 + 2.59 + 0.60 = 8.94

3. About what is the cost per pound of the 3 pounds of cookies you selected? Show your work. I will be 48 oz about 4 pounds. I add 16 16 16 48 oz

End-of-Year Assessment Goals

The End-of-Year Assessment (pages 234–241) provides an additional opportunity that you may use as part of your balanced assessment plan. It covers many of the important concepts and skills presented in *Fourth Grade Everyday Mathematics.* It should be used to complement the ongoing and periodic assessments that appear within lessons and at the end of units. The following tables provide the goals for all the problems in Part A and Part B of the End-of-Year Assessment.

Part A Recognizing Student Achievement

Problems 1–20 provide summative information and may be used for grading purposes.

Problem(s)	Description	Grade-Level Goal
1	Solve problems involving fractional parts of a collection.	Number and Numeration Goal 2
2	Find multiples.	Number and Numeration Goal 3
3	Find factors.	Number and Numeration Goal 3
4	Rename fractions as decimals and percents.	Number and Numeration Goal 5
5	Compare fractions.	Number and Numeration Goal 6
6	Order fractions.	Number and Numeration Goal 6
7a, 7b	Multiply a multidigit whole number by a 2-digit whole number.	Operations and Computation Goal 4
7c, 7d	Divide a multidigit whole number by 1-digit whole number.	Operations and Computation Goal 4
8a, 8b	Add fractions.	Operations and Computation Goal 5
8c, 8d	Subtract fractions.	Operations and Computation Goal 5
9	Use given data to create a line graph.	Data and Chance Goal 1
10	Describe events using basic probability terms.	Data and Chance Goal 3
11a, 11b	Solve problems involving fractional parts of a region.	Number and Numeration Goal 2
11c	Rename a fraction as a percent.	Number and Numeration Goal 5
11d, 11e	Predict the outcomes of spinner experiments.	Data and Chance Goal 4
12	Use strategies to find the areas of a rectangle, parallelogram, and triangle.	Measurement and Reference Frames Goal 2

Problem(s)	Description *continued*	Grade-Level Goal
13	Calculate the volume of a rectangular prism.	Measurement and Reference Frames Goal 2
14	Describe relationships among U.S. customary and metric units of length.	Measurement and Reference Frames Goal 3
15	Use ordered pairs of numbers to locate and plot points on a coordinate grid.	Measurement and Reference Frames Goal 4
16	Estimate the measures of angles.	Measurement and Reference Frames Goal 1
17	Identify geometric solids.	Geometry Goal 2
18	Identify reflections, rotations, and translations.	Geometry Goal 3
19	Complete a pattern and describe a rule.	Patterns, Functions, and Algebra Goal 1
20	Insert parentheses to make true number sentences.	Patterns, Functions, and Algebra Goal 3

Part B Informing Instruction

Problems 21–27 provide formative information.

Problem(s)	Description	Grade-Level Goal
21	Solve "percent-of" problems.	Number and Numeration Goal 2
22	Rename fractions as decimals and percents.	Number and Numeration Goal 5
23	Compare fractions and decimals less than 1.	Number and Numeration Goal 6
24	Multiply and divide decimals.	Operations and Computation Goal 4
25	Estimate sums and differences of fractions and mixed numbers.	Operations and Computation Goal 5
26	Measure angles with a protractor.	Measurement and Reference Frames Goal 1
27	Interpret a circle graph.	Data and Chance Goal 2

Assessment Masters

Contents

Progress Check

Unit 1 154
Unit 2 159
Unit 3 164
Unit 4 169
Unit 5 174
Unit 6 179
Unit 7 184
Unit 8 189
Unit 9 195
Unit 10 200
Unit 11 206
Unit 12 211
Progress Check Answers Unit 1 . . .216
Progress Check Answers Unit 2 . . .217
Progress Check Answers Unit 3 . . .218
Progress Check Answers Unit 4 . . .219
Progress Check Answers Unit 5 . . .220
Progress Check Answers Unit 6 . . .221
Progress Check Answers Unit 7 . . .222
Progress Check Answers Unit 8 . . .223
Progress Check Answers Unit 9 . . .224
Progress Check Answers Unit 10 . .225
Progress Check Answers Unit 11 . .226
Progress Check Answers Unit 12 . .227
Mid-Year Assessment 228
End-of-Year Assessment 234
Mid-Year and End-of-Year Assessment Answers 242

Class Checklists and Individual Profiles of Progress

Unit 1 246
Unit 2 250
Unit 3 254
Unit 4 258
Unit 5 262
Unit 6 266
Unit 7 270
Unit 8 274
Unit 9 278
Unit 10 282
Unit 11 286
Unit 12 290
Quarter 1 .294
Quarter 2 .296
Quarter 3 .298
Quarter 4 .300

General Masters (students' masters in italics)

Individual Profile of Progress 302
Class Checklist 303
Evaluating My Math Class 304
My Math Class 305
Weekly Math Log 306
Math Log 307
Number-Story Math Log 308
Sample Math Work 309
Discussion of My Math Work 310
Exit Slip 311
Parent Reflections 312

Name Date Time

LESSON 1•9

Self Assessment

Progress Check 1

Think about each skill listed below. Assess your own progress by checking the most appropriate box.

Skills	I can do this on my own and explain how to do it.	I can do this on my own.	I can do this if I get help or look at an example.
1. Know addition and subtraction facts.			
2. Identify, draw, and label line segments, lines, and rays.			
3. Identify and draw parallel and intersecting line segments.			
4. Describe sides and angles of polygons.			
5. Use a compass and straightedge to construct geometric figures.			

Name ____________________ Date ____________ Time ____________

Written Assessment

Progress Check 1

Part A

Use a straightedge or the Geometry Template to complete Problems 1–4.

1. Draw a quadrangle that has 4 right angles and is not a square.

What kind of quadrangle is this?

____

2. Draw a quadrangle with 1 pair of parallel sides and no right angles.

What kind of quadrangle is this?

____

3. Draw $\overline{AB}$ parallel to $\overline{CD}$.

4. Draw $\overleftrightarrow{EM}$. Draw $\overleftrightarrow{TX}$ so that $\overleftrightarrow{EM}$ and $\overleftrightarrow{TX}$ intersect.

For Problems 5–8, there may be more than one correct name for the geometric figure. Put a check mark beside all of the correct names.

5. ____ $\overline{OP}$

____ $\overleftrightarrow{OP}$

____ $\overleftrightarrow{PO}$

P O

6. ____ $\overline{LA}$

____ $\overrightarrow{AL}$

____ $\overrightarrow{LA}$

A L

7. ____ quadrangle

____ polygon

____ parallelogram

8. ____ square

____ rhombus

____ parallelogram

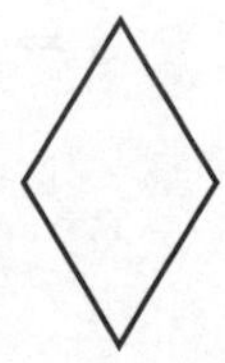

Name ______________________ Date ______________________ Time ______________________

LESSON 1•9

Written Assessment *continued*

9.

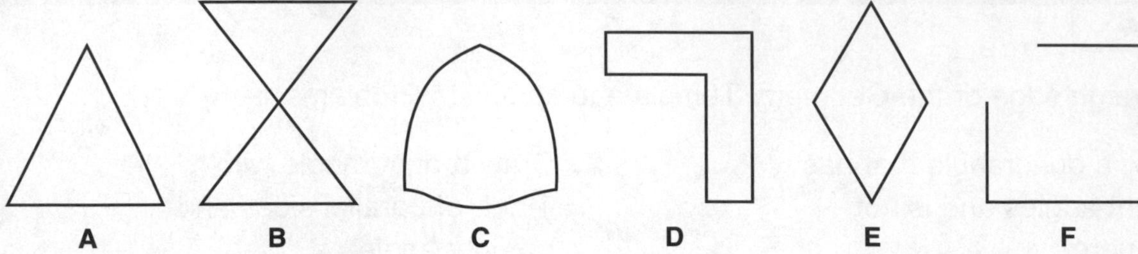

a. Which of the above shapes are NOT polygons? ______________________

b. Choose two of the shapes that are not polygons. Tell why each one is not a polygon.

____

____

10. Add mentally.

0 + 5 = ______

9 + 1 = ______

5 + 5 = ______

3 + 2 = ______

1 + 6 = ______

2 + 4 = ______

7 + 3 = ______

3 + 3 = ______

5 + 1 = ______

4 + 6 = ______

6 + 6 = ______

1 + 8 = ______

4 + 8 = ______

7 + 5 = ______

9 + 4 = ______

3 + 8 = ______

8 + 6 = ______

6 + 7 = ______

9 + 9 = ______

9 + 6 = ______

8 + 8 = ______

7 + 9 = ______

3 + 9 = ______

5 + 8 = ______

11. Subtract mentally.

7 − 2 = ____

6 − 2 = ____

11 − 8 = ____

4 − 1 = ____

12 − 4 = ____

12 − 7 = ____

15 − 6 = ____

13 − 7 = ____

6 − 5 = ____

5 − 3 = ____

10 − 4 = ____

11 − 9 = ____

16 − 8 = ____

14 − 6 = ____

17 − 9 = ____

14 − 9 = ____

10 − 7 = ____

6 − 3 = ____

9 − 6 = ____

12 − 6 = ____

13 − 9 = ____

11 − 4 = ____

15 − 8 = ____

18 − 9 = ____

Name Date Time

LESSON 1•9 **Written Assessment** *continued*

Part B

12. Part of each polygon below is hidden. One of the 3 polygons is a **parallelogram,** another is a **trapezoid,** and another is a regular **hexagon.** Write the correct name of each polygon on the line.

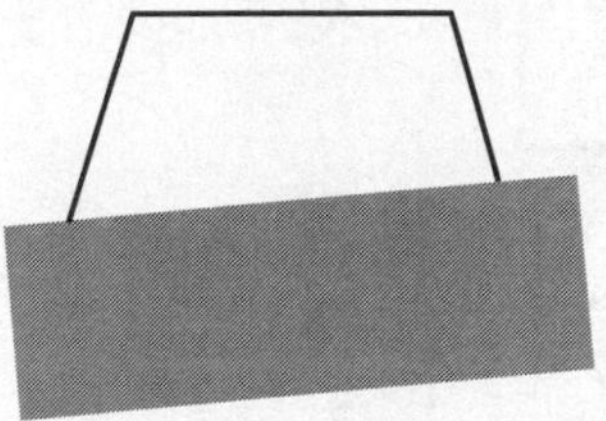

_______________ _______________ _______________

Use a straightedge, the Geometry Template, or a compass to draw each of the geometric figures in Problems 13–16.

13. **perpendicular** line segments

14. **concave** polygon

15. **concentric** circles

16. a polygon that is **congruent** to the one shown below

Name Date Time

Open Response

Progress Check 1

Properties of Polygons

Ben's teacher Ms. Lopez asked him to sort the polygons below into 2 groups. Ms. Lopez said Ben must sort the polygons according to their properties.

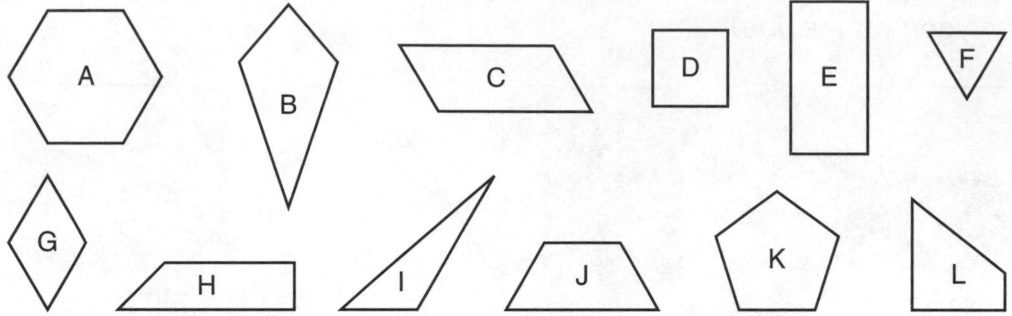

1. So far, Ben has put some of the polygons into two groups. Write the letters of at least 2 more polygons that could go into each group.

Group 1	Group 2
G A	*E L*

All of the polygons in Group 1 have this property or properties in common:

____

____

____

____

All of the polygons in Group 2 have this property or properties in common:

____

____

____

____

Try This

2. Ms. Lopez gave Ben one more polygon. Does Polygon M belong in one of the groups above? Explain why or why not.

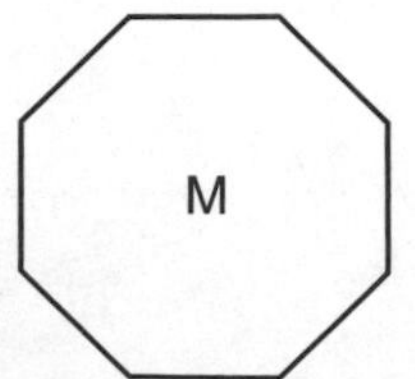

____

____

____

Name Date Time

LESSON 2·10

Self Assessment

Progress Check 2

Think about each skill listed below. Assess your own progress by checking the most appropriate box.

Skills	I can do this on my own and explain how to do it.	I can do this on my own.	I can do this if I get help or look at an example.
1. Read and write large numbers.			
2. Fill in name-collection boxes.			
3. Add multidigit numbers.			
4. Subtract multidigit numbers.			
5. Make ballpark estimates for addition and subtraction problems.			
6. Create and read a bar graph.			
7. Find the minimum, maximum, range, median, and mode of a data set.			

Name Date Time

LESSON 2•10

Written Assessment

Progress Check 2

Part A

Add or subtract with a paper-and-pencil algorithm.

1. 129 + 462	**2.** 507 + 1,829	**3.** 4,326 + 2,974
4. 924 − 648	**5.** 208 − 72	**6.** 4,361 − 2,498

7. Draw a polygon with at least one right angle.
Mark the right angle(s) with a square corner symbol.

8. Is the polygon you drew a parallelogram? ______ Explain. ______________________

____

Name ____________ Date ____________ Time ____________

Written Assessment *continued*

The students in Ivan's class are selling rolls of wrapping paper to raise money for their school. Use Ivan's chart to answer the following questions:

Number of Rolls Sold	Number of Students
20	////
21	//
22	~~////~~
23	//
24	///
25	~~////~~ /
26	
27	/
28	/

9. How many students sold 22 rolls of wrapping paper? ______ students

10. What is the maximum number of rolls sold? ______

11. What is the range of the number of rolls sold? ______

12. What is the mode (most frequent number) of rolls sold? ______

13. What is the median (or typical number) of rolls sold by the students? ______

14. Explain how you found the median.

____

____

____

15. Make a bar graph of the data.

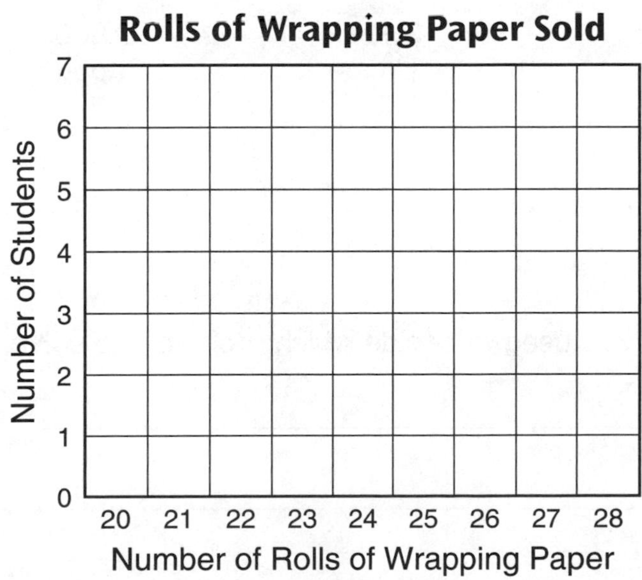

Name Date Time

Written Assessment *continued*

Part B

16. Su Lin wanted to show the number 27 on her calculator. The 7-key on her calculator was broken, so this is what she did:

3 [×] 8 [+] 3 [Enter =] 27

Show two other ways to show 27 without using the 7-key. Try to use different numbers and operations.

a. ____________________ **b.** ____________________

17. Measure the line segments to the nearest $\frac{1}{2}$ centimeter.

a. ____ About _______ cm

b. ______________________________ About _______ cm

18. Draw a line segment 12.5 centimeters long.

19. Solve *only* those problems with a sum or difference *greater than* 2,500.

a. $\begin{array}{r} 1{,}859 \\ +\ 2{,}098 \\ \hline \end{array}$ **b.** $\begin{array}{r} 1{,}132 \\ +\ 1{,}246 \\ \hline \end{array}$ **c.** $\begin{array}{r} 3{,}127 \\ -\ 1{,}989 \\ \hline \end{array}$ **d.** $\begin{array}{r} 6{,}800 \\ -\ 3{,}229 \\ \hline \end{array}$

20. Explain the estimation strategy you used to decide which problems to solve.

____

____

____

Name Date Time

Open Response

Jelly Bean Data

Mr. Evans gave bags of jelly beans to students in his class. Each student counted the jelly beans in the bag and wrote the number on the board. Then the students found the landmarks for the class data.

Minimum 9 **Maximum 18** **Mode 12** **Median 13**

1. Suppose there were 11 students in Mr. Evans's class. List the number of jelly beans each student could have reported to get the landmarks listed above.

2. Explain how you found your answer.

3. Display your data on a line plot or bar graph.
Be sure to include a **title** and **labels** for your display.

Name Date Time

Self Assessment

Progress Check 3

Think about each skill listed below. Assess your own progress by checking the most appropriate box.

Skills	I can do this on my own and explain how to do it.	I can do this on my own.	I can do this if I get help or look at an example.
1. Find multiples and factors.			
2. Solve addition and subtraction number stories.			
3. Know multiplication facts.			
4. Know division facts.			
5. Use a map scale.			
6. Solve "What's My Rule?" problems.			
7. Solve open sentences.			
8. Use parentheses.			

Name ______ Date ______ Time ______

Written Assessment

Progress Check 3

Part A

Fill in the missing number in each Fact Triangle.

1. 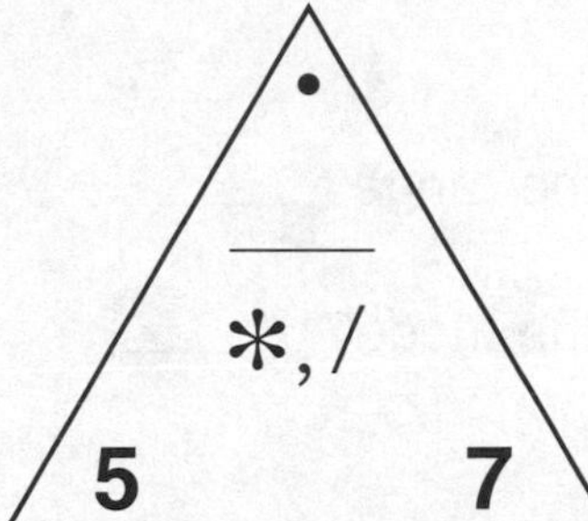

2. 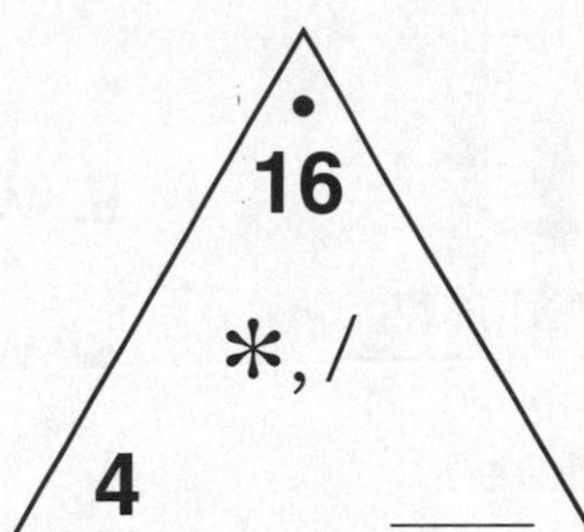

3. 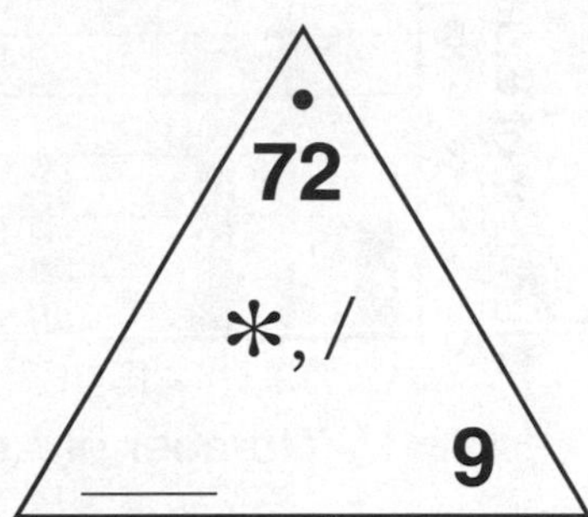

Write T if the number sentence is true, F if it is false, or ? if you can't tell.

4. $6 * 8 = 48$ ______

5. $9 * 6$ ______

6. $3 * 3 = 45 / 5$ ______

7. $4 * 6 < 30$ ______

8. $3 * (4 + 5) = 17$ ______

9. $(7 * 4) \div 2 > 3 * 7$ ______

Make a true sentence by filling in the missing number.

10. ______ $= (8 * 9) + 13$

11. ______ $= (12 - 5) * 5$

12. $(14 - 6) + (32 / 8) =$ ______

13. $(12 \div 4) * (24 \div 4) =$ ______

Make a true sentence by inserting parentheses.

14. $30 - 15 + 2 = 13$

15. $56 / 8 + 48 = 1$

16. $26 - 3 + 13 = 10$

17. $6 * 4 + 57 = 81$

Name Date Time

LESSON 3•12

Written Assessment *continued*

18. Use the bar graph to answer the questions.

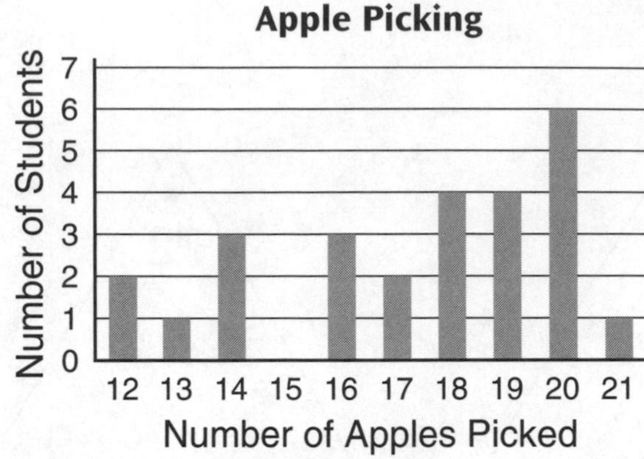

a. What is the median number of apples picked?

______

b. What is the range? ______

c. What is the mode? ______

Write a number model and solve the addition and subtraction number stories.

19. A European eel can live up to 88 years. A giant tortoise can live about 62 years longer. About how long can a giant tortoise live?

Number model: ______________________________ __________ years

20. The Golden Gate Bridge was completed in 1937. The length of its main span is 4,200 feet. The San Francisco Bay Bridge was completed in 1936. The length of its main span is 2,310 feet. How much longer is the Golden Gate Bridge than the San Francisco Bay Bridge?

Number model: ______________________________ __________ feet

21. Complete the "What's My Rule?" table and state the rule.

Rule: ______

in	out
6	24
4	16
5	
	28
3	
	32

22. List all the factors of 30.

____

____

Name Date Time

LESSON 3•12

Written Assessment *continued*

Part B

Solve the open sentences.

23. $19 = 12 + x$ Solution: ______

24. $4 * n = 16$ Solution: ______

25. $z / 3 = 6$ Solution: ______

26. $x / 6 = 5$ Solution: ______

27. $17 - x = 8$ Solution: ______

28. $4 * 5 = 30 - t$ Solution: ______

Use the map and map scale to answer the following questions.

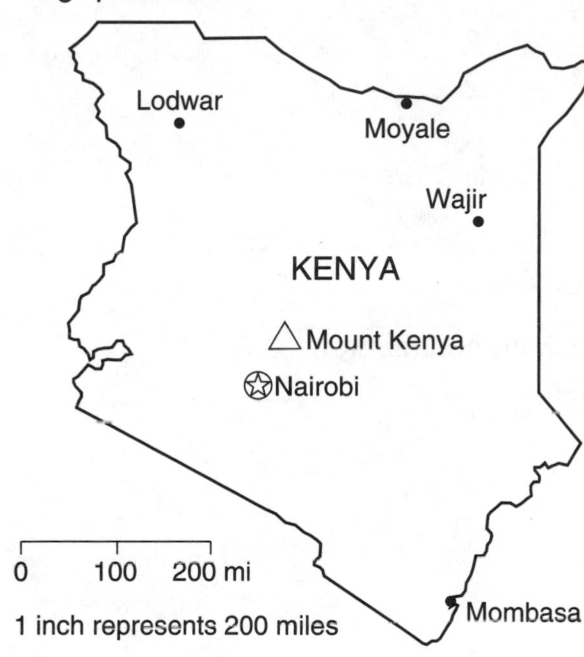

29. The distance between Mombasa and Wajir is about ______ inches on the map.

That represents about ______ miles.

30. The distance between Nairobi and Lodwar is about ______ inches on the map.

That represents about ______ miles.

31. Complete the Venn diagram. Use at least 10 numbers.

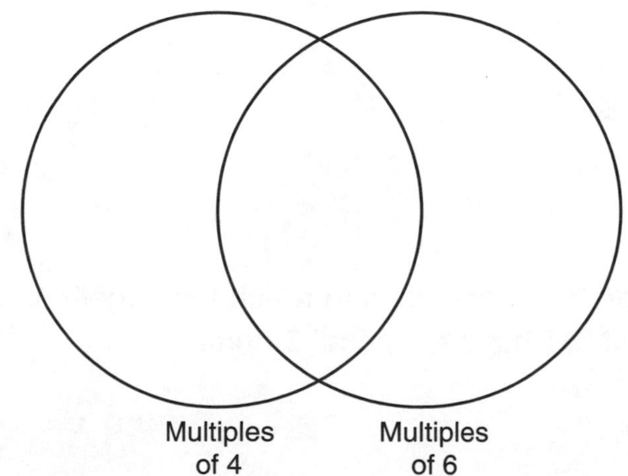

Name Date Time

LESSON 3•12

Open Response

Progress Check 3

Name That Number

Kato was playing a game of *Name That Number*. He had the following five number cards and target number:

Cards

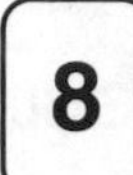

3 **2** **8** **6** **5**

Target

12

His teacher, Ms. Ayers, asked everyone to record their thinking. Here is what Kato wrote:

$$5 + (6 + 8) \div 2 - 3 = 12$$
$$6 * 2 + (8 - 5) - 3 = 12$$
$$3 * 2 + (8 + 5) - 6 = 12$$

1. Ms. Ayers saw that Kato had made mistakes in writing two of his number sentences.

- Circle the two number sentences with mistakes.
- Explain in words how Kato can correct each number sentence. (Hint: The numbers are in the correct order.)

2. Describe two more ways to reach the target number of 12. You do NOT have to use all 5 numbers.

Name Date Time

LESSON 4•11

Self Assessment

Progress Check 4

Think about each skill listed below. Assess your own progress by checking the most appropriate box.

Skills	I can do this on my own and explain how to do it.	I can do this on my own.	I can do this if I get help or look at an example.
1. Read decimals through thousandths.			
2. Write decimals through thousandths.			
3. Compare and order decimals through thousandths.			
4. Add decimals like these: \$23.62 + \$7.95 15.8 + 2.23			
5. Subtract decimals like these: \$14.35 − \$6.27 5.9 − 4.61			
6. Measure objects to the nearest centimeter.			
7. Measure objects to the nearest $\frac{1}{2}$ centimeter.			

Name Date Time

LESSON 4•11

Written Assessment

Progress Check 4

Part A

Write > or < to make a true number sentence.

1. 5.46 _____ 5.9

2. 0.45 _____ 0.7

3. 4.8 + 6.9 _____ 3.4 + 7.7

4. 3.85 − 3.46 _____ 9.1 − 6.2

5. Write the following numbers in order from smallest to largest.

0.001, 4.3, 4.05, 0.6, 0.06, 0.1

_____ _____ _____ _____ _____ _____

smallest largest

6. Write 2 numbers between 0 and 1. Use decimals. _____ _____

7. Write 2 numbers between 1 and 2. Use decimals. _____ _____

8. Use your ruler to measure the line segment to the nearest centimeter.

About _____ cm

9. Use your ruler to measure the line segment to the nearest $\frac{1}{2}$ centimeter.

About _____ cm

10. Draw a line segment that is 12.5 centimeters long.

11. List the first ten multiples of 8.

_____, _____, _____, _____, _____, _____, _____, _____, _____, _____

12. List the factor pairs of 28.

_____ and _____ _____ and _____ _____ and _____

Name _______________ Date _______________ Time _______________

LESSON 4•11 **Written Assessment** *continued*

Add or subtract mentally or with a paper-and-pencil algorithm.

13. \$12.34 + \$7.45 = __________

14. __________ = 9.6 + 0.8

15. 41.12 + 6.9 = __________

16. \$15.46 − \$9.23 = __________

17. __________ = 12.8 − 2.9

18. 34.3 − 26.51 = __________

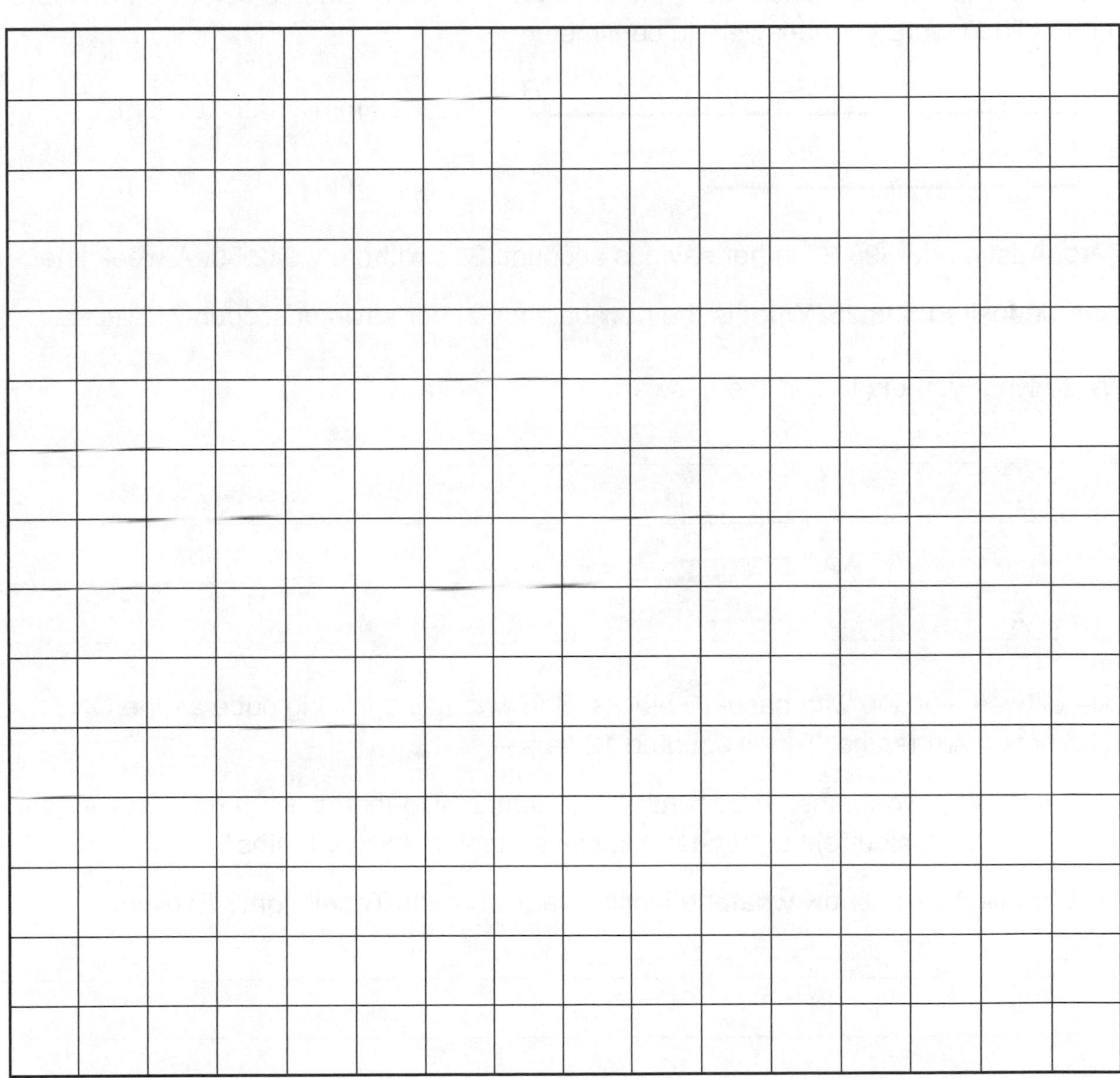

Solve each open sentence.

19. $r + 129 = 254$ $r =$ __________

20. $93 - p = 37$ $p =$ __________

21. $w * 6 = 54$ $w =$ __________

22. $56 / g = 7$ $g =$ __________

Name Date Time

LESSON 4•11

Written Assessment *continued*

Part B

Write each decimal as a fraction.

23. 0.4 = ______ **24.** 0.34 = ______ **25.** 0.674 = ______

Use your ruler to measure and record the length of the line segments below to the nearest millimeter. Then write your answers in centimeters.

26. *A* ______________________ *B* ______ mm ______ cm

27. *C* ________________ *D* ______ mm ______ cm

28. Mrs. Austin had $98.37 in her savings account. She withdrew $42.50. A week later, she deposited $38.25. What is the new balance in her savings account? ________

Write what you did to find the answer.

____

____

____

____

29. Teneil was working with base-10 blocks. She was using the big cube as the ONE. The flats were tenths. Teneil counted 12 flats—

"one-tenth, two-tenths, three-tenths, four-tenths, five-tenths, six-tenths, seven-tenths, eight-tenths, nine-tenths, ten-tenths, eleven-tenths, twelve-tenths"

She wrote 0.12 to show what the blocks were worth. Is Teneil right? Explain.

____

____

____

____

Name Date Time

Open Response

Progress Check 4

Forming a Relay Team

Mrs. Wong, the gym teacher, wants to form 3 teams for a 200-yard relay race. There will be 4 students on each team. Each student will run 50 yards.

The table at the right shows how long it took some fourth-grade students to run 50 yards the last time they had a race. They were timed to the nearest tenth of a second.

Runner	Time (seconds)
Art	6.3
Bruce	7.0
Jamal	7.4
Doug	7.9
Al	8.3
Will	8.8
Linda	6.2
Sue	7.6
Pat	7.7
Mary	8.1
Alba	8.4
Joyce	8.5

1. Help Mrs. Wong create 3 teams that will be fairly evenly matched. She will use their times from the last race to predict about how fast they will run in the relay race.

Write the names of the four students that you think should be on each team.

Estimate about how long you think it will take each team to complete the race.

Names of 4 Students on Each Team	**Estimated Team Time**
Team 1: ______________________	About: ___.___ seconds
Team 2: ______________________	About: ___.___ seconds
Team 3: ______________________	About: ___.___ seconds

2. Explain how you made your teams so that they would be fairly matched.

Name Date Time

LESSON 5•12

Self Assessment

Progress Check 5

Think about each skill listed below. Assess your own progress by checking the most appropriate box.

Skills	I can do this on my own and explain how to do it.	I can do this on my own.	I can do this if I get help or look at an example.
1. Multiply numbers like these: 23 ∗ 5 214 ∗ 3			
2. Multiply numbers like these: 26 ∗ 31 78 ∗ 64			
3. Estimate sums like this: 493 + 262 is about 800			
4. Add and subtract decimals like these: 8.4 + 6.3 14.75 − 8.32			
5. Measure line segments in inches and centimeters.			
6. Complete a "What's My Rule?" table.			

Name Date Time

LESSON 5•12

Written Assessment

Progress Check 5

Part A

Circle the number closest to the sum. Write a number model for the estimate.

1. 486 + 732   900   1,200   1,500   1,800

Number model: ______________________________

2. 515 + 987 + 264   1,000   1,400   1,800   2,200

Number model: ______________________________

Use the partial-products algorithm to multiply.

3. 5 * 57 = ______________

4. 42 * 6 = ______________

5. 241 * 3 = ______________

6. 32 * 50 = ______________

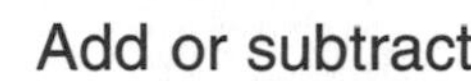
Add or subtract.

7. 9.6 + 7.3 = ______________

8. 2.63 + 4.15 = ______________

9. 8.9 − 5.3 − ______________

10. 12.86 − 9.34 = ______________

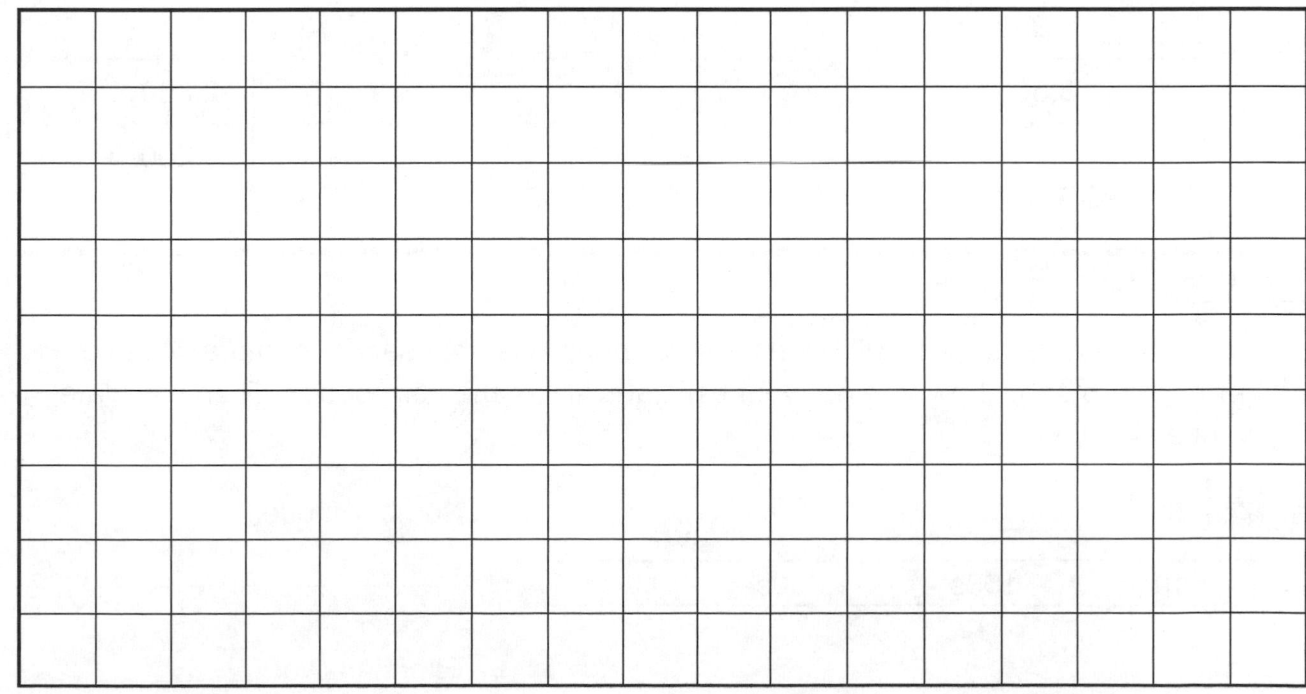

Name Date Time

LESSON 5•12 **Written Assessment** *continued*

11. Explain the mistake Marvice made when she solved this problem:

$$\begin{array}{r} 0.55 \\ -0.4 \\ \hline 0.51 \end{array}$$

____

____

____

Find the correct answer. __________

12. Measure the line segment to the nearest $\frac{1}{4}$ inch and 0.5 centimeter.

____

About __________ inches About __________ centimeters

Complete the "What's My Rule?" tables. State the rule, if necessary.

13. Rule: Multiply by 5.

in	out
6	
60	
	350
	3,500
40	

14. Rule: * 20

in	out
7	
30	
	400
	1,200
50	

15. Rule: __________

in	out
8	560
9	630
3	
	2,800
	4,200

Part B

Estimate whether the answer will be in the tens, hundreds, thousands, or more. Write a number model to show how you got your estimate. Circle the correct box. Then calculate the exact answer.

16. 74 * 53

10s	100s	1,000s	10,000s

a. Number model:

____

b. Exact answer: __________

LESSON 5•12

Written Assessment *continued*

17. An opossum sleeps an average of 19 hours per day. How many hours does an opossum sleep during a 4-week time period?

10s	100s	1,000s	10,000s

a. Number model: ______________

b. Exact answer: __________ hours

On average, 11,000 babies are born in the United States each day.

18. About how many babies are born in one week? ______________ babies

19. About how many babies are born in one month? ______________ babies

20. Are more or less than a million babies born in the U.S. in a year? __________

Explain your answer.

____

____

21. Rami measured the line segment shown below. He said, "The line segment is $5\frac{1}{4}$ inches long." Do you think Rami measured correctly? Explain your answer.

0 1 2 3 4 5 6
inches

____

____

____

Name Date Time

Open Response

Progress Check 5

Walking Away with a Million Dollars

You will need the following information to solve the problem below:

You can cover a **sheet** of paper with about six $100 bills.

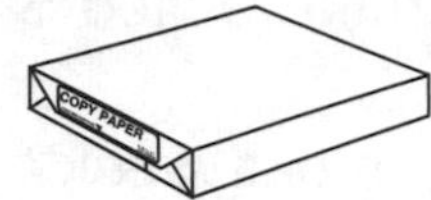

There are 500 sheets in one **ream** of paper.

There are 10 reams in one **carton.**

Imagine that you have inherited one million dollars. The bank has only $700,000 in $100 bills. The bank gives you the rest of the money in $20 bills and $10 bills. Your suitcase will hold as much as 1 carton of paper.

Will one million dollars fit in your suitcase?
Show all of your work. Explain what you did to solve the problem.

Name Date Time

Self Assessment

Progress Check 6

Think about each skill listed below. Assess your own progress by checking the most appropriate box.

Skills	I can do this on my own and explain how to do it.	I can do this on my own.	I can do this if I get help or look at an example.
1. Divide numbers like these: 322 ÷ 4, 457 ÷ 3.			
2. Divide numbers like these: 181 ÷ 66, 719 ÷ 12.			
3. Round numbers to the nearest ten thousand.			
4. Measure angles like these: 25°, 60°, 155°.			
5. Draw angles like these: 30°, 95°, 160°.			
6. Plot ordered number pairs on a coordinate grid.			

Name Date Time

Written Assessment

Progress Check 6

Part A

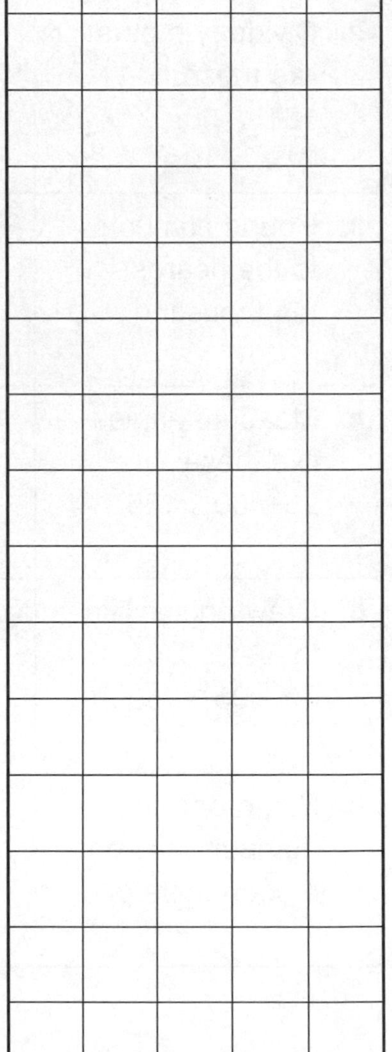

`1. There are 38 cookies in a box. Tina and her two sisters decide to share them equally. How many whole cookies will each girl get?

Number model: ________________

Answer: ______ cookies

2. Grace baked 76 muffins for a class breakfast. She put the muffins on plates. Each plate holds 8 muffins. How many plates were needed to hold all of the muffins?

Number model: ________________

Answer: ______ plates

Divide. If there is a remainder, write it as a fraction.

3. $5\overline{)84}$ Answer: ______

4. $168 \div 8$ Answer: ______

5. Mrs. Green wants to buy a washing machine and pay for it in 1 year. L-Mart offers two plans, and she wants to choose the cheaper one.

Plan A: $7 each week; a total of 52 payments.
Plan B: $27 each month; a total of 12 payments.

Which plan would cost less? __________

Explain your answer.

____

____

____

Name Date Time

LESSON 6•11

Written Assessment *continued*

For each angle, circle the type. Then measure and record your measurements.

6. angle type: acute right obtuse

∠*BCA*: ________ °

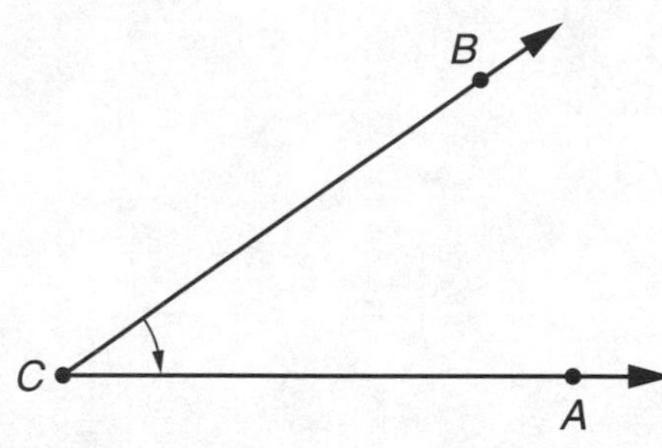

7. angle type: acute right obtuse

∠*EDF*: ________ °

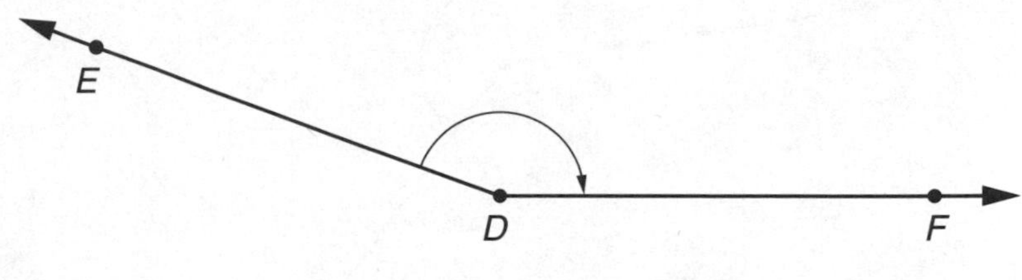

8. Plot and label each point on the coordinate grid.

A (5,2)

B (3,2)

C (1,1)

D (1,2)

E (3,5)

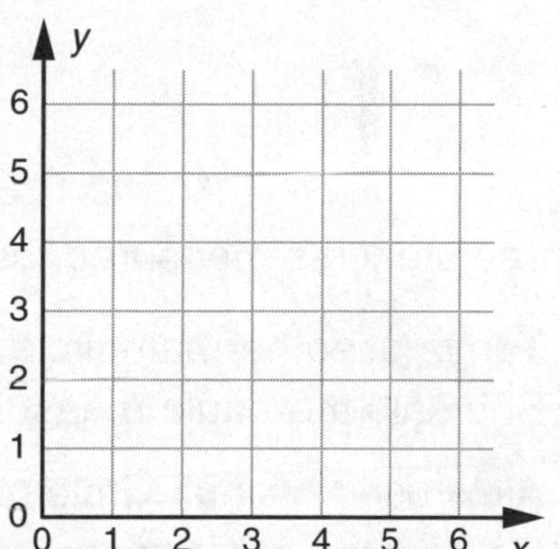

9. Insert parentheses to make these number sentences true.

a. 4 + 6 ∗ 3 = 30

b. 36 = 8 ∗ 2 + 5 ∗ 4

c. 2 + 7 ∗ 6 = 2 ∗ 2 ∗ 11

d. 9 + 6 ∗ 3 ÷ 3 = 9

10. Round these numbers to the nearest ten thousand.

a. 670,299 ________

b. 7,239,041 ________

c. 22,513,748 ________

d. 380,755,119 ________

LESSON 6•11

Written Assessment *continued*

Part B

11. Measure reflex angle *HGI*. ________ °

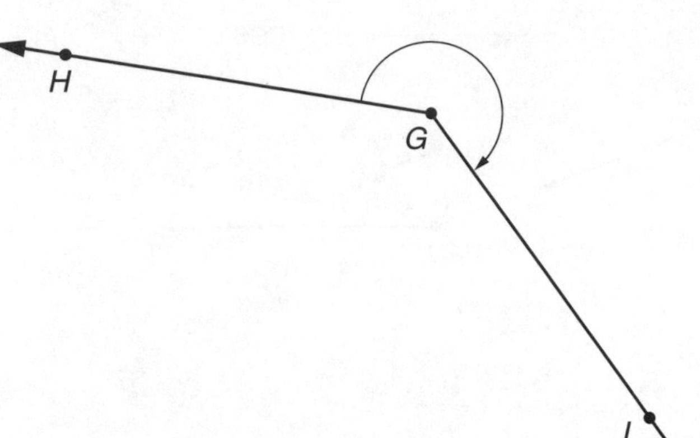

12. Draw reflex angle *ZYX* so that it measures 265°.

13. Three students measured the angle to the right.

- Tonya used her half-circle protractor. She said the angle measures about 50°.
- Alexi used his half-circle protractor. He said the angle measures about 130°.
- José used his full-circle protractor. He said the angle measures about 310°.

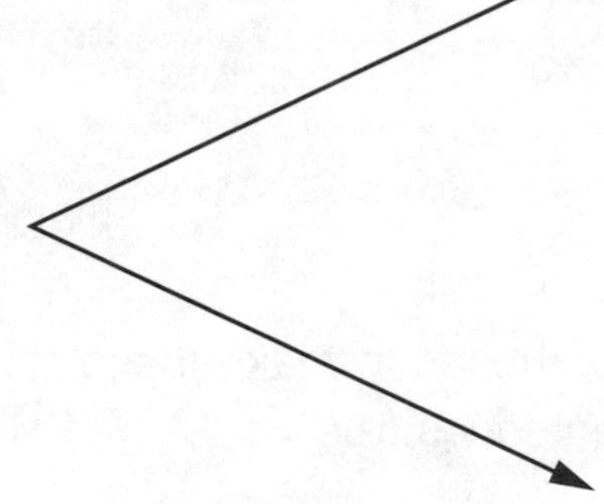

Use your half-circle protractor and your full-circle protractor to measure the angle. Do you agree with Tonya, Alexi, or José? Why?

____

____

____

Divide. If there is a remainder, write it as a fraction.

14. 314 / 12

Answer: ________

15. $26\overline{)494}$

Answer: ________

Name Date Time

LESSON 6•11

Open Response

Progress Check 6

A Trip to Adventure Land

The students in Ms. Brown's and Mr. Ron's classes at Ridge Elementary School are going on a field trip to Adventure Land. There are 28 students in each class.

Mr. Ron's class secretary has the following information about admission prices:

Adventure Land
Special Group Rates:
One Class—$60.00
Adults (1 for every 10 students)—Free

It costs $80.00 to rent a bus for a day. One bus can hold 66 people.

Calculate the amount of money each student needs to pay for the trip. Explain your strategy below.

Name Date Time

LESSON 7•13

Self Assessment

Progress Check 7

Think about each skill listed below. Assess your own progress by checking the most appropriate box.

Skills	I can do this on my own and explain how to do it.	I can do this on my own.	I can do this if I get help or look at an example.
1. Solve "fraction-of" problems like these: $\frac{1}{4}$ of 8 $\frac{4}{5}$ of 30			
2. Find equivalent fractions.			
3. Compare fractions like these: $\frac{1}{4}$ and $\frac{1}{10}$ $\frac{2}{5}$ and $\frac{2}{9}$			
4. Divide multidigit numbers like these: 492 / 7 684 / 5			
5. Add fractions like these: $\frac{1}{6} + \frac{2}{6}$ $\frac{1}{3} + \frac{1}{6}$ $\frac{1}{2} + \frac{1}{3}$			
6. Use a fraction to describe the probability of an event.			

Name Date Time

Written Assessment

Progress Check 7

Part A

For each fraction, write two equivalent fractions.

1. $\frac{1}{2}$ _____, _____ **2.** $\frac{1}{3}$ _____, _____ **3.** $\frac{6}{8}$ _____, _____

Write >, <, or = to make each number sentence true.

4. $\frac{1}{6}$ _____ $\frac{1}{8}$ **5.** $\frac{11}{12}$ _____ $\frac{5}{12}$ **6.** $\frac{2}{3}$ _____ $\frac{8}{12}$

Write each set of fractions in order from smallest to largest.

7. $\frac{2}{10}$, $\frac{9}{10}$, $\frac{7}{10}$, $\frac{1}{10}$, $\frac{5}{10}$ _____ _____ _____ _____ _____
smallest largest

8. $\frac{1}{7}$, $\frac{1}{2}$, $\frac{1}{5}$, $\frac{1}{10}$, $\frac{1}{3}$ _____ _____ _____ _____ _____
smallest largest

Use pattern blocks to help solve Problems 9 and 10.

9. If the red trapezoid is the whole, what fraction of the whole is

a. 1 green triangle? _____ **b.** 1 blue rhombus? _____

10. Suppose the green triangle is $\frac{1}{2}$ of the whole. Which pattern block is

a. 1 whole? _______________ **b.** $1\frac{1}{2}$ wholes? _______________

11. Liam had 9 quarters. He spent $\frac{1}{3}$ of them on video games.

a. How many quarters did he spend? _____ quarters

b. How many quarters does he have left? _____ quarters

c. How much money does he have left? $_____._____

LESSON 7•13

Written Assessment *continued*

12. A bag contains

2 blue blocks,

3 purple blocks,

4 green blocks, and

1 yellow block.

You put your hand in the bag and pull out a block. About what fraction of the time would you expect to get a yellow block? ______

13. Plot and label each point on the coordinate grid.

A (4,1)

B (3,4)

C (1,5)

D (2,2)

E (2,5)

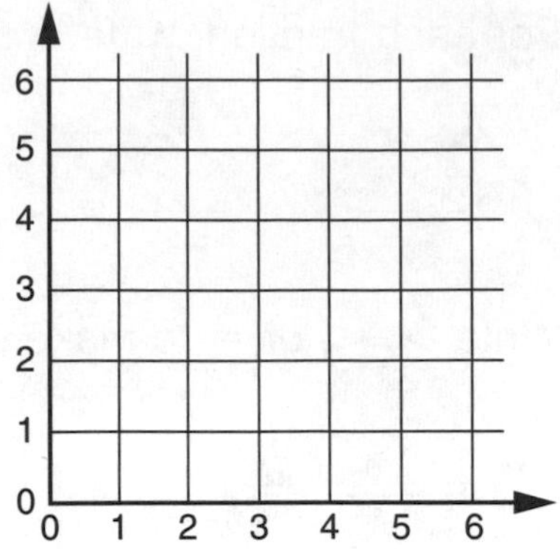

Multiply and divide. Use paper-and-pencil algorithms of your choice.

14. 47 * 23 = ________

15. ________ = 97 * 31

16. 93 ÷ 4 = ________

17. 7)542 = ________

Name Date Time

LESSON 7•13

Written Assessment *continued*

Part B

18. Which fraction is larger: $\frac{6}{7}$ or $\frac{9}{10}$? ______ Explain how you know.

______

______

______

______

19. Make a spinner.

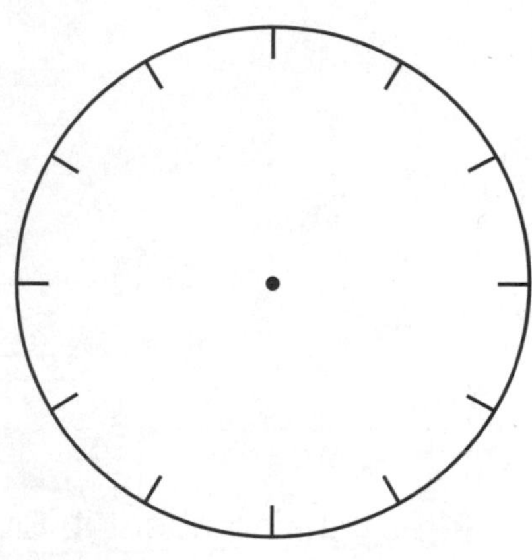

a. Color it so that the paper clip will land on red about $\frac{1}{2}$ of the time and on blue about $\frac{1}{3}$ of the time. Color the rest yellow.

b. About what fraction of the time should you expect the paper clip to land on yellow? ______

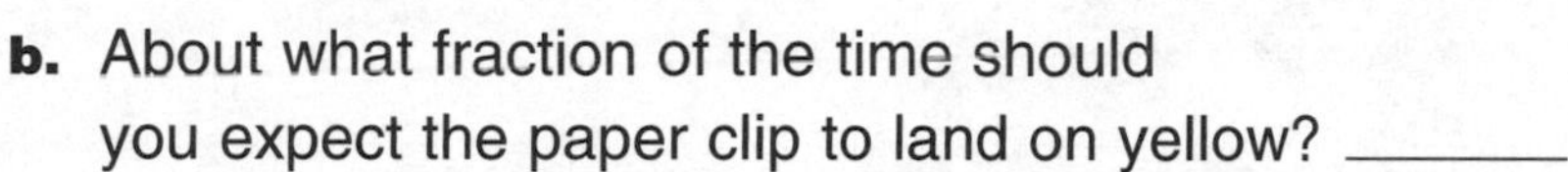

Add or subtract. Use pattern blocks to help you.

20. $\frac{1}{6} + \frac{4}{6} =$ ______

21. $\frac{1}{6} + \frac{1}{3} =$ ______

22. $\frac{5}{6} - \frac{3}{6} =$ ______

23. $\frac{2}{3} - \frac{1}{6} =$ ______

24. It took Denise $\frac{3}{4}$ of an hour to drive from Zion to Platt and $\frac{1}{2}$ hour to drive from Platt to Rome. To figure out her total driving time, Denise wrote the following number model: $\frac{3}{4} + \frac{1}{2} = \frac{4}{6}$.

Do you agree that it took her about $\frac{4}{6}$ of an hour? ______ Explain.

______

______

______

______

Name Date Time

Open Response

Progress Check 7

Queen Arlene's Dilemma

1. Queen Arlene has a problem. She wants to divide her land among her 3 children. She wants her oldest daughter to get $\frac{1}{2}$ of the land and her younger daughters to each get $\frac{1}{3}$ of the land. Can she do it? Explain your answer.

2. After thinking about it, Queen Arlene decides to keep $\frac{1}{2}$ of her land and have her 3 children divide the other $\frac{1}{2}$. She still wants the oldest daughter to get more land than her sisters. Think of a way to use fractions to divide the land. Explain your answer.

Name Date Time

LESSON 8•9

Self Assessment

Progress Check 8

Think about each skill listed below. Assess your own progress by checking the most appropriate box.

Skills	I can do this on my own and explain how to do it.	I can do this on my own.	I can do this if I get help or look at an example.
1. Add and subtract fractions.			
2. Make a scale drawing.			
3. Determine the probability of an event.			
4. Find the perimeter of a polygon.			
5. Count squares and fractions of squares to find the area of a polygon.			
6. Use a formula to find the area of a rectangle, parallelogram, and triangle.			

Name Date Time

LESSON 8•9

Written Assessment

Progress Check 8

Part A

Find the perimeter of each polygon.

1.

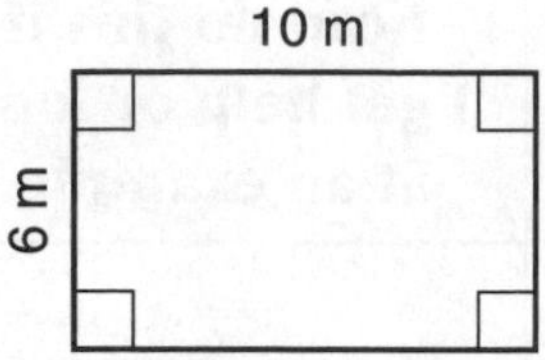

Number model:

____

Perimeter = ________ m

2.

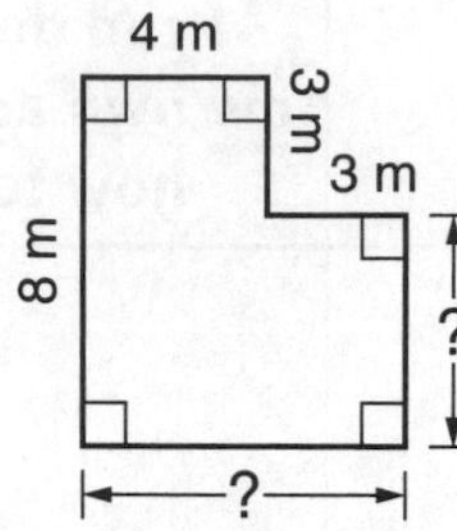

Number model:

____

Perimeter = ________ m

Find the area of each polygon.

3.

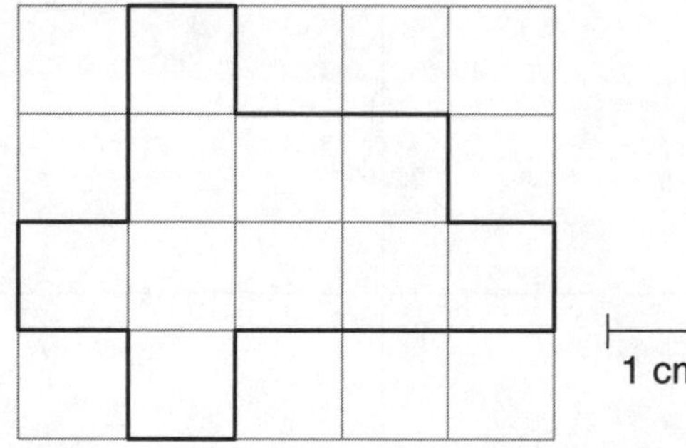

Area = ________ square centimeters

4.

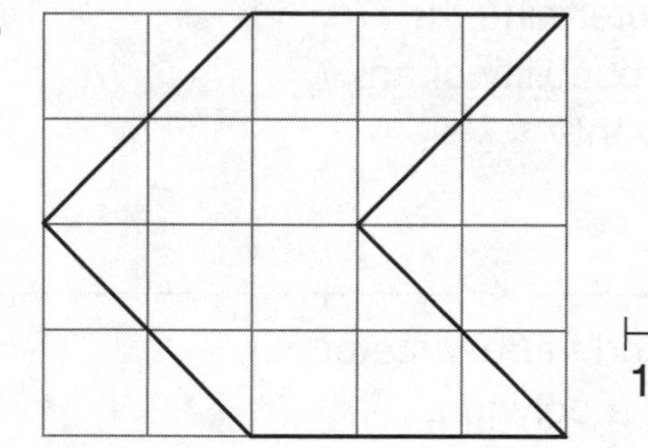

Area = ________ square centimeters

5. Draw a rectangle with an area of 12 square centimeters and a perimeter of 16 centimeters.

Name ____________ Date ____________ Time ____________

LESSON 8•9

Written Assessment *continued*

6. Mrs. Lopez wants to tile her kitchen floor. The room is 10 feet wide and 12 feet long. How many 1-square-foot tiles does she need to cover the floor?

__________ tiles

7. Suppose Mrs. Lopez chooses smaller tiles that are only 6 inches on each side. How many 6-inch tiles would she need to cover her kitchen floor?

__________ tiles

Explain the strategy you used to solve the problem.

____

____

Add or subtract.

8. $\frac{1}{5} + \frac{2}{5} =$ ______ **9.** ______ $= \frac{4}{9} + \frac{1}{3}$ **10.** $\frac{8}{10} - \frac{5}{10} =$ ______ **11.** ______ $= \frac{7}{10} - \frac{1}{2}$

12. If you spin the spinner 600 times, how many times would you expect it to land

on blue? __________

on green? __________

on orange? __________

on white? __________

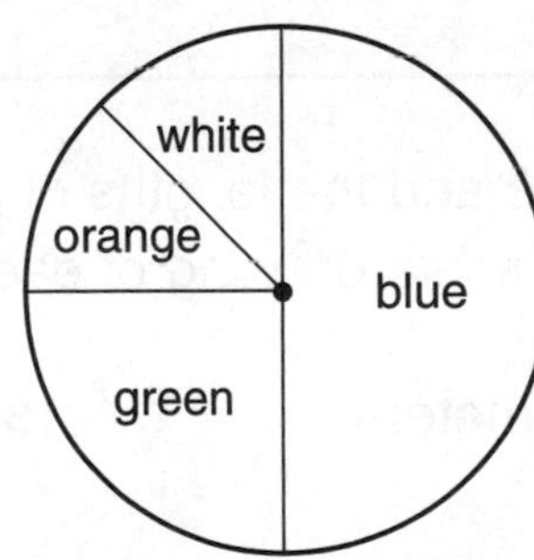

13. A jar contains 12 blue blocks, 5 red blocks, 6 orange blocks, and 2 green blocks.

You put your hand in the jar and, without looking, pull out a block. About what fraction of the time would you expect to get a red block?

____

Name Date Time

Written Assessment *continued*

Part B

Formulas		
Rectangle	Parallelogram	Triangle
Area = base ∗ height	Area = base ∗ height	Area = $\frac{1}{2}$ ∗ (base ∗ height)

Complete. Measure each with a centimeter ruler.

14. base = ______ cm perimeter = ______ cm

height = ______ cm Area = ______ cm^2

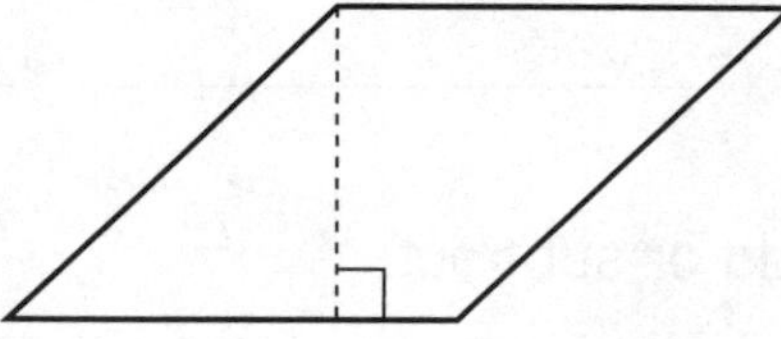

15. base = ______ cm perimeter = ______ cm

height = ______ cm Area = ______ cm^2

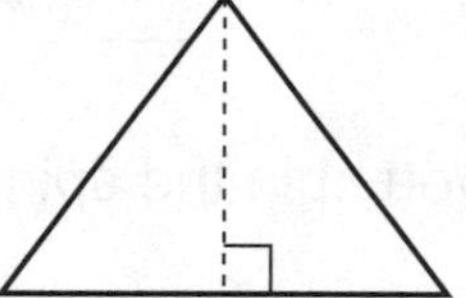

16. base = ______ cm perimeter = ______ cm

height = ______ cm Area = ______ cm^2

In each problem below, a scale and the lengths of the sides of a rectangle are given. Make a scale drawing of each rectangle.

17. Scale: 1 cm represents 5 meters

Dimensions of rectangle:
15 meters by 35 meters

18. Scale: 1 cm represents 10 meters

Dimensions of rectangle:
40 meters by 55 meters

Name Date Time

LESSON 8•9

Open Response

Progress Check 8

Comparing Areas

Carefully cut out each of the shapes below.

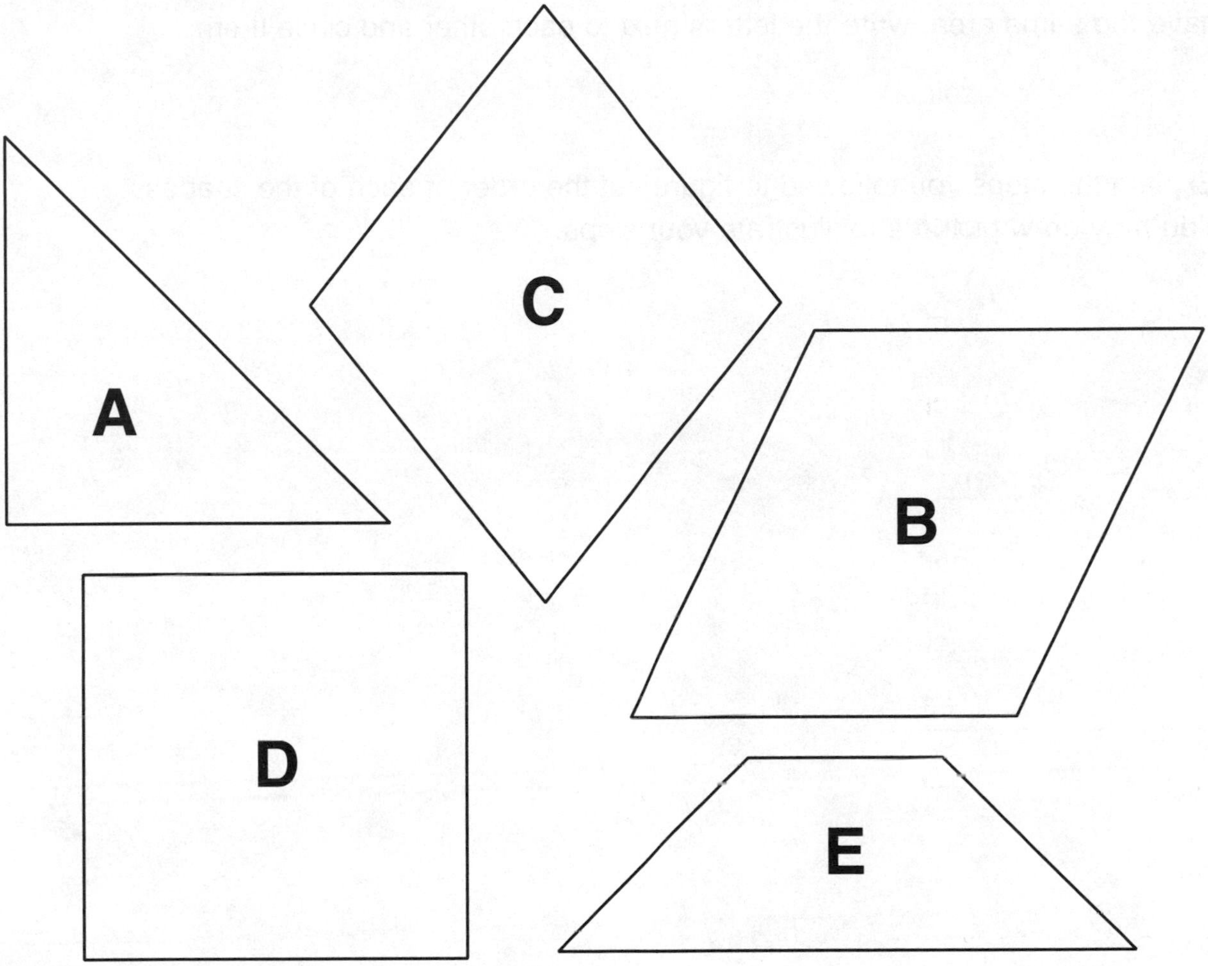

Name Date Time

Open Response *continued*

Progress Check 8

Comparing Areas

1. Arrange shapes A–D in order of their area. (You may not measure with a ruler.) List the letters of the shapes from largest to smallest. If some shapes have the same area, write the letters next to each other and circle them.

2. Explain the steps you followed to figure out the order of each of the shapes. You may draw pictures to illustrate your steps.

Try This

3. Compare shapes A and E. Tell which has the larger area. Explain how you compared the shapes.

Name Date Time

Self Assessment

Progress Check 9

Think about each skill listed below. Assess your own progress by checking the most appropriate box.

Skills	I can do this on my own and explain how to do it.	I can do this on my own.	I can do this if I get help or look at an example.
1. Solve "fraction-of" problems like these: $\frac{1}{4}$ of 20 $\frac{3}{5}$ of 15			
2. Solve discount number stories.			
3. Rename fractions like these as decimals and percents: $\frac{15}{100}, \frac{6}{10}, \frac{3}{4}, \frac{1}{5}$			
4. Solve decimal multiplication and division problems like these: 4.5 * 7 56.7 / 5 9.82 * 6 345.6 / 4			
5. Find the area and perimeter of rectangles, parallelograms, and triangles.			
6. Use parentheses in number sentences.			

Name Date Time

Written Assessment

Progress Check 9

Part A

1. Gloria made 15 out of 20 shots in the school basketball free-throw contest.

a. What fraction of the shots did she make? ____________

b. What percent of the shots did she make? ____________

c. At this rate, how many shots would she make if she took 100 shots? ____________ shots

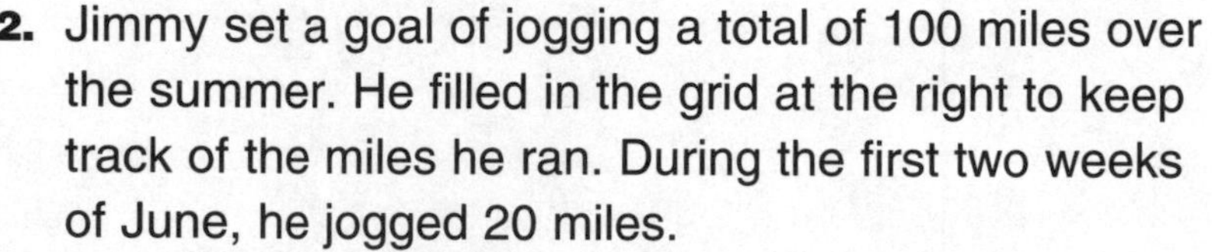

2. Jimmy set a goal of jogging a total of 100 miles over the summer. He filled in the grid at the right to keep track of the miles he ran. During the first two weeks of June, he jogged 20 miles.

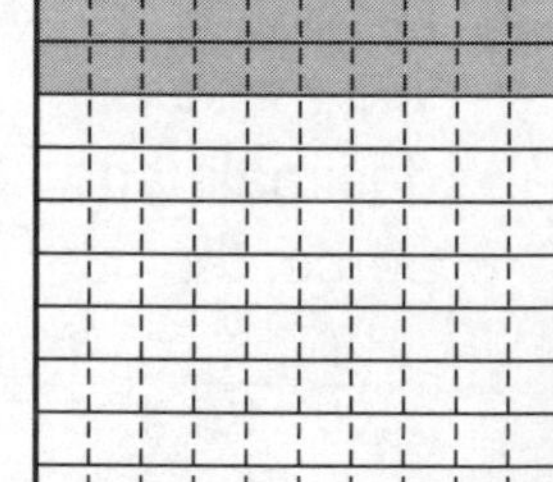

a. What fraction of 100 miles did he jog in 2 weeks? ____________

b. What percent of 100 miles did he jog? ____________

c. At this rate, how many weeks will it take him to jog 100 miles? ____________ weeks

3. Fill in the table of equivalent fractions, decimals, and percents.

Fraction	Decimal	Percent
$\frac{3}{10}$		
$\frac{1}{2}$		
		25%
$\frac{3}{4}$		
	0.80	
$\frac{5}{5}$		

Name Date Time

LESSON 9•10 **Written Assessment** *continued*

4. Use a calculator to rename each fraction as a decimal.

a. $\frac{7}{16}$ = ____________ **b.** $\frac{3}{25}$ = ____________ **c.** $\frac{6}{32}$ = ____________

5. Use a calculator to rename each fraction as a percent.

a. $\frac{3}{8}$ = ____________ **b.** $\frac{15}{16}$ = ____________ **c.** $\frac{3}{96}$ = ____________

6. Shade 40% of the grid at the right.

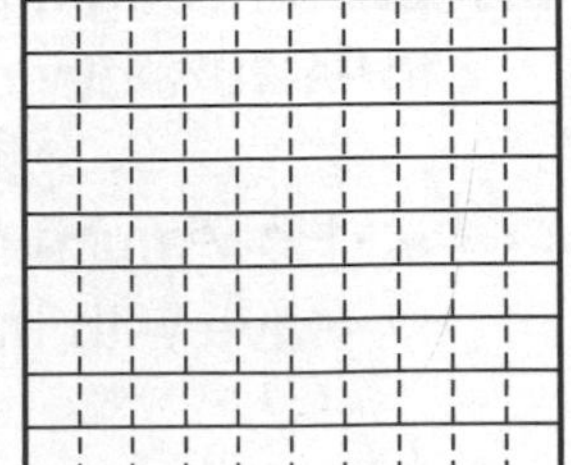

a. What fraction of the grid did you shade? ____________

b. Write this fraction as a decimal. ____________

c. What percent of the grid is NOT shaded? ____________

Find the area and perimeter of each polygon. Write number models to show what you did to get the answers. Include the correct units.

7.

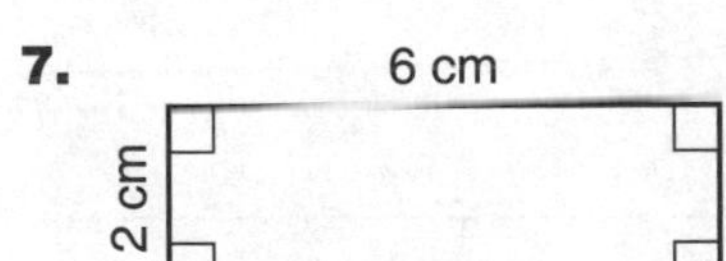

Area = ____________ Number model: ____________

Perimeter = ____________ Number model: ____________

8.

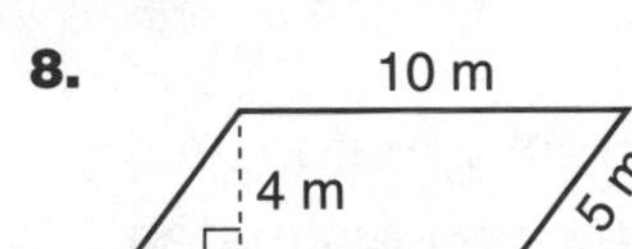

Area = ____________ Number model: ____________

Perimeter = ____________ Number model: ____________

9.

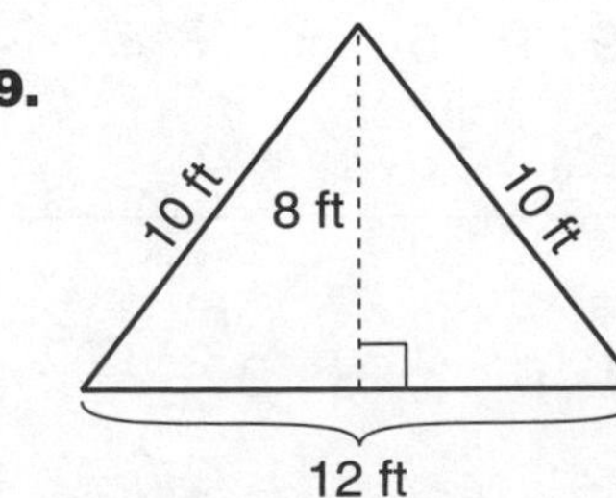

Area = ____________ Number model: ____________

Perimeter = ____________ Number model: ____________

Name Date Time

LESSON 9•10

Written Assessment *continued*

10. Insert parentheses to make each number sentence true.

a. 40 + 30 * 7 = 490

b. 7 = 45 − 16 + 22

c. 55 − 30 / 5 = 5

d. 50 = 13 + 7 + 5 * 2

Part B

11. Susan bought a coat that cost $150. She had a coupon for a 10% discount.

a. How much money did she save with the discount? __________

b. How much did she pay for the coat? __________

12. Randy plans to buy a color television. The model he wants costs $200 at L-Mart and $220 at Al's Department Store. In spring, L-Mart put that television on sale at a savings of $\frac{1}{4}$ off the regular price. Al's Department Store offered a 30% discount on all items.

a. At which store should Randy buy the television? ______________

b. Explain your answer.

____

____

____

For each problem below, the multiplication or division has been done correctly, but the decimal point is missing in the answer. Write a number model to show how you estimated the answer. Then correctly place the decimal point in the answer.

13. 56 * 4.2 = 2 3 5 2

Number model: ______________

14. 0.47 * 85 = 3 9 9 5

Number model: ______________

15. 91.3 / 4 = 2 2 8 2 5

Number model: ______________

16. 297.1 / 3 = 9 9 0 3 3 3

Number model: ______________

Name Date Time

LESSON 9•10

Open Response

Progress Check 9

Designing a Floor

Mrs. Wyman is tiling her floor in a colorful pattern. She knows what colors she wants to use and what percent of the floor each color will be.

1. Find how many tiles of each color Mrs. Wyman needs. Show and explain your work.

Color	Percent of Tiles	Number of Tiles
Blue	40%	
Red	25%	
Yellow	20%	
Green	10%	
Orange		
Total		160

2. Make a design using Mrs. Wyman's tiles on the grid below.

Name Date Time

LESSON **10•7**

Self Assessment

Progress Check 10

Think about each skill listed below. Assess your own progress by checking the most appropriate box.

Skills	I can do this on my own and explain how to do it.	I can do this on my own.	I can do this if I get help or look at an example.
1. Give fraction, decimal, and percent equivalencies.			
2. Add positive and negative numbers.			
3. Use a mirror to draw reflections (flips).			
4. Identify shapes with line symmetry, and draw lines of symmetry.			
5. Identify and describe translations (slides).			
6. Identify and describe rotations (turns).			

Name Date Time

Written Assessment

Progress Check 10

Part A

Use your Geometry Template to complete Problems 1–4.

1. Draw a shape that has no lines of symmetry.

2. Draw a shape that has exactly 1 line of symmetry. Draw the line of symmetry.

3. Draw a shape that has exactly 2 lines of symmetry. Draw the lines of symmetry.

4. Draw a shape that has more than 2 lines of symmetry. Draw the lines of symmetry.

5. Which figure below is a translation (slide) of the original figure? ______

Original

A

B

C

6. Which figure below shows the original figure rotated (turned) clockwise $\frac{1}{4}$-turn? ______

Original

A

B

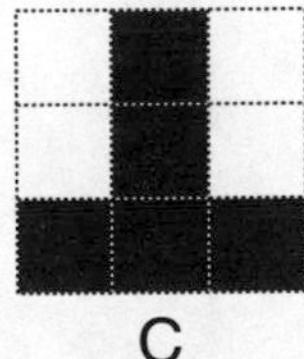
C

Name Date Time

LESSON 10·7 **Written Assessment** *continued*

7. Use a transparent mirror to draw the reflection of the preimage.

8. Use a transparent mirror to draw the other half of the figure across the line of symmetry.

9. Complete the table with equivalent names.

Fraction	Decimal	Percent
$\frac{4}{5}$		
		20%
	0.75	
		6%

10. Add or subtract.

a. $\frac{3}{5} + \frac{1}{5} =$ ________

b. ________ $= \frac{4}{12} + \frac{1}{4}$

c. ________ $= \frac{7}{8} - \frac{2}{8}$

d. $\frac{5}{6} - \frac{1}{2} =$ ________

Name Date Time

LESSON 10•7

Written Assessment *continued*

Part B

11. Add.

a. $-7 + 8 =$ ________

b. $5 + (-2) =$ ________

c. ________ $= -4 + (-6)$

d. ________ $= -9 + 3$

12. Omar had $15.72 in his piggy bank. Then his mother gave him $5.50 for doing his weekly chores. He went to the store with his sister but forgot his money. He borrowed $25.00 from her and spent it all on a new computer game. How much money will Omar have after he repays his sister? Show your work.

Number model: ________________________________

Answer: ________________________________

13. Angle *TUV* is an ________ (acute or obtuse) angle.

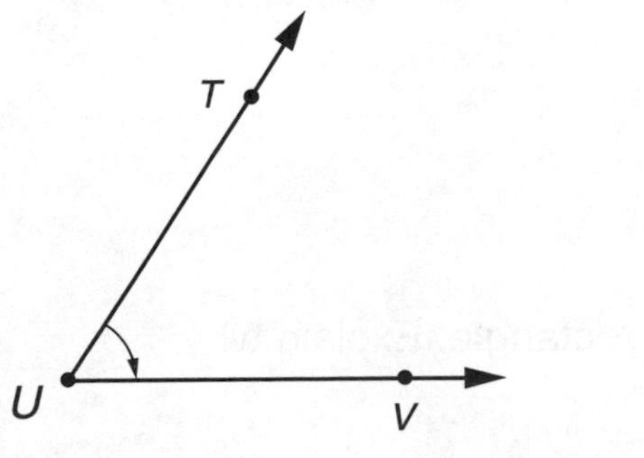

Measure of $\angle TUV =$ ________ °

14. Insert the decimal point in each answer.

a. $9.8 * 6 =$ 5 8 8

b. 1 1 3 6 $= 1.42 * 8$

c. 2 9 4 6 $= 147.3 \div 5$

d. $36.4 \div 8 =$ 4 5 5

Name Date Time

LESSON 10•7

Open Response

Pentominoes

1. Cut out the pentominoes on page 205. Use them to cover the rectangles below in different ways. You must use in each of your solutions. Record your solutions by tracing the pentominoes.

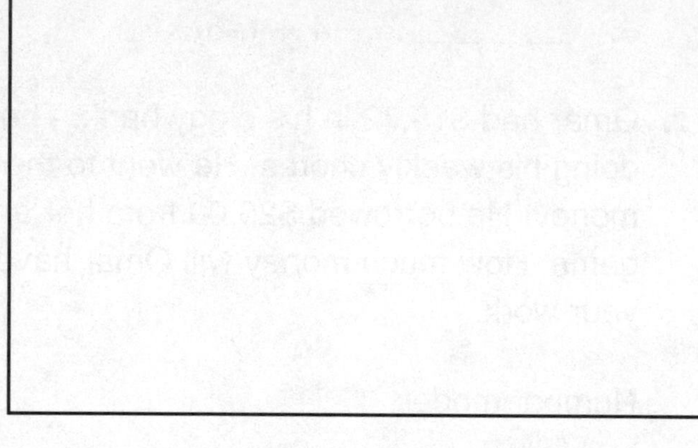

2. Explain the strategy you used to position in your solutions. Include the words *flip, slide,* and *turn* in your explanation.

3. cannot be used as one of the pieces to cover a rectangle. Explain why this is true.

Name Date Time

LESSON 10•7

Pentominoes *continued*

Name Date Time

LESSON 11•8

Self Assessment

Progress Check 11

Think about each skill listed below. Assess your own progress by checking the most appropriate box.

Skills	I can do this on my own and explain how to do it.	I can do this on my own.	I can do this if I get help or look at an example.
1. Add positive and negative numbers.			
2. Subtract positive and negative numbers.			
3. Describe events using terms such as: *certain, likely, very unlikely,* and *impossible.*			
4. Count cubes to find the volume of a rectangular prism.			
5. Use a formula to find the volume of a rectangular prism.			
6. Identify, describe, and compare solid figures such as: *rectangular prisms, pyramids,* and *cones.*			

Name Date Time

LESSON 11•8

Written Assessment

Progress Check 11

Part A

1. Each object below has the shape of a geometric solid. Name the geometric solid.

a.

____

b.

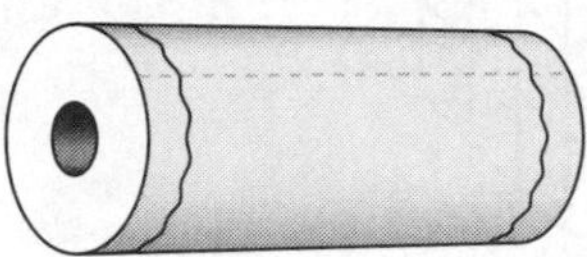

____

2. How many faces does the pentagonal pyramid have? ________ faces

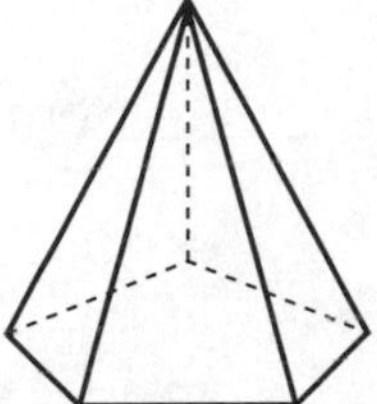

3. Mark *X*s on the vertices of the triangular prism.

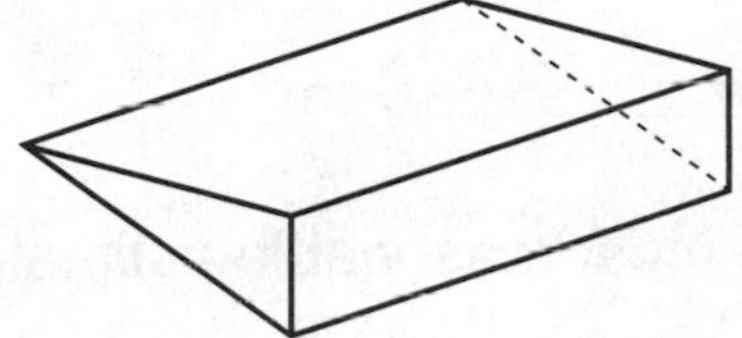

4. How many edges does the rectangular pyramid have? ________ edges

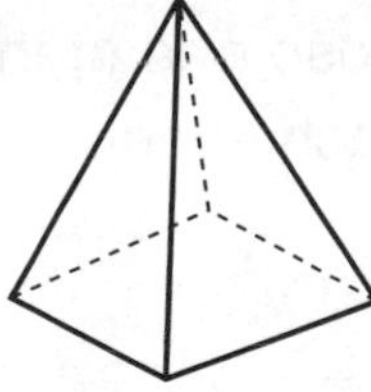

5. Name the shape of the base of the pyramid below. ______________

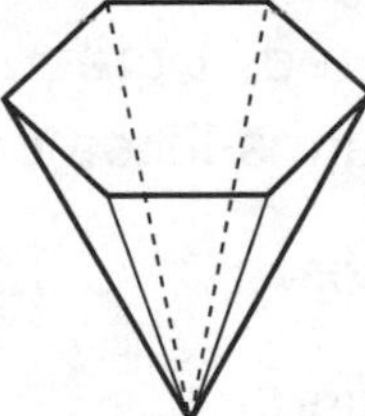

6. Describe the geometric solid to the right. Use the words *vertex, base, face, edge,* and *congruent* in your description.

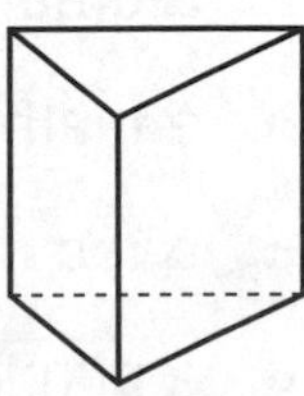

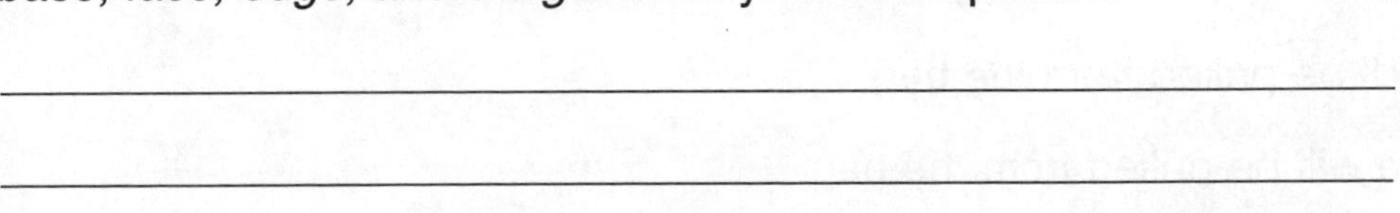

Name Date Time

LESSON 11•8

Written Assessment *continued*

Find the volume of each stack of centimeter cubes.

7.

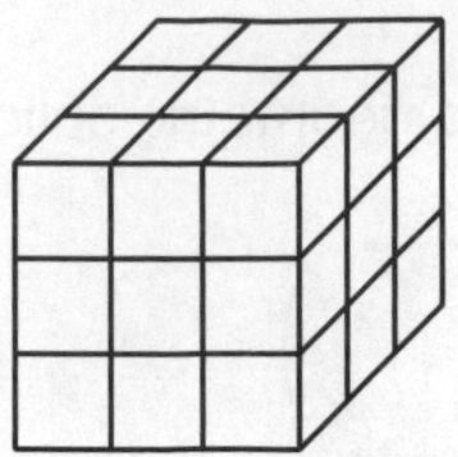

Volume = ________ cm^3

8.

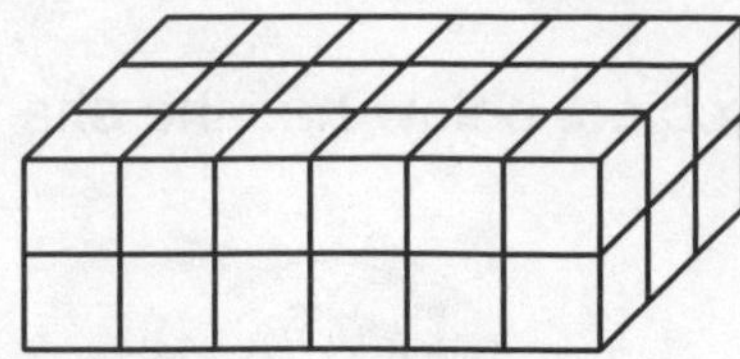

Volume = ________ cm^3

9.

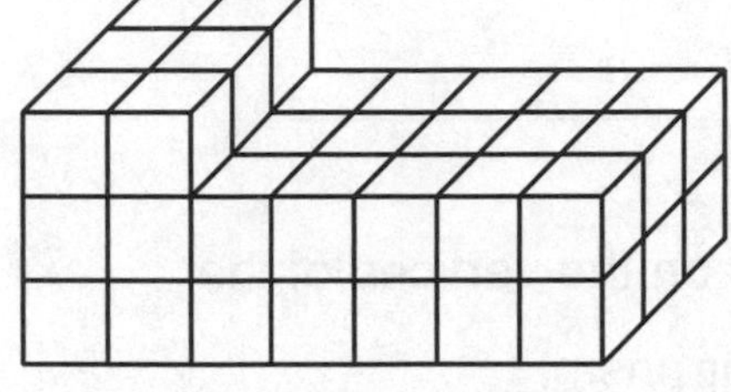

Volume = ________ cm^3

10.

Volume = ________ cm^3

11. Circle the most reasonable estimate for each weight.

a. A box of cereal might weigh about 1.8 oz 18 oz 180 oz

b. A pencil might weigh about 0.5 g 5 g 50 g

c. A female adult might weigh about 65 kg 650 kg 6,500 kg

12. There are 6 red, 1 green, and 3 blue marbles in a bag. Choose one of the probability terms listed below to describe the likelihood of each event.

impossible *certain* *very unlikely* *likely*

Without looking,

a. a green marble will be pulled from the bag. ____________

b. a marble will be pulled from the bag. ____________

c. a red marble will be pulled from the bag. ____________

d. a purple marble will be pulled from the bag. ____________

Name Date Time

LESSON 11•8

Written Assessment *continued*

Part B

Calculate the volume of each rectangular prism.

Volume of a rectangular prism = area of base * height	$V = B * h$

13.

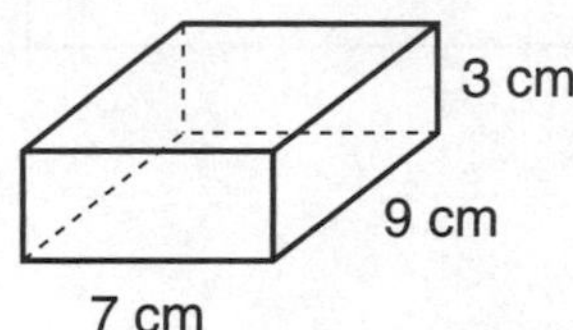

Number model: ____________

Volume = ________ cm^3

14.

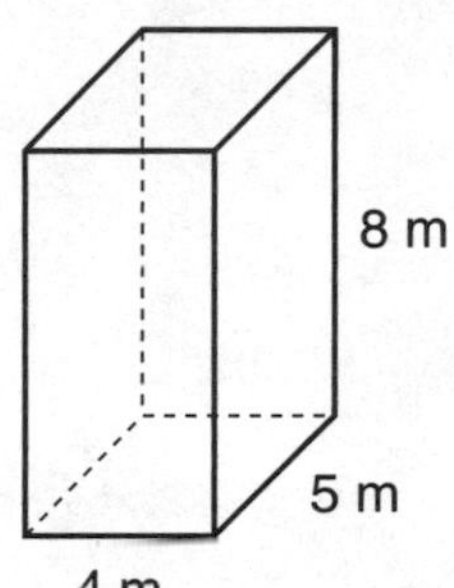

Number model: ____________

Volume = ________ m^3

Add.

15. 14 + (−8) = ________

16. (−20) + 9 = ________

17. ________ = −5 + (−13)

18. ________ = 6 + (−6)

Subtract.

19. −10 − (−7) = ________

20. −12 − 7 = ________

21. ________ = −6 − (−8)

22. ________ = 14 − (−3)

Multiply or divide. Be sure to include the decimal point in your answer.

23. 4.5 * 63 = ________

24. ________ = 0.72 * 9

25. 12.6 ÷ 6 = ________

26. ________ = 78.5 ÷ 5

Name Date Time

Open Response

Progress Check 11

Record Rainfall

According to the National Weather Service, the most rain that fell in the United States in a 24-hour period was 42 inches. This happened in Alvin, Texas, on July 25 and 26, 1979.

Imagine that it rained 42 inches in your classroom. About how many pounds would the water weigh?

Hints: 1 cubic foot of water weighs about 62.5 pounds. 1 ton equal 2,000 pounds.

1. List the information you need to solve the problem.

2. Explain your plan for solving the problem.

3. If 42 inches of rainwater fell in a classroom that is 27 feet long and 24 feet wide, about how many pounds would the rainwater weigh? Show all of your work.

Name Date Time

LESSON 12•7

Self Assessment

Progress Check 12

Think about each skill listed below. Assess your own progress by checking the most appropriate box.

Skills	I can do this on my own and explain how to do it.	I can do this on my own.	I can do this if I get help or look at an example.
1. Find factors and factor pairs.			
2. Compare and order positive and negative fractions.			
3. Add positive and negative numbers.			
4. Subtract positive and negative numbers.			
5. Solve rate problems.			
6. Convert among U.S. customary units of capacity.			
7. Solve open sentences.			

Name Date Time

LESSON 12•7

Written Assessment

Progress Check 12

Part A

1. The Davis family drove 280 miles to visit relatives. It took 5 hours. At that rate, about how many miles did the Davises drive in 3 hours? About _______ miles

Fill in the rate table, if needed.

Hours			3		5
Miles					280

2. Jan earned $19.50 last week for mowing 3 lawns. At that rate, what would Jan earn for mowing 5 lawns? _______

Fill in the rate table, if needed.

Lawns			3		5
Dollars			19.50		

3. Tina works 7 hours per day, 5 days per week. She earns $56.00 per day.

a. How much does she earn per hour? _______

b. How much does she earn per week? _______

4. List the factor pairs of 40.

_______ and _______ _______ and _______

_______ and _______ _______ and _______

5. Name all the factors of 64.

____

Name Date Time

LESSON 12•7

Written Assessment *continued*

6. Insert <, >, or = to make a true number sentence.

a. −25 ________ 22

b. 0 ________ −2

c. −10 ________ −100

d. −82 ________ −64

7. Order the numbers from smallest to largest.

−30, 4, 15, −2, 17, −8

________ ________ ________ ________ ________ ________

smallest largest

8. Use the diagram to help you solve the problems.

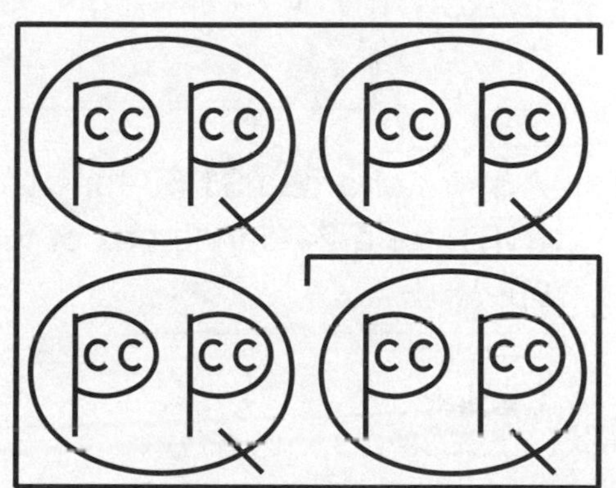

a. ________ c = 2 gal

b. 10 qt = ________ gal ________ qt

c. 22 c = ________ qt ________ pt

d. 13 pt = ________ qt ________ pt

e. 15 qt = ________ c

9. Calculate the volume.

a.

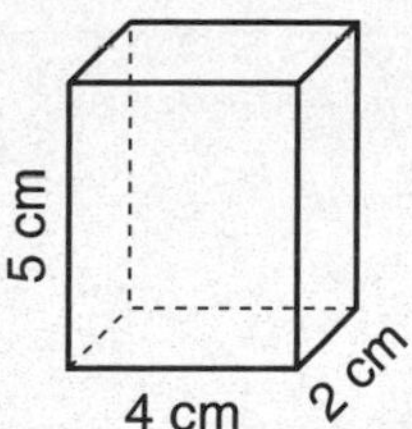

Number model: ________________

Volume = ________ cm^3

b.

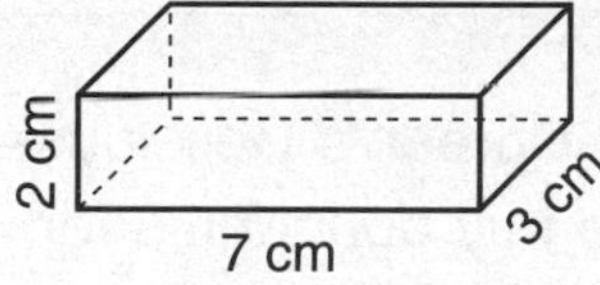

Number model: ________________

Volume = ________ cm^3

10. Solve the open sentences.

a. 0.930 + 3.59 = *y* *y* = ________

b. 51.9 + *b* = 69.07 *b* = ________

c. 1.89 − 0.206 = *q* *q* = ________

d. 1.46 = *k* − 0.028 *k* = ________

Name _______________ Date _______________ Time _______________

LESSON 12•7

Written Assessment *continued*

Part B

11. Order the fractions from smallest to largest.

a. $-\frac{10}{7}$, $\frac{1}{7}$, $-\frac{7}{7}$, $\frac{4}{7}$, $-\frac{5}{7}$ _______ _______ _______ _______ _______
smallest largest

b. $\frac{6}{12}$, $-\frac{1}{3}$, $\frac{2}{9}$, $\frac{15}{20}$, $\frac{4}{4}$ _______ _______ _______ _______ _______
smallest largest

12. It was reported that on New Year's Day in 1907, Theodore Roosevelt shook hands with 8,513 people. Does this seem reasonable? Explain your answer.

____

____

____

13. A store charges \$1.58 for a 20-ounce box of Puff Flakes cereal and \$1.72 for a 24-ounce box of the same cereal. Which is the better buy?

____

Explain why.

____

____

____

14. Joey goes to Doreen's Delicious Doughnuts to buy doughnuts for the class party. What is the least amount of money he will have to pay for 30 doughnuts?

____

Explain.

____

____

____

____

Name Date Time

Open Response

Progress Check 12

Buying Cookies

Raheem and India volunteered to buy cookies for the class party. They wanted at least 4 different kinds of cookies, and they wanted to spend as little money as possible. They decided that 3 pounds of cookies would be enough. When they went to the store, they saw these prices for packages of cookies:

mint creams $2.79/lb

fudge marshmallow . . . . $1.69/12 oz

sugar wafers . . . . $2.99/8 oz

vanilla wafers . . . . $1.39/11 oz

chocolate chip . . . .$2.39/12 oz

oatmeal . . . . $2.03/17 oz

windmill $2.59/lb

ginger snaps . . . . $0.60/8 oz

1. What 4 packages of cookies would you recommend they buy so that they have a total of about 3 pounds and they spend as little money as possible? Show all of your work, and explain how you found your answer. *Hint:* 1 pound = 16 ounces

2. If they follow your recommendations, how much money will they spend on cookies? Show your work.

3. About what is the cost per pound of the 3 pounds of cookies you selected? Show your work.

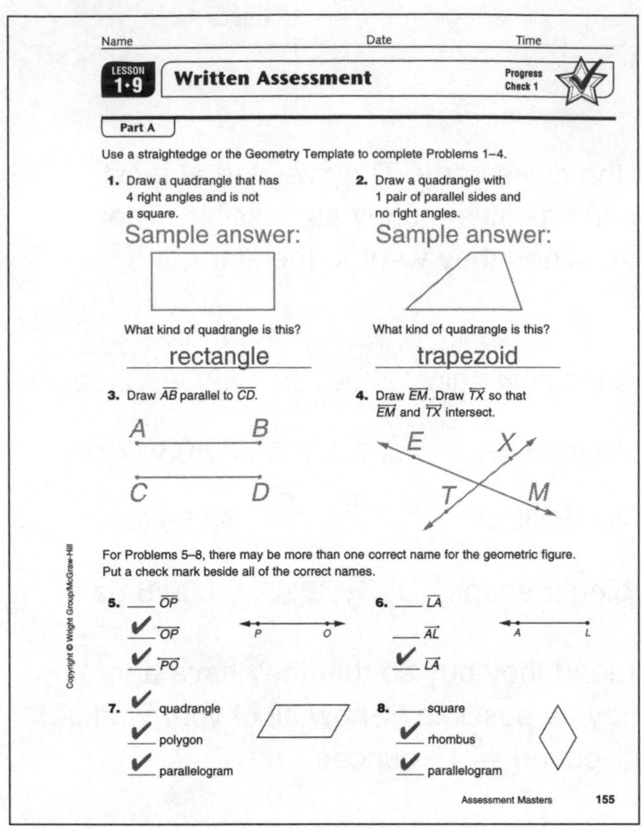

Name Date Time

LESSON 1•9 **Written Assessment** Progress Check 1

Part A

Use a straightedge or the Geometry Template to complete Problems 1–4.

1. Draw a quadrangle that has 4 right angles and is not a square.

Sample answer:

What kind of quadrangle is this? rectangle

2. Draw a quadrangle with 1 pair of parallel sides and no right angles.

Sample answer:

What kind of quadrangle is this? trapezoid

3. Draw $\overline{AB}$ parallel to $\overline{CD}$.

A B
C D

4. Draw $\overleftrightarrow{EM}$. Draw $\overleftrightarrow{TX}$ so that $\overleftrightarrow{EM}$ and $\overleftrightarrow{TX}$ intersect.

E X T M

For Problems 5–8, there may be more than one correct name for the geometric figure. Put a check mark beside all of the correct names.

5. ___ $\overline{OP}$
✔ $\overleftrightarrow{OP}$
✔ $\overleftrightarrow{PO}$

P O

6. ___ $\overline{LA}$
___ $\overrightarrow{AL}$
✔ $\overrightarrow{LA}$

A L

7. ✔ quadrangle
✔ polygon
✔ parallelogram

8. ___ square
✔ rhombus
✔ parallelogram

Copyright © Wright Group/McGraw-Hill

Assessment Masters 155

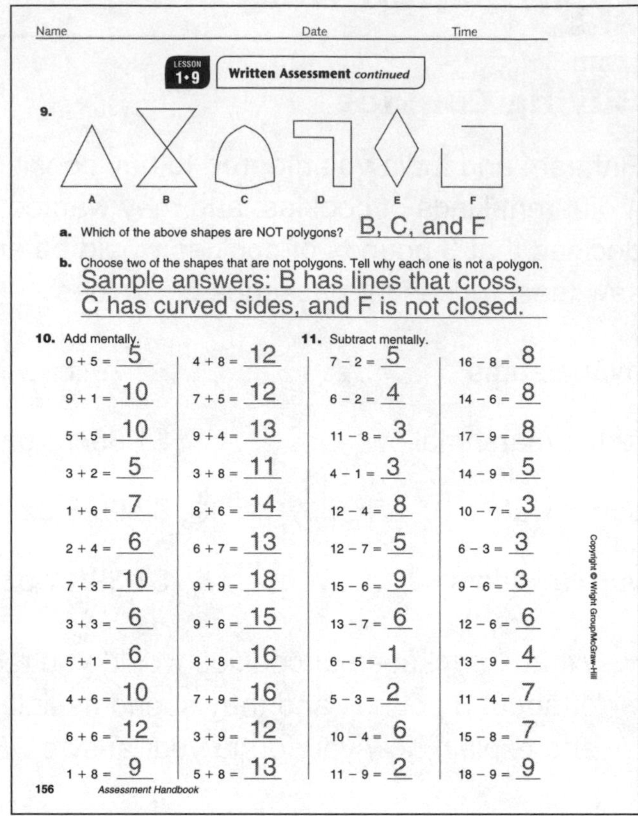

Name Date Time

LESSON 1•9 **Written Assessment** *continued*

9.

A B C D E F

a. Which of the above shapes are NOT polygons? B, C, and F

b. Choose two of the shapes that are not polygons. Tell why each one is not a polygon.
Sample answers: B has lines that cross, C has curved sides, and F is not closed.

10. Add mentally.

11. Subtract mentally.

0 + 5 = 5	4 + 8 = 12	7 − 2 = 5	16 − 8 = 8
9 + 1 = 10	7 + 5 = 12	6 − 2 = 4	14 − 6 = 8
5 + 5 = 10	9 + 4 = 13	11 − 8 = 3	17 − 9 = 8
3 + 2 = 5	3 + 8 = 11	4 − 1 = 3	14 − 9 = 5
1 + 6 = 7	8 + 6 = 14	12 − 4 = 8	10 − 7 = 3
2 + 4 = 6	6 + 7 = 13	12 − 7 = 5	6 − 3 = 3
7 + 3 = 10	9 + 9 = 18	15 − 6 = 9	9 − 6 = 3
3 + 3 = 6	9 + 6 = 15	13 − 7 = 6	12 − 6 = 6
5 + 1 = 6	8 + 8 = 16	6 − 5 = 1	13 − 9 = 4
4 + 6 = 10	7 + 9 = 16	5 − 3 = 2	11 − 4 = 7
6 + 6 = 12	3 + 9 = 12	10 − 4 = 6	15 − 8 = 7
1 + 8 = 9	5 + 8 = 13	11 − 9 = 2	18 − 9 = 9

Copyright © Wright Group/McGraw-Hill

156 Assessment Handbook

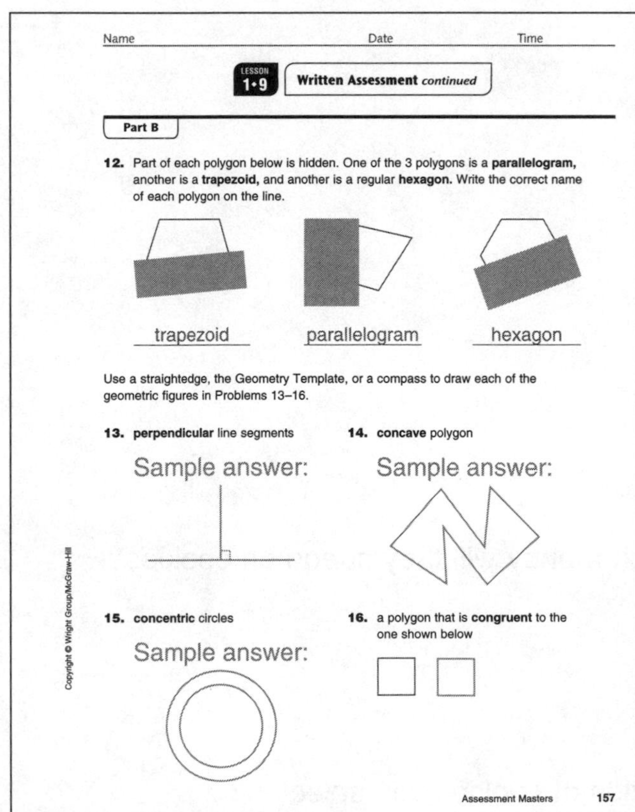

Name Date Time

LESSON 1•9 **Written Assessment** *continued*

Part B

12. Part of each polygon below is hidden. One of the 3 polygons is a **parallelogram,** another is a **trapezoid,** and another is a regular **hexagon.** Write the correct name of each polygon on the line.

trapezoid parallelogram hexagon

Use a straightedge, the Geometry Template, or a compass to draw each of the geometric figures in Problems 13–16.

13. perpendicular line segments

Sample answer:

14. concave polygon

Sample answer:

15. concentric circles

Sample answer:

16. a polygon that is **congruent** to the one shown below

Copyright © Wright Group/McGraw-Hill

Assessment Masters 157

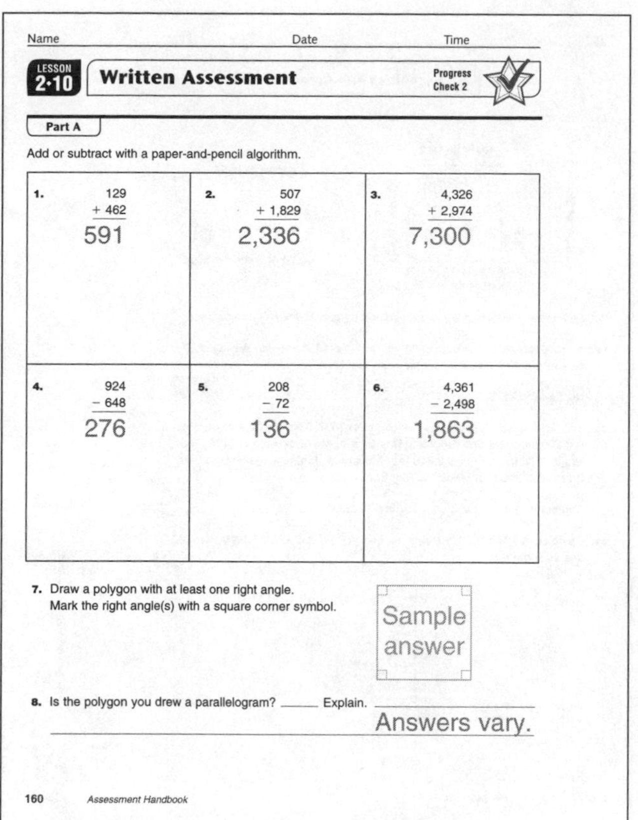

Name Date Time

LESSON 2·10 **Written Assessment** Progress Check 2

Part A

Add or subtract with a paper-and-pencil algorithm.

1. 129 + 462 = 591	**2.** 507 + 1,829 = 2,336	**3.** 4,326 + 2,974 = 7,300
4. 924 − 648 = 276	**5.** 208 − 72 = 136	**6.** 4,361 − 2,498 = 1,863

7. Draw a polygon with at least one right angle. Mark the right angle(s) with a square corner symbol.

Sample answer

8. Is the polygon you drew a parallelogram? ____ Explain. Answers vary.

160 *Assessment Handbook*

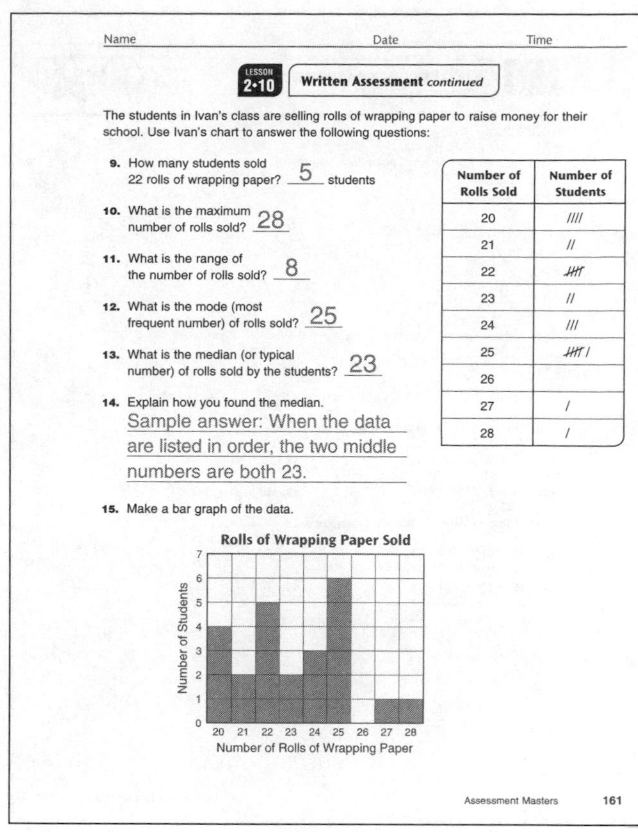

Name Date Time

LESSON 2·10 **Written Assessment** *continued*

The students in Ivan's class are selling rolls of wrapping paper to raise money for their school. Use Ivan's chart to answer the following questions:

9. How many students sold 22 rolls of wrapping paper? 5 students

10. What is the maximum number of rolls sold? 28

11. What is the range of the number of rolls sold? 8

12. What is the mode (most frequent number) of rolls sold? 25

13. What is the median (or typical number) of rolls sold by the students? 23

14. Explain how you found the median.
Sample answer: When the data are listed in order, the two middle numbers are both 23.

Number of Rolls Sold	Number of Students
20	////
21	//
22	~~////~~
23	//
24	///
25	~~////~~ /
26	
27	/
28	/

15. Make a bar graph of the data.

Assessment Masters 161

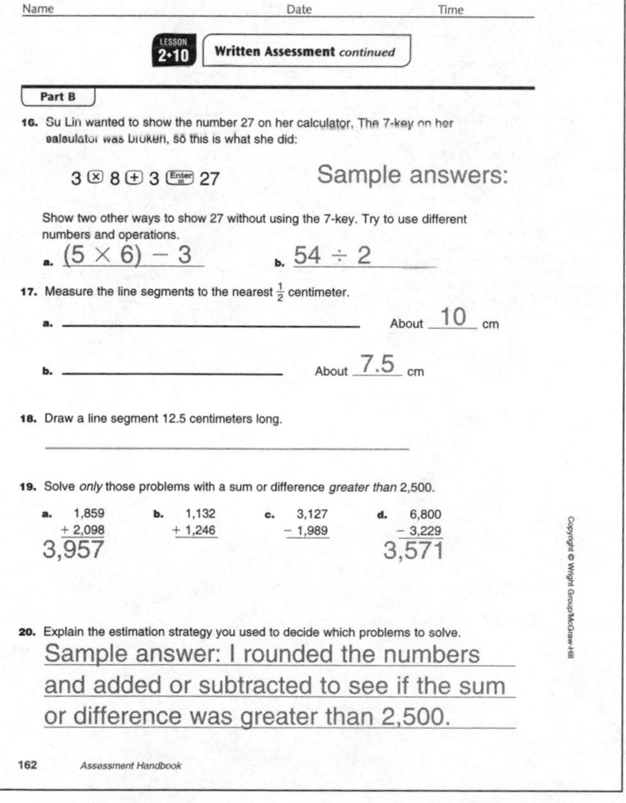

Name Date Time

LESSON 2·10 **Written Assessment** *continued*

Part B

16. Su Lin wanted to show the number 27 on her calculator. The 7-key on her calculator was broken, so this is what she did:

3 ⊗ 8 ⊕ 3 (Enter) 27

Sample answers:

Show two other ways to show 27 without using the 7-key. Try to use different numbers and operations.

a. $(5 \times 6) - 3$ **b.** $54 \div 2$

17. Measure the line segments to the nearest $\frac{1}{2}$ centimeter.

a. ________ About 10 cm

b. ________ About 7.5 cm

18. Draw a line segment 12.5 centimeters long.

19. Solve *only* those problems with a sum or difference *greater than* 2,500.

a. 1,859 + 2,098 = 3,957 **b.** 1,132 + 1,246 **c.** 3,127 − 1,989 **d.** 6,800 − 3,229 = 3,571

20. Explain the estimation strategy you used to decide which problems to solve.
Sample answer: I rounded the numbers and added or subtracted to see if the sum or difference was greater than 2,500.

162 *Assessment Handbook*

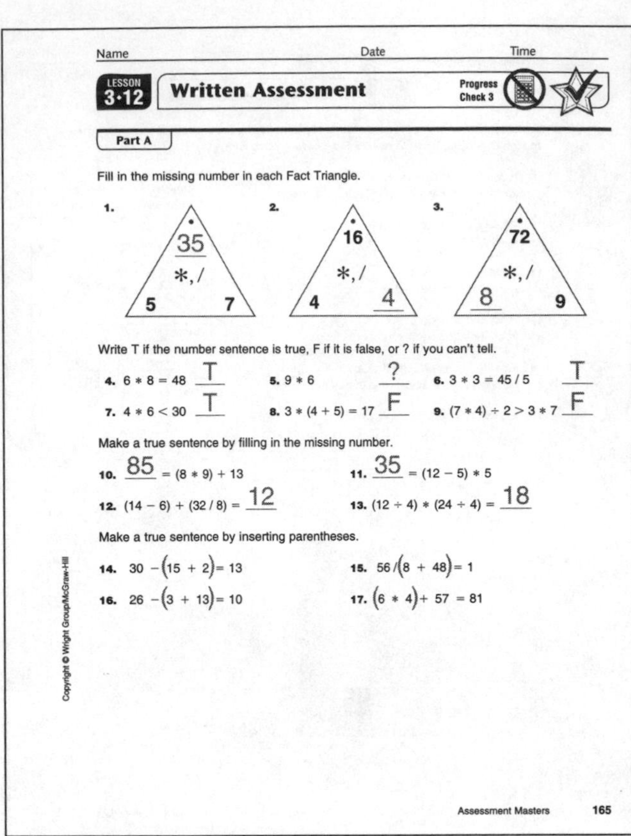

Name Date Time

LESSON 3·12 **Written Assessment** Progress Check 3

Part A

Fill in the missing number in each Fact Triangle.

Write T if the number sentence is true, F if it is false, or ? if you can't tell.

4. 6 * 8 = 48 T
5. 9 * 6 ?
6. 3 * 3 = 45 / 5 T
7. 4 * 6 < 30 T
8. 3 * (4 + 5) = 17 F
9. (7 * 4) ÷ 2 > 3 * 7 F

Make a true sentence by filling in the missing number.

10. 85 = (8 * 9) + 13
11. 35 = (12 − 5) * 5
12. (14 − 6) + (32 / 8) = 12
13. (12 ÷ 4) * (24 ÷ 4) = 18

Make a true sentence by inserting parentheses.

14. 30 − (15 + 2) = 13
15. 56 / (8 + 48) = 1
16. 26 − (3 + 13) = 10
17. (6 * 4) + 57 = 81

Assessment Masters 165

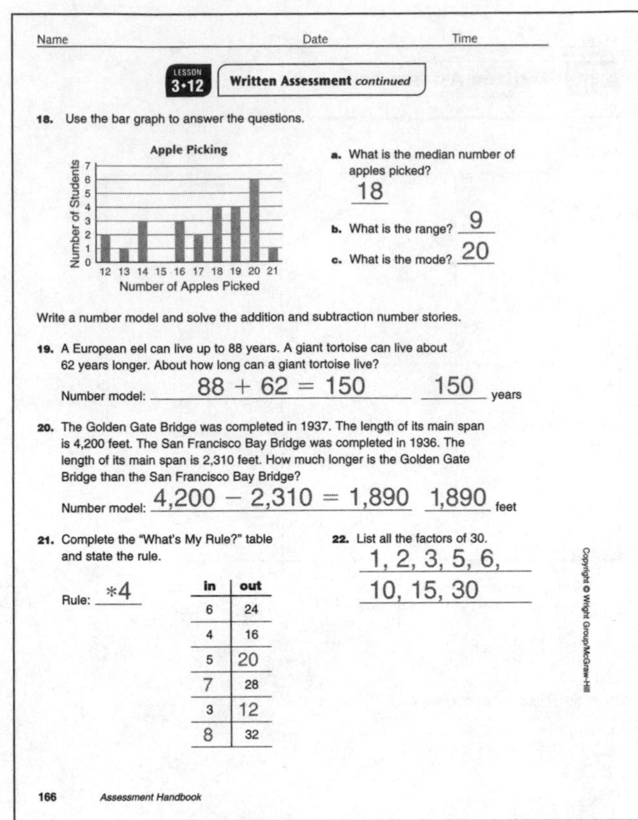

Name Date Time

LESSON 3·12 **Written Assessment** *continued*

18. Use the bar graph to answer the questions.

a. What is the median number of apples picked? 18

b. What is the range? 9

c. What is the mode? 20

Write a number model and solve the addition and subtraction number stories.

19. A European eel can live up to 88 years. A giant tortoise can live about 62 years longer. About how long can a giant tortoise live?

Number model: 88 + 62 = 150 150 years

20. The Golden Gate Bridge was completed in 1937. The length of its main span is 4,200 feet. The San Francisco Bay Bridge was completed in 1936. The length of its main span is 2,310 feet. How much longer is the Golden Gate Bridge than the San Francisco Bay Bridge?

Number model: 4,200 − 2,310 = 1,890 1,890 feet

21. Complete the "What's My Rule?" table and state the rule.

Rule: *4

in	out
6	24
4	16
5	20
7	28
3	12
8	32

22. List all the factors of 30.

1, 2, 3, 5, 6, 10, 15, 30

166 *Assessment Handbook*

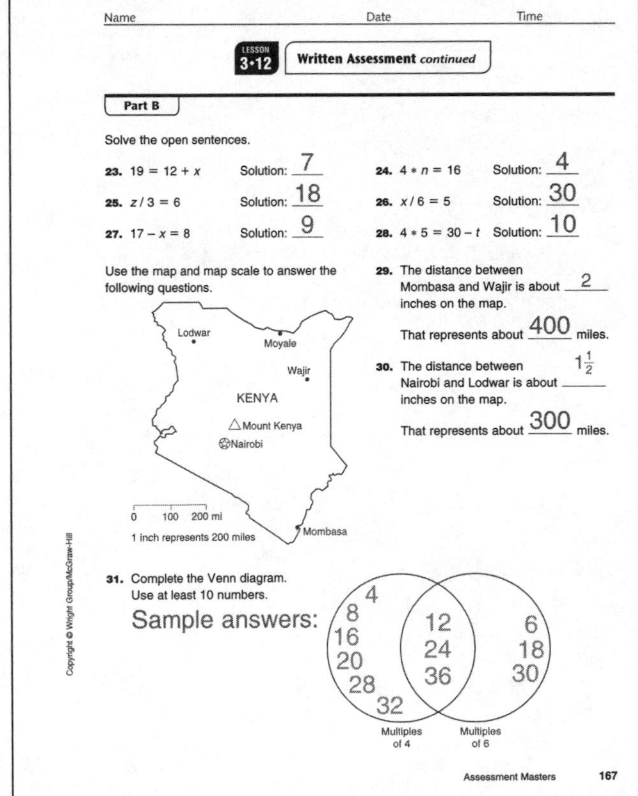

Name Date Time

LESSON 3·12 **Written Assessment** *continued*

Part B

Solve the open sentences.

23. 19 = 12 + *x* Solution: 7
24. 4 * *n* = 16 Solution: 4
25. *z* / 3 = 6 Solution: 18
26. *x* / 6 = 5 Solution: 30
27. 17 − *x* = 8 Solution: 9
28. 4 * 5 = 30 − *t* Solution: 10

Use the map and map scale to answer the following questions.

29. The distance between Mombasa and Wajir is about 2 inches on the map.

That represents about 400 miles.

30. The distance between Nairobi and Lodwar is about $1\frac{1}{2}$ inches on the map.

That represents about 300 miles.

31. Complete the Venn diagram. Use at least 10 numbers.

Sample answers:

Assessment Masters 167

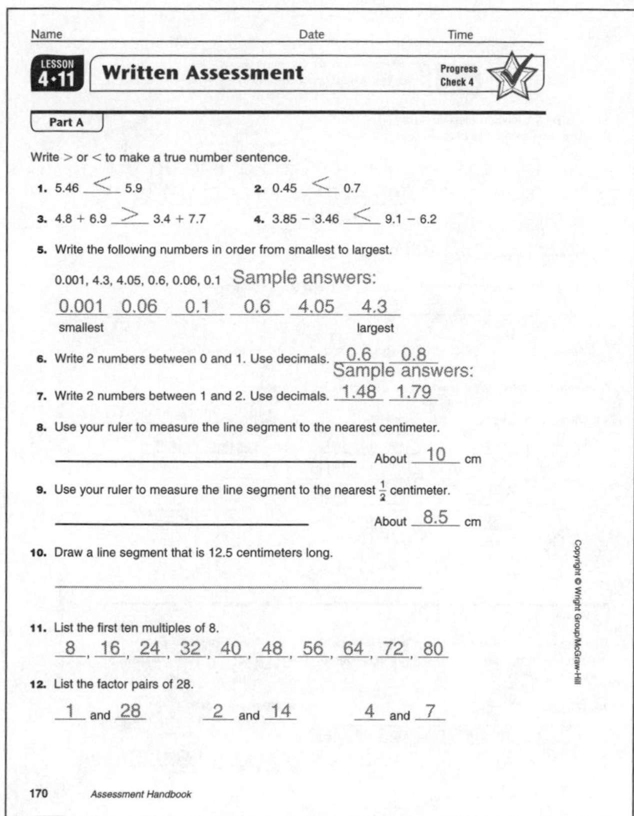
Name Date Time

LESSON 4•11 **Written Assessment** Progress Check 4

Part A

Write > or < to make a true number sentence.

1. 5.46 __<__ 5.9
2. 0.45 __<__ 0.7
3. 4.8 + 6.9 __>__ 3.4 + 7.7
4. 3.85 − 3.46 __<__ 9.1 − 6.2
5. Write the following numbers in order from smallest to largest.

   0.001, 4.3, 4.05, 0.6, 0.06, 0.1 Sample answers:

   0.001, 0.06, 0.1, 0.6, 4.05, 4.3

   smallest ... largest
6. Write 2 numbers between 0 and 1. Use decimals. 0.6 0.8

   Sample answers:
7. Write 2 numbers between 1 and 2. Use decimals. 1.48 1.79
8. Use your ruler to measure the line segment to the nearest centimeter.

   About __10__ cm
9. Use your ruler to measure the line segment to the nearest $\frac{1}{2}$ centimeter.

   About __8.5__ cm
10. Draw a line segment that is 12.5 centimeters long.
11. List the first ten multiples of 8.

    8, 16, 24, 32, 40, 48, 56, 64, 72, 80
12. List the factor pairs of 28.

    1 and 28 2 and 14 4 and 7

170 *Assessment Handbook*

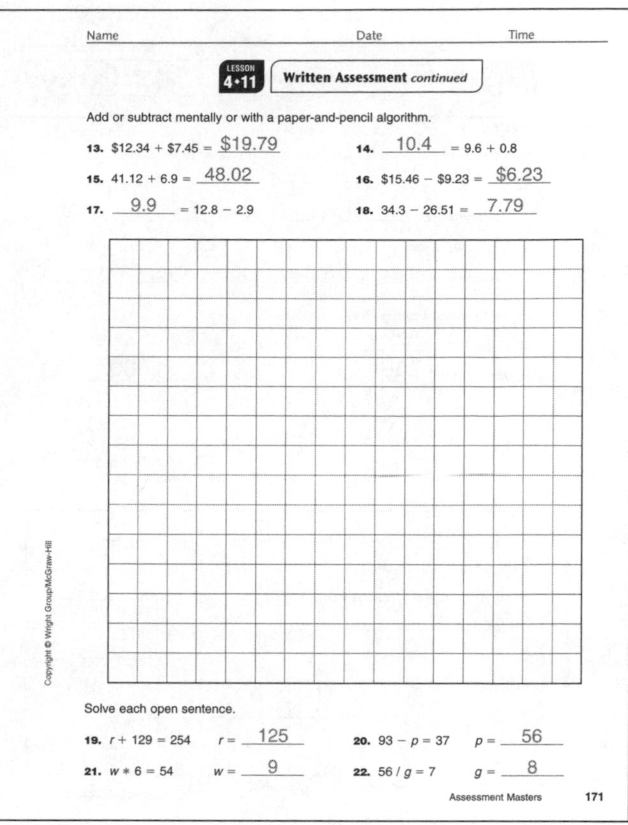
Name Date Time

LESSON 4•11 **Written Assessment** *continued*

Add or subtract mentally or with a paper-and-pencil algorithm.

13. $12.34 + $7.45 = __$19.79__
14. __10.4__ = 9.6 + 0.8
15. 41.12 + 6.9 = __48.02__
16. $15.46 − $9.23 = __$6.23__
17. __9.9__ = 12.8 − 2.9
18. 34.3 − 26.51 = __7.79__

Solve each open sentence.

19. $r + 129 = 254$ $r =$ __125__
20. $93 - p = 37$ $p =$ __56__
21. $w * 6 = 54$ $w =$ __9__
22. $56 / g = 7$ $g =$ __8__

Assessment Masters 171

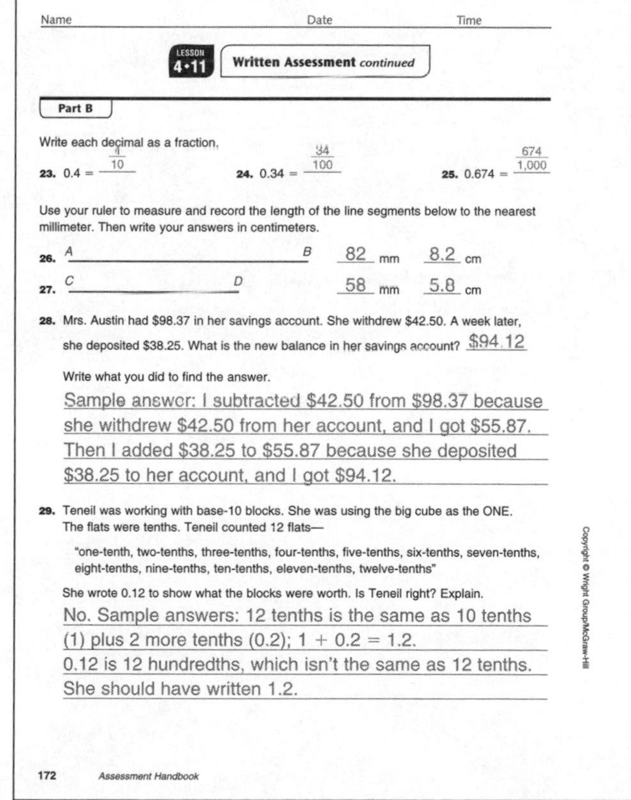
Name Date Time

LESSON 4•11 **Written Assessment** *continued*

Part B

Write each decimal as a fraction.

23. 0.4 = $\frac{4}{10}$
24. 0.34 = $\frac{34}{100}$
25. 0.674 = $\frac{674}{1,000}$

Use your ruler to measure and record the length of the line segments below to the nearest millimeter. Then write your answers in centimeters.

26. A ——— B __82__ mm __8.2__ cm
27. C ——— D __58__ mm __5.8__ cm
28. Mrs. Austin had $98.37 in her savings account. She withdrew $42.50. A week later, she deposited $38.25. What is the new balance in her savings account? __$94.12__

    Write what you did to find the answer.

    Sample answer: I subtracted $42.50 from $98.37 because she withdrew $42.50 from her account, and I got $55.87. Then I added $38.25 to $55.87 because she deposited $38.25 to her account, and I got $94.12.
29. Teneil was working with base-10 blocks. She was using the big cube as the ONE. The flats were tenths. Teneil counted 12 flats—

    "one-tenth, two-tenths, three-tenths, four-tenths, five-tenths, six-tenths, seven-tenths, eight-tenths, nine-tenths, ten-tenths, eleven-tenths, twelve-tenths"

    She wrote 0.12 to show what the blocks were worth. Is Teneil right? Explain.

    No. Sample answers: 12 tenths is the same as 10 tenths (1) plus 2 more tenths (0.2); 1 + 0.2 = 1.2. 0.12 is 12 hundredths, which isn't the same as 12 tenths. She should have written 1.2.

172 *Assessment Handbook*

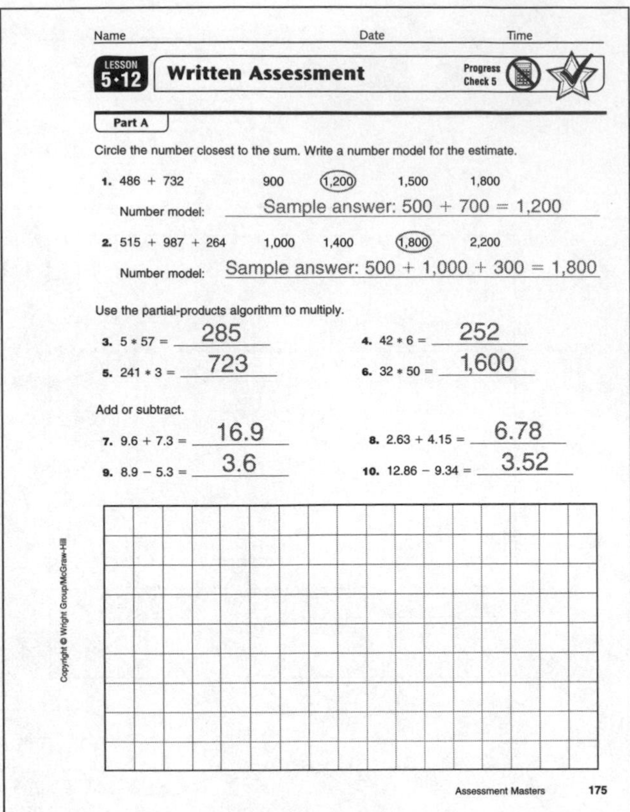

Name Date Time

LESSON 5·12 **Written Assessment** Progress Check 5

Part A

Circle the number closest to the sum. Write a number model for the estimate.

1. 486 + 732 — 900 (1,200) 1,500 1,800

Number model: Sample answer: 500 + 700 = 1,200

2. 515 + 987 + 264 — 1,000 1,400 (1,800) 2,200

Number model: Sample answer: 500 + 1,000 + 300 = 1,800

Use the partial-products algorithm to multiply.

3. 5 * 57 = 285
4. 42 * 6 = 252
5. 241 * 3 = 723
6. 32 * 50 = 1,600

Add or subtract.

7. 9.6 + 7.3 = 16.9
8. 2.63 + 4.15 = 6.78
9. 8.9 − 5.3 = 3.6
10. 12.86 − 9.34 = 3.52

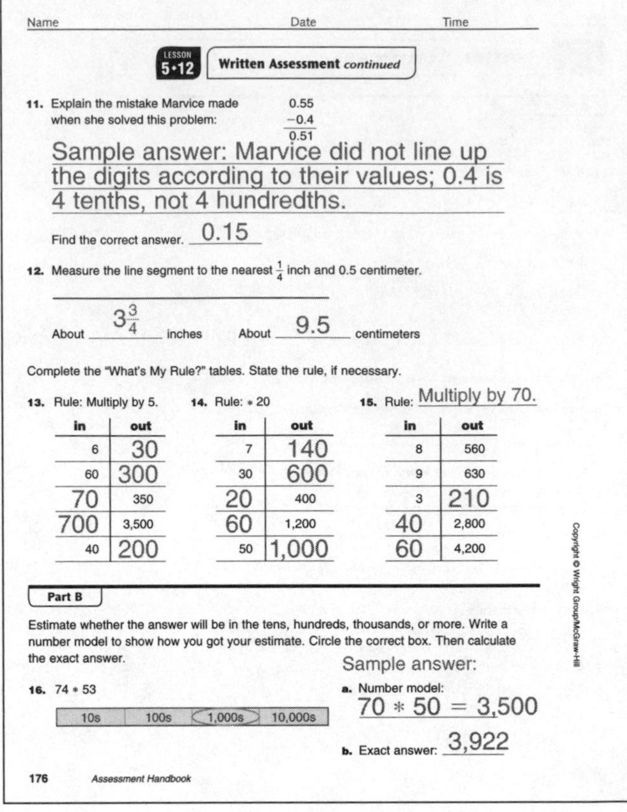

Name Date Time

LESSON 5·12 **Written Assessment** *continued*

11. Explain the mistake Marvice made when she solved this problem:

0.55
−0.4
0.51

Sample answer: Marvice did not line up the digits according to their values; 0.4 is 4 tenths, not 4 hundredths.

Find the correct answer. 0.15

12. Measure the line segment to the nearest $\frac{1}{4}$ inch and 0.5 centimeter.

About $3\frac{3}{4}$ inches About 9.5 centimeters

Complete the "What's My Rule?" tables. State the rule, if necessary.

13. Rule: Multiply by 5.

in	out
6	30
60	300
70	350
700	3,500
40	200

14. Rule: * 20

in	out
7	140
30	600
20	400
60	1,200
50	1,000

15. Rule: Multiply by 70.

in	out
8	560
9	630
3	210
40	2,800
60	4,200

Part B

Estimate whether the answer will be in the tens, hundreds, thousands, or more. Write a number model to show how you got your estimate. Circle the correct box. Then calculate the exact answer.

16. 74 * 53

10s | 100s | (1,000s) | 10,000s

Sample answer:

a. Number model: 70 * 50 = 3,500

b. Exact answer: 3,922

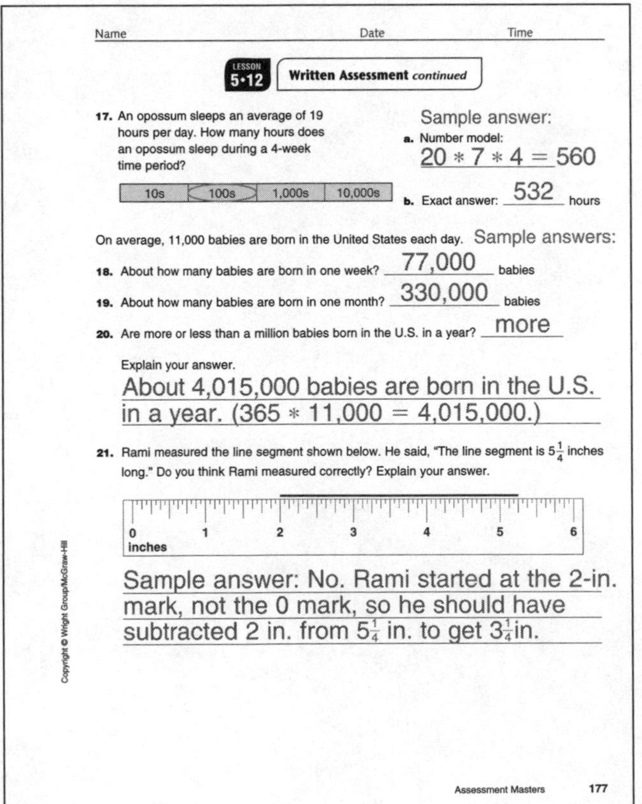

Name Date Time

LESSON 5·12 **Written Assessment** *continued*

17. An opossum sleeps an average of 19 hours per day. How many hours does an opossum sleep during a 4-week time period?

10s | (100s) | 1,000s | 10,000s

Sample answer:

a. Number model: 20 * 7 * 4 = 560

b. Exact answer: 532 hours

On average, 11,000 babies are born in the United States each day. Sample answers:

18. About how many babies are born in one week? 77,000 babies

19. About how many babies are born in one month? 330,000 babies

20. Are more or less than a million babies born in the U.S. in a year? more

Explain your answer.

About 4,015,000 babies are born in the U.S. in a year. (365 * 11,000 = 4,015,000.)

21. Rami measured the line segment shown below. He said, "The line segment is $5\frac{1}{4}$ inches long." Do you think Rami measured correctly? Explain your answer.

Sample answer: No. Rami started at the 2-in. mark, not the 0 mark, so he should have subtracted 2 in. from $5\frac{1}{4}$ in. to get $3\frac{1}{4}$ in.

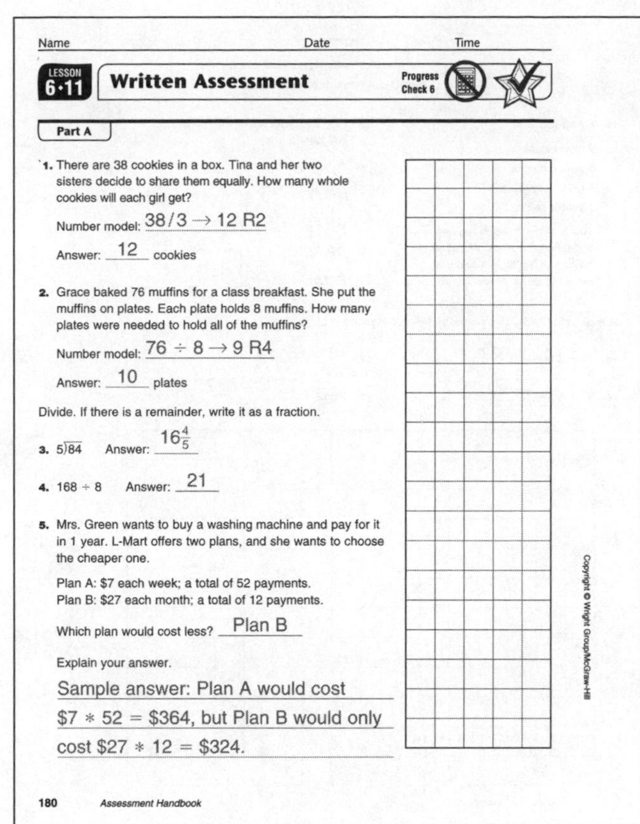

Name Date Time

LESSON 6·11 **Written Assessment** Progress Check 6

Part A

1. There are 38 cookies in a box. Tina and her two sisters decide to share them equally. How many whole cookies will each girl get?

   Number model: 38 / 3 → 12 R2

   Answer: 12 cookies

2. Grace baked 76 muffins for a class breakfast. She put the muffins on plates. Each plate holds 8 muffins. How many plates were needed to hold all of the muffins?

   Number model: $76 \div 8 \rightarrow 9$ R4

   Answer: 10 plates

Divide. If there is a remainder, write it as a fraction.

3. 5)84 Answer: $16\frac{4}{5}$

4. 168 ÷ 8 Answer: 21

5. Mrs. Green wants to buy a washing machine and pay for it in 1 year. L-Mart offers two plans, and she wants to choose the cheaper one.

   Plan A: $7 each week; a total of 52 payments.
   Plan B: $27 each month; a total of 12 payments.

   Which plan would cost less? Plan B

   Explain your answer.

   Sample answer: Plan A would cost $7 * 52 = $364, but Plan B would only cost $27 * 12 = $324.

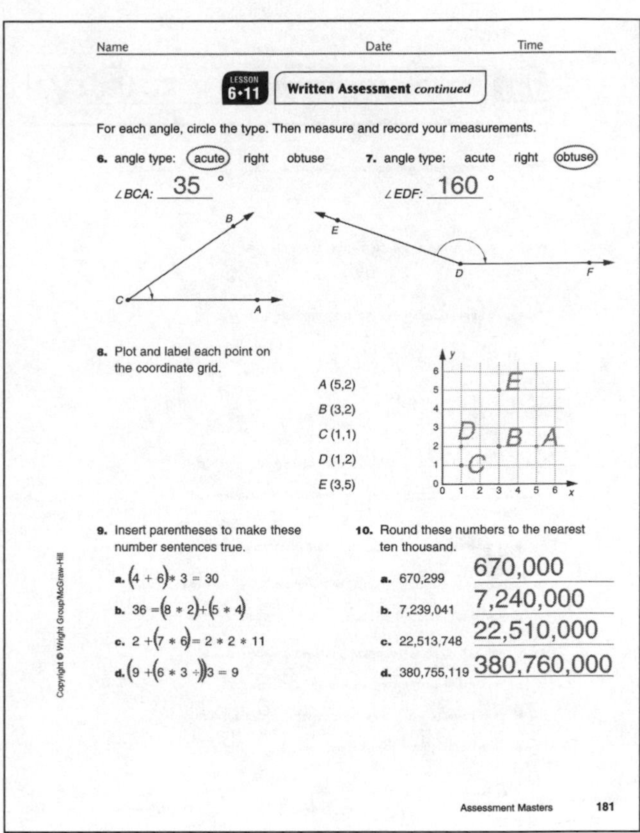

Name Date Time

LESSON 6·11 **Written Assessment** *continued*

For each angle, circle the type. Then measure and record your measurements.

6. angle type: (acute) right obtuse

   ∠BCA: 35 °

7. angle type: acute right (obtuse)

   ∠EDF: 160 °

8. Plot and label each point on the coordinate grid.

   A (5,2)
   B (3,2)
   C (1,1)
   D (1,2)
   E (3,5)

9. Insert parentheses to make these number sentences true.

   a. (4 + 6) * 3 = 30
   b. 36 = (8 * 2) + (5 * 4)
   c. 2 + (7 * 6) = 2 * 2 * 11
   d. (9 + (6 * 3 ÷)) 3 = 9

10. Round these numbers to the nearest ten thousand.

   a. 670,299 670,000
   b. 7,239,041 7,240,000
   c. 22,513,748 22,510,000
   d. 380,755,119 380,760,000

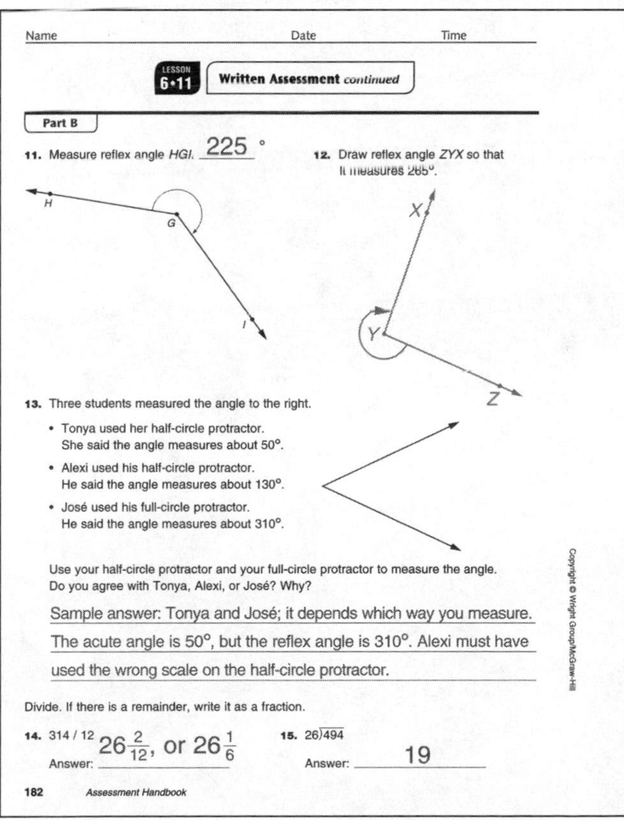

Name Date Time

LESSON 6·11 **Written Assessment** *continued*

Part B

11. Measure reflex angle HGI. 225 °

12. Draw reflex angle ZYX so that it measures 285°.

13. Three students measured the angle to the right.

   - Tonya used her half-circle protractor. She said the angle measures about 50°.
   - Alexi used his half-circle protractor. He said the angle measures about 130°.
   - José used his full-circle protractor. He said the angle measures about 310°.

   Use your half-circle protractor and your full-circle protractor to measure the angle. Do you agree with Tonya, Alexi, or José? Why?

   Sample answer: Tonya and José; it depends which way you measure. The acute angle is 50°, but the reflex angle is 310°. Alexi must have used the wrong scale on the half-circle protractor.

Divide. If there is a remainder, write it as a fraction.

14. 314 / 12 Answer: $26\frac{2}{12}$, or $26\frac{1}{6}$

15. 26)494 Answer: 19

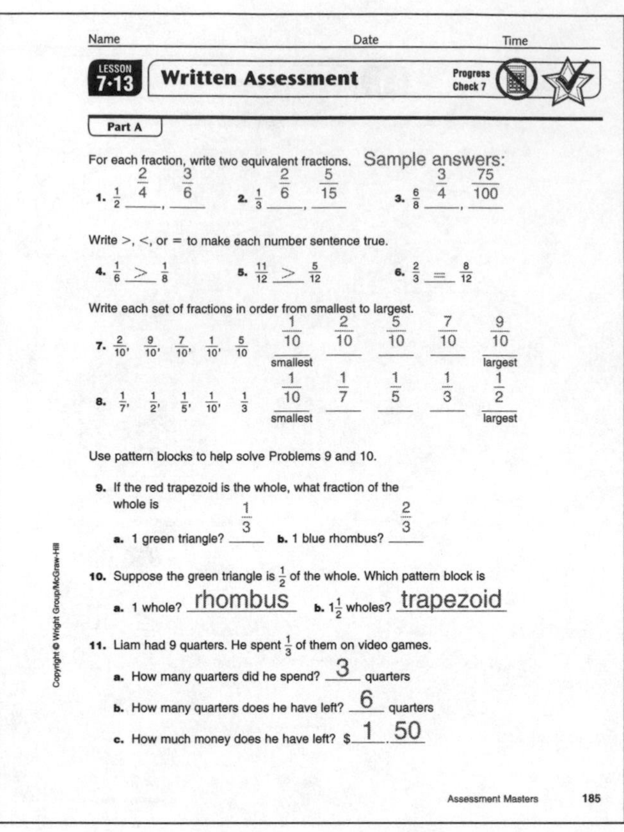

Name Date Time

LESSON 7·13 **Written Assessment** Progress Check 7

Part A

For each fraction, write two equivalent fractions. Sample answers:

1. $\frac{1}{2}$ $\frac{2}{4}$, $\frac{3}{6}$ 2. $\frac{1}{3}$ $\frac{2}{6}$, $\frac{5}{15}$ 3. $\frac{6}{8}$ $\frac{3}{4}$, $\frac{75}{100}$

Write >, <, or = to make each number sentence true.

4. $\frac{1}{6} > \frac{1}{8}$ 5. $\frac{11}{12} > \frac{5}{12}$ 6. $\frac{2}{3} = \frac{8}{12}$

Write each set of fractions in order from smallest to largest.

7. $\frac{2}{10}$, $\frac{9}{10}$, $\frac{7}{10}$, $\frac{1}{10}$, $\frac{5}{10}$ — $\frac{1}{10}$ (smallest), $\frac{2}{10}$, $\frac{5}{10}$, $\frac{7}{10}$, $\frac{9}{10}$ (largest)

8. $\frac{1}{7}$, $\frac{1}{2}$, $\frac{1}{5}$, $\frac{1}{10}$, $\frac{1}{3}$ — $\frac{1}{10}$ (smallest), $\frac{1}{7}$, $\frac{1}{5}$, $\frac{1}{3}$, $\frac{1}{2}$ (largest)

Use pattern blocks to help solve Problems 9 and 10.

9. If the red trapezoid is the whole, what fraction of the whole is
 a. 1 green triangle? $\frac{1}{3}$ b. 1 blue rhombus? $\frac{2}{3}$

10. Suppose the green triangle is $\frac{1}{2}$ of the whole. Which pattern block is
 a. 1 whole? rhombus b. $1\frac{1}{2}$ wholes? trapezoid

11. Liam had 9 quarters. He spent $\frac{1}{3}$ of them on video games.
 a. How many quarters did he spend? 3 quarters
 b. How many quarters does he have left? 6 quarters
 c. How much money does he have left? \$1.50

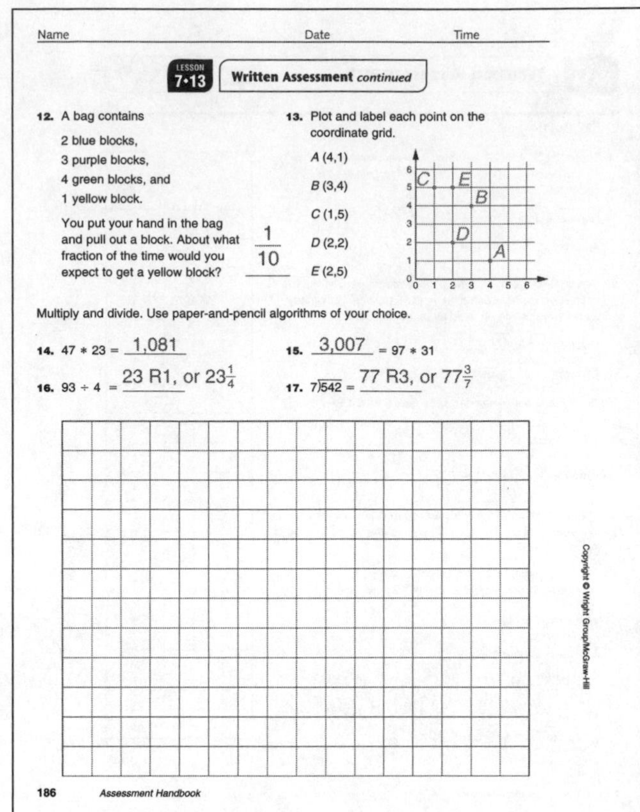

Name Date Time

LESSON 7·13 **Written Assessment** *continued*

12. A bag contains
 2 blue blocks,
 3 purple blocks,
 4 green blocks, and
 1 yellow block.
 You put your hand in the bag and pull out a block. About what fraction of the time would you expect to get a yellow block? $\frac{1}{10}$

13. Plot and label each point on the coordinate grid.
 A (4,1)
 B (3,4)
 C (1,5)
 D (2,2)
 E (2,5)

Multiply and divide. Use paper-and-pencil algorithms of your choice.

14. 47 * 23 = 1,081 15. 3,007 = 97 * 31

16. 93 ÷ 4 = 23 R1, or $23\frac{1}{4}$ 17. 7)542 = 77 R3, or $77\frac{3}{7}$

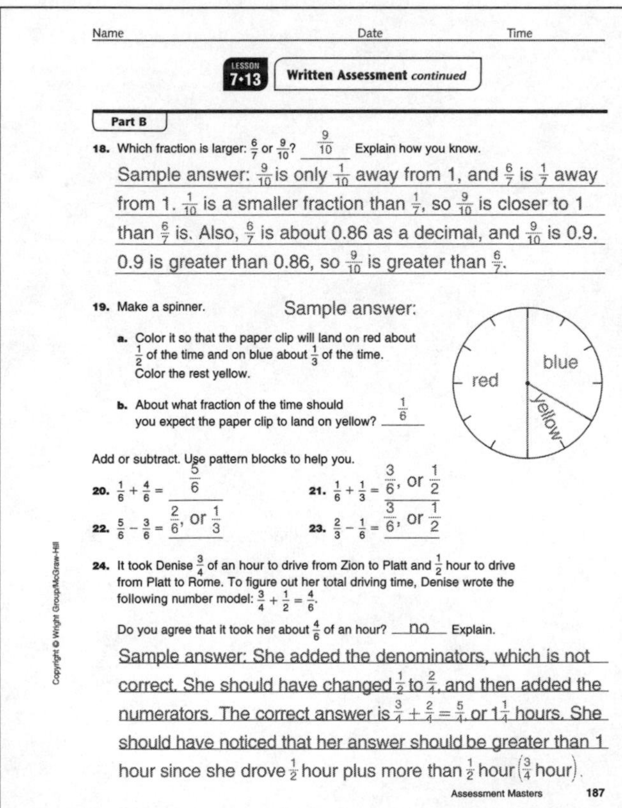

Name Date Time

LESSON 7·13 **Written Assessment** *continued*

Part B

18. Which fraction is larger: $\frac{6}{7}$ or $\frac{9}{10}$? $\frac{9}{10}$ Explain how you know.
 Sample answer: $\frac{9}{10}$ is only $\frac{1}{10}$ away from 1, and $\frac{6}{7}$ is $\frac{1}{7}$ away from 1. $\frac{1}{10}$ is a smaller fraction than $\frac{1}{7}$, so $\frac{9}{10}$ is closer to 1 than $\frac{6}{7}$ is. Also, $\frac{6}{7}$ is about 0.86 as a decimal, and $\frac{9}{10}$ is 0.9. 0.9 is greater than 0.86, so $\frac{9}{10}$ is greater than $\frac{6}{7}$.

19. Make a spinner. Sample answer:
 a. Color it so that the paper clip will land on red about $\frac{1}{2}$ of the time and on blue about $\frac{1}{3}$ of the time. Color the rest yellow.
 b. About what fraction of the time should you expect the paper clip to land on yellow? $\frac{1}{6}$

Add or subtract. Use pattern blocks to help you.

20. $\frac{1}{6} + \frac{4}{6} = \frac{5}{6}$ 21. $\frac{1}{6} + \frac{1}{3} = \frac{3}{6}$, or $\frac{1}{2}$

22. $\frac{5}{6} - \frac{3}{6} = \frac{2}{6}$, or $\frac{1}{3}$ 23. $\frac{2}{3} - \frac{1}{6} = \frac{3}{6}$, or $\frac{1}{2}$

24. It took Denise $\frac{3}{4}$ of an hour to drive from Zion to Platt and $\frac{1}{2}$ hour to drive from Platt to Rome. To figure out her total driving time, Denise wrote the following number model: $\frac{3}{4} + \frac{1}{2} = \frac{4}{6}$.
 Do you agree that it took her about $\frac{4}{6}$ of an hour? no Explain.
 Sample answer: She added the denominators, which is not correct. She should have changed $\frac{1}{2}$ to $\frac{2}{4}$, and then added the numerators. The correct answer is $\frac{3}{4} + \frac{2}{4} = \frac{5}{4}$, or $1\frac{1}{4}$ hours. She should have noticed that her answer should be greater than 1 hour since she drove $\frac{1}{2}$ hour plus more than $\frac{1}{2}$ hour ($\frac{3}{4}$ hour).

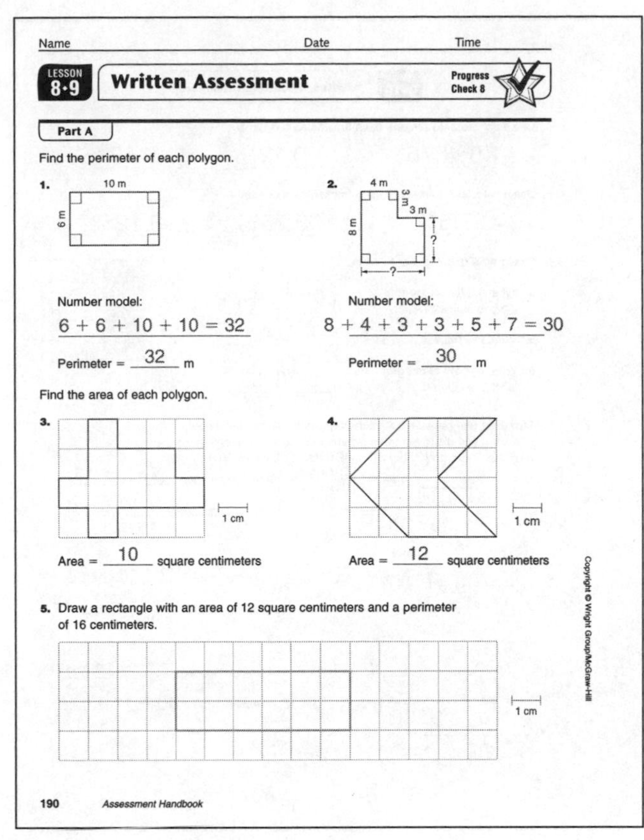
Name Date Time

LESSON 8•9 **Written Assessment** Progress Check 8

Part A

Find the perimeter of each polygon.

1. (10 m by 6 m rectangle)

Number model: $6 + 6 + 10 + 10 = 32$

Perimeter = 32 m

2. (4 m, 3 m, 3 m, 8 m, ?, ?)

Number model: $8 + 4 + 3 + 3 + 5 + 7 = 30$

Perimeter = 30 m

Find the area of each polygon.

3. Area = 10 square centimeters

4. Area = 12 square centimeters

5. Draw a rectangle with an area of 12 square centimeters and a perimeter of 16 centimeters.

190 *Assessment Handbook*

Copyright © Wright Group/McGraw-Hill

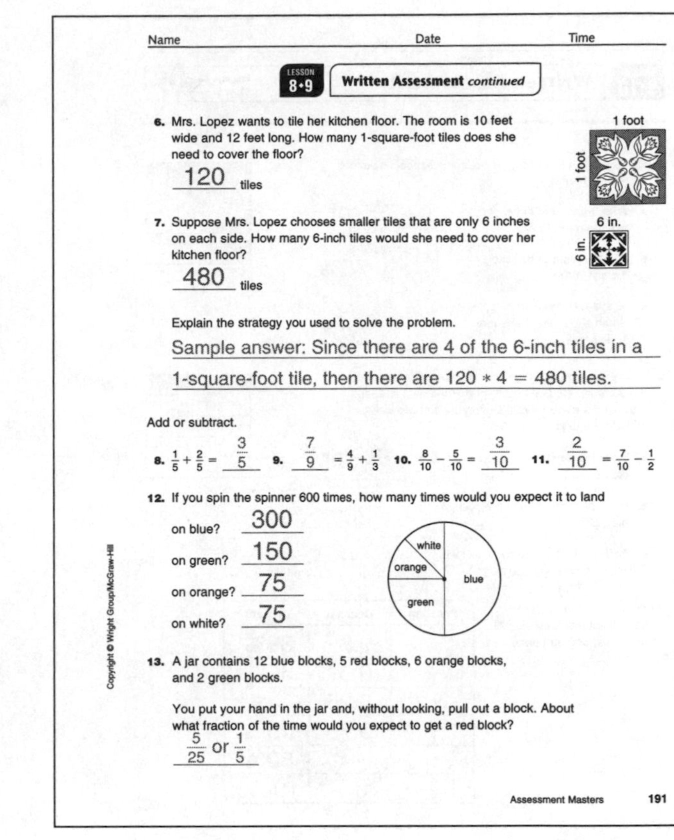
Name Date Time

LESSON 8•9 **Written Assessment** *continued*

6. Mrs. Lopez wants to tile her kitchen floor. The room is 10 feet wide and 12 feet long. How many 1-square-foot tiles does she need to cover the floor?

120 tiles

7. Suppose Mrs. Lopez chooses smaller tiles that are only 6 inches on each side. How many 6-inch tiles would she need to cover her kitchen floor?

480 tiles

Explain the strategy you used to solve the problem.

Sample answer: Since there are 4 of the 6-inch tiles in a 1-square-foot tile, then there are $120 * 4 = 480$ tiles.

Add or subtract.

8. $\frac{1}{5} + \frac{2}{5} = \frac{3}{5}$ 9. $\frac{7}{9} = \frac{4}{9} + \frac{1}{3}$ 10. $\frac{8}{10} - \frac{5}{10} = \frac{3}{10}$ 11. $\frac{2}{10} = \frac{7}{10} - \frac{1}{2}$

12. If you spin the spinner 600 times, how many times would you expect it to land

on blue? 300

on green? 150

on orange? 75

on white? 75

13. A jar contains 12 blue blocks, 5 red blocks, 6 orange blocks, and 2 green blocks.

You put your hand in the jar and, without looking, pull out a block. About what fraction of the time would you expect to get a red block?

$\frac{5}{25}$ or $\frac{1}{5}$

Copyright © Wright Group/McGraw-Hill

Assessment Masters 191

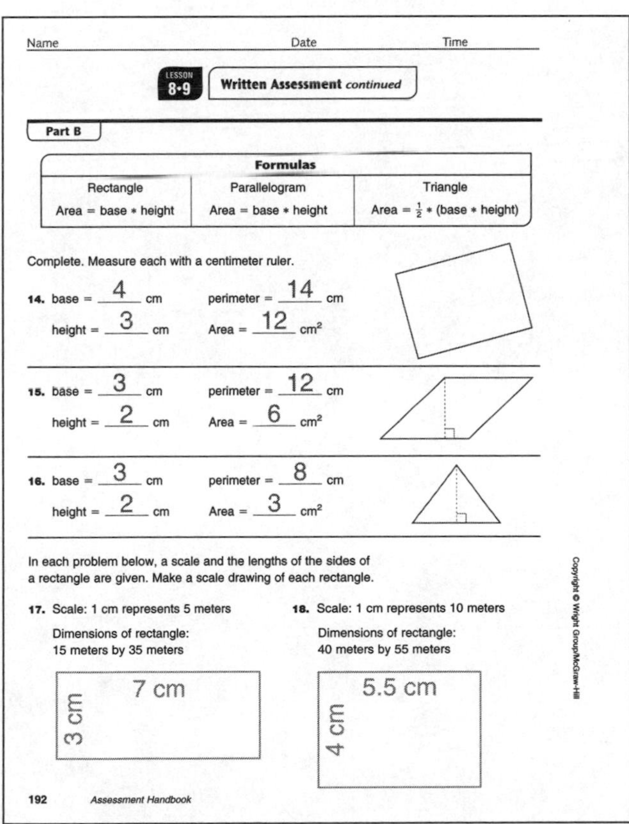
Name Date Time

LESSON 8•9 **Written Assessment** *continued*

Part B

Formulas		
Rectangle	Parallelogram	Triangle
Area = base * height	Area = base * height	Area = $\frac{1}{2}$ * (base * height)

Complete. Measure each with a centimeter ruler.

14. base = 4 cm perimeter = 14 cm
height = 3 cm Area = 12 cm²

15. base = 3 cm perimeter = 12 cm
height = 2 cm Area = 6 cm²

16. base = 3 cm perimeter = 8 cm
height = 2 cm Area = 3 cm²

In each problem below, a scale and the lengths of the sides of a rectangle are given. Make a scale drawing of each rectangle.

17. Scale: 1 cm represents 5 meters
Dimensions of rectangle: 15 meters by 35 meters

7 cm, 3 cm

18. Scale: 1 cm represents 10 meters
Dimensions of rectangle: 40 meters by 55 meters

5.5 cm, 4 cm

192 *Assessment Handbook*

Copyright © Wright Group/McGraw-Hill

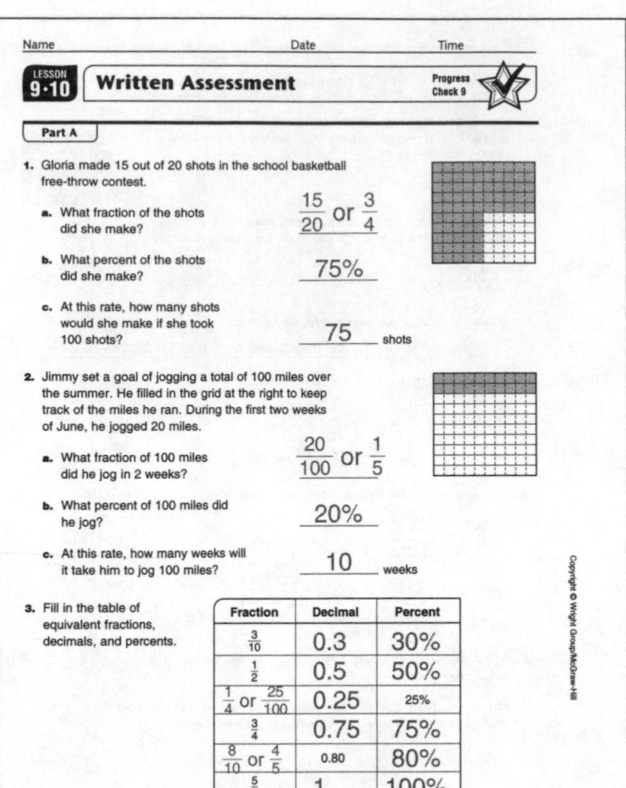

Name Date Time

LESSON 9•10 **Written Assessment** Progress Check 9

Part A

1. Gloria made 15 out of 20 shots in the school basketball free-throw contest.
   a. What fraction of the shots did she make? $\frac{15}{20}$ or $\frac{3}{4}$
   b. What percent of the shots did she make? 75%
   c. At this rate, how many shots would she make if she took 100 shots? 75 shots

2. Jimmy set a goal of jogging a total of 100 miles over the summer. He filled in the grid at the right to keep track of the miles he ran. During the first two weeks of June, he jogged 20 miles.
   a. What fraction of 100 miles did he jog in 2 weeks? $\frac{20}{100}$ or $\frac{1}{5}$
   b. What percent of 100 miles did he jog? 20%
   c. At this rate, how many weeks will it take him to jog 100 miles? 10 weeks

3. Fill in the table of equivalent fractions, decimals, and percents.

Fraction	Decimal	Percent
$\frac{3}{10}$	0.3	30%
$\frac{1}{2}$	0.5	50%
$\frac{1}{4}$ or $\frac{25}{100}$	0.25	25%
$\frac{3}{4}$	0.75	75%
$\frac{8}{10}$ or $\frac{4}{5}$	0.80	80%
$\frac{5}{5}$	1	100%

196 *Assessment Handbook*

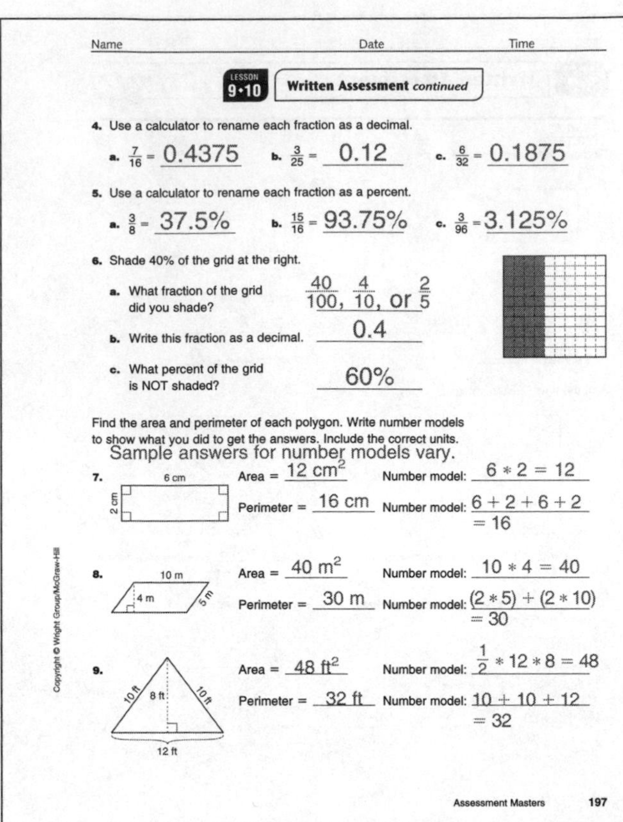

Name Date Time

LESSON 9•10 **Written Assessment** *continued*

4. Use a calculator to rename each fraction as a decimal.
   a. $\frac{7}{16}$ = 0.4375 b. $\frac{3}{25}$ = 0.12 c. $\frac{6}{32}$ = 0.1875

5. Use a calculator to rename each fraction as a percent.
   a. $\frac{3}{8}$ = 37.5% b. $\frac{15}{16}$ = 93.75% c. $\frac{3}{96}$ = 3.125%

6. Shade 40% of the grid at the right.
   a. What fraction of the grid did you shade? $\frac{40}{100}$, $\frac{4}{10}$, or $\frac{2}{5}$
   b. Write this fraction as a decimal. 0.4
   c. What percent of the grid is NOT shaded? 60%

Find the area and perimeter of each polygon. Write number models to show what you did to get the answers. Include the correct units.

Sample answers for number models vary.

7. (6 cm, 2 cm) Area = 12 cm² Number model: $6 * 2 = 12$
   Perimeter = 16 cm Number model: $6 + 2 + 6 + 2 = 16$

8. (10 m, 4 m, 5 m) Area = 40 m² Number model: $10 * 4 = 40$
   Perimeter = 30 m Number model: $(2 * 5) + (2 * 10) = 30$

9. (10 ft, 10 ft, 8 ft, 12 ft) Area = 48 ft² Number model: $\frac{1}{2} * 12 * 8 = 48$
   Perimeter = 32 ft Number model: $10 + 10 + 12 = 32$

Copyright © Wright Group/McGraw-Hill

Assessment Masters 197

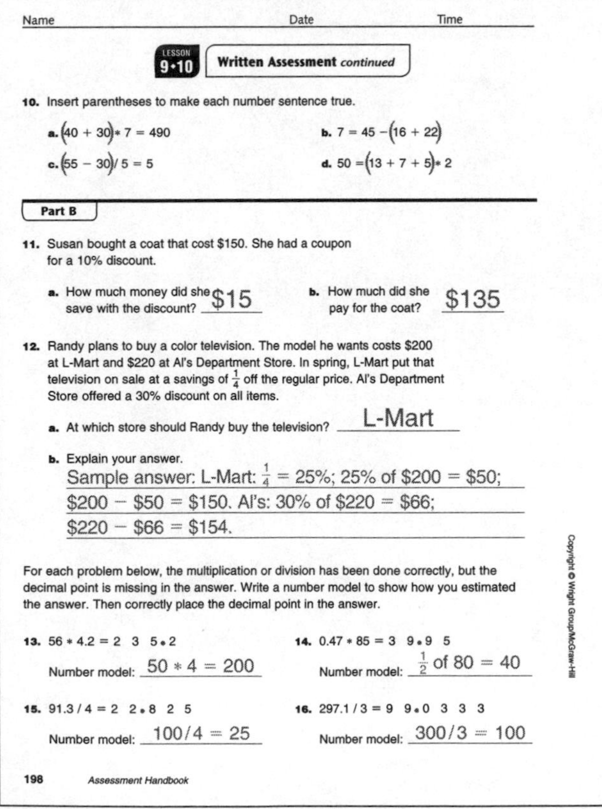

Name Date Time

LESSON 9•10 **Written Assessment** *continued*

10. Insert parentheses to make each number sentence true.
    a. $(40 + 30) * 7 = 490$
    b. $7 = 45 - (16 + 22)$
    c. $(55 - 30) / 5 = 5$
    d. $50 = (13 + 7 + 5) * 2$

Part B

11. Susan bought a coat that cost $150. She had a coupon for a 10% discount.
    a. How much money did she save with the discount? $15
    b. How much did she pay for the coat? $135

12. Randy plans to buy a color television. The model he wants costs $200 at L-Mart and $220 at Al's Department Store. In spring, L-Mart put that television on sale at a savings of $\frac{1}{4}$ off the regular price. Al's Department Store offered a 30% discount on all items.
    a. At which store should Randy buy the television? L-Mart
    b. Explain your answer.
    Sample answer: L-Mart: $\frac{1}{4}$ = 25%; 25% of $200 = $50; $200 − $50 = $150. Al's: 30% of $220 = $66; $220 − $66 = $154.

For each problem below, the multiplication or division has been done correctly, but the decimal point is missing in the answer. Write a number model to show how you estimated the answer. Then correctly place the decimal point in the answer.

13. 56 ∗ 4.2 = 2 3 5 • 2
    Number model: $50 * 4 = 200$

14. 0.47 ∗ 85 = 3 9 • 9 5
    Number model: $\frac{1}{2}$ of 80 = 40

15. 91.3 / 4 = 2 2 • 8 2 5
    Number model: $100 / 4 = 25$

16. 297.1 / 3 = 9 9 • 0 3 3 3
    Number model: $300 / 3 = 100$

Copyright © Wright Group/McGraw-Hill

198 *Assessment Handbook*

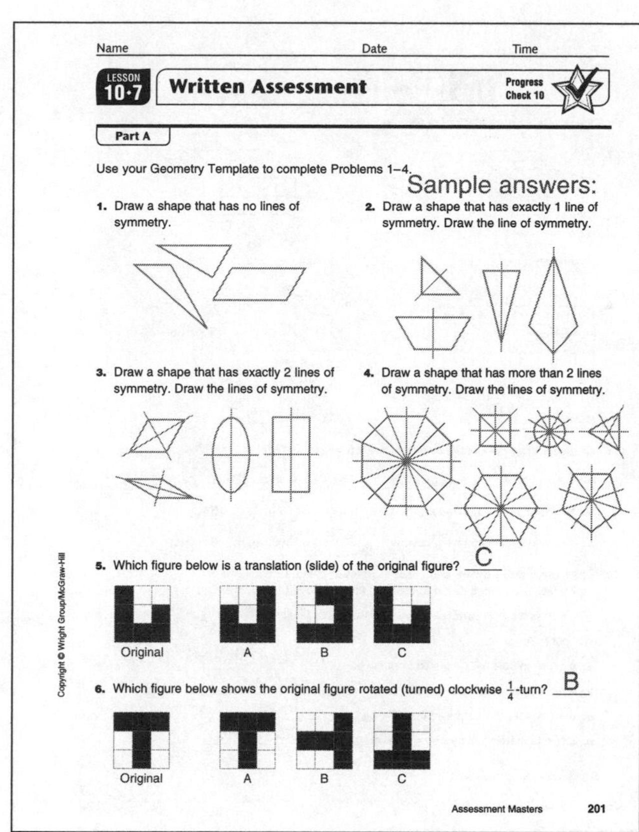

Name Date Time

LESSON 10•7 **Written Assessment** Progress Check 10

Part A

Use your Geometry Template to complete Problems 1–4.

Sample answers:

1. Draw a shape that has no lines of symmetry.
2. Draw a shape that has exactly 1 line of symmetry. Draw the line of symmetry.
3. Draw a shape that has exactly 2 lines of symmetry. Draw the lines of symmetry.
4. Draw a shape that has more than 2 lines of symmetry. Draw the lines of symmetry.
5. Which figure below is a translation (slide) of the original figure? C

Original A B C

6. Which figure below shows the original figure rotated (turned) clockwise $\frac{1}{4}$-turn? B

Original A B C

Copyright © Wright Group/McGraw-Hill

Assessment Masters 201

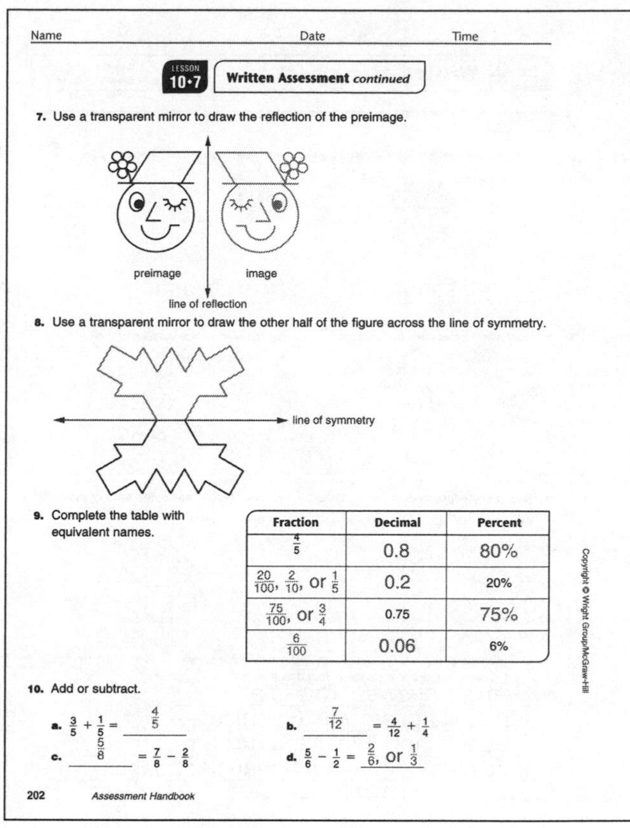

Name Date Time

LESSON 10•7 **Written Assessment** *continued*

7. Use a transparent mirror to draw the reflection of the preimage.

8. Use a transparent mirror to draw the other half of the figure across the line of symmetry.

9. Complete the table with equivalent names.

Fraction	Decimal	Percent
$\frac{4}{5}$	0.8	80%
$\frac{20}{100}$, $\frac{2}{10}$, or $\frac{1}{5}$	0.2	20%
$\frac{75}{100}$, or $\frac{3}{4}$	0.75	75%
$\frac{6}{100}$	0.06	6%

10. Add or subtract.

a. $\frac{3}{5} + \frac{1}{5} = \frac{4}{5}$

b. $\frac{7}{12} = \frac{4}{12} + \frac{1}{4}$

c. $\frac{5}{8} = \frac{7}{8} - \frac{2}{8}$

d. $\frac{5}{6} - \frac{1}{2} = \frac{2}{6}$, or $\frac{1}{3}$

Copyright © Wright Group/McGraw-Hill

202 *Assessment Handbook*

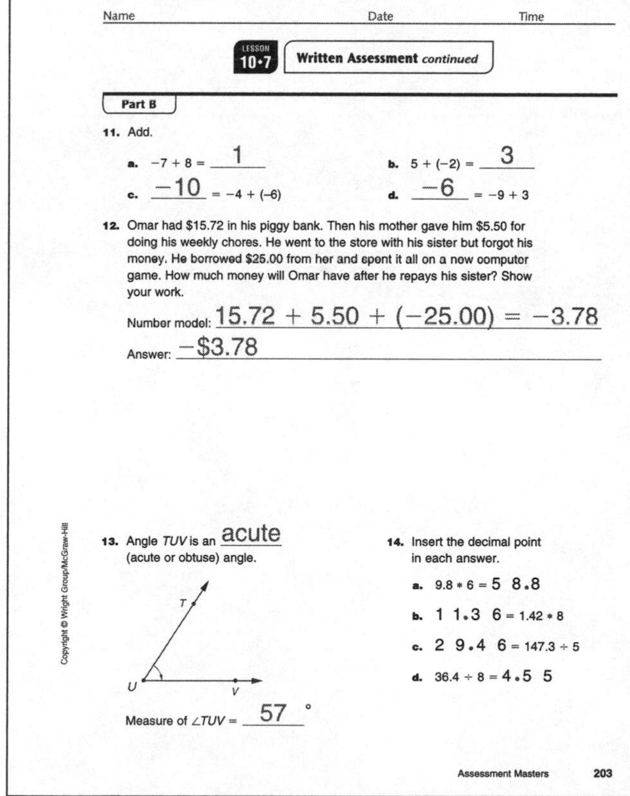

Name Date Time

LESSON 10•7 **Written Assessment** *continued*

Part B

11. Add.

a. $-7 + 8 = 1$

b. $5 + (-2) = 3$

c. $-10 = -4 + (-6)$

d. $-6 = -9 + 3$

12. Omar had $15.72 in his piggy bank. Then his mother gave him $5.50 for doing his weekly chores. He went to the store with his sister but forgot his money. He borrowed $25.00 from her and spent it all on a new computer game. How much money will Omar have after he repays his sister? Show your work.

Number model: $15.72 + 5.50 + (-25.00) = -3.78$

Answer: $-\$3.78$

13. Angle *TUV* is an acute (acute or obtuse) angle.

Measure of $\angle TUV =$ 57 °

14. Insert the decimal point in each answer.

a. $9.8 * 6 = 58.8$

b. $11.36 = 1.42 * 8$

c. $29.46 = 147.3 \div 5$

d. $36.4 \div 8 = 4.55$

Copyright © Wright Group/McGraw-Hill

Assessment Masters 203

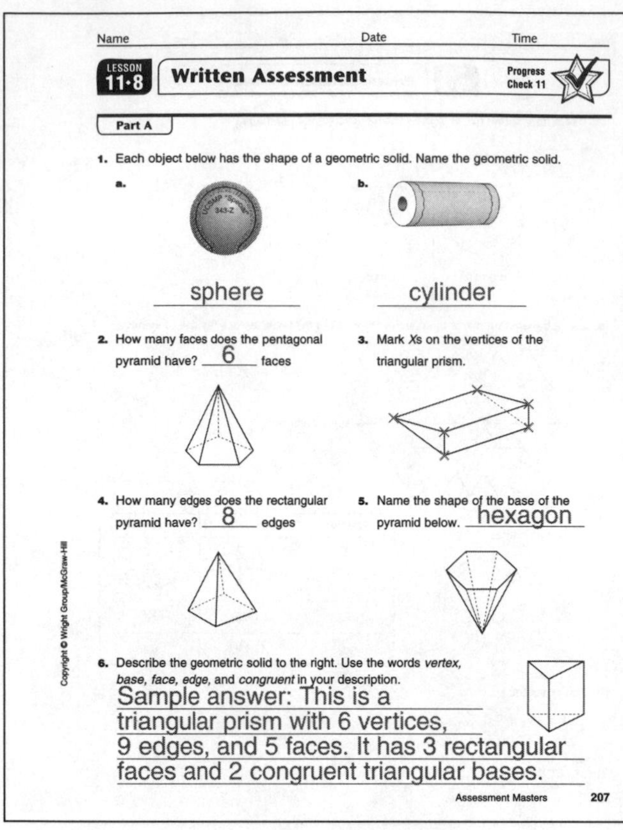

Name Date Time

LESSON 11•8 **Written Assessment** Progress Check 11

Part A

1. Each object below has the shape of a geometric solid. Name the geometric solid.

a. sphere

b. cylinder

2. How many faces does the pentagonal pyramid have? 6 faces

3. Mark Xs on the vertices of the triangular prism.

4. How many edges does the rectangular pyramid have? 8 edges

5. Name the shape of the base of the pyramid below. hexagon

6. Describe the geometric solid to the right. Use the words *vertex, base, face, edge,* and *congruent* in your description.

Sample answer: This is a triangular prism with 6 vertices, 9 edges, and 5 faces. It has 3 rectangular faces and 2 congruent triangular bases.

Copyright © Wright Group/McGraw-Hill

Assessment Masters 207

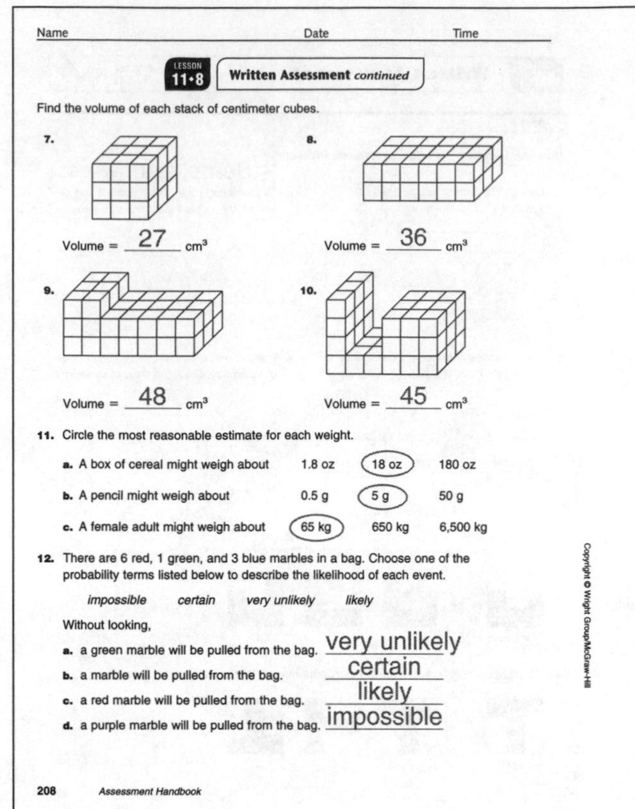

Name Date Time

LESSON 11•8 **Written Assessment** *continued*

Find the volume of each stack of centimeter cubes.

7. Volume = 27 cm^3

8. Volume = 36 cm^3

9. Volume = 48 cm^3

10. Volume = 45 cm^3

11. Circle the most reasonable estimate for each weight.

a. A box of cereal might weigh about	1.8 oz	(18 oz)	180 oz
b. A pencil might weigh about	0.5 g	(5 g)	50 g
c. A female adult might weigh about	(65 kg)	650 kg	6,500 kg

12. There are 6 red, 1 green, and 3 blue marbles in a bag. Choose one of the probability terms listed below to describe the likelihood of each event.

impossible *certain* *very unlikely* *likely*

Without looking,

a. a green marble will be pulled from the bag. very unlikely

b. a marble will be pulled from the bag. certain

c. a red marble will be pulled from the bag. likely

d. a purple marble will be pulled from the bag. impossible

Copyright © Wright Group/McGraw-Hill

208 *Assessment Handbook*

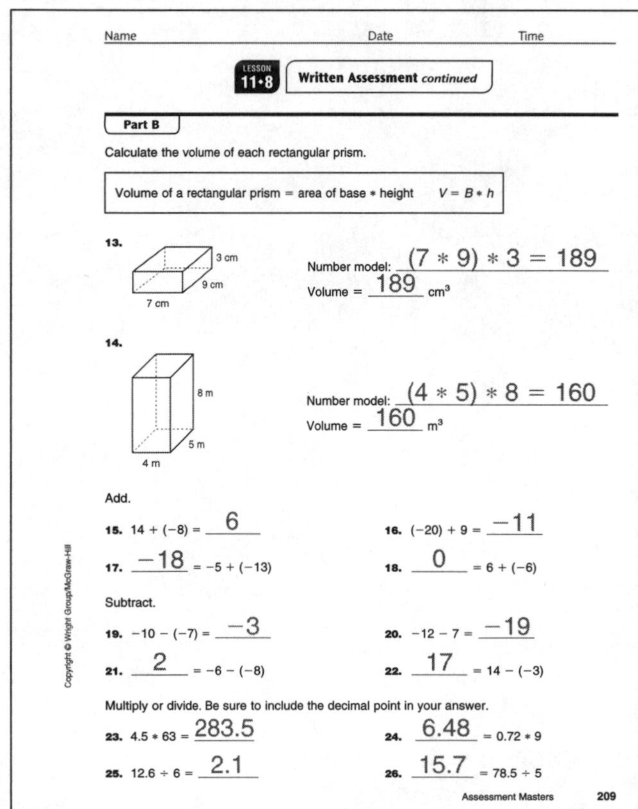

Name Date Time

LESSON 11•8 **Written Assessment** *continued*

Part B

Calculate the volume of each rectangular prism.

Volume of a rectangular prism = area of base * height $V = B * h$

13. 3 cm, 9 cm, 7 cm

Number model: $(7 * 9) * 3 = 189$

Volume = 189 cm^3

14. 8 m, 5 m, 4 m

Number model: $(4 * 5) * 8 = 160$

Volume = 160 m^3

Add.

15. $14 + (-8) =$ 6

16. $(-20) + 9 =$ -11

17. -18 $= -5 + (-13)$

18. 0 $= 6 + (-6)$

Subtract.

19. $-10 - (-7) =$ -3

20. $-12 - 7 =$ -19

21. 2 $= -6 - (-8)$

22. 17 $= 14 - (-3)$

Multiply or divide. Be sure to include the decimal point in your answer.

23. $4.5 * 63 =$ 283.5

24. 6.48 $= 0.72 * 9$

25. $12.6 \div 6 =$ 2.1

26. 15.7 $= 78.5 \div 5$

Copyright © Wright Group/McGraw-Hill

Assessment Masters 209

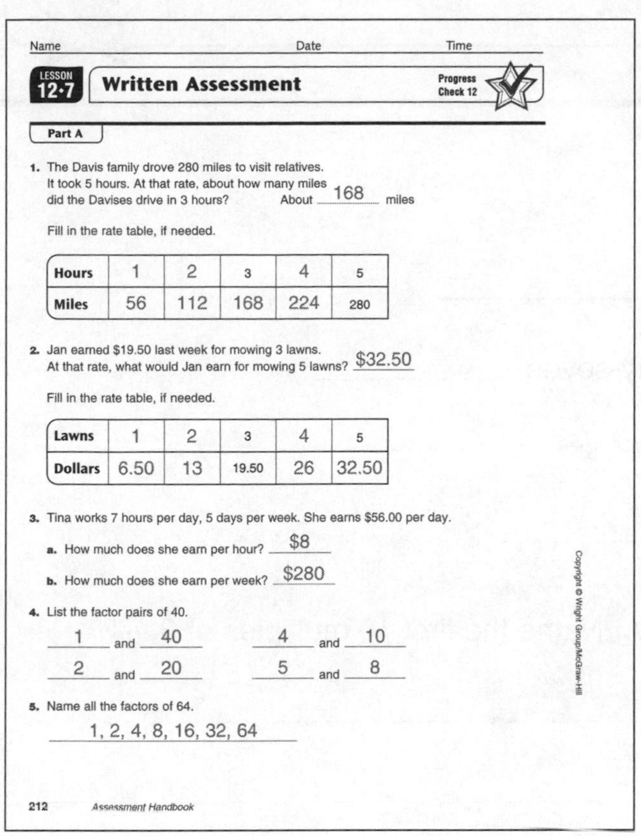

Name Date Time

LESSON 12·7 **Written Assessment** Progress Check 12

Part A

1. The Davis family drove 280 miles to visit relatives. It took 5 hours. At that rate, about how many miles did the Davises drive in 3 hours? About 168 miles

Fill in the rate table, if needed.

Hours	1	2	3	4	5
Miles	56	112	168	224	280

2. Jan earned $19.50 last week for mowing 3 lawns. At that rate, what would Jan earn for mowing 5 lawns? $32.50

Fill in the rate table, if needed.

Lawns	1	2	3	4	5
Dollars	6.50	13	19.50	26	32.50

3. Tina works 7 hours per day, 5 days per week. She earns $56.00 per day.
   a. How much does she earn per hour? $8
   b. How much does she earn per week? $280

4. List the factor pairs of 40.
   1 and 40   4 and 10
   2 and 20   5 and 8

5. Name all the factors of 64.
   1, 2, 4, 8, 16, 32, 64

212 Assessment Handbook

Copyright © Wright Group/McGraw-Hill

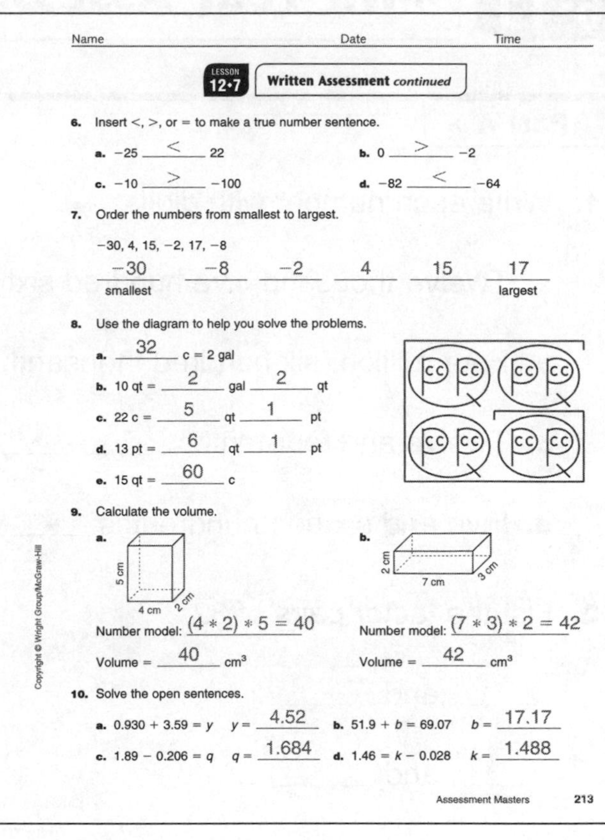

Name Date Time

LESSON 12·7 **Written Assessment** *continued*

6. Insert <, >, or = to make a true number sentence.
   a. −25 < 22   b. 0 > −2
   c. −10 > −100   d. −82 < −64

7. Order the numbers from smallest to largest.
   −30, 4, 15, −2, 17, −8
   −30 (smallest), −8, −2, 4, 15, 17 (largest)

8. Use the diagram to help you solve the problems.
   a. 32 c = 2 gal
   b. 10 qt = 2 gal 2 qt
   c. 22 c = 5 qt 1 pt
   d. 13 pt = 6 qt 1 pt
   e. 15 qt = 60 c

9. Calculate the volume.
   a. (5 cm, 4 cm, 2 cm) Number model: $(4 * 2) * 5 = 40$ Volume = 40 cm^3
   b. (2 cm, 7 cm, 3 cm) Number model: $(7 * 3) * 2 = 42$ Volume = 42 cm^3

10. Solve the open sentences.
   a. $0.930 + 3.59 = y$ $y =$ 4.52   b. $51.9 + b = 69.07$ $b =$ 17.17
   c. $1.89 - 0.206 = q$ $q =$ 1.684   d. $1.46 = k - 0.028$ $k =$ 1.488

Assessment Masters 213

Copyright © Wright Group/McGraw-Hill

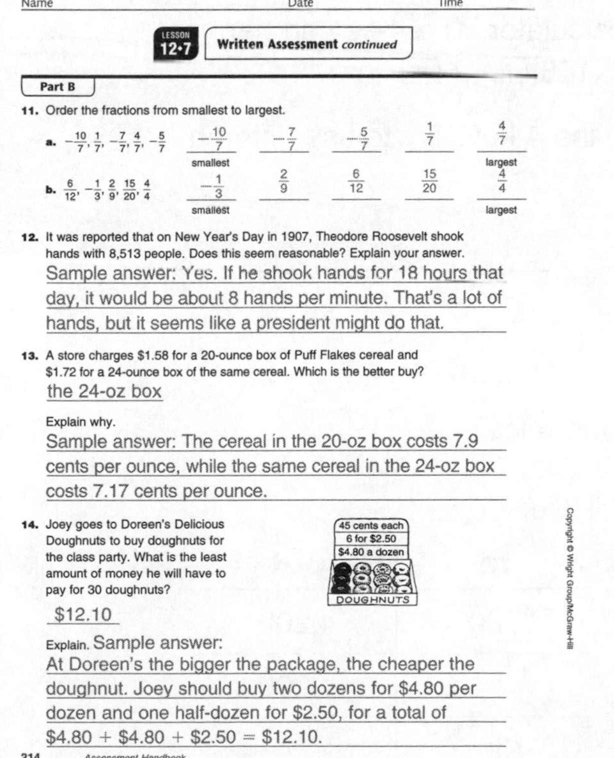

Name Date Time

LESSON 12·7 **Written Assessment** *continued*

Part B

11. Order the fractions from smallest to largest.
   a. $\frac{10}{7}, \frac{1}{7}, \frac{7}{7}, \frac{4}{7}, \frac{5}{7}$ $-\frac{10}{7}$ (smallest), $-\frac{7}{7}$, $-\frac{5}{7}$, $\frac{1}{7}$, $\frac{4}{7}$ (largest)
   b. $\frac{6}{12}, -\frac{1}{3}, \frac{2}{9}, \frac{15}{20}, \frac{4}{4}$ $-\frac{1}{3}$ (smallest), $\frac{2}{9}$, $\frac{6}{12}$, $\frac{15}{20}$, $\frac{4}{4}$ (largest)

12. It was reported that on New Year's Day in 1907, Theodore Roosevelt shook hands with 8,513 people. Does this seem reasonable? Explain your answer.
   Sample answer: Yes. If he shook hands for 18 hours that day, it would be about 8 hands per minute. That's a lot of hands, but it seems like a president might do that.

13. A store charges $1.58 for a 20-ounce box of Puff Flakes cereal and $1.72 for a 24-ounce box of the same cereal. Which is the better buy?
   the 24-oz box
   Explain why.
   Sample answer: The cereal in the 20-oz box costs 7.9 cents per ounce, while the same cereal in the 24-oz box costs 7.17 cents per ounce.

14. Joey goes to Doreen's Delicious Doughnuts to buy doughnuts for the class party. What is the least amount of money he will have to pay for 30 doughnuts?
   45 cents each / 6 for $2.50 / $4.80 a dozen / DOUGHNUTS
   $12.10
   Explain. Sample answer:
   At Doreen's the bigger the package, the cheaper the doughnut. Joey should buy two dozens for $4.80 per dozen and one half-dozen for $2.50, for a total of $4.80 + $4.80 + $2.50 = $12.10.

214 Assessment Handbook

Copyright © Wright Group/McGraw-Hill

Name Date Time

LESSON 6•11

Mid-Year Assessment

Part A

1. Write each number with digits.

a. Twelve thousand, five hundred sixty-five ___________

b. Four million, six hundred thousand, twenty-seven ___________

c. Twelve and four-tenths ___________

d. Five and sixteen-hundredths ___________

2. List the factor pairs of 32.

______ and ______

______ and ______

______ and ______

3. Name the first 10 multiples of 9.

______ ______ ______ ______ ______

______ ______ ______ ______ ______

4. Nishi wanted to show the number 54 on her calculator. The 4-key on her calculator was broken, so this is what she did: 108 [÷] 2 [=]

Find two other ways to show 54 without using the 4-key. Try to use different numbers and operations.

a. ____

b. ____

Complete the "What's My Rule?" tables and state the rules.

5. Rule: ___________

in	out
600	1,500
	1,200
400	
1,200	2,100
800	

6. Rule: ___________

in	out
700	4,200
	1,200
50	
8,000	4,800
	2,400

Name _______________ Date _______________ Time _______________

Mid-Year Assessment *continued*

Solve. Use paper-and-pencil algorithms.

7. A gallon of skim milk costs $3.09 at the Gem supermarket and $4.19 at the 6-to-Midnight convenience store. How much more does a gallon of milk cost at the convenience store?

$ _______________

8. Keena bought some supplies for school. The crayons cost $1.29, the notebooks cost $2.49, and the pencils cost $0.89. How much did Keena spend in all?

$ _______________

9. _______________ = 3,551 + 2,279

10. 2,653 − 1,289 = _______________

11. 7 * 128 = _______________

12. _______________ = 385 / 7

LESSON 6•11

Mid-Year Assessment *continued*

13. A farm stand sells apples. The farmer records how many pounds of each type of apple are sold per day. Below are the results of Monday's sales:

18 Red Delicious	25 Gala	24 Fuji
21 Granny Smith	17 Empire	14 Pink Lady

Create a bar graph using the data above. Include labels and a title.

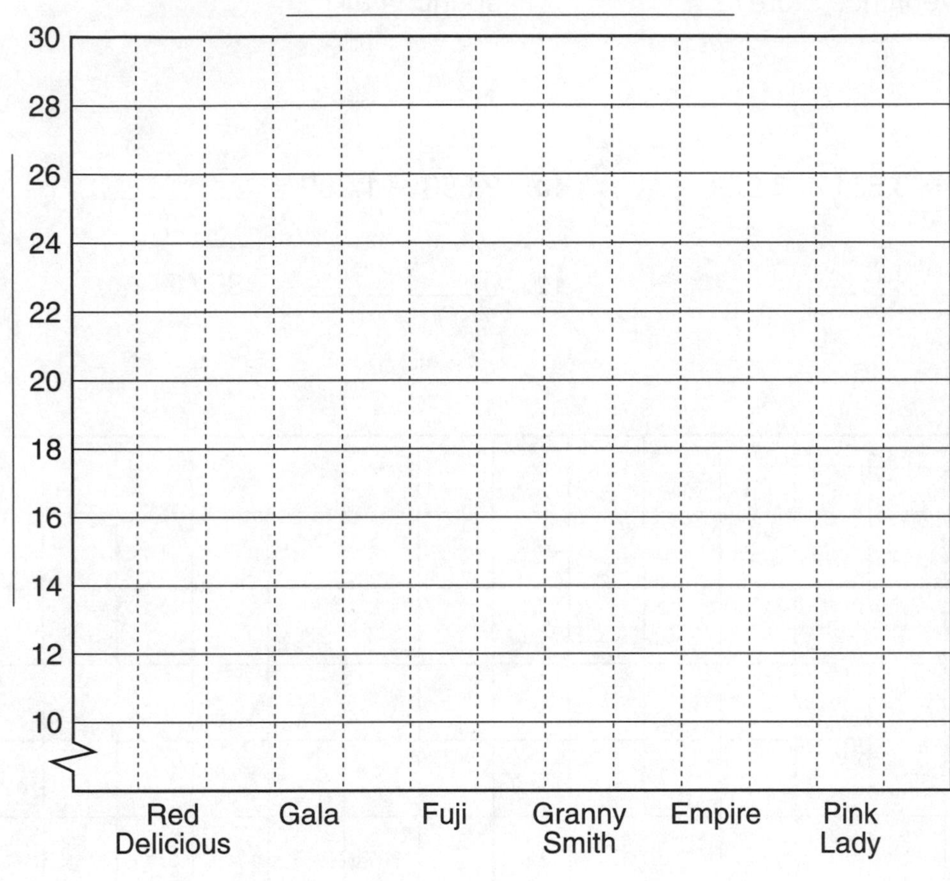

14. As part of her science project on sleep, Ama asked 13 students in her class how many hours, to the nearest half-hour, they had slept the night before. Here are the results of her survey:

Number of hours of sleep: 7, 10.5, 8, 8, 9, 10, 10, 7.5, 9.5, 9, 8, 8.5, 8

a. What is the median number of hours the students slept? ________

b. What is the mode? ________

c. What is the minimum number of hours slept? ________

d. What is the maximum number of hours slept? ________

e. What is the range of hours they slept? ________

Name Date Time

LESSON 6•11

Mid-Year Assessment *continued*

15. Measure the line segment to the nearest inch.

________ in.

16. Measure the line segment to the nearest $\frac{1}{2}$ inch.

________ in.

17. Measure the line segment to the nearest $\frac{1}{4}$ inch.

________ in.

18. Measure the line segment to the nearest centimeter.

________ cm

19. Measure the line segment to the nearest half-centimeter.

________ cm

20. Draw $\overrightarrow{QR}$ parallel to $\overleftrightarrow{ST}$. Draw line segment *WX* so that it intersects ray *QR* and line *ST*.

S *T*

Name Date Time

LESSON 6•11

Mid-Year Assessment *continued*

Use your Geometry Template to complete Problems 21–24.

21. Draw a quadrangle that has two pairs of parallel sides and is not a square.

What kind of quadrangle is this?

____

22. Draw a regular polygon.

Name the polygon.

____

23. Draw a trapezoid.

How many pairs of parallel sides does it have? ______

24. Draw a shape that is not a polygon.

The shape is not a polygon because

____

____

25. Find the solution of each open sentence.

a. $32 = x * 8$ Solution: ______

b. $7 * y = 42$ Solution: ______

c. $m / 9 = 5$ Solution: ______

d. $54 / s = 6$ Solution: ______

26. Tell whether each number sentence is true or false.

a. $(5 * 6) + 13 = 43$ ________

b. $(81 / 9) - (36 / 4) = 3$ ________

c. $30 - (4 * 7) = 2$ ________

d. $(12 - 6) * 32 = 36$ ________

Name Date Time

Mid-Year Assessment *continued*

Part B

27. Insert >, <, or = to make each number sentence true.

a. 10^3 ________ 10,000 **b.** 10^6 ________ 1,000,000 **c.** 1,000 ________ 10^2

28. Rename each decimal as a fraction.

a. 0.2 = ____________ **b.** 0.75 = ____________ **c.** 0.84 = ____________

Solve. Use a paper-and-pencil algorithm.

29. 49 * 67 = __________	**30.** __________ = 251 * 35	**31.** 786 / 24 = __________

32. Landon picked 5 different number cards from a deck numbered 0–18. He did not pick a 7. The mean of the 5 cards is 7. Name 5 cards that Landon might have picked.

________ ________ ________ ________ ________

33. Complete.

a. 1.5 m = ________ cm **b.** 56 cm = ________ mm

c. 0.2 m = ________ cm **d.** 0.8 m = ________ mm

Name Date Time

LESSON 12•7

End-of-Year Assessment

Part A

1. Complete.

a. $\frac{1}{8}$ of 24 = ______ **b.** 3 = $\frac{1}{4}$ of ______

c. ______ = $\frac{4}{7}$ of 14 **d.** 10 = $\frac{2}{3}$ of ______

e. $\frac{6}{5}$ of 20 = ______ **f.** $\frac{4}{3}$ of ______ = 24

2. Is 127 a multiple of 7? ________

How do you know? ________________________________

3. Is 4 a factor of 88? ________

How do you know? ________________________________

4. Write each fraction as a decimal and as a percent.

a. $\frac{34}{100}$ = ______ . ______ = ______%

b. $\frac{7}{10}$ = ______ . ______ = ______%

c. $\frac{3}{4}$ = ______ . ______ = ______%

d. $\frac{4}{5}$ = ______ . ______ = ______%

e. $\frac{2}{100}$ = ______ . ______ = ______%

f. $\frac{15}{10}$ = ______ . ______ = ______%

5. Insert >, <, or = to make each number sentence true.

a. $\frac{3}{5}$ ______ $\frac{2}{5}$ **b.** $\frac{1}{4}$ ______ $\frac{1}{6}$ **c.** $\frac{2}{3}$ ______ $\frac{9}{10}$

d. Explain how you solved Problem 5c.

____

____

Name Date Time

LESSON 12•7

End-of-Year Assessment *continued*

6. Order the fractions from smallest to largest.

$\frac{5}{6}$, $\frac{1}{3}$, $\frac{1}{10}$, $\frac{19}{20}$, $\frac{2}{5}$ ______ ______ ______ ______ ______

smallest largest

7. Multiply or divide. Show your work.

a. 45 ∗ 23 = ______ **b.** ______ = 86 ∗ 74

c. ______ = 486 / 6 **d.** 895 ÷ 7 = ______

8. Add or subtract.

a. $\frac{1}{5} + \frac{3}{5} =$ ______ **b.** $\frac{1}{3} + \frac{3}{6} =$ ______

c. ______ $= \frac{3}{4} - \frac{1}{4}$ **d.** ______ $= \frac{7}{8} - \frac{1}{2}$

Name Date Time

End-of-Year Assessment *continued*

9. The table shows the number of people who attended lacrosse games each week during the spring season. Create a line graph to show the data. Use a straightedge to connect the data points. Label each axis and include a title.

Week	Number of People
1	60
2	80
3	40
4	100
5	100
6	80
7	120
8	110

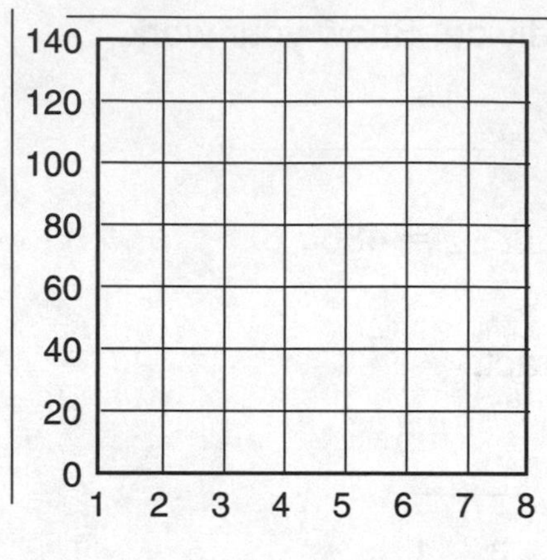

10. Use the following terms to complete the statements below.

impossible
likely
unlikely
very likely

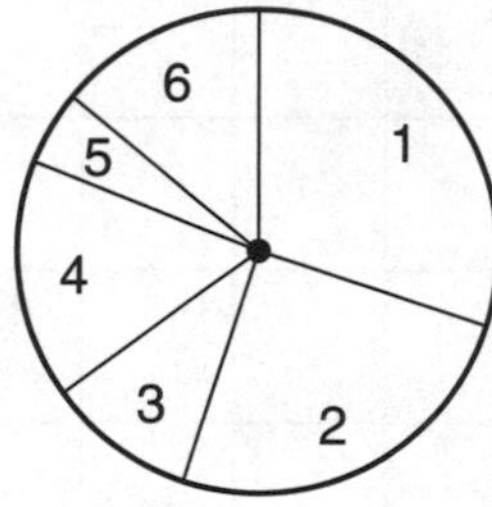

a. It is ____________________ that the spinner will land on a number less than or equal to 2.

b. It is ____________________ that the spinner will land on a number not equal to 5.

c. It is ____________________ that the spinner will land on a number less than $\frac{9}{10}$.

d. It is ____________________ that the spinner will land on 5.

LESSON 12•7

End-of-Year Assessment *continued*

11. Complete.

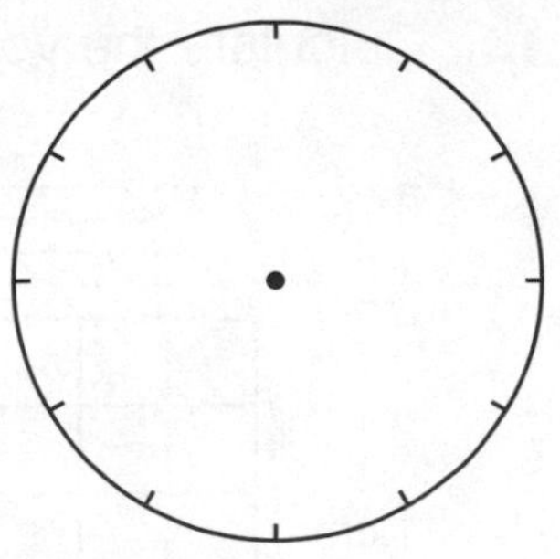

a. Color $\frac{1}{4}$ of the spinner at the right.

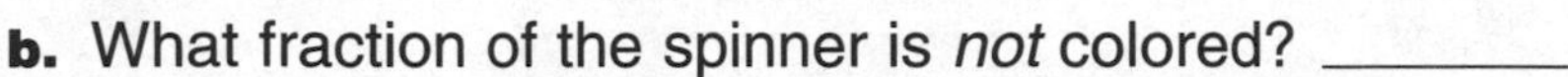

b. What fraction of the spinner is *not* colored? ______

c. What *percent* of the spinner is colored? ______

d. If you spin the spinner 100 times, about how many times would you expect it to land on the colored part? ______ times

e. If you spin the spinner 300 times, about how many times would you expect it to land on the colored part? ______ times

12. Use these formulas to calculate the areas of the figures below.

Rectangle	Parallelogram	Triangle
Area = base $*$ height	Area = base $*$ height	Area = $\frac{1}{2}$ $*$ (base $*$ height)

a.

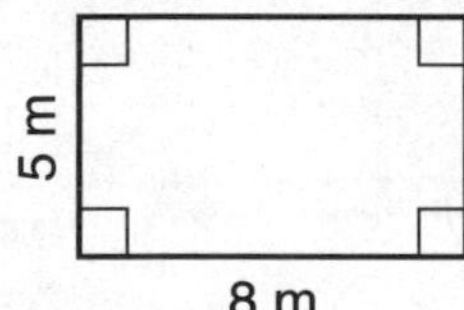

Number model: ______________

Area = __________

b.

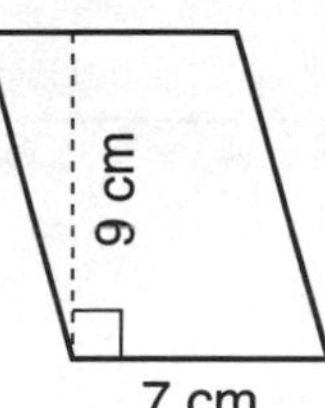

Number model: ______________

Area = __________

c.

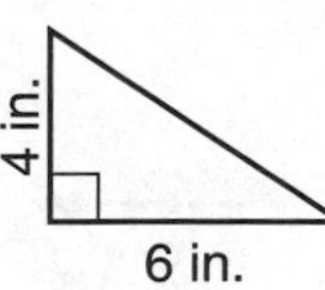

Number model: ______________

Area = __________

Name Date Time

LESSON 12•7

End-of-Year Assessment *continued*

13. Calculate the volume of each rectangular prism.

a.

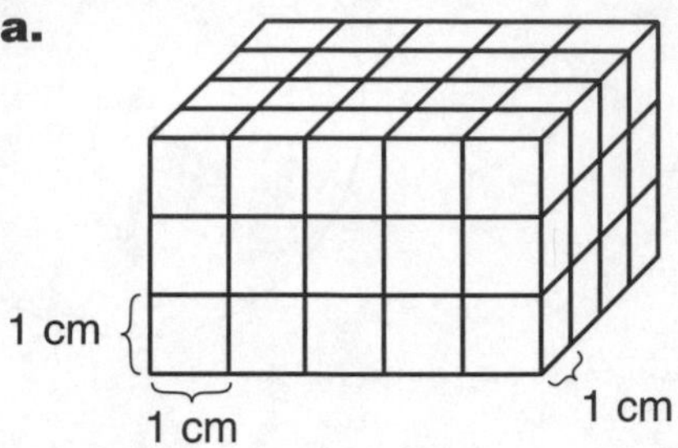

Volume = ________ cm^3

b.

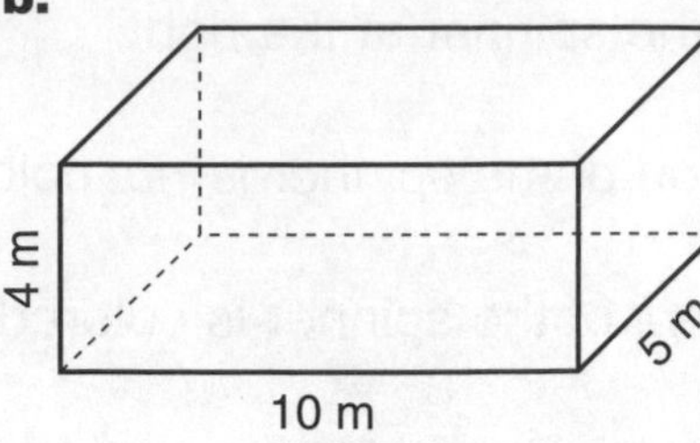

Volume = ________ m^3

14. Complete.

a. 72 in. = ________ yd

b. 10 yd = ________ ft

c. 56 cm = ________ mm

d. 63 cm = ________ m

15. Complete.

a. Draw a triangle at (5,4).

b. Draw a square at (1,5).

c. What shape is located at (2,3)? ____________

d. What shape is located at (3,2)? ________________

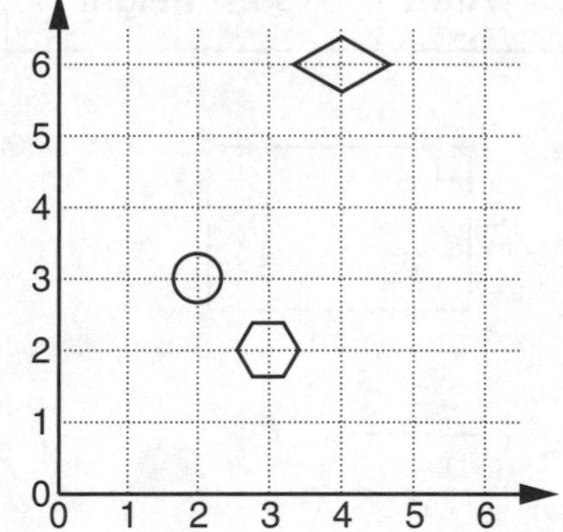

16. Estimate the measure of each angle. Do not use a protractor.

a.

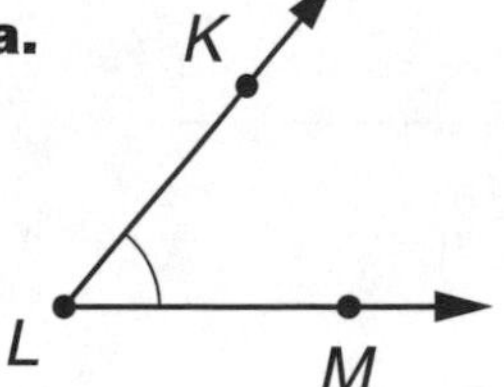

∠*KLM* is an ____________ (acute or obtuse) angle.

∠*KLM* measures about ____________°.

b.

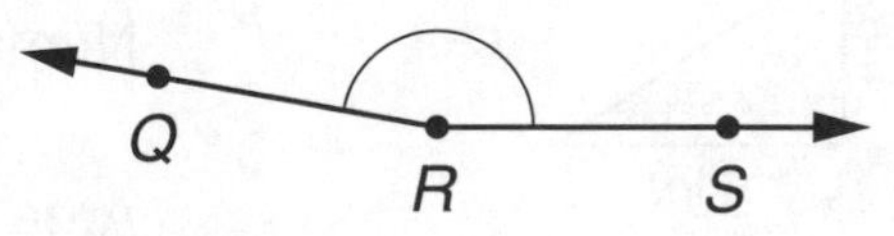

∠*QRS* is an ____________ (acute or obtuse) angle.

∠*QRS* measures about ____________°.

Name Date Time

End-of-Year Assessment *continued*

17. The objects below have the shapes of geometric solids. Name the solids.

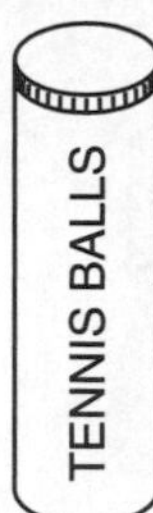

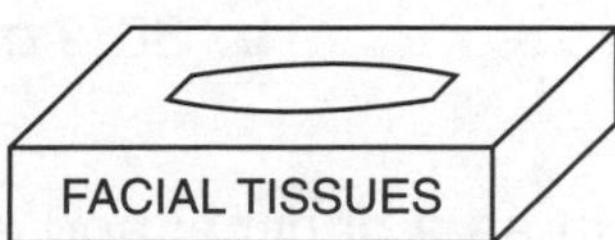

a. ____________________ **b.** ____________________

18. Label each figure as a *reflection, rotation,* or *translation* of the original figure. Use each word one time only.

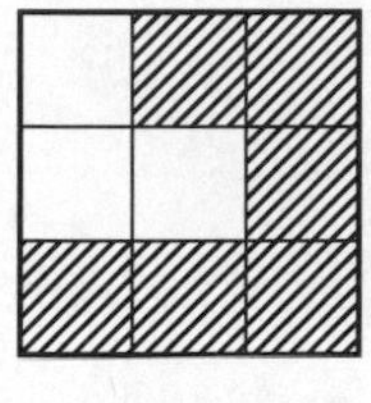
original

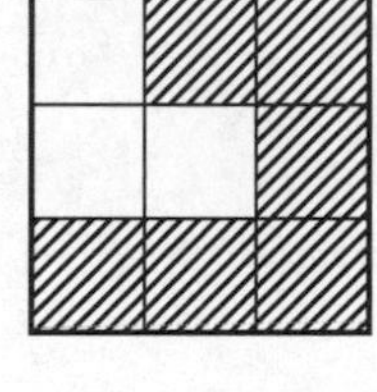
____

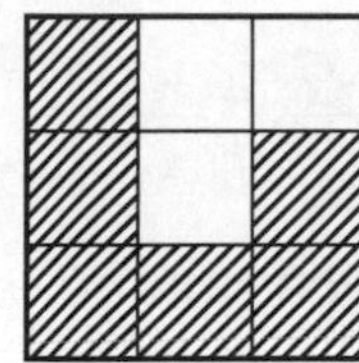
____

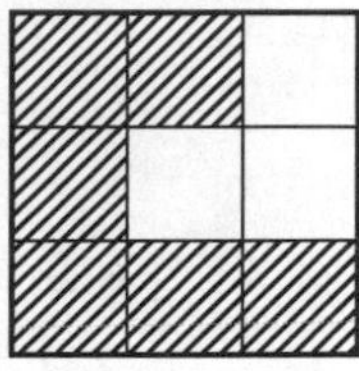
____

19. Complete the pattern and describe the rule.

Rule: _______________

5, 75, 145, 215, 285, ________, ________, ________

20. Insert parentheses to make each number sentence true.

a. $120 - 60 + 20 = 40$

b. $160 = 160 - 80 * 2$

c. $90 = 270 \div 90 \div 30$

d. $14 + 10 \div 2 * 6 = 2$

Name Date Time

LESSON 12•7

End-of-Year Assessment *continued*

Part B

21. Complete.

a. 25% of 24 = ________ **b.** 30% of 50 = ________ **c.** 150% of 14 = ________

22. Write each fraction as a decimal and as a percent.

a. $\frac{17}{20}$ = ________ . ________ = ________%

b. $\frac{1}{3}$ = ________ . ________ = ________%

c. $\frac{4}{16}$ = ________ . ________ = ________%

d. $\frac{3}{50}$ = ________ . ________ = ________%

23. Insert >, <, or = to make each number sentence true.

a. $-\frac{1}{4}$ ________ $-\frac{3}{4}$

b. $-\frac{4}{10}$ ________ $-\frac{4}{5}$

c. -14.6 ________ -12.8

d. -0.6 ________ $-\frac{3}{5}$

24. Multiply and divide. Show your work.

a. ____________ = 4.5 ∗ 6.9

b. 212.4 / 9 = ____________

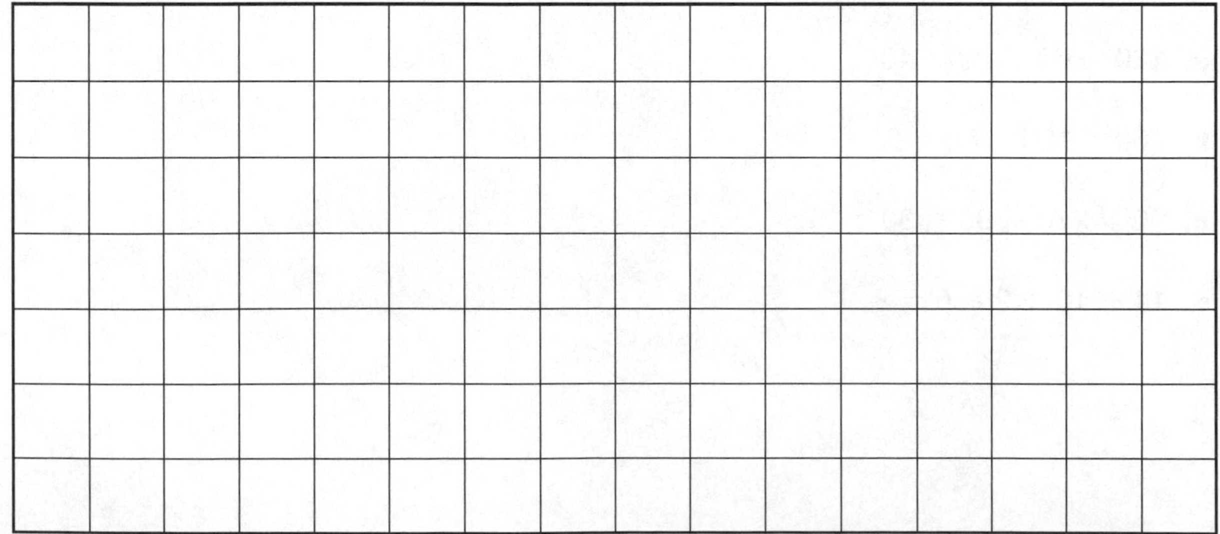

End-of-Year Assessment *continued*

25. Estimate. Is the sum or difference closest to 0, 1, or 2?

a. $\frac{1}{5} + \frac{1}{8}$ ________

b. $1\frac{2}{3} + \frac{1}{2}$ ________

c. $2\frac{1}{12} - \frac{9}{10}$ ________

d. $\frac{7}{8} - \frac{5}{6}$ ________

26. Use your protractor. Measure each angle below to the nearest degree.

a.

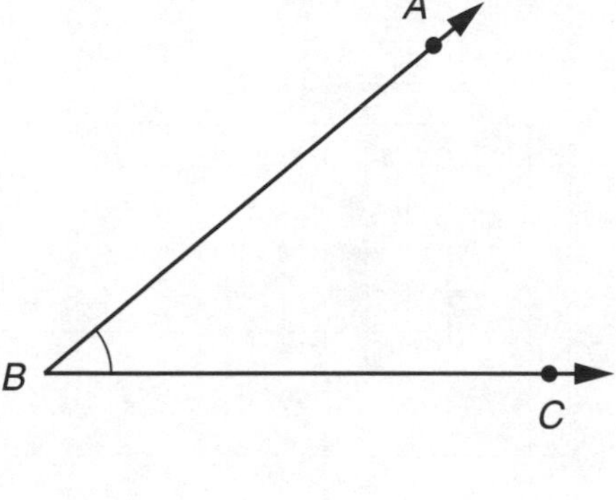

b.

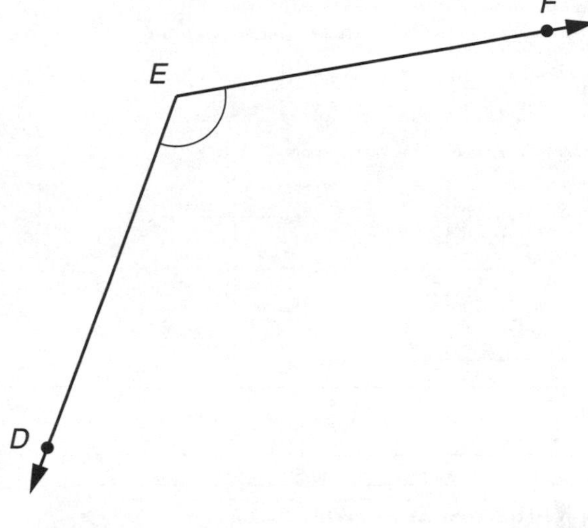

$\angle ABC$ measures ________°.

$\angle DEF$ measures ________°.

27. Austin surveyed the students in his class to find out which breakfast drinks they like best. Use the circle graph to answer the questions below.

a. What is the least favorite breakfast drink?

____

b. Do more students like cranberry juice or water? ____________

c. Which drink is more popular than milk?

____

Favorite Breakfast Drink

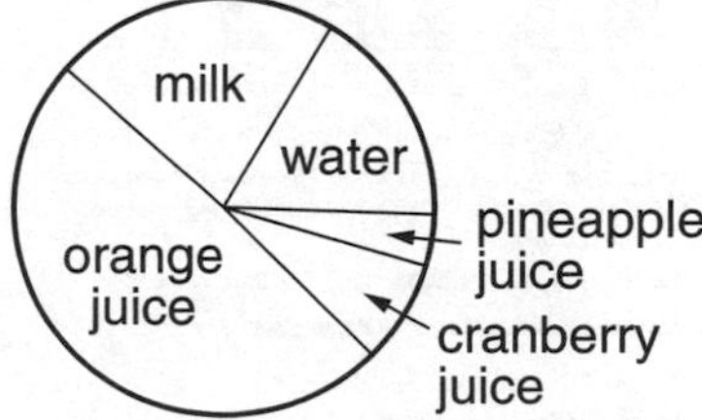

Name Date Time

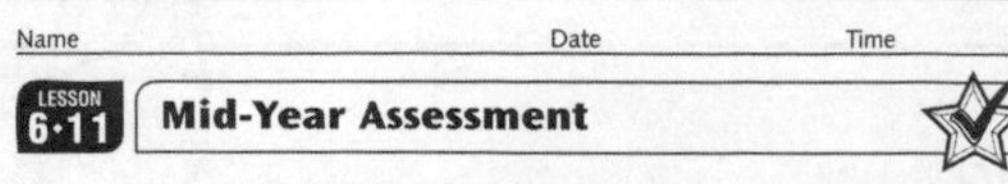

LESSON 6·11 **Mid-Year Assessment**

Part A

1. Write each number with digits.
   a. Twelve thousand, five hundred sixty-five 12,565
   b. Four million, six hundred thousand, twenty-seven 4,600,027
   c. Twelve and four-tenths 12.4
   d. Five and sixteen-hundredths 5.16

2. List the factor pairs of 32.
   1 and 32
   2 and 16
   4 and 8

3. Name the first 10 multiples of 9.
   9 18 27 36 45
   54 63 72 81 90

4. Nishi wanted to show the number 54 on her calculator. The 4-key on her calculator was broken, so this is what she did: 108 [÷] 2 [=]

   Find two other ways to show 54 without using the 4-key. Try to use different numbers and operations.
   a. Sample answer: 18 [×] 3 [=]
   b. Sample answer: 27 [+] 27 [=]

Complete the "What's My Rule?" tables and state the rules.

5. Rule: + 900

in	out
600	1,500
300	1,200
400	1,300
1,200	2,100
800	1,700

6. Rule: * 6

in	out
700	4,200
200	1,200
50	300
8,000	4,800
400	2,400

Name Date Time

LESSON 6·11 **Mid-Year Assessment** *continued*

Solve. Use paper-and-pencil algorithms.

7. A gallon of skim milk costs \$3.09 at the Gem supermarket and \$4.19 at the 6-to-Midnight convenience store. How much more does a gallon of milk cost at the convenience store?
   \$ 1.10

8. Keena bought some supplies for school. The crayons cost \$1.29, the notebooks cost \$2.49, and the pencils cost \$0.89. How much did Keena spend in all?
   \$ 4.67

9. 5,830 = 3,551 + 2,279

10. 2,653 − 1,289 = 1,364

11. 7 * 128 = 896

12. 55 = 385 / 7

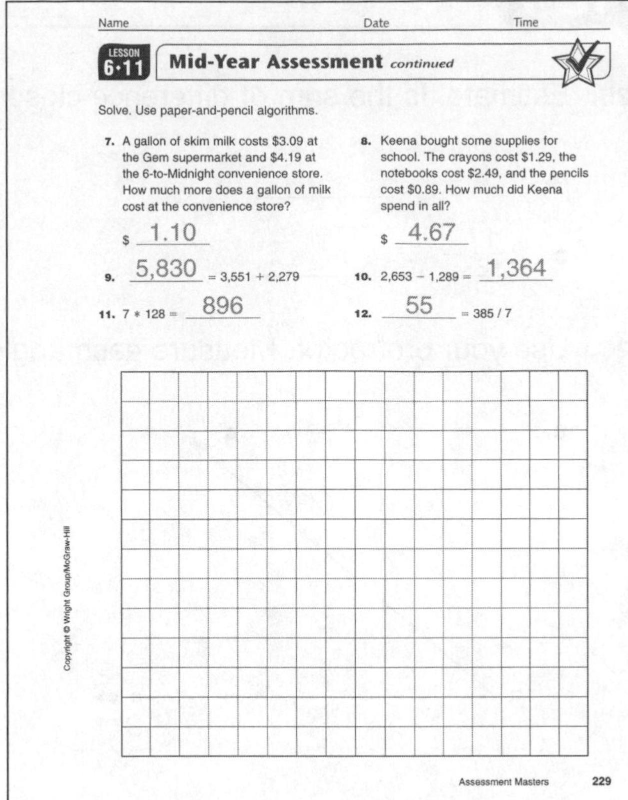

Name Date Time

LESSON 6·11 **Mid-Year Assessment** *continued*

13. A farm stand sells apples. The farmer records how many pounds of each type of apple are sold per day. Below are the results of Monday's sales:

    18 Red Delicious 25 Gala 24 Fuji
    21 Granny Smith 17 Empire 14 Pink Lady

    Create a bar graph using the data above. Include labels and a title.

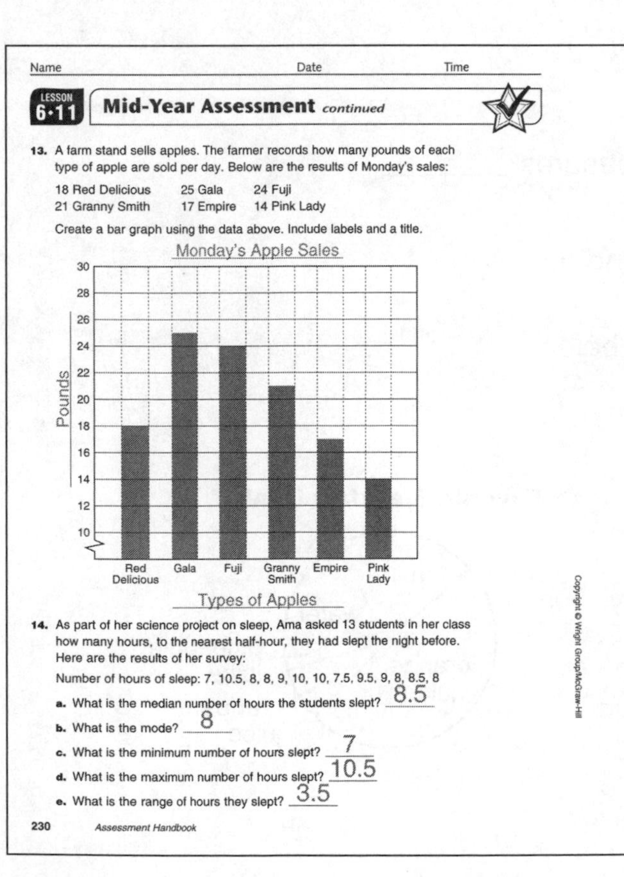

14. As part of her science project on sleep, Ama asked 13 students in her class how many hours, to the nearest half-hour, they had slept the night before. Here are the results of her survey:

    Number of hours of sleep: 7, 10.5, 8, 8, 9, 10, 10, 7.5, 9.5, 9, 8, 8.5, 8
    a. What is the median number of hours the students slept? 8.5
    b. What is the mode? 8
    c. What is the minimum number of hours slept? 7
    d. What is the maximum number of hours slept? 10.5
    e. What is the range of hours they slept? 3.5

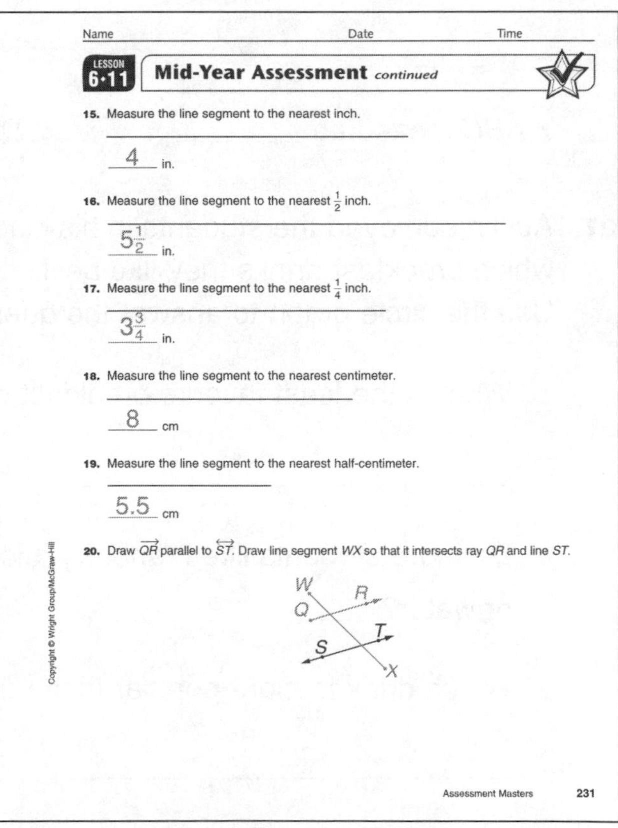

Name Date Time

LESSON 6·11 **Mid-Year Assessment** *continued*

15. Measure the line segment to the nearest inch.
    4 in.

16. Measure the line segment to the nearest $\frac{1}{2}$ inch.
    $5\frac{1}{2}$ in.

17. Measure the line segment to the nearest $\frac{1}{4}$ inch.
    $3\frac{3}{4}$ in.

18. Measure the line segment to the nearest centimeter.
    8 cm

19. Measure the line segment to the nearest half-centimeter.
    5.5 cm

20. Draw $\overrightarrow{QR}$ parallel to $\overleftrightarrow{ST}$. Draw line segment WX so that it intersects ray QR and line ST.

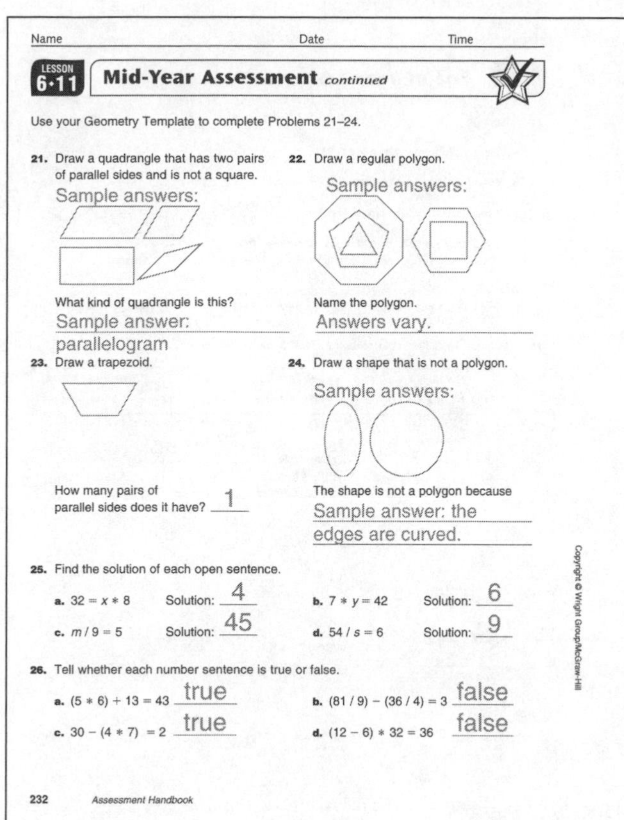

Name Date Time

LESSON 6·11 **Mid-Year Assessment** *continued*

Use your Geometry Template to complete Problems 21–24.

21. Draw a quadrangle that has two pairs of parallel sides and is not a square.

Sample answers:

What kind of quadrangle is this? Sample answer: parallelogram

22. Draw a regular polygon.

Sample answers:

Name the polygon. Answers vary.

23. Draw a trapezoid.

How many pairs of parallel sides does it have? 1

24. Draw a shape that is not a polygon.

Sample answers:

The shape is not a polygon because Sample answer: the edges are curved.

25. Find the solution of each open sentence.

a. $32 = x * 8$ Solution: 4

b. $7 * y = 42$ Solution: 6

c. $m / 9 = 5$ Solution: 45

d. $54 / s = 6$ Solution: 9

26. Tell whether each number sentence is true or false.

a. $(5 * 6) + 13 = 43$ true

b. $(81 / 9) - (36 / 4) = 3$ false

c. $30 - (4 * 7) = 2$ true

d. $(12 - 6) * 32 = 36$ false

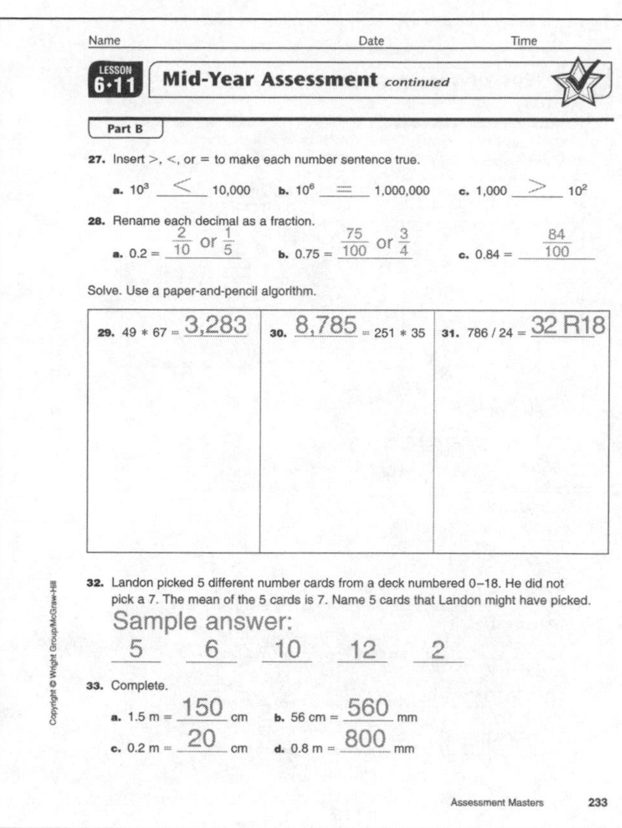

Name Date Time

LESSON 6·11 **Mid-Year Assessment** *continued*

Part B

27. Insert >, <, or = to make each number sentence true.

a. 10^3 < 10,000

b. 10^6 = 1,000,000

c. 1,000 > 10^2

28. Rename each decimal as a fraction.

a. $0.2 = \frac{2}{10}$ or $\frac{1}{5}$

b. $0.75 = \frac{75}{100}$ or $\frac{3}{4}$

c. $0.84 = \frac{84}{100}$

Solve. Use a paper-and-pencil algorithm.

29. $49 * 67 =$ 3,283	**30.** 8,785 $= 251 * 35$	**31.** $786 / 24 =$ 32 R18

32. Landon picked 5 different number cards from a deck numbered 0–18. He did not pick a 7. The mean of the 5 cards is 7. Name 5 cards that Landon might have picked.

Sample answer: 5 6 10 12 2

33. Complete.

a. 1.5 m = 150 cm

b. 56 cm = 560 mm

c. 0.2 m = 20 cm

d. 0.8 m = 800 mm

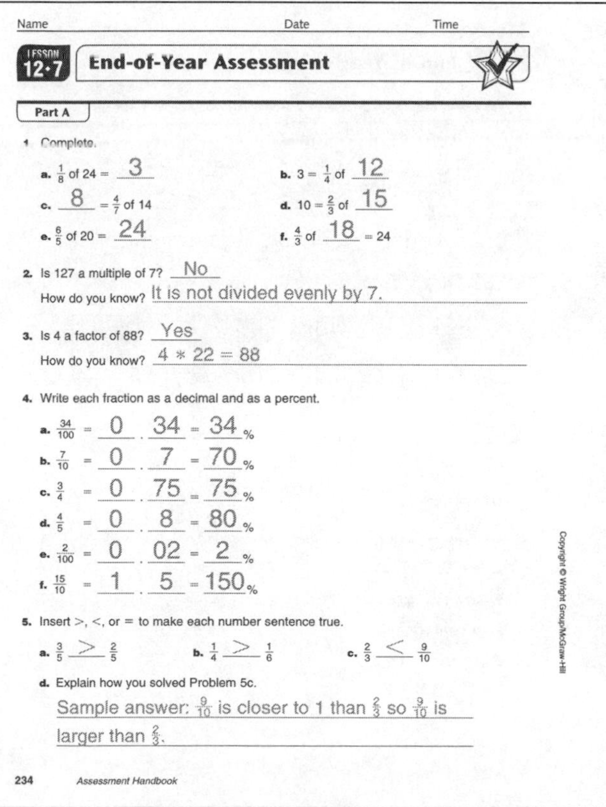

Name Date Time

LESSON 12·7 **End-of-Year Assessment**

Part A

1. Complete.

a. $\frac{1}{8}$ of 24 = 3

b. $3 = \frac{1}{4}$ of 12

c. 8 $= \frac{4}{7}$ of 14

d. $10 = \frac{2}{3}$ of 15

e. $\frac{6}{5}$ of 20 = 24

f. $\frac{4}{3}$ of 18 = 24

2. Is 127 a multiple of 7? No

How do you know? It is not divided evenly by 7.

3. Is 4 a factor of 88? Yes

How do you know? $4 * 22 = 88$

4. Write each fraction as a decimal and as a percent.

a. $\frac{34}{100}$ = 0.34 = 34%

b. $\frac{7}{10}$ = 0.7 = 70%

c. $\frac{3}{4}$ = 0.75 = 75%

d. $\frac{4}{5}$ = 0.8 = 80%

e. $\frac{2}{100}$ = 0.02 = 2%

f. $\frac{15}{10}$ = 1.5 = 150%

5. Insert >, <, or = to make each number sentence true.

a. $\frac{3}{5} > \frac{2}{5}$

b. $\frac{1}{4} > \frac{1}{6}$

c. $\frac{2}{3} < \frac{9}{10}$

d. Explain how you solved Problem 5c.

Sample answer: $\frac{9}{10}$ is closer to 1 than $\frac{2}{3}$ so $\frac{9}{10}$ is larger than $\frac{2}{3}$.

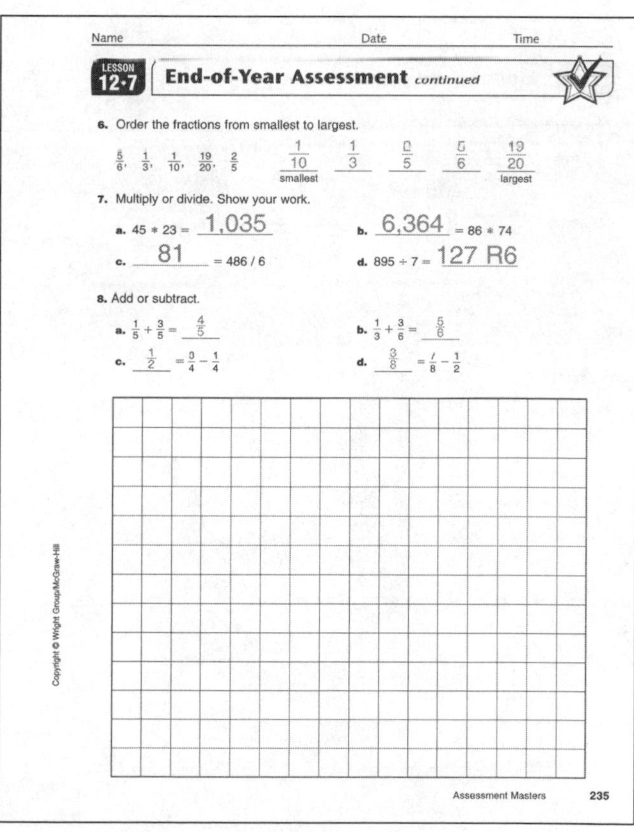

Name Date Time

LESSON 12·7 **End-of-Year Assessment** *continued*

6. Order the fractions from smallest to largest.

$\frac{5}{6}, \frac{1}{3}, \frac{1}{10}, \frac{19}{20}, \frac{2}{5}$

$\frac{1}{10}$ (smallest), $\frac{1}{3}$, $\frac{2}{5}$, $\frac{5}{6}$, $\frac{19}{20}$ (largest)

7. Multiply or divide. Show your work.

a. $45 * 23 =$ 1,035

b. 6,364 $= 86 * 74$

c. 81 $= 486 / 6$

d. $895 \div 7 =$ 127 R6

8. Add or subtract.

a. $\frac{1}{5} + \frac{3}{5} = \frac{4}{5}$

b. $\frac{1}{3} + \frac{3}{6} = \frac{5}{6}$

c. $\frac{1}{2} = \frac{3}{4} - \frac{1}{4}$

d. $\frac{3}{8} = \frac{7}{8} - \frac{1}{2}$

Name Date Time

9. The table shows the number of people who attended lacrosse games each week during the spring season. Create a line graph to show the data. Use a straightedge to connect the data points. Label each axis and include a title.

Week	Number of People
1	60
2	80
3	40
4	100
5	100
6	80
7	120
8	110

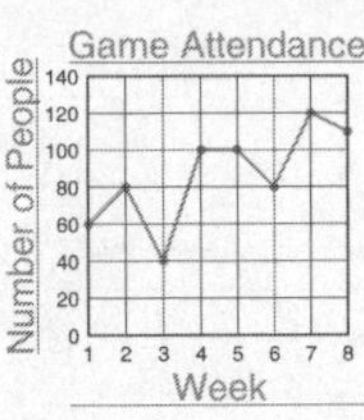

10. Use the following terms to complete the statements below.

impossible
likely
unlikely
very likely

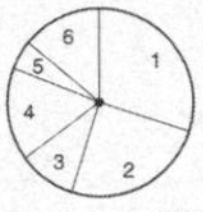

a. It is likely that the spinner will land on a number less than or equal to 2.

b. It is very likely that the spinner will land on a number not equal to 5.

c. It is impossible that the spinner will land on a number less than $\frac{9}{10}$.

d. It is unlikely that the spinner will land on 5.

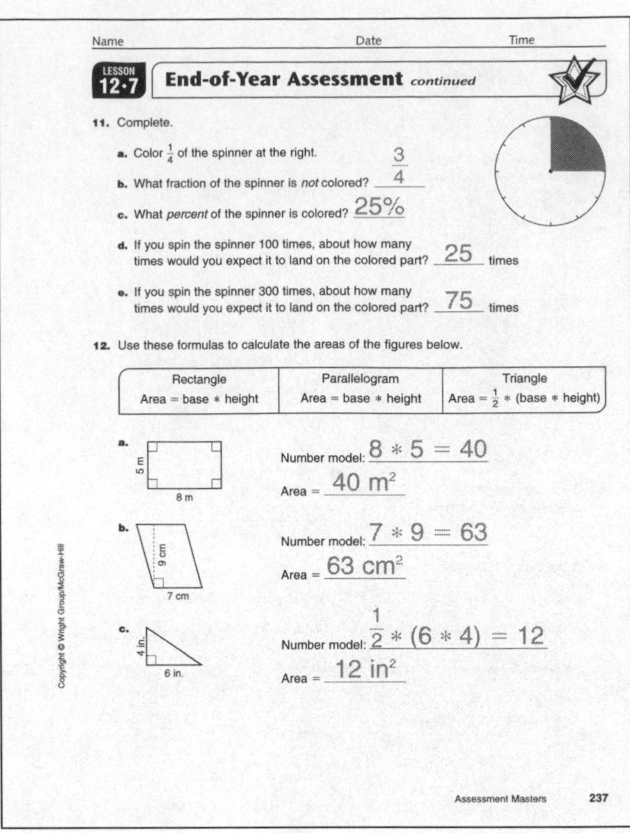

Name Date Time

LESSON 12·7 **End-of-Year Assessment** *continued*

11. Complete.

a. Color $\frac{1}{4}$ of the spinner at the right.

b. What fraction of the spinner is *not* colored? $\frac{3}{4}$

c. What *percent* of the spinner is colored? 25%

d. If you spin the spinner 100 times, about how many times would you expect it to land on the colored part? 25 times

e. If you spin the spinner 300 times, about how many times would you expect it to land on the colored part? 75 times

12. Use these formulas to calculate the areas of the figures below.

Rectangle	Parallelogram	Triangle
Area = base * height	Area = base * height	Area = $\frac{1}{2}$ * (base * height)

a. 5 m, 8 m
Number model: 8 * 5 = 40
Area = 40 m^2

b. 9 cm, 7 cm
Number model: 7 * 9 = 63
Area = 63 cm^2

c. 4 in., 6 in.
Number model: $\frac{1}{2}$ * (6 * 4) = 12
Area = 12 in^2

Copyright © Wright Group/McGraw-Hill

Assessment Masters 237

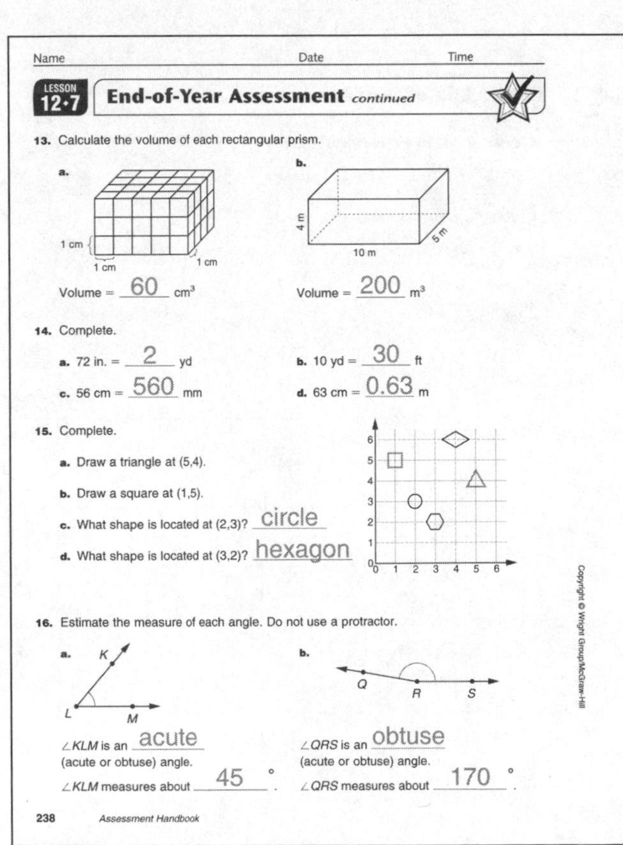

Name Date Time

LESSON 12·7 **End-of-Year Assessment** *continued*

13. Calculate the volume of each rectangular prism.

a. 1 cm, 1 cm, 1 cm
Volume = 60 cm^3

b. 4 m, 10 m, 5 m
Volume = 200 m^3

14. Complete.

a. 72 in. = 2 yd
b. 10 yd = 30 ft
c. 56 cm = 560 mm
d. 63 cm = 0.63 m

15. Complete.

a. Draw a triangle at (5,4).
b. Draw a square at (1,5).
c. What shape is located at (2,3)? circle
d. What shape is located at (3,2)? hexagon

16. Estimate the measure of each angle. Do not use a protractor.

a. ∠*KLM* is an acute (acute or obtuse) angle.
∠*KLM* measures about 45°.

b. ∠*QRS* is an obtuse (acute or obtuse) angle.
∠*QRS* measures about 170°.

Copyright © Wright Group/McGraw-Hill

238 Assessment Handbook

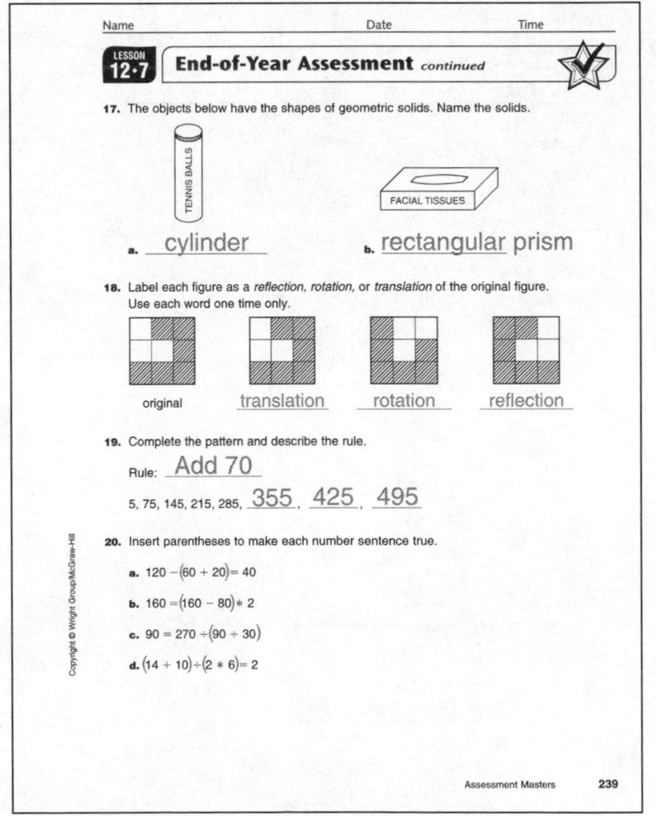

Name Date Time

LESSON 12·7 **End-of-Year Assessment** *continued*

17. The objects below have the shapes of geometric solids. Name the solids.

TENNIS BALLS
FACIAL TISSUES

a. cylinder
b. rectangular prism

18. Label each figure as a *reflection, rotation,* or *translation* of the original figure. Use each word one time only.

original translation rotation reflection

19. Complete the pattern and describe the rule.

Rule: Add 70

5, 75, 145, 215, 285, 355, 425, 495

20. Insert parentheses to make each number sentence true.

a. 120 − (60 + 20) = 40
b. 160 = (160 − 80) * 2
c. 90 = 270 ÷ (90 ÷ 30)
d. (14 + 10) ÷ (2 * 6) = 2

Copyright © Wright Group/McGraw-Hill

Assessment Masters 239

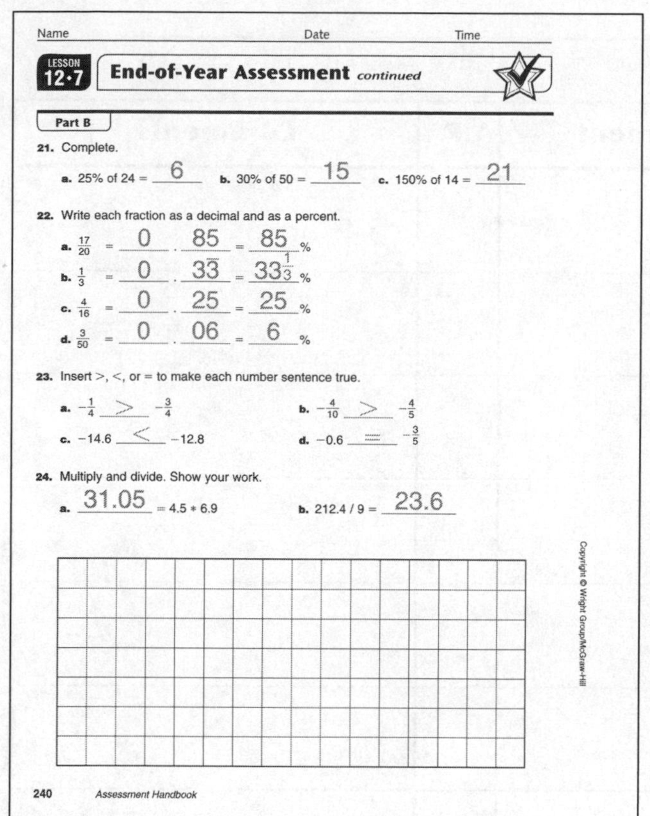

Name Date Time

LESSON 12·7

End-of-Year Assessment *continued*

Part B

21. Complete.

a. 25% of 24 = 6 **b.** 30% of 50 = 15 **c.** 150% of 14 = 21

22. Write each fraction as a decimal and as a percent.

a. $\frac{17}{20}$ = 0.85 = 85%

b. $\frac{1}{3}$ = 0.$\overline{33}$ = $33\frac{1}{3}$%

c. $\frac{4}{16}$ = 0.25 = 25%

d. $\frac{3}{50}$ = 0.06 = 6%

23. Insert >, <, or = to make each number sentence true.

a. $-\frac{1}{4}$ > $-\frac{3}{4}$ **b.** $-\frac{4}{10}$ > $-\frac{4}{5}$

c. −14.6 < −12.8 **d.** −0.6 = $-\frac{3}{5}$

24. Multiply and divide. Show your work.

a. 31.05 = 4.5 ∗ 6.9 **b.** 212.4 / 9 = 23.6

Copyright © Wright Group/McGraw-Hill

240 *Assessment Handbook*

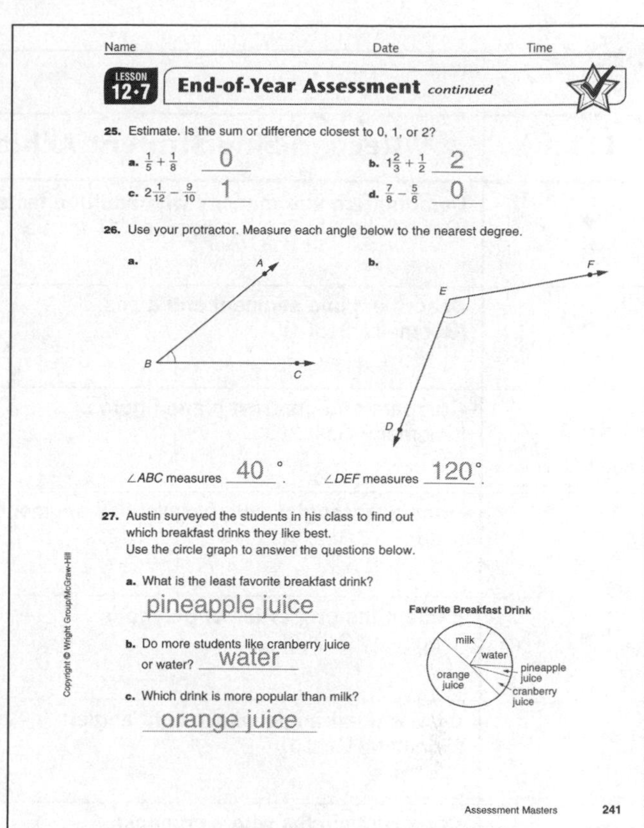

Name Date Time

LESSON 12·7

End-of-Year Assessment *continued*

25. Estimate. Is the sum or difference closest to 0, 1, or 2?

a. $\frac{1}{5} + \frac{1}{8}$ 0 **b.** $1\frac{2}{3} + \frac{1}{2}$ 2

c. $2\frac{1}{12} - \frac{9}{10}$ 1 **d.** $\frac{7}{8} - \frac{5}{6}$ 0

26. Use your protractor. Measure each angle below to the nearest degree.

a. **b.**

∠*ABC* measures 40°. ∠*DEF* measures 120°.

27. Austin surveyed the students in his class to find out which breakfast drinks they like best. Use the circle graph to answer the questions below.

a. What is the least favorite breakfast drink? pineapple juice

b. Do more students like cranberry juice or water? water

c. Which drink is more popular than milk? orange juice

Copyright © Wright Group/McGraw-Hill

Assessment Masters 241

Unit 1

Individual Profile of Progress

Name ______________________ Date ____________

Lesson	Recognizing Student Achievement	A.P.*	Comments
1◆1	**Demonstrate automaticity with addition facts.** [Operations and Computation Goal 1]		
1◆2	**Describe a line segment and a line.** [Geometry Goal 1]		
1◆3	**Compare and contrast plane figures.** [Geometry Goal 2]		
1◆4	**Draw quadrangles with parallel line segments.** [Geometry Goal 1]		
1◆5	**Explain the properties of polygons.** [Geometry Goal 2]		
1◆6	**Draw a quadrangle with 1 right angle.** [Geometry Goal 1]		
1◆7	**Construct circles with a compass.** [Geometry Goal 2]		
1◆8	**Demonstrate automaticity with subtraction facts.** [Operations and Computation Goal 1]		

*Assess Progress: 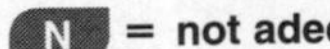 A = adequate progress  N = not adequate progress N/A = not assessed

Unit 1

Individual Profile of Progress

Name _______________ Date _______________

Problem(s)	Progress Check 1	A.P.*	Comments
Oral/Slate Assessment			
1	**Describe a geometric figure such as a trapezoid.** [Geometry Goals 1 and 2]		
2	**Point out examples of line segments, lines, rays, right angles, and parallel line segments in the classroom.** [Geometry Goal 1]		
3	**Draw geometric figures—rhombus, right angle, hexagon, parallel line segments, trapezoid, and triangle.** [Geometry Goals 1 and 2]		
4	**Solve basic addition and subtraction facts.** [Operations and Computation Goal 1]		
Written Assessment Part A			
1, 2	**Draw quadrangles.** [Geometry Goals 1 and 2]		
3, 4	**Draw parallel and intersecting lines and line segments.** [Geometry Goal 1]		
5, 6	**Name lines and rays.** [Geometry Goal 1]		
7, 8	**Name polygons.** [Geometry Goal 2]		
9	**Identify properties of polygons.** [Geometry Goal 2]		
10, 11	**Solve addition and subtraction facts.** [Operations and Computation Goal 1]		
Written Assessment Part B			
12	**Identify polygons.** [Geometry Goal 2]		
13	**Draw perpendicular line segments.** [Geometry Goal 1]		
14	**Draw a concave polygon.** [Geometry Goal 2]		
15	**Draw concentric circles.** [Geometry Goal 2]		
16	**Draw a polygon congruent to a given polygon.** [Geometry Goal 2]		

*Assess Progress:  A 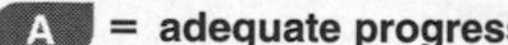 = adequate progress 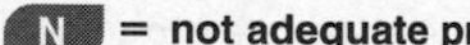 N = not adequate progress  N/A = not assessed

Formative Assessments

Unit 1 Class Checklist:

Recognizing Student Achievement

Class ______________________

Date ______________________

Names	1•1 Demonstrate automaticity with addition facts. [Operations and Computation Goal 1]	1•2 Describe a line segment and a line. [Geometry Goal 1]	1•3 Compare and contrast plane figures. [Geometry Goal 2]	1•4 Draw quadrangles with parallel line segments. [Geometry Goal 1]	1•5 Explain the properties of polygons. [Geometry Goal 2]	1•6 Draw a quadrangle with 1 right angle. [Geometry Goal 1]	1•7 Construct circles with a compass. [Geometry Goal 2]	1•8 Demonstrate automaticity with subtraction facts. [Operations and Computation Goal 1]
1.								
2.								
3.								
4.								
5.								
6.								
7.								
8.								
9.								
10.								
11.								
12.								
13.								
14.								
15.								
16.								
17.								
18.								
19.								
20.								
21.								
22.								
23.								
24.								
25.								

Assess Progress: 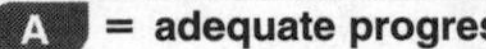  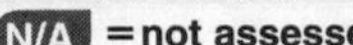

A = adequate progress N = not adequate progress N/A = not assessed

Unit 1

Class Checklist:

Progress Check 1

Class ____________________

Date ____________________

	Oral/Slate				Written Part A						Written Part B				
Names	**1. Describe a geometric figure such as a trapezoid.** [Geometry Goals 1 and 2]	**2. Point out examples of line segments, lines, rays, right angles, and parallel line segments in the classroom.** [Geometry Goal 1]	**3. Draw geometric figures—rhombus, right angle, hexagon, parallel line segments, trapezoid, and triangle.** [Geometry Goals 1 and 2]	**4. Solve basic addition and subtraction facts.** [Operations and Computation Goal 1]	**1, 2. Draw quadrangles.** [Geometry Goals 1 and 2]	**3, 4. Draw parallel and intersecting lines and line segments.** [Geometry Goal 1]	**5, 6. Name lines and rays.** [Geometry Goal 1]	**7, 8. Name polygons.** [Geometry Goal 2]	**9. Identify properties of polygons.** [Geometry Goal 2]	**10, 11. Solve addition and subtraction facts.** [Operations and Computation Goal 1]	**12. Identify polygons.** [Geometry Goal 2]	**13. Draw perpendicular line segments.** [Geometry Goal 1]	**14. Draw a concave polygon.** [Geometry Goal 2]	**15. Draw concentric circles.** [Geometry Goal 2]	**16. Draw a polygon congruent to a given polygon.** [Geometry Goal 2]
1.															
2.															
3.															
4.															
5.															
6.															
7.															
8.															
9.															
10.															
11.															
12.															
13.															
14.															
15.															
16.															
17.															
18.															
19.															
20.															
21.															
22.															
23.															
24.															
25.															

Assess Progress: 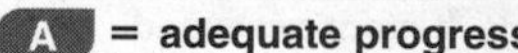 A = adequate progress 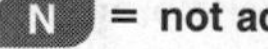 N = not adequate progress 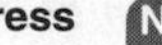 N/A = not assessed **Formative Assessments**

Unit 2 Individual Profile of Progress

Name ________________________ Date ________

Lesson	Recognizing Student Achievement	A.P.*	Comments
2◆1	**Demonstrate automaticity with extended addition facts.** [Operations and Computation Goal 1]		
2◆2	**Give equivalent names for whole numbers.** [Number and Numeration Goal 4]		
2◆3	**Identify the value of digits in whole numbers.** [Number and Numeration Goal 1]		
2◆4	**Identify places in whole numbers and the values of the digits in those places.** [Number and Numeration Goal 1]		
2◆5	**Demonstrate automaticity with basic addition facts.** [Operations and Computation Goal 1]		
2◆6	**Identify the maximum, minimum, range, and mode of a data set.** [Data and Chance Goal 2]		
2◆7	**Solve multidigit addition problems.** [Operations and Computation Goal 2]		
2◆8	**Use data landmarks and a bar graph to draw conclusions about a data set.** [Data and Chance Goal 2]		
2◆9	**Solve multidigit subtraction problems.** [Operations and Computation Goal 2]		

***Assess Progress:** 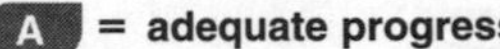 **A = adequate progress**  **N = not adequate progress** 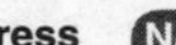 **N/A = not assessed**

Unit 2

Individual Profile of Progress

Name Date

Problem(s)	Progress Check 2	A.P.*	Comments
Oral/Slate Assessment			
1	**Read numbers and identify the values of digits in specified places.** [Number and Numeration Goal 1]		
2	**Explain how to find the mode, median, and range of a data set.** [Data and Chance Goal 2]		
3	**Read and write numbers and then identify the values of digits in specified places.** [Number and Numeration Goal 1]		
4	**Draw geometric shapes to match descriptions.** [Geometry Goal 2]		
Written Assessment Part A			
1–6	**Add and subtract multidigit numbers.** [Operations and Computation Goal 2]		
7	**Draw a polygon. Mark the right angles.** [Geometry Goal 2]		
8	**Explain whether or not a given polygon is a parallelogram.** [Geometry Goal 2]		
9–14	**Interpret a tally chart and find the maximum, range, mode, and median for a set of data.** [Data and Chance Goals 1 and 2]		
15	**Construct a bar graph.** [Data and Chance Goal 1]		
Written Assessment Part B			
16	**Write equivalent names for numbers.** [Number and Numeration Goal 4]		
17	**Measure line segments to the nearest half-centimeter.** [Measurement and Reference Frames Goal 1]		
18	**Draw a line segment to the nearest half-centimeter.** [Measurement and Reference Frames Goal 1]		
19	**Estimate sums and differences; solve multidigit addition and subtraction problems.** [Operations and Computation Goals 2 and 6]		
20	**Describe a strategy for estimating sums and differences.** [Operations and Computation Goal 6]		

*Assess Progress: 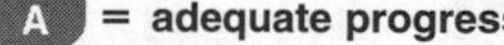 A = adequate progress 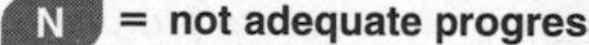 N = not adequate progress 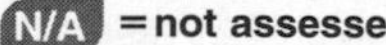 N/A = not assessed

Unit 2

Class Checklist:

Recognizing Student Achievement

Class ____________________

Date ____________________

Names	2•1 Demonstrate automaticity with extended addition facts. [Operations and Computation Goal 1]	2•2 Give equivalent names for whole numbers. [Number and Numeration Goal 4]	2•3 Identify the value of digits in whole numbers. [Number and Numeration Goal 1]	2•4 Identify places in whole numbers and the values of the digits in those places. [Number and Numeration Goal 1]	2•5 Demonstrate automaticity with basic addition facts. [Operations and Computation Goal 1]	2•6 Identify the maximum, minimum, range, and mode of a data set. [Data and Chance Goal 2]	2•7 Solve multidigit addition problems. [Operations and Computation Goal 2]	2•8 Use data landmarks and a bar graph to draw conclusions about a data set. [Data and Chance Goal 2]	2•9 Solve multidigit subtraction problems. [Operations and Computation Goal 2]
1.									
2.									
3.									
4.									
5.									
6.									
7.									
8.									
9.									
10.									
11.									
12.									
13.									
14.									
15.									
16.									
17.									
18.									
19.									
20.									
21.									
22.									
23.									
24.									
25.									

Assess Progress: 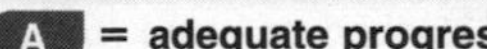 A = adequate progress  N = not adequate progress N/A = not assessed

Unit 2

Class Checklist:

Progress Check 2

Class ____________________

Date ____________________

Names	Oral/Slate				Written: Part A					Written: Part B				
	1. Read numbers and identify the values of digits in specified places. [Number and Numeration Goal 1]	**2. Explain how to find the mode, median, and range of a data set.** [Data and Chance Goal 2]	**3. Read and write numbers and then identify the values of digits in specified places.** [Number and Numeration Goal 1]	**4. Draw geometric shapes to match descriptions.** [Geometry Goal 2]	**1–6. Add and subtract multidigit numbers.** [Operations and Computation Goal 2]	**7. Draw a polygon. Mark the right angles.** [Geometry Goal 2]	**8. Explain whether or not a given polygon is a parallelogram.** [Geometry Goal 2]	**9–14. Interpret a tally chart and find the maximum, range, mode, and median for a set of data.** [Data and Chance Goals 1 and 2]	**15. Construct a bar graph.** [Data and Chance Goal 1]	**16. Write equivalent names for numbers.** [Number and Numeration Goal 4]	**17. Measure line segments to the nearest half-centimeter.** [Measurement and Reference Frames Goal 1]	**18. Draw a line segment to the nearest half-centimeter.** [Measurement and Reference Frames Goal 1]	**19. Estimate sums and differences; solve multidigit addition and subtraction problems.** [Operations and Computation Goals 2 and 6]	**20. Describe a strategy for estimating sums and differences.** [Operations and Computation Goal 6]
1.														
2.														
3.														
4.														
5.														
6.														
7.														
8.														
9.														
10.														
11.														
12.														
13.														
14.														
15.														
16.														
17.														
18.														
19.														
20.														
21.														
22.														
23.														
24.														
25.														

Assess Progress: 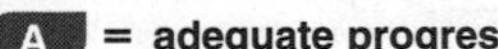 A = adequate progress 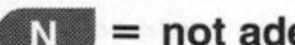 N = not adequate progress  N/A = not assessed **Formative Assessments**

Unit 3

Individual Profile of Progress

Name Date

Lesson	Recognizing Student Achievement	A.P.*	Comments
3◆1	**Use rules to complete "What's My Rule?" tables.** [Patterns, Functions, and Algebra Goal 1]		
3◆2	**Use numerical expressions involving one or more of the basic four operations to give equivalent names for whole numbers.** [Number and Numeration Goal 4]		
3◆3	**Estimate reasonable solutions for whole-number addition and subtraction problems.** [Operations and Computation Goal 6]		
3◆4	**Demonstrate automaticity with multiplication facts through 10 ∗ 10.** [Operations and Computation Goal 3]		
3◆5	**Use conventional notation to write multiplication and division number sentences.** [Patterns, Functions, and Algebra Goal 2]		
3◆6	**Solve multidigit addition and subtraction problems.** [Operations and Computation Goal 2]		
3◆7	**Use a map scale to estimate distances.** [Operations and Computation Goal 7]		
3◆8	**Use and explain a strategy for solving an addition number story.** [Operations and Computation Goal 2]		
3◆9	**Determine whether number sentences are true or false.** [Patterns, Functions, and Algebra Goal 2]		
3◆10	**Demonstrate proficiency with basic division facts.** [Operations and Computation Goal 3]		
3◆11	**Use and explain a strategy for solving open number sentences.** [Patterns, Functions, and Algebra Goal 2]		

*Assess Progress:  A = adequate progress  N = not adequate progress  N/A = not assessed

Unit 3

Individual Profile of Progress

Name ____________________ Date ____________

Problem(s)	Progress Check 3	A.P.*	Comments
Oral/Slate Assessment			
1	**Explain and provide examples for the meaning of *factor*, *multiple*, and *product*.** [Number and Numeration Goal 3]		
2	**Explain why "18 divided by 6 (18 / 6)" is not a number sentence.** [Patterns, Functions, and Algebra Goal 2]		
3	**Solve multiplication and division facts.** [Operations and Computation Goal 3]		
4	**Use a map scale to write the distance it represents.** [Operations and Computation Goal 7]		
Written Assessment Part A			
1–3	**Fill in missing Fact Triangle numbers.** [Operations and Computation Goal 3; Patterns, Functions, and Algebra Goal 2]		
4–9	**Tell whether a number sentence is true, false, or "can't tell."** [Operations and Computation Goal 3; Patterns, Functions, and Algebra Goals 2 and 3]		
10–13	**Make a true sentence by filling in a missing number.** [Operations and Computation Goal 3; Patterns, Functions, and Algebra Goals 2 and 3]		
14–17	**Make a true sentence by inserting parentheses.** [Operations and Computation Goal 3; Patterns, Functions, and Algebra Goals 2 and 3]		
18	**Use a bar graph to find the median, range, and mode of a data set.** [Data and Chance Goal 2]		
19, 20	**Solve addition and subtraction number stories.** [Operations and Computation Goal 2]		
21	**Solve "What's My Rule?" problems.** [Operations and Computation Goal 3]		
22	**Name factors of 24.** [Number and Numeration Goal 3]		
Written Assessment Part B			
23–28	**Solve an open sentence.** [Patterns, Functions, and Algebra Goal 2]		
29, 30	**Use a map and map scale.** [Operations and Computation Goal 7; Measurement and Reference Frames Goal 1]		
31	**Complete a Venn diagram with multiples.** [Number and Numeration Goal 3]		

*Assess Progress: 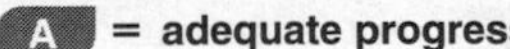 A = adequate progress 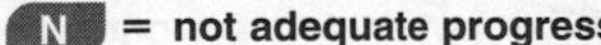 N = not adequate progress 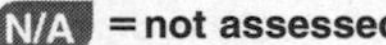 N/A = not assessed

Formative Assessments

Unit 3

Class Checklist:

Recognizing Student Achievement

Class ______________________

Date ______________________

	Use rules to complete "What's My Rule?" tables. [Patterns, Functions, and Algebra Goal 1]	**Use numerical expressions involving one or more of the basic four operations to give equivalent names for whole numbers.** [Number and Numeration Goal 4]	**Estimate reasonable solutions for whole-number addition and subtraction problems.** [Operations and Computation Goal 6]	**Demonstrate automaticity with multiplication facts through 10 * 10.** [Operations and Computation Goal 3]	**Use conventional notation to write multiplication and division number sentences.** [Patterns, Functions, and Algebra Goal 2]	**Solve multidigit addition and subtraction problems.** [Operations and Computation Goal 2]	**Use a map scale to estimate distances.** [Operations and Computation Goal 7]	**Use and explain a strategy for solving an addition number story.** [Operations and Computation Goal 2]	**Determine whether number sentences are true or false.** [Patterns, Functions, and Algebra Goal 2]	**Demonstrate proficiency with basic division facts.** [Operations and Computation Goal 3]	**Use and explain a strategy for solving open number sentences.** [Patterns, Functions, and Algebra Goal 2]
Names	**3•1**	**3•2**	**3•3**	**3•4**	**3•5**	**3•6**	**3•7**	**3•8**	**3•9**	**3•10**	**3•11**
1.											
2.											
3.											
4.											
5.											
6.											
7.											
8.											
9.											
10.											
11.											
12.											
13.											
14.											
15.											
16.											
17.											
18.											
19.											
20.											
21.											
22.											
23.											
24.											
25.											

Assess Progress: **A** = adequate progress **N** = not adequate progress **N/A** = not assessed

Unit 3

Class Checklist:

Progress Check 3:

Class ____________

Date ____________

Names	Oral/Slate				Written: Part A								Written: Part B		
	1. **Explain and provide examples for the meaning of *factor, multiple,* and *product.*** [Number and Numeration Goal 3]	2. **Explain why "18 divided by 6 (18 / 6)" is not a number sentence.** [Patterns, Functions, and Algebra Goal 2]	3. **Solve multiplication and division facts.** [Operations and Computation Goal 3]	4. **Use a map scale to write the distance it represents.** [Operations and Computation Goal 7]	1–3. **Fill in missing Fact Triangle numbers.** [Operations and Computation Goal 3; Patterns, Functions, and Algebra Goal 2]	4–9. **Tell whether a number sentence is true, false, or "can't tell."** [Operations and Computation Goal 3; Patterns, Functions, and Algebra Goals 2 and 3]	10–13. **Make a true sentence by filling in a missing number.** [Operations and Computation Goal 3; Patterns, Functions, and Algebra Goals 2 and 3]	14–17. **Make a true sentence by inserting parentheses.** [Operations and Computation Goal 3; Patterns, Functions, and Algebra Goals 2 and 3]	18. **Use a bar graph to find the median, range, and mode of a data set.** [Data and Chance Goal 2]	19, 20. **Solve addition and subtraction number stories.** [Operations and Computation Goal 2]	21. **Solve "What's My Rule?" problems.** [Operations and Computation Goal 3]	22. **Name factors of 24.** [Number and Numeration Goal 3]	23–28. **Solve an open sentence.** [Patterns, Functions, and Algebra Goal 2]	29, 30. **Use a map and map scale.** [Operations and Computation Goal 7; Measurement and Reference Frames Goal 1]	31. **Complete a Venn diagram with multiples.** [Number and Numeration Goal 3]
1.															
2.															
3.															
4.															
5.															
6.															
7.															
8.															
9.															
10.															
11.															
12.															
13.															
14.															
15.															
16.															
17.															
18.															
19.															
20.															
21.															
22.															
23.															
24.															
25.															

Assess Progress: 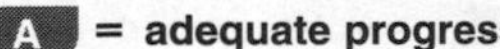 A = adequate progress  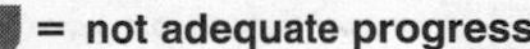 N = not adequate progress  N/A = not assessed **Formative Assessments**

Individual Profile of Progress

Name Date

Lesson	Recognizing Student Achievement	A.P.*	Comments
4◆1	**Identify the values of digits in whole numbers.** [Number and Numeration Goal 1]		
4◆2	**Identify the values of decimal digits.** [Number and Numeration Goal 1]		
4◆3	**Compare decimals through hundredths.** [Number and Numeration Goal 6]		
4◆4	**Estimate sums of decimals and explain the estimation strategy.** [Operations and Computation Goal 6]		
4◆5	**Identify the value of decimal digits.** [Number and Numeration Goal 1]		
4◆6	**Identify data landmarks.** [Data and Chance Goal 2]		
4◆7	**Write decimals through hundredths.** [Number and Numeration Goal 1]		
4◆8	**Measure line segments to the nearest centimeter.** [Measurement and Reference Frames Goal 1]		
4◆9	**Compare decimals through thousandths.** [Number and Numeration Goal 6]		
4◆10	**Demonstrate automaticity with multiplication facts.** [Operations and Computation Goal 3]		

*Assess Progress: 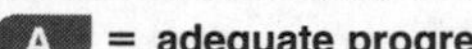 A = adequate progress  N = not adequate progress N/A = not assessed

Individual Profile of Progress

Name ______________________ Date ______________

Problem(s)	Progress Check 4	A.P.*	Comments
Oral/Slate Assessment			
1	**Read aloud 1-, 2-, and 3-place decimals.** [Number and Numeration Goal 1]		
2	**Solve decimal addition and subtraction problems and describe the strategy used to estimate the answer to each problem.** [Operations and Computation Goal 6]		
3	**Write 1-, 2-, and 3-place decimals.** [Number and Numeration Goal 1]		
4	**Convert metric measurements.** [Measurement and Reference Frames Goal 3]		
Written Assessment Part A			
1–4	**Insert > or < to make true number sentences.** [Number and Numeration Goal 6; Operations and Computation Goal 2; Patterns, Functions, and Algebra Goal 2]		
5	**Order decimals.** [Number and Numeration Goal 6]		
6, 7	**Write numbers between 2 whole numbers.** [Number and Numeration Goal 6]		
8	**Measure line segments to the nearest centimeter.** [Measurement and Reference Frames Goal 1]		
9, 10	**Measure and draw line segments to the nearest $\frac{1}{2}$ centimeter.** [Measurement and Reference Frames Goal 1]		
11, 12	**Write factors and multiples.** [Number and Numeration Goal 3]		
13–18	**Add and subtract decimals.** [Operations and Computation Goal 2]		
19–22	**Solve open sentences.** [Patterns, Functions, and Algebra Goal 2]		
Written Assessment Part B			
23–25	**Rename decimals as fractions with 10, 100, and 1,000 in the denominator.** [Number and Numeration Goal 5]		
26, 27	**Measure line segments to the nearest millimeter.** [Measurement and Reference Frames Goals 1 and 3]		
28	**Solve a decimal addition and subtraction number story.** [Operations and Computation Goal 2]		
29	**Identify decimal digits and express their value.** [Number and Numeration Goal 1]		

 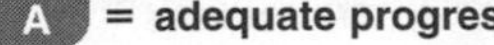  

*Assess Progress: A = adequate progress N = not adequate progress N/A = not assessed **Formative Assessments**

Class Checklist:
Recognizing Student Achievement

Class ____________________

Date ____________________

	Identify the values of digits in whole numbers. [Number and Numeration Goal 1]	Identify the values of decimal digits. [Number and Numeration Goal 1]	Compare decimals through hundredths. [Number and Numeration Goal 6]	Estimate sums of decimals and explain the estimation strategy. [Operations and Computation Goal 6]	Identify the value of decimal digits. [Number and Numeration Goal 1]	Identify data landmarks. [Data and Chance Goal 2]	Write decimals through hundredths. [Number and Numeration Goal 1]	Measure line segments to the nearest centimeter. [Measurement and Reference Frames Goal 1]	Compare decimals through thousandths. [Number and Numeration Goal 6]	Demonstrate automaticity with multiplication facts. [Operations and Computation Goal 3]
Names	**4•1**	**4•2**	**4•3**	**4•4**	**4•5**	**4•6**	**4•7**	**4•8**	**4•9**	**4•10**
1.										
2.										
3.										
4.										
5.										
6.										
7.										
8.										
9.										
10.										
11.										
12.										
13.										
14.										
15.										
16.										
17.										
18.										
19.										
20.										
21.										
22.										
23.										
24.										
25.										

Assess Progress: 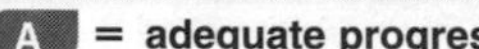 **A = adequate progress**  **N = not adequate progress**  **N/A = not assessed**

Unit 4

Class Checklist:

Progress Check 4

Class ____________________

Date ____________________

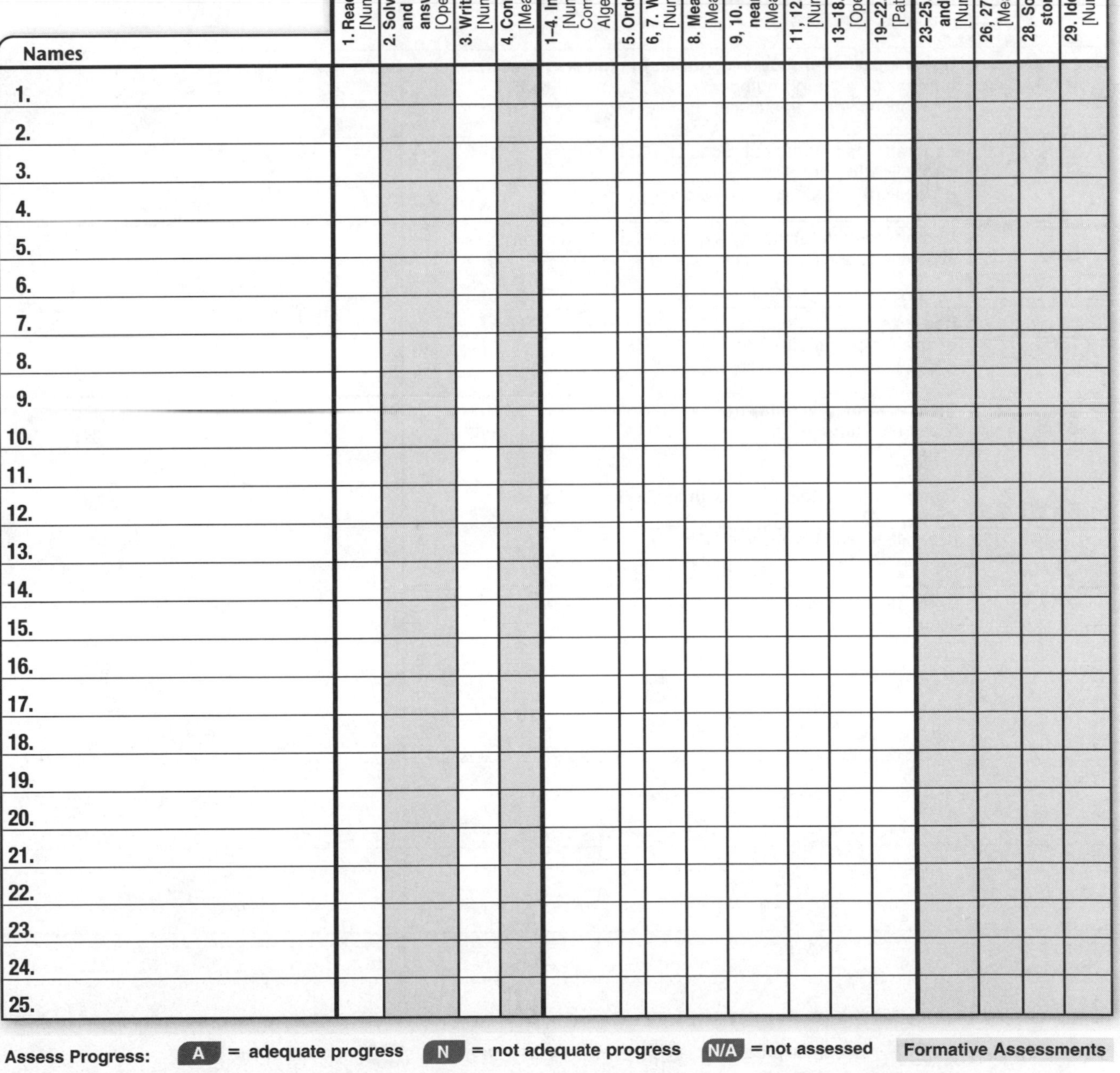

Names	Oral/Slate				Written: Part A								Written: Part B			
	1. Read aloud 1-, 2-, and 3-place decimals. [Number and Numeration Goal 1]	**2. Solve decimal addition and subtraction problems and describe the strategy used to estimate the answer to each problem.** [Operations and Computation Goal 6]	**3. Write 1-, 2-, and 3-place decimals.** [Number and Numeration Goal 1]	**4. Convert metric measurements.** [Measurement and Reference Frames Goal 3]	**1–4. Insert > or < to make true number sentences.** [Number and Numeration Goal 6; Operations and Computation Goal 2; Patterns, Functions, and Algebra Goal 2]	**5. Order decimals.** [Number and Numeration Goal 6]	**6, 7. Write numbers between 2 whole numbers.** [Number and Numeration Goal 6]	**8. Measure line segments to the nearest centimeter.** [Measurement and Reference Frames Goal 1]	**9, 10. Measure and draw line segments to the nearest $\frac{1}{2}$ centimeter.** [Measurement and Reference Frames Goal 1]	**11, 12. Write factors and multiples.** [Number and Numeration Goal 3]	**13–18. Add and subtract decimals.** [Operations and Computation Goal 2]	**19–22. Solve open sentences.** [Patterns, Functions, and Algebra Goal 2]	**23–25. Rename decimals as fractions with 10, 100, and 1,000 in the denominator.** [Number and Numeration Goal 5]	**26, 27. Measure line segments to the nearest millimeter.** [Measurement and Reference Frames Goals 1 and 3]	**28. Solve a decimal addition and subtraction number story.** [Operations and Computation Goal 2]	**29. Identify decimal digits and express their value.** [Number and Numeration Goal 1]
1.																
2.																
3.																
4.																
5.																
6.																
7.																
8.																
9.																
10.																
11.																
12.																
13.																
14.																
15.																
16.																
17.																
18.																
19.																
20.																
21.																
22.																
23.																
24.																
25.																

Assess Progress: A = adequate progress N = not adequate progress N/A = not assessed **Formative Assessments**

Individual Profile of Progress

Name Date

Lesson	Recognizing Student Achievement	A.P.*	Comments
5♦1	**Explain how to use basic facts to compute fact extensions.** [Operations and Computation Goal 3]		
5♦2	**Determine whether a number sentence is true or false.** [Patterns, Functions, and Algebra Goal 2]		
5♦3	**Explain how estimation was used to solve addition problems.** [Operations and Computation Goal 6]		
5♦4	**Use the Distributive Property of Multiplication over Addition to find partial products.** [Patterns, Functions, and Algebra Goal 4]		
5♦5	**Use the partial-products algorithm to multiply a 1-digit number by a 2-digit number.** [Operations and Computation Goal 4]		
5♦6	**Estimate reasonable solutions to whole-number multiplication problems.** [Operations and Computation Goal 6]		
5♦7	**Demonstrate automaticity with basic multiplication facts.** [Operations and Computation Goal 3]		
5♦8	**Use extended multiplication facts in a problem-solving situation.** [Operations and Computation Goal 3]		
5♦9	**Describe numeric patterns.** [Patterns, Functions, and Algebra Goal 1]		
5♦10	**Demonstrate automaticity with multiplication facts through 10 * 10.** [Operations and Computation Goal 3]		
5♦11	**Compare numbers up to 1 billion.** [Number and Numeration Goal 6]		

*Assess Progress: 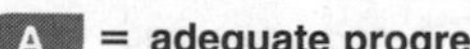 A = adequate progress 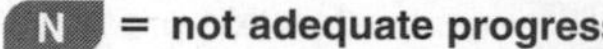 N = not adequate progress 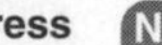 N/A = not assessed

Unit 5

Individual Profile of Progress

Name _______________ Date _______________

Problem(s)	Progress Check 5	A.P.*	Comments
Oral/Slate Assessment			
1	**Read aloud numbers through the billions.** [Number and Numeration Goal 1]		
2	**Describe the strategy used to estimate the sum of addition problems.** [Operations and Computation Goal 6]		
3	**Use exponential notation to name powers of 10.** [Number and Numeration Goal 4]		
4	**Determine place value through the billions in numbers.** [Number and Numeration Goal 1]		
Written Assessment Part A			
1, 2	**Estimate sums.** [Operations and Computation Goal 6]		
3–6	**Multiply multidigit whole numbers.** [Operations and Computation Goal 4; Patterns, Functions, and Algebra Goal 4]		
7–11	**Add and subtract decimals.** [Operations and Computation Goal 2]		
12	**Measure to the nearest $\frac{1}{4}$ in. and 0.5 cm.** [Measurement and Reference Frames Goal 1]		
13–15	**Multiply using "What's My Rule?" tables.** [Operations and Computation Goal 3; Patterns, Functions, and Algebra Goal 1]		
Written Assessment Part B			
16a, 17a	**Estimate products.** [Operations and Computation Goal 6]		
16b, 17b	**Multiply multidigit whole numbers.** [Operations and Computation Goal 4; Patterns, Functions, and Algebra Goal 4]		
18–20	**Multiply using extended facts.** [Number and Numeration Goal 6; Operations and Computation Goal 3]		
21	**Measure to the nearest $\frac{1}{4}$ in. and 0.5 cm when the 0-mark of the ruler is not positioned at the end of an object.** [Measurement and Reference Frames Goal 1]		

*Assess Progress:  A = adequate progress 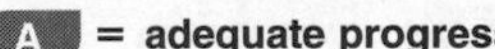 N = not adequate progress  N/A = not assessed 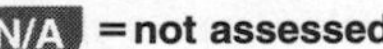 Formative Assessments

Class Checklist:

Recognizing Student Achievement

Class ______________________

Date ______________________

Names	5•1 Explain how to use basic facts to compute fact extensions. [Operations and Computation Goal 3]	5•2 Determine whether a number sentence is true or false. [Patterns, Functions, and Algebra Goal 2]	5•3 Explain how estimation was used to solve addition problems. [Operations and Computation Goal 6]	5•4 Use the Distributive Property of Multiplication over Addition to find partial products. [Patterns, Functions, and Algebra Goal 4]	5•5 Use the partial-products algorithm to multiply a 1-digit number by a 2-digit number. [Operations and Computation Goal 4]	5•6 Estimate reasonable solutions to whole-number multiplication problems. [Operations and Computation Goal 6]	5•7 Demonstrate automaticity with basic multiplication facts. [Operations and Computation Goal 3]	5•8 Use extended multiplication facts in a problem-solving situation. [Operations and Computation Goal 3]	5•9 Describe numeric patterns. [Patterns, Functions, and Algebra Goal 1]	5•10 Demonstrate automaticity with multiplication facts through 10 * 10. [Operations and Computation Goal 3]	5•11 Compare numbers up to 1 billion. [Number and Numeration Goal 6]
1.											
2.											
3.											
4.											
5.											
6.											
7.											
8.											
9.											
10.											
11.											
12.											
13.											
14.											
15.											
16.											
17.											
18.											
19.											
20.											
21.											
22.											
23.											
24.											
25.											

Assess Progress: A = adequate progress  N = not adequate progress 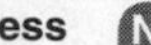 N/A = not assessed

Unit 5

Class Checklist:

Progress Check 5

Class ______________________

Date ______________________

Names	Oral/Slate				Written: Part A					Written: Part B			
	1. Read aloud numbers through the billions. [Number and Numeration Goal 1]	**2. Describe the strategy used to estimate the sum of addition problems.** [Operations and Computation Goal 6]	**3. Use exponential notation to name powers of 10.** [Number and Numeration Goal 4]	**4. Determine place value through the billions in numbers.** [Number and Numeration Goal 1]	**1, 2. Estimate sums.** [Operations and Computation Goal 6]	**3–6. Multiply multidigit whole numbers.** [Operations and Computation Goal 4; Patterns, Functions, and Algebra Goal 4]	**7–11. Add and subtract decimals.** [Operations and Computation Goal 2]	**12. Measure to the nearest $\frac{1}{4}$ in. and 0.5 cm.** [Measurement and Reference Frames Goal 1]	**13–15. Multiply using "What's My Rule?" tables.** [Operations and Computation Goal 3; Patterns, Functions, and Algebra Goal 1]	**16a, 17a. Estimate products.** [Operations and Computation Goal 6]	**16b, 17b. Multiply multidigit whole numbers.** [Operations and Computation Goal 4; Patterns, Functions, and Algebra Goal 4]	**18–20. Multiply using extended facts.** [Number and Numeration Goal 6; Operations and Computation Goal 3]	**21. Measure to the nearest $\frac{1}{4}$ in. and 0.5 cm when the 0-mark of the ruler is not positioned at the end of an object.** [Measurement and Reference Frames Goal 1]
1.													
2.													
3.													
4.													
5.													
6.													
7.													
8.													
9.													
10.													
11.													
12.													
13.													
14.													
15.													
16.													
17.													
18.													
19.													
20.													
21.													
22.													
23.													
24.													
25.													

Assess Progress: 

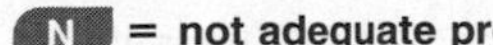

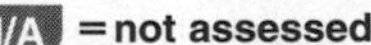

Formative Assessments

Unit 6

Individual Profile of Progress

Name _______________ Date _______________

Lesson	Recognizing Student Achievement	A.P.*	Comments
6◆1	**Write number models to represent number stories.** [Patterns, Functions, and Algebra Goal 2]		
6◆2	**Solve open sentences involving multiplication and division facts.** [Patterns, Functions, and Algebra Goal 2]		
6◆3	**Solve division problems and number stories with 1-digit divisors and 2-digit dividends.** [Operations and Computation Goal 4]		
6◆4	**Solve decimal addition and subtraction problems.** [Operations and Computation Goal 2]		
6◆5	**Create a bar graph.** [Data and Chance Goal 1]		
6◆6	**Draw angles less than or greater than 90°.** [Measurement and Reference Frames Goal 1]		
6◆7	**Identify places in decimals and the values of the digits in those places.** [Number and Numeration Goal 1]		
6◆8	**Compare coordinate grid systems.** [Measurement and Reference Frames Goal 4]		
6◆9	**Solve multidigit multiplication number stories.** [Operations and Computation Goal 4]		
6◆10	**Solve problems involving the division of multidigit whole numbers by 1-digit divisors.** [Operations and Computation Goal 4]		

***Assess Progress:** 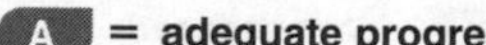 **A = adequate progress**  **N = not adequate progress**  **N/A = not assessed**

Unit 6 Individual Profile of Progress

Name Date

Problem(s)	Progress Check 6	A.P.*	Comments
Oral/Slate Assessment			
1	**Explain and show how parentheses can be used when writing a number model for a number story.** [Patterns, Functions, and Algebra Goal 3]		
2	**Solve a number story and explain how to show the remainder.** [Operations and Computation Goal 4]		
3	**Draw an example of an acute, an obtuse, a straight, and a reflex angle.** [Geometry Goal 1]		
4	**Name countries found at specified latitudes and longitudes.** [Measurement and Reference Frames Goal 4]		
Written Assessment Part A			
1, 2	**Solve division number stories; interpret remainders.** [Operations and Computation Goal 4]		
3, 4	**Divide multidigit numbers by 1-digit divisors; express remainders as fractions.** [Operations and Computation Goal 4]		
5	**Multiply multidigit numbers and compare them.** [Operations and Computation Goal 4]		
6, 7	**Classify and measure angles.** [Measurement and Reference Frames Goal 1; Geometry Goal 1]		
8	**Plot points on a coordinate grid.** [Measurement and Reference Frames Goal 4]		
9	**Insert parentheses.** [Patterns, Functions, and Algebra Goal 3]		
10	**Round numbers.** [Operations and Computation Goal 6]		
Written Assessment Part B			
11–13	**Draw and measure angles.** [Measurement and Reference Frames Goal 1]		
14, 15	**Divide multidigit numbers by 2-digit divisors; express remainders as fractions.** [Operations and Computation Goal 4]		

*Assess Progress:  A  = adequate progress  N = not adequate progress 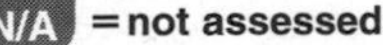 N/A = not assessed **Formative Assessments**

Unit 6

Class Checklist:

Recognizing Student Achievement

Class ____________________

Date ____________________

Names	6•1 Write number models to represent number stories. [Patterns, Functions, and Algebra Goal 2]	6•2 Solve open sentences involving multiplication and division facts. [Patterns, Functions, and Algebra Goal 2]	6•3 Solve division problems and number stories with 1-digit divisors and 2-digit dividends. [Operations and Computation Goal 4]	6•4 Solve decimal addition and subtraction problems. [Operations and Computation Goal 2]	6•5 Create a bar graph. [Data and Chance Goal 1]	6•6 Draw angles less than or greater than 90°. [Measurement and Reference Frames Goal 1]	6•7 Identify places in decimals and the values of the digits in those places. [Number and Numeration Goal 1]	6•8 Compare coordinate grid systems. [Measurement and Reference Frames Goal 4]	6•9 Solve multidigit multiplication number stories. [Operations and Computation Goal 4]	6•10 Solve problems involving the division of multidigit whole numbers by 1-digit divisors. [Operations and Computation Goal 4]
1.										
2.										
3.										
4.										
5.										
6.										
7.										
8.										
9.										
10.										
11.										
12.										
13.										
14.										
15.										
16.										
17.										
18.										
19.										
20.										
21.										
22.										
23.										
24.										
25.										

Assess Progress: **A** = adequate progress **N** = not adequate progress **N/A** = not assessed

Unit 6

Class Checklist:
Progress Check 6

Class ______________________

Date ______________________

Names	Oral/Slate: 1. Explain and show how parentheses can be used when writing a number model for a number story. [Patterns, Functions, and Algebra Goal 3]	Oral/Slate: 2. Solve a number story and explain how to show the remainder. [Operations and Computation Goal 4]	Oral/Slate: 3. Draw an example of an acute, an obtuse, a straight, and a reflex angle. [Geometry Goal 1]	Oral/Slate: 4. Name countries found at specified latitudes and longitudes. [Measurement and Reference Frames Goal 4]	Written, Part A: 1, 2. Solve division number stories; interpret remainders. [Operations and Computation Goal 4]	Written, Part A: 3, 4. Divide multidigit numbers by 1-digit divisors; express remainders as fractions. [Operations and Computation Goal 4]	Written, Part A: 5. Multiply multidigit numbers and compare them. [Operations and Computation Goal 4]	Written, Part A: 6, 7. Classify and measure angles. [Measurement and Reference Frames Goal 1; Geometry Goal 1]	Written, Part A: 8. Plot points on a coordinate grid. [Measurement and Reference Frames Goal 4]	Written, Part A: 9. Insert parentheses. [Patterns, Functions, and Algebra Goal 3]	Written, Part A: 10. Round numbers. [Operations and Computation Goal 6]	Written, Part B: 11–13. Draw and measure angles. [Measurement and Reference Frames Goal 1]	Written, Part B: 14, 15. Divide multidigit numbers by 2-digit divisors; express remainders as fractions. [Operations and Computation Goal 4]
1.													
2.													
3.													
4.													
5.													
6.													
7.													
8.													
9.													
10.													
11.													
12.													
13.													
14.													
15.													
16.													
17.													
18.													
19.													
20.													
21.													
22.													
23.													
24.													
25.													

Assess Progress: A = adequate progress 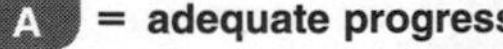  N = not adequate progress 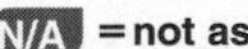 N/A = not assessed   Formative Assessments

Individual Profile of Progress

Name ______________________ Date ______________

Lesson	Recognizing Student Achievement	A.P.*	Comments
7◆1	**Explain that fractions are equal parts of a whole.** [Number and Numeration Goal 2]		
7◆2	**Solve "fraction-of" problems.** [Number and Numeration Goal 2]		
7◆3	**Use a basic probability term to describe the likelihood of an event.** [Data and Chance Goal 3]		
7◆4	**Explain the relationship between a whole and its fractional parts.** [Number and Numeration Goal 2]		
7◆5	**Use pattern blocks to solve fraction addition problems.** [Operations and Computation Goal 5]		
7◆6	**Estimate the measure of an angle.** [Measurement and Reference Frames Goal 1]		
7◆7	**Describe a method for determining fraction equivalency.** [Number and Numeration Goal 5]		
7◆8	**Rename tenths and hundredths as decimals.** [Number and Numeration Goal 5]		
7◆9	**Compare fractions and explain strategies.** [Number and Numeration Goal 6]		
7◆10	**Compare fractions.** [Number and Numeration Goal 6]		
7◆11	**Express the probability of an event as a fraction.** [Data and Chance Goal 4]		
7◆12	**Predict the outcome of an experiment and test the predictions using manipulatives.** [Data and Chance Goal 4]		

*Assess Progress: 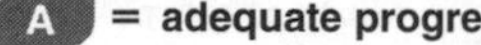 A = adequate progress  N = not adequate progress  N/A = not assessed

Individual Profile of Progress

Name Date

Problem(s)	Progress Check 7	A.P.*	Comments
Oral/Slate Assessment			
1	**Compare pairs of fractions and explain which is the greater.** [Number and Numeration Goal 6]		
2	**Use probability language to describe the likelihood of specified events.** [Data and Chance Goal 3]		
3	**Write equivalent decimals for fractions with denominators of 10 or 100 and write equivalent fractions for decimals.** [Number and Numeration Goal 5]		
4	**Solve "fraction-of" problems.** [Number and Numeration Goal 2]		
Written Assessment Part A			
1–3	**Write equivalent fractions.** [Number and Numeration Goal 5]		
4–6	**Compare fractions.** [Number and Numeration Goals 5 and 6]		
7, 8	**Order fractions.** [Number and Numeration Goal 6]		
9–11	**Name fractions of regions or collections; find the ONE.** [Number and Numeration Goal 2]		
12	**Calculate expected probability of an event.** [Data and Chance Goal 4]		
13	**Plot coordinates on a grid.** [Measurement and Reference Frames Goal 4]		
14, 15	**Multiply multidigit numbers.** [Operations and Computation Goal 4]		
16, 17	**Divide multidigit numbers by one-digit divisors.** [Operations and Computation Goal 4]		
Written Assessment Part B			
18	**Explain a strategy to compare fractions.** [Number and Numeration Goal 6]		
19	**Create a spinner, and predict the probability of an event.** [Data and Chance Goal 4]		
20–23	**Add and subtract fractions.** [Operations and Computation Goal 5]		
24	**Solve a fraction number story.** [Number and Numeration Goal 2; Operations and Computation Goal 5]		

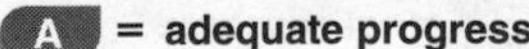
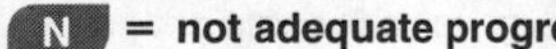
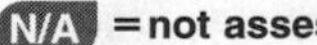

*Assess Progress: A = adequate progress N = not adequate progress N/A = not assessed **Formative Assessments**

Unit 7 Class Checklist:
Recognizing Student Achievement

Class ______________________

Date ______________________

Names	7•1 Explain that fractions are equal parts of a whole. [Number and Numeration Goal 2]	7•2 Solve "fraction-of" problems. [Number and Numeration Goal 2]	7•3 Use a basic probability term to describe the likelihood of an event. [Data and Chance Goal 3]	7•4 Explain the relationship between a whole and its fractional parts. [Number and Numeration Goal 2]	7•5 Use pattern blocks to solve fraction addition problems. [Operations and Computation Goal 5]	7•6 Estimate the measure of an angle. [Measurement and Reference Frames Goal 1]	7•7 Describe a method for determining fraction equivalency. [Number and Numeration Goal 5]	7•8 Rename tenths and hundredths as decimals. [Number and Numeration Goal 5]	7•9 Compare fractions and explain strategies. [Number and Numeration Goal 6]	7•10 Compare fractions. [Number and Numeration Goal 6]	7•11 Express the probability of an event as a fraction. [Data and Chance Goal 4]	7•12 Predict the outcome of an experiment and test the predictions using manipulatives. [Data and Chance Goal 4]
1.												
2.												
3.												
4.												
5.												
6.												
7.												
8.												
9.												
10.												
11.												
12.												
13.												
14.												
15.												
16.												
17.												
18.												
19.												
20.												
21.												
22.												
23.												
24.												
25.												

Assess Progress: A = adequate progress N = not adequate progress N/A = not assessed

Unit 7 Class Checklist:

Progress Check 7

Class ______________________

Date ______________________

Names	Oral/Slate				Written											
					Part A								Part B			
	1. Compare pairs of fractions and explain which is the greater. [Number and Numeration Goal 6]	**2. Use probability language to describe the likelihood of specified events.** [Data and Chance Goal 3]	**3. Write equivalent decimals for fractions with denominators of 10 or 100 and write equivalent fractions for decimals.** [Number and Numeration Goal 5]	**4. Solve "fraction-of" problems.** [Number and Numeration Goal 2]	**1–3. Write equivalent fractions.** [Number and Numeration Goal 5]	**4–6. Compare fractions.** [Number and Numeration Goals 5 and 6]	**7, 8. Order fractions.** [Number and Numeration Goal 6]	**9–11. Name fractions of regions or collections; find the ONE.** [Number and Numeration Goal 2]	**12. Calculate expected probability of an event.** [Data and Chance Goal 4]	**13. Plot coordinates on a grid.** [Measurement and Reference Frames Goal 4]	**14, 15. Multiply multidigit numbers.** [Operations and Computation Goal 4]	**16, 17. Divide multidigit numbers by one-digit divisors.** [Operations and Computation Goal 4]	**18. Explain a strategy to compare fractions.** [Number and Numeration Goal 6]	**19. Create a spinner, and predict the probability of an event.** [Data and Chance Goal 4]	**20–23. Add and subtract fractions.** [Operations and Computation Goal 5]	**24. Solve a fraction number story.** [Number and Numeration Goal 2; Operations and Computation Goal 5]
1.																
2.																
3.																
4.																
5.																
6.																
7.																
8.																
9.																
10.																
11.																
12.																
13.																
14.																
15.																
16.																
17.																
18.																
19.																
20.																
21.																
22.																
23.																
24.																
25.																

Assess Progress: 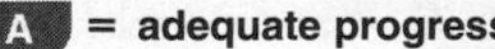 A = adequate progress 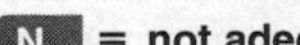 N = not adequate progress  N/A = not assessed **Formative Assessments**

Individual Profile of Progress

Name ______________________ Date ______________

Lesson	Recognizing Student Achievement	A.P.*	Comments
8◆1	**Rename fractions with denominators of 10 and 100 as decimals and percents.** [Number and Numeration Goal 5]		
8◆2	**Use data to create a line graph.** [Data and Chance Goal 1]		
8◆3	**Count squares and half squares to find the area of a polygon.** [Measurement and Reference Frames Goal 2]		
8◆4	**Count unit squares and fractions of unit squares to estimate the area of an irregular figure.** [Measurement and Reference Frames Goal 2]		
8◆5	**Find the perimeter of a figure.** [Measurement and Reference Frames Goal 2]		
8◆6	**Solve fraction addition and subtraction problems.** [Operations and Computation Goal 5]		
8◆7	**Describe a strategy for finding and comparing the area of a square and a polygon.** [Measurement and Reference Frames Goal 2]		
8◆8	**Calculate the probability of an event.** [Data and Chance Goal 4]		

***Assess Progress:** 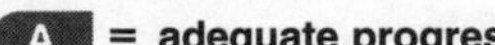 **A = adequate progress** 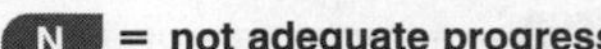 **N = not adequate progress** 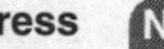 **N/A = not assessed**

Unit 8

Individual Profile of Progress

Name ______________________________ Date ______________

Problem(s)	Progress Check 8	A.P.*	Comments
Oral/Slate Assessment			
1	**Explain the differences between *area* and *perimeter*.** [Measurement and Reference Frames Goal 2]		
2	**Order groups of fractions and explain how to do so.** [Number and Numeration Goal 6]		
3	**Solve problems that require interpreting a map scale.** [Operations and Computation Goal 7]		
4	**Write equivalent decimals for fractions with denominators of 10 or 100 and write equivalent fractions for decimals.** [Number and Numeration Goal 5]		
Written Assessment Part A			
1, 2	**Find the perimeter of a polygon.** [Measurement and Reference Frames Goal 2]		
3, 4	**Find the area of a polygon drawn on a grid.** [Measurement and Reference Frames Goal 2]		
5	**Draw a rectangle with a given area and perimeter.** [Measurement and Reference Frames Goal 2]		
6, 7	**Solve number stories involving area.** [Measurement and Reference Frames Goal 2]		
8–11	**Add and subtract fractions.** [Operations and Computation Goal 5]		
12	**Predict the outcomes of a spinner experiment.** [Data and Chance Goal 4]		
13	**Express the probability of a block-drawing event as a fraction.** [Data and Chance Goal 4]		
Written Assessment Part B			
14–16	**Use formulas to find the area of a rectangle, parallelogram, and triangle.** [Measurement and Reference Frames Goals 1 and 2]		
17, 18	**Use a scale to draw rectangles with given dimensions.** [Operations and Computation Goal 7; Measurement and Reference Frames Goal 1]		

*Assess Progress:  A = adequate progress 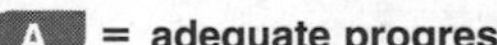 N = not adequate progress 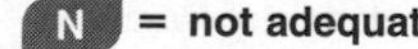 N/A = not assessed  Formative Assessments

Unit 8 Class Checklist:

Recognizing Student Achievement

Class ______________________

Date ______________________

Names	8•1 Rename fractions with denominators of 10 and 100 as decimals and percents. [Number and Numeration Goal 5]	8•2 Use data to create a line graph. [Data and Chance Goal 1]	8•3 Count squares and half squares to find the area of a polygon. [Measurement and Reference Frames Goal 2]	8•4 Count unit squares and fractions of unit squares to estimate the area of an irregular figure. [Measurement and Reference Frames Goal 2]	8•5 Find the perimeter of a figure. [Measurement and Reference Frames Goal 2]	8•6 Solve fraction addition and subtraction problems. [Operations and Computation Goal 5]	8•7 Describe a strategy for finding and comparing the area of a square and a polygon. [Measurement and Reference Frames Goal 2]	8•8 Calculate the probability of an event. [Data and Chance Goal 4]
1.								
2.								
3.								
4.								
5.								
6.								
7.								
8.								
9.								
10.								
11.								
12.								
13.								
14.								
15.								
16.								
17.								
18.								
19.								
20.								
21.								
22.								
23.								
24.								
25.								

Assess Progress: 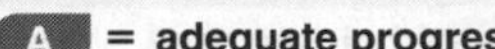 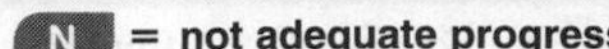 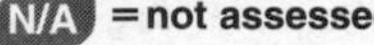

Unit 8

Class Checklist:
Progress Check 8

Class ____________________

Date ____________________

Names	Oral/Slate				Written: Part A							Written: Part B	
	1. Explain the differences between *area* and *perimeter*. [Measurement and Reference Frames Goal 2]	**2. Order groups of fractions and explain how to do so.** [Number and Numeration Goal 6]	**3. Solve problems that require interpreting a map scale.** [Operations and Computation Goal 7]	**4. Write equivalent decimals for fractions with denominators of 10 or 100 and write equivalent fractions for decimals.** [Number and Numeration Goal 5]	**1, 2. Find the perimeter of a polygon.** [Measurement and Reference Frames Goal 2]	**3, 4. Find the area of a polygon drawn on a grid.** [Measurement and Reference Frames Goal 2]	**5. Draw a rectangle with a given area and perimeter.** [Measurement and Reference Frames Goal 2]	**6, 7. Solve number stories involving area.** [Measurement and Reference Frames Goal 2]	**8–11. Add and subtract fractions.** [Operations and Computation Goal 5]	**12. Predict the outcomes of a spinner experiment.** [Data and Chance Goal 4]	**13. Express the probability of a block-drawing event as a fraction.** [Data and Chance Goal 4]	**14–16. Use formulas to find the area of a rectangle, parallelogram, and triangle.** [Measurement and Reference Frames Goals 1 and 2]	**17, 18. Use a scale to draw rectangles with given dimensions.** [Operations and Computation Goal 7; Measurement and Reference Frames Goal 1]
1.													
2.													
3.													
4.													
5.													
6.													
7.													
8.													
9.													
10.													
11.													
12.													
13.													
14.													
15.													
16.													
17.													
18.													
19.													
20.													
21.													
22.													
23.													
24.													
25.													

Assess Progress: 

= adequate progress 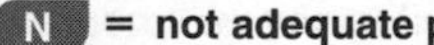

= not adequate progress 

= not assessed **Formative Assessments**

Unit 9

Individual Profile of Progress

Name ______________________ Date ______________

Lesson	Recognizing Student Achievement	A.P.*	Comments
9◆1	**Find equivalent fractions.** [Number and Numeration Goal 5]		
9◆2	**Rename fourths, fifths, tenths, and hundredths as decimals and percents.** [Number and Numeration Goal 5]		
9◆3	**Rename fourths, fifths, tenths, and hundredths as decimals and percents.** [Number and Numeration Goal 5]		
9◆4	**Solve "fraction-of" problems.** [Number and Numeration Goal 2]		
9◆5	**Divide a multidigit whole number by a 1-digit divisor.** [Operations and Computation Goal 4]		
9◆6	**Interpret a map scale.** [Operations and Computation Goal 7]		
9◆7	**Draw conclusions from a data representation.** [Data and Chance Goal 2]		
9◆8	**Estimate the product of a whole number and a decimal.** [Operations and Computation Goal 6]		
9◆9	**Estimate the quotient of a decimal divided by a whole number.** [Operations and Computation Goal 6]		

*Assess Progress: 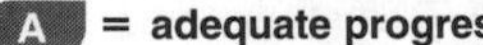 A = adequate progress 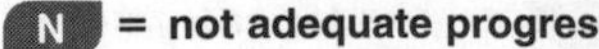 N = not adequate progress  N/A = not assessed

Unit 9

Individual Profile of Progress

Name ______________________ Date ______________

Problem(s)	Progress Check 9	A.P.*	Comments
Oral/Slate Assessment			
1	**Solve division number sentences and explain strategy used to place the decimal point in the quotient.** [Operations and Computation Goal 6]		
2	**Solve multiplication number sentences and explain strategy used to place the decimal point in the product.** [Operations and Computation Goal 6]		
3	**Rename fractions as equivalent decimals and percents.** [Number and Numeration Goal 5]		
4	**Solve "percent-of" and "fraction-of" problems.** [Number and Numeration Goal 2]		
Written Assessment Part A			
1, 2	**Write a ratio as a fraction and a percent. Interpret a percent.** [Number and Numeration Goal 2]		
3	**Fill in a table of equivalent fractions, decimals, and percents.** [Number and Numeration Goal 5]		
4	**Use a calculator to rename fractions as decimals.** [Number and Numeration Goal 5]		
5	**Use a calculator to rename fractions as percents.** [Number and Numeration Goal 5]		
6	**Shade a percent of a region. Write the percent as a fraction and as a decimal.** [Number and Numeration Goal 2]		
7–9	**Find the area and perimeter of a rectangle, parallelogram, and a triangle.** [Measurement and Reference Frames Goal 2]		
10	**Insert parentheses to make number sentences true.** [Patterns, Functions, and Algebra Goal 3]		
Written Assessment Part B			
11, 12	**Use the percent of discount to calculate the discount and sale price of an item. Compare a fraction of a discount and a percent of a discount.** [Number and Numeration Goal 2]		
13, 14	**Use an estimation strategy to multiply decimals by whole numbers.** [Operations and Computation Goal 6]		
15, 16	**Use an estimation strategy to divide decimals by whole numbers.** [Operations and Computation Goal 6]		

*Assess Progress:  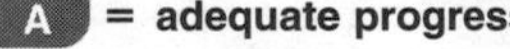 A = adequate progress 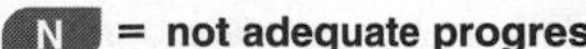 N = not adequate progress  N/A = not assessed

Class Checklist:

Recognizing Student Achievement

Class ____________________

Date ____________________

Names	9•1 Find equivalent fractions. [Number and Numeration Goal 5]	9•2 Rename fourths, fifths, tenths, and hundredths as decimals and percents. [Number and Numeration Goal 5]	9•3 Rename fourths, fifths, tenths, and hundredths as decimals and percents. [Number and Numeration Goal 5]	9•4 Solve "fraction-of" problems. [Number and Numeration Goal 2]	9•5 Divide a multidigit whole number by a 1-digit divisor. [Operations and Computation Goal 4]	9•6 Interpret a map scale. [Operations and Computation Goal 1]	9•7 Draw conclusions from a data representation. [Data and Chance Goal 2]	9•8 Estimate the product of a whole number and a decimal. [Operations and Computation Goal 6]	9•9 Estimate the quotient of a decimal divided by a whole number. [Operations and Computation Goal 6]
1.									
2.									
3.									
4.									
5.									
6.									
7.									
8.									
9.									
10.									
11.									
12.									
13.									
14.									
15.									
16.									
17.									
18.									
19.									
20.									
21.									
22.									
23.									
24.									
25.									

Assess Progress: **A** = adequate progress **N** = not adequate progress **N/A** = not assessed

Unit 9

Class Checklist:

Progress Check 9

Class ______________________

Date ______________________

	Oral/Slate				Written: Part A							Written: Part B		
Names	**1. Solve division number sentences and explain strategy used to place the decimal point in the quotient.** [Operations and Computation Goal 6]	**2. Solve multiplication number sentences and explain strategy used to place the decimal point in the product.** [Operations and Computation Goal 6]	**3. Rename fractions as equivalent decimals and percents.** [Number and Numeration Goal 5]	**4. Solve "percent-of" and "fraction-of" problems.** [Number and Numeration Goal 2]	**1, 2. Write a ratio as a fraction and a percent. Interpret a percent.** [Number and Numeration Goal 2]	**3. Fill in a table of equivalent fractions, decimals, and percents.** [Number and Numeration Goal 5]	**4. Use a calculator to rename fractions as decimals.** [Number and Numeration Goal 5]	**5. Use a calculator to rename fractions as percents.** [Number and Numeration Goal 5]	**6. Shade a percent of a region. Write the percent as a fraction and as a decimal.** [Number and Numeration Goal 2]	**7–9. Find the area and perimeter of a rectangle, parallelogram, and a triangle.** [Measurement and Reference Frames Goal 2]	**10. Insert parentheses to make number sentences true.** [Patterns, Functions, and Algebra Goal 3]	**11, 12. Use the percent of discount to calculate the discount and sale price of an item. Compare a fraction of a discount and a percent of a discount.** [Number and Numeration Goal 2]	**13, 14. Use an estimation strategy to multiply decimals by whole numbers.** [Operations and Computation Goal 6]	**15, 16. Use an estimation strategy to divide decimals by whole numbers.** [Operations and Computation Goal 6]
1.														
2.														
3.														
4.														
5.														
6.														
7.														
8.														
9.														
10.														
11.														
12.														
13.														
14.														
15.														
16.														
17.														
18.														
19.														
20.														
21.														
22.														
23.														
24.														
25.														

Assess Progress: 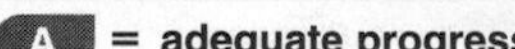 A = adequate progress  N 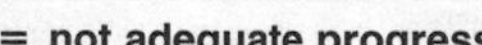 = not adequate progress  N/A = not assessed **Formative Assessments**

Individual Profile of Progress

Name Date

Lesson	Recognizing Student Achievement	A.P.*	Comments
10◆1	**Plot points in the first quadrant of a coordinate grid.** [Measurement and Reference Frames Goal 4]		
10◆2	**Compare fractions.** [Number and Numeration Goal 6]		
10◆3	**Sketch and describe a reflection.** [Geometry Goal 3]		
10◆4	**Describe a pattern and use it to solve problems.** [Patterns, Functions, and Algebra Goal 1]		
10◆5	**Identify and sketch an example of a reflection and identify examples of translations and rotations.** [Geometry Goal 3]		
10◆6	**Express the probability of an event as a fraction.** [Data and Chance Goal 4]		

*Assess Progress: 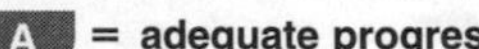 A = adequate progress 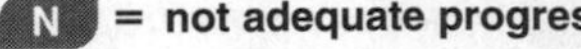 N = not adequate progress  N/A = not assessed

Individual Profile of Progress

Name ____________________ Date ____________

Problem(s)	Progress Check 10	A.P.*	Comments
Oral/Slate Assessment			
1	**Solve addition problems involving positive and negative numbers and explain solution strategies.** [Operations and Computation Goal 2]		
2	**Solve addition and subtraction problems involving fractions and explain solution strategies.** [Operations and Computation Goal 5]		
3	**Write equivalent decimals and percents for fractions.** [Number and Numeration Goal 5]		
4	**Draw and identify different types of angles.** [Measurement and Reference Frames Goal 1]		
Written Assessment Part A			
1–4	**Draw shapes with no, one, two, or multiple lines of symmetry.** [Geometry Goal 3]		
5	**Identify a translation.** [Geometry Goal 3]		
6	**Identify a rotation.** [Geometry Goal 3]		
7	**Use a transparent mirror to draw the reflection of the preimage.** [Geometry Goal 3]		
8	**Use a transparent mirror to draw the other half of the figure across the line of symmetry.** [Geometry Goal 3]		
9	**Give fraction, decimal, and percent equivalents.** [Number and Numeration Goal 5]		
10	**Add and subtract fractions.** [Operations and Computation Goal 5]		
Written Assessment Part B			
11	**Add positive and negative integers.** [Operations and Computation Goal 2]		
12	**Solve a number story involving addition of positive and negative integers.** [Operations and Computation Goal 2]		
13	**Identify and measure an angle.** [Measurement and Reference Frames Goal 1]		
14	**Estimate the products and quotients of problems involving decimals.** [Operations and Computation Goal 6]		

*Assess Progress: 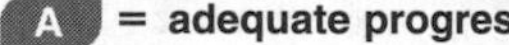 A = adequate progress 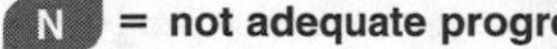 N = not adequate progress  N/A = not assessed **Formative Assessments**

Class Checklist:

Recognizing Student Achievement

Class ______________________

Date ______________________

Names	10•1 Plot points in the first quadrant of a coordinate grid. [Measurement and Reference Frames Goal 4]	10•2 Compare fractions. [Number and Numeration Goal 6]	10•3 Sketch and describe a reflection. [Geometry Goal 3]	10•4 Describe a pattern and use it to solve problems. [Patterns, Functions, and Algebra Goal 1]	10•5 Identify and sketch an example of a reflection and identify examples of translations and rotations. [Geometry Goal 3]	10•6 Express the probability of an event as a fraction. [Data and Chance Goal 4]
1.						
2.						
3.						
4.						
5.						
6.						
7.						
8.						
9.						
10.						
11.						
12.						
13.						
14.						
15.						
16.						
17.						
18.						
19.						
20.						
21.						
22.						
23.						
24.						
25.						

Assess Progress: 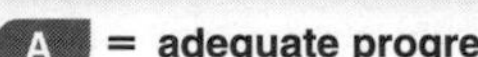 A = adequate progress 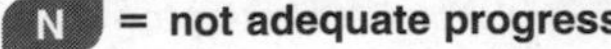 N = not adequate progress 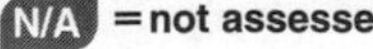 N/A = not assessed

Class Checklist:

Progress Check 10

Class ______________________

Date ______________________

	Oral/Slate				Written										
					Part A							Part B			
Names	1. Solve addition problems involving positive and negative numbers and explain solution strategies. [Operations and Computation Goal 2]	2. Solve addition and subtraction problems involving fractions and explain solution strategies. [Operations and Computation Goal 5]	3. Write equivalent decimals and percents for fractions. [Number and Numeration Goal 5]	4. Draw and identify different types of angles. [Measurement and Reference Frames Goal 1]	1–4. Draw shapes with no, one, two, or multiple lines of symmetry. [Geometry Goal 3]	5. Identify a translation. [Geometry Goal 3]	6. Identify a rotation. [Geometry Goal 3]	7. Use a transparent mirror to draw the reflection of the preimage. [Geometry Goal 3]	8. Use a transparent mirror to draw the other half of the figure across the line of symmetry. [Geometry Goal 3]	9. Give fraction, decimal, and percent equivalents. [Number and Numeration Goal 5]	10. Add and subtract fractions. [Operations and Computation Goal 5]	11. Add positive and negative integers. [Operations and Computation Goal 2]	12. Solve a number story involving addition of positive and negative integers. [Operations and Computation Goal 2]	13. Identify and measure an angle. [Measurement and Reference Frames Goal 1]	14. Estimate the products and quotients of problems involving decimals. [Operations and Computation Goal 6]
1.															
2.															
3.															
4.															
5.															
6.															
7.															
8.															
9.															
10.															
11.															
12.															
13.															
14.															
15.															
16.															
17.															
18.															
19.															
20.															
21.															
22.															
23.															
24.															
25.															

Assess Progress: 

= adequate progress 

= not adequate progress 

= not assessed **Formative Assessments**

Individual Profile of Progress

Name ______________________ Date ______________

Lesson	Recognizing Student Achievement	A.P.*	Comments
11◆1	**Describe a translation.** [Geometry Goal 3]		
11◆2	**Describe a rectangular prism.** [Geometry Goal 2]		
11◆3	**Find multiples of whole numbers less than 10.** [Number and Numeration Goal 3]		
11◆4	**Solve multiplication and division facts.** [Operations and Computation Goal 3]		
11◆5	**Find the volume of stacks of centimeter cubes.** [Measurement and Reference Frames Goal 2]		
11◆6	**Identify an example of a rotation.** [Geometry Goal 3]		
11◆7	**Describe the relationships among U.S. customary units of length and among metric units of length.** [Measurement and Reference Frames Goal 3]		

*Assess Progress: 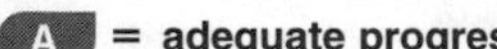 A = adequate progress 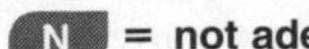 N = not adequate progress  N/A = not assessed

Individual Profile of Progress

Name Date

Problem(s)	Progress Check 11	A.P.*	Comments
Oral/Slate Assessment			
1	**Round numbers to the nearest tenth and explain how.** [Operations and Computation Goal 6]		
2	**Using centimeter cubes, build rectangular prisms with given volumes or dimensions.** [Measurement and Reference Frames Goal 2; Geometry Goal 2]		
3	**Solve problems involving equivalent measures.** [Measurement and Reference Frames Goal 3]		
4	**Solve problems involving equivalent capacities.** [Measurement and Reference Frames Goal 3]		
Written Assessment Part A			
1	**Name the geometric solid.** [Geometry Goal 2]		
2	**Identify pentagonal pyramid faces.** [Geometry Goal 2]		
3	**Mark the vertices of a triangular prism.** [Geometry Goal 2]		
4	**Identify rectangular pyramid edges.** [Geometry Goal 2]		
5	**Name the base of a pyramid.** [Geometry Goal 2]		
6	**Describe a triangular prism.** [Geometry Goal 2]		
7–10	**Find the volume of a stack of centimeter cubes.** [Measurement and Reference Frames Goal 2]		
11	**Make reasonable weight estimates.** [Measurement and Reference Frames Goal 1]		
12	**Use probability terms to describe events.** [Data and Chance Goal 3]		
Written Assessment Part B			
13, 14	**Use a volume formula.** [Measurement and Reference Frames Goal 2]		
15–18	**Add signed numbers.** [Operations and Computation Goal 2]		
19–22	**Subtract signed numbers.** [Operations and Computation Goal 2]		
23–26	**Multiply and divide using decimals.** [Operations and Computation Goal 4]		

*Assess Progress:  A = adequate progress 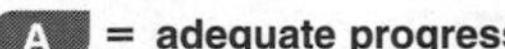 N = not adequate progress  N/A = not assessed 

Class Checklist:
Recognizing Student Achievement

Class ______

Date ______

Names	11•1 Describe a translation. [Geometry Goal 3]	11•2 Describe a rectangular prism. [Geometry Goal 2]	11•3 Find multiples of whole numbers less than 10. [Number and Numeration Goal 3]	11•4 Solve multiplication and division facts. [Operations and Computation Goal 3]	11•5 Find the volume of stacks of centimeter cubes. [Measurement and Reference Frames Goal 2]	11•6 Identify an example of a rotation. [Geometry Goal 3]	11•7 Describe the relationships among U.S. customary units of length and among metric units of length. [Measurement and Reference Frames Goal 3]
1.							
2.							
3.							
4.							
5.							
6.							
7.							
8.							
9.							
10.							
11.							
12.							
13.							
14.							
15.							
16.							
17.							
18.							
19.							
20.							
21.							
22.							
23.							
24.							
25.							

Assess Progress: 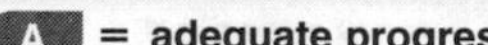 **A = adequate progress** 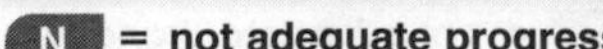 **N = not adequate progress** **N/A = not assessed**

Unit 11 Class Checklist:
Progress Check 11

Class ____________________

Date ____________________

	Oral/Slate				Written														
					Part A										Part B			
Names	1. Round numbers to the nearest tenth and explain how. [Operations and Computation Goal 6]	2. Using centimeter cubes, build rectangular prisms with given volumes or dimensions. [Measurement and Reference Frames Goal 2; Geometry Goal 2]	3. Solve problems involving equivalent measures. [Measurement and Reference Frames Goal 3]	4. Solve problems involving equivalent capacities. [Measurement and Reference Frames Goal 3]	1. Name the geometric solid. [Geometry Goal 2]	2. Identify pentagonal pyramid faces. [Geometry Goal 2]	3. Mark the vertices of a triangular prism. [Geometry Goal 2]	4. Identify rectangular pyramid edges. [Geometry Goal 2]	5. Name the base of a pyramid. [Geometry Goal 2]	6. Describe a triangular prism. [Geometry Goal 2]	7–10. Find the volume of a stack of centimeter cubes. [Measurement and Reference Frames Goal 2]	11. Make reasonable weight estimates. [Measurement and Reference Frames Goal 1]	12. Use probability terms to describe events. [Data and Chance Goal 3]	13, 14. Use a volume formula. [Measurement and Reference Frames Goal 2]	15–18. Add signed numbers. [Operations and Computation Goal 2]	19–22. Subtract signed numbers. [Operations and Computation Goal 2]	23–26. Multiply and divide using decimals. [Operations and Computation Goal 4]
1.																		
2.																		
3.																		
4.																		
5.																		
6.																		
7.																		
8.																		
9.																		
10.																		
11.																		
12.																		
13.																		
14.																		
15.																		
16.																		
17.																		
18.																		
19.																		
20.																		
21.																		
22.																		
23.																		
24.																		
25.																		

Assess Progress: 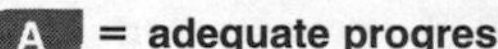 A = adequate progress  N = not adequate progress 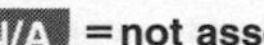 N/A = not assessed **Formative Assessments**

Individual Profile of Progress

Name ______________________ Date ______________

Lesson	Recognizing Student Achievement	A.P.*	Comments
12♦1	**Compare integers between 100 and –100.** [Number and Numeration Goal 6]		
12♦2	**Describe a rule for a pattern and use the rule to solve problems.** [Patterns, Functions, and Algebra Goal 1]		
12♦3	**Use given data to create a line graph.** [Data and Chance Goal 1]		
12♦4	**Insert grouping symbols to make number sentences true.** [Patterns, Functions, and Algebra Goal 3]		
12♦5	**Use scaling to model multiplication and division.** [Operations and Computation Goal 7]		
12♦6	**Demonstrate automaticity with multiplication facts through 10 ∗ 10.** [Operations and Computation Goal 3]		

*Assess Progress: 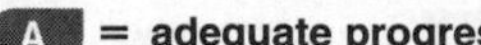 A = adequate progress 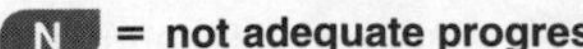 N = not adequate progress 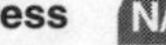 N/A = not assessed

Unit 12

Individual Profile of Progress

Name ____________________ Date ____________

Problem(s)	Progress Check 12	A.P.*	Comments
Oral/Slate Assessment			
1	**Solve addition and subtraction problems involving positive and negative integers and explain solution strategies.** [Operations and Computation Goal 2]		
2	**Determine equivalence of quantities measured in different U.S. customary units of capacity.** [Measurement and Reference Frames Goal 3]		
3	**Solve rate problems.** [Operations and Computation Goal 7]		
4	**Solve problems involving unit prices, rounding answers to the nearest tenth of a cent.** [Operations and Computation Goal 7]		
Written Assessment Part A			
1–3	**Solve rate problems.** [Operations and Computation Goal 7]		
4, 5	**Find factors and factor pairs.** [Number and Numeration Goal 3]		
6	**Compare integers.** [Number and Numeration Goal 6]		
7	**Order integers.** [Number and Numeration Goal 6]		
8	**Find equivalent capacities.** [Measurement and Reference Frames Goal 3]		
9	**Calculate volume.** [Measurement and Reference Frames Goal 2]		
10	**Solve open sentences.** [Patterns, Functions, and Algebra Goal 2]		
Written Assessment Part B			
11	**Compare and order fractions.** [Number and Numeration Goal 6]		
12	**Determine the reasonableness of a statistic.** [Data and Chance Goal 2]		
13	**Determine which box of cereal is the better buy.** [Operations and Computation Goal 7]		
14	**Make informed consumer decisions.** [Operations and Computation Goal 7]		

*Assess Progress:   A = adequate progress  N = not adequate progress  N/A = not assessed

Class Checklist:
Recognizing Student Achievement

Class ____________________

Date ____________________

Names	12•1 Compare integers between 100 and –100. [Number and Numeration Goal 6]	12•2 Describe a rule for a pattern and use the rule to solve problems. [Patterns, Functions, and Algebra Goal 1]	12•3 Use given data to create a line graph. [Data and Chance Goal 1]	12•4 Insert grouping symbols to make number sentences true. [Patterns, Functions, and Algebra Goal 3]	12•5 Use scaling to model multiplication and division. [Operations and Computation Goal 7]	12•6 Demonstrate automaticity with multiplication facts through 10 * 10. [Operations and Computation Goal 3]
1.						
2.						
3.						
4.						
5.						
6.						
7.						
8.						
9.						
10.						
11.						
12.						
13.						
14.						
15.						
16.						
17.						
18.						
19.						
20.						
21.						
22.						
23.						
24.						
25.						

Assess Progress: A = adequate progress N = not adequate progress N/A = not assessed

Class Checklist:
Progress Check 12

Class ______________________

Date ______________________

Names	Oral/Slate				Written: Part A							Written: Part B			
	1. Solve addition and subtraction problems involving positive and negative integers and explain solution strategies. [Operations and Computation Goal 2]	**2. Determine equivalence of quantities measured in different U.S. customary units of capacity.** [Measurement and Reference Frames Goal 3]	**3. Solve rate problems.** [Operations and Computation Goal 7]	**4. Solve problems involving unit prices, rounding answers to the nearest tenth of a cent.** [Operations and Computation Goal 7]	**1–3. Solve rate problems.** [Operations and Computation Goal 7]	**4, 5. Find factors and factor pairs.** [Number and Numeration Goal 3]	**6. Compare integers.** [Number and Numeration Goal 6]	**7. Order integers.** [Number and Numeration Goal 6]	**8. Find equivalent capacities.** [Measurement and Reference Frames Goal 3]	**9. Calculate volume.** [Measurement and Reference Frames Goal 2]	**10. Solve open sentences.** [Patterns, Functions, and Algebra Goal 2]	**11. Compare and order fractions.** [Number and Numeration Goal 6]	**12. Determine the reasonableness of a statistic.** [Data and Chance Goal 2]	**13. Determine which box of cereal is the better buy.** [Operations and Computation Goal 7]	**14. Make informed consumer decisions.** [Operations and Computation Goal 7]
1.															
2.															
3.															
4.															
5.															
6.															
7.															
8.															
9.															
10.															
11.															
12.															
13.															
14.															
15.															
16.															
17.															
18.															
19.															
20.															
21.															
22.															
23.															
24.															
25.															

Assess Progress: 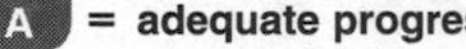 **A = adequate progress**  **N = not adequate progress**  **N/A = not assessed** **Formative Assessments**

Quarterly Checklist: Quarter 1

Names		Number and Numeration				Operations and Computation													
	Goal	4	1	1	4	1	1	1	1	2	2	6	3	2	7	2	3		
	Lesson	2•2	2•3	2•4	3•2	1•1	1•8	2•1	2•5	2•7	2•9	3•3	3•4	3•6	3•7	3•8	3•10		
	Date																		
1.																			
2.																			
3.																			
4.																			
5.																			
6.																			
7.																			
8.																			
9.																			
10.																			
11.																			
12.																			
13.																			
14.																			
15.																			
16.																			
17.																			
18.																			
19.																			
20.																			
21.																			
22.																			

Quarterly Checklist: Quarter 1

Names	Data and Chance				Measurement and Reference Frames				Geometry						Patterns, Functions, and Algebra			
Goal	2	2							1	2	1	2	1	2	1	2	2	2
Lesson	2•6	2•8							1•2	1•3	1•4	1•5	1•6	1•7	3•1	3•5	3•9	3•11
Date																		
1.																		
2.																		
3.																		
4.																		
5.																		
6.																		
7.																		
8.																		
9.																		
10.																		
11.																		
12.																		
13.																		
14.																		
15.																		
16.																		
17.																		
18.																		
19.																		
20.																		
21.																		
22.																		

Quarterly Checklist: Quarter 2

		Number and Numeration									Operations and Computation												
	Goal	1	1	6	1	1	6	6	1		6	3	3	6	4	6	3	3	3	4	2	4	4
	Lesson	4•1	4•2	4•3	4•5	4•7	4•9	5•11	6•7		4•4	4•10	5•1	5•3	5•5	5•6	5•7	5•8	5•10	6•3	6•4	6•9	6•10
Names	Date																						
1.																							
2.																							
3.																							
4.																							
5.																							
6.																							
7.																							
8.																							
9.																							
10.																							
11.																							
12.																							
13.																							
14.																							
15.																							
16.																							
17.																							
18.																							
19.																							
20.																							
21.																							
22.																							

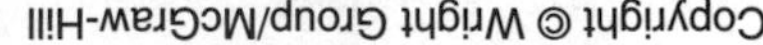

Quarterly Checklist: Quarter 2

Names	Data and Chance				Measurement and Reference Frames				Geometry				Patterns, Functions, and Algebra									
Goal	2	1			1	1	4						2	4	1	2	2					
Lesson	4•6	6•5			4•8	6•6	6•8						5•2	5•4	5•9	6•1	6•2					
Date																						
1.																						
2.																						
3.																						
4.																						
5.																						
6.																						
7.																						
8.																						
9.																						
10.																						
11.																						
12.																						
13.																						
14.																						
15.																						
16.																						
17.																						
18.																						
19.																						
20.																						
21.																						
22.																						

Quarterly Checklist: Quarter 3

Names		Number and Numeration												Operations and Computation						
	Goal	2	2	2	5	5	6	6	5	5	5	5	2	5	5	4	7	6	6	
	Lesson	7•1	7•2	7•4	7•7	7•8	7•9	7•10	8•1	9•1	9•2	9•3	9•4	7•5	8•6	9•5	9•6	9•8	9•9	
	Date																			
1.																				
2.																				
3.																				
4.																				
5.																				
6.																				
7.																				
8.																				
9.																				
10.																				
11.																				
12.																				
13.																				
14.																				
15.																				
16.																				
17.																				
18.																				
19.																				
20.																				
21.																				
22.																				

Quarterly Checklist: Quarter 3

Names		Data and Chance						Measurement and Reference Frames						Geometry				Patterns, Functions, and Algebra			
	Goal	3	4	4	1	4	2	1	2	2	2	2									
	Lesson	7•3	7•11	7•12	8•2	8•8	9•7	7•6	8•3	8•4	8•5	8•7									
	Date																				
1.																					
2.																					
3.																					
4.																					
5.																					
6.																					
7.																					
8.																					
9.																					
10.																					
11.																					
12.																					
13.																					
14.																					
15.																					
16.																					
17.																					
18.																					
19.																					
20.																					
21.																					
22.																					

Quarterly Checklist: Quarter 4

Names		Number and Numeration				Operations and Computation				Data and Chance				
	Goal	6	3	6		3	7	3		4	1			
	Lesson	10•2	11•3	12•1		11•4	12•5	12•6		10•6	12•3			
	Date													
1.														
2.														
3.														
4.														
5.														
6.														
7.														
8.														
9.														
10.														
11.														
12.														
13.														
14.														
15.														
16.														
17.														
18.														
19.														
20.														
21.														
22.														

Quarterly Checklist: Quarter 4

Names		Measurement and Reference Frames				Geometry					Patterns, Functions, and Algebra			
	Goal	4	2	3		3	3	3	2	3	1	1	3	
	Lesson	10•1	11•5	11•7		10•3	10•5	11•1	11•2	11•6	10•4	12•2	12•4	
	Date													
1.														
2.														
3.														
4.														
5.														
6.														
7.														
8.														
9.														
10.														
11.														
12.														
13.														
14.														
15.														
16.														
17.														
18.														
19.														
20.														
21.														
22.														

Unit

Individual Profile of Progress

Name Date

Lesson	Recognizing Student Achievement	A.P.*	Comments

*Assess Progress: 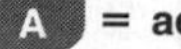 A = adequate progress  N = not adequate progress 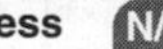 N/A = not assessed

Unit

Class Checklist:

Recognizing Student Achievement

Class ____________________

Date ____________________

Names								
1.								
2.								
3.								
4.								
5.								
6.								
7.								
8.								
9.								
10.								
11.								
12.								
13.								
14.								
15.								
16.								
17.								
18.								
19.								
20.								
21.								
22.								
23.								
24.								
25.								

Assess Progress: 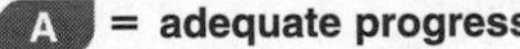 **A = adequate progress** 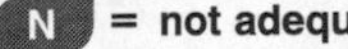 **N = not adequate progress**  **N/A = not assessed**

Name Date

Evaluating My Math Class

Interest Inventory

Dislike a Lot 1	Dislike 2	Neither Like nor Dislike 3	Like 4	Like a Lot 5

Use the scale above to describe how you feel about:

1. your math class. ______
2. working with a partner or in a group. ______
3. working by yourself. ______
4. solving problems. ______
5. making up problems for others to solve. ______
6. finding new ways to solve problems. ______
7. challenges in math class. ______
8. playing mathematical games. ______
9. working on Study Links. ______
10. working on projects that take more than a day to complete. ______
11. Which math lesson has been your favorite so far? Why?

Name Date

My Math Class

Interest Inventory

1. In math class, I am good at ______________________________

____

____

____

2. One thing I like about math is ______________________________

____

____

____

3. One thing I find difficult in mathematics class is ______________________________

____

____

____

4. The most interesting thing I have learned in math so far this year is ______________________________

____

____

____

5. Outside school, I used mathematics when I ______________________________

____

____

____

6. I would like to know more about ______________________________

____

____

____

Name ______________________ Date ______________________

Weekly Math Log

1. What did you study in math this week?

2. Many ideas in math are related to other ideas within math. Think about how the topic(s) you studied in class this week relate to other topics you learned before.

   Your reflection can include what you learned in previous years.

Name Date

Math Log

Name _______________________________ Date _______________

Number-Story Math Log

1. Write an easy number story that uses mathematical ideas that you have studied recently. Solve the problem.

Number Story _______________________________

____

____

____

____

____

Solution _______________________________

____

____

____

____

2. Write a difficult number story that uses mathematical ideas that you have studied recently. If you can, solve the number story. If you are not able to solve it, explain what you need to know to solve it.

Number Story _______________________________

____

____

____

____

____

Solution _______________________________

____

____

____

____

Name Date

Sample Math Work

Attach a sample of your work to this form.

1. This work is an example of:

2. This work shows that I can:

OPTIONAL

3. This work shows that I still need to improve:

Name Date

Discussion of My Math Work

Attach a sample of your work to this page. Tell what you think is important about your sample.

Name Date Time

Exit Slip

Name Date Time

Exit Slip

Name Date

Parent Reflections

Use some of the following questions (or your own) and tell us how you see your child progressing in mathematics.

Do you see evidence of your child using mathematics at home?

What do you think are your child's strengths and challenges in mathematics?

Does your child demonstrate responsibility for completing Study Links?

What thoughts do you have about your child's progress in mathematics?

Copyright © Wright Group/McGraw-Hill

Glossary

Assessment Management System An online management system designed to track student, class, school, and district progress toward Grade-Level Goals.

Class Checklists Recording tools that can be used to keep track of a class's progress on specific Grade-Level Goals.

Content for Assessment Material that is important for students to learn and is the focus of assessment. *Everyday Mathematics* highlights this content through Grade-Level Goals.

Contexts for Assessment Ongoing, periodic, and external assessments based on products or observations.

Enrichment activities Optional activities that apply or deepen students' understanding.

Evidence from Assessment Information about student knowledge, skills, and dispositions collected from observations or products.

External Assessments Assessments that are independent of the curriculum, for example, standardized tests.

Formative Assessments Assessments that provide information about students' current knowledge and abilities so that teachers can plan future instruction more effectively and so that students can identify their own areas of weakness or strength.

Grade-Level Goals Mathematical goals organized by content strand and articulated across grade levels from Kindergarten through Grade 6.

Individual Profile of Progress A recording tool that can be used to keep track of student progress on specific Grade-Level Goals.

Informing Instruction note These notes in the *Teacher's Lesson Guide* suggest how to use observations of students' work to adapt instruction by describing common errors and misconceptions in students' thinking and alerting the teacher to multiple solution strategies or unique insights students might offer.

Making Adequate Progress On a trajectory to meet a Grade-Level Goal.

Math Boxes Collections of problems designed to provide distributed practice. Math Boxes revisit content from prior units to build and maintain important concepts and skills. One or two problems on each page preview content from the next unit.

Mental Math and Reflexes Exercises at three levels of difficulty that prepare students for the lesson, build mental-arithmetic skills, and help teachers quickly assess individual strengths and weaknesses.

Observational Assessments Assessments based on observing students during daily activities or periodic assessments.

Ongoing Assessments Assessments based on students' everyday work during regular classroom instruction.

Open Response task An extended response assessment included in the Progress Check lesson of each unit.

Periodic Assessments Formal assessments that are built into a curriculum such as the end-of-unit Progress Checks.

Portfolios Collections of student products and observations that provide opportunities for students to reflect on their mathematical growth and for teachers to understand and document that growth.

Product Assessments Assessments based on student work from daily activities or from periodic assessments.

Program Evaluation Assessment intended to reveal how well a program of instruction is working. A school district, for example, might carry out program evaluation to identify schools with strong mathematics programs so that their success can be replicated.

Program Goals The fifteen cross-grade goals in *Everyday Mathematics* that weave the program together across grade levels. They form an organizing framework that supports both curriculum and assessment. Every Grade-Level Goal is linked to a Program Goal.

Progress Check lesson The last lesson in every unit. Progress Check lessons include a student Self Assessment, an Oral and Slate Assessment, a Written Assessment, and an Open Response task.

Purposes of Assessment The reasons for assessment, which include providing information that can be used to plan future instruction, identifying what students have achieved during a period of time, and evaluating the quality of the mathematics program.

Readiness Activities Optional activities in many lessons that preview lesson content or provide alternative routes of access for learning concepts and skills.

Recognizing Student Achievement note A feature in many lessons that highlights specific tasks used to monitor students' progress toward Grade-Level Goals. The notes identify the expectations for a student who is making adequate progress and point to skills or strategies that some students might be able to demonstrate.

Rubric A set of suggested guidelines for scoring assessment activities.

Student Self Assessment The individual reflection included in the Progress Check lesson of each unit.

Summative Assessments Assessments that aim to measure student growth and achievement, for example, an assessment to determine whether students have learned certain material by the end of a fixed period of study such as a semester or a course.

Writing/Reasoning Prompt A question linked to a specific Math Boxes problem. Writing/Reasoning Prompts provide students with opportunities to respond to questions that extend and deepen their mathematical thinking.

Written Progress Check The Written Assessment included in the Progress Check lesson of each unit.

Index

Adequate progress. *See* Making adequate progress
Assessment. *See* Balanced Assessment; Content Assessed; Contexts for Assessment; External Assessment; Formative Assessment; Ongoing Assessment; Periodic Assessment; Purposes of Assessment; and Sources of Evidence for Assessment; Summative Assessment
Assessment Management System, 28–30
Assessment Masters, 153–215. See Open Response task, assessment masters; Self Assessment masters; Written Assessment, masters.
Assessment Overviews, 51–149

Balanced Assessment, 2–6, 7, 8, 16, 18, 20–21, 29–30
  creating a plan, 4, 7

Checklists. *See* Class Checklists; Individual Profiles of Progress
  using checklists, 25–27
Class Checklists, 25–27
  general master, 303
  masters, Unit 1: 248–249, Unit 2: 252–253, Unit 3: 256–257, Unit 4: 260–261, Unit 5: 264–265, Unit 6: 268–269, Unit 7: 272–273, Unit 8: 276–277, Unit 9: 280–281, Unit 10: 284–285, Unit 11: 288–289, Unit 12: 292–293
  quarterly checklists, 26, 294–301
Content Assessed, 5–6
Contexts for Assessment, 3–4

End-of-Year Assessment Answers, 242–245
End-of-Year Assessment Masters, 234–241
End-of-Year Assessment Goals, 150–151
End-of-Year written assessment, 4, 18, 20, 28
Enrichment activities, 12–14
Exit Slips, 4, 8, 10–11, 15
  master, 311
External Assessment, 3–4, 8, 18, 24

Formative Assessment, 2, 7, 19, 20
Frequently Asked Questions, 31–35

Game record sheets, 4, 8, 10, 12
General Masters, 302–312
  Class Checklist, 303
  Discussion of My Math Work, 16, 310
  Evaluating My Math Class, 17, 304
  Exit Slip, 311
  Individual Profile of Progress, 302
  Math Log, 307
  My Math Class, 17, 305
  Number-Story Math Log, 17, 308
  Parent Reflections, 312
  Sample Math Work, 16, 309
  Weekly Math Log, 17, 306
Grade-Level Goals, 6–7, 10–14, 19–22, 25, 27–34, 37–50
  adequate progress toward, 7, 10–14, 19, 25, 27–30, 32–34
  definition of, 6, 32
  exposure to versus mastery of, 6, 32, 34–35
  table, 37–50
Grading, 30, 34

Informing Instruction notes, 4, 8, 9, 19
Individual Profiles of Progress, 25–26
  general master, 302
  masters, Unit 1: 246–247, Unit 2: 250–251, Unit 3: 254–255, Unit 4: 258–259, Unit 5: 262–263, Unit 6: 266–267, Unit 7: 270–271, Unit 8: 274–275, Unit 9: 278–279, Unit 10: 282–283, Unit 11: 286–287, Unit 12: 290–291

Journal pages, 4, 8, 10

Kid Watching, 4, 8

Making adequate progress
- based on a rubric, 27
- definition of, 27, 32–33
- in Recognizing Student Achievement notes, 10–14, 27, 29, 32–33
- in Written Assessments, 19

Math Boxes, 4, 8, 10–12, 15, 24, 33
Math Logs, 15, 17, 306–308
Mental Math and Reflexes, 4, 8, 10–11, 20
Mid-Year Assessment Answers, 242–245
Mid-Year Assessment masters, 228–233
Mid-Year Assessment Goals, 100–101
Mid-Year written assessment, 4, 18, 20, 28

O

Observations, 4, 8, 18, 26, 30
Ongoing Assessment, 3–4, 8–17, 25–26, 28
- by unit, Unit 1: 52–53, Unit 2: 60–61, Unit 3: 68–69, Unit 4: 76–77, Unit 5: 84–85, Unit 6: 92–93, Unit 7: 102–103, Unit 8: 110–111, Unit 9: 118–119, Unit 10: 126–127, Unit 11: 134–135, Unit 12: 142–143

Open Response tasks, 4, 18, 21–22, 24, 28
- assessment masters, 158, 163, 168, 173, 178, 183, 188, 193–194, 199, 204–205, 210, 215
- by unit, Unit 1: 55–56, Unit 2: 63–64, Unit 3: 71–72, Unit 4: 79–80, Unit 5: 87–88, Unit 6: 95–96, Unit 7: 105–106, Unit 8: 113–114, Unit 9: 121–122, Unit 10: 129–130, Unit 11: 137–138, Unit 12: 145–146

Oral and Slate Assessments, 20
Outside tests, 24

P

Parent Reflections, 17, 312
Performance-based assessments, 24, 32–33
Periodic Assessment, 3, 4, 18–23, 25–26
- by unit, Unit 1: 54–59, Unit 2: 62–67, Unit 3: 70–75, Unit 4: 78–83, Unit 5: 86–91, Unit 6: 94–99, Unit 7: 104–109, Unit 8: 112–117, Unit 9: 120–125, Unit 10: 128–133, Unit 11: 136–141, Unit 12: 144–149

Planning tips, 7
Portfolios, 4, 8, 15, 16–17, 26
Product Assessment, 16–17, 26
Products 4, 8, 18
Program Goals, 5–6, 29, 32, 37–50
- definition of, 5–6
- table list, 37–50
  - Data and Chance, 5, 44–45
  - Geometry, 5, 48
  - Measurement and Reference Frames, 5, 46–47
  - Number and Numeration, 5, 37–39
  - Operations and Computation, 5, 40–43
  - Patterns, Functions, and Algebra, 5, 49–50
- track progress toward, 32

Program Evaluation, 2
Progress Check Oral/Slate Assessments, 4, 18, 20, 28, 33, 34
Progress Check Written Assessments, 4, 18, 19, 20, 28, 33, 34, 154–215, 216–227
Purposes of Assessment, 2

Readiness activities, 12–14, 21
Recognizing Student Achievement notes, 4, 8, 10–14, 25–29, 32–34
Record-Keeping, 25–28, 34
- *Assessment Management System*, 28–30
- options for recording data on checklists, 27

Rubrics, 22–23, 27, 29

Self Assessment Masters, 21, 154, 159, 164, 169, 174, 179, 184, 189, 195, 200, 206, 211
Student Reports, 29
Student Self Assessment, 4, 21
Sources of Evidence for Assessment, 4
Summative Assessment, 2, 7, 19–20

Written Assessments, 4, 8, 19–20
- masters, Unit 1: 155–157, Unit 2: 160–162, Unit 3: 165–167, Unit 4: 170–172, Unit 5: 175–177, Unit 6: 180–182, Unit 7: 185–187, Unit 8: 190–192, Unit 9: 196–198, Unit 10: 201–203, Unit 11: 207–209, Unit 12: 212–214

Writing/Reasoning Prompts for Math Boxes, 4, 8, 15